Contents

Foreword

When I began research for this biographical study three years after Langston Hughes's death, I was a graduate student of comparative literature. I had met Hughes briefly in Paris in 1965 and was deeply interested in his influence on Francophone poets of the Caribbean and Africa, and in his social protest writings. By 1969, in the flurry of interest in "black studies," I had accepted a publisher's offer to write a short book on Hughes in a series of African and Afro-American biographies.

At that time, the late Arna Bontemps, a mentor and friend, was literary executor of the Langston Hughes Estate and also acting curator of the James Weldon Johnson Memorial Collection at the Yale University Library, where he was processing the vast collection of Hughes's papers in preparation for his own definitive biography of the late poet. Bontemps had been named in Hughes's will to write his biography, and I used to say to him in jest that, as literary executor, curator of the JWJ Collection, and biographer, he had "all the keys to the kingdom": he alone could unlock the vast storehouse of Hughes materials. Having known me since I was an undergraduate, and having read some of my published pieces, Bontemps was quick to encourage me in my Hughes project. "Go find whatever you can," he told me, "wherever you can find it, and I'll give you all the help I can." This meant literally that—but it also meant that most of the Hughes papers at Yale would be unopen to me until he finished his own book.

Bontemps died in 1973, leaving no trace of a Hughes biography. By then, the small series of books in which mine was to be included had died also. Shortly before, Bontemps had granted his permission for an anthology I had compiled of some of Hughes's hitherto uncollected prose and poetry— *Good Morning, Revolution: Uncollected Social Protest Writings by Langston Hughes* (Lawrence Hill & Co., 1973). The response from reviewers and friends was encouraging enough for me to decide to continue my research on Langston Hughes. For the next seven years I continued researching, interviewing, and writing, taking other editorial assignments and jobs to keep me going while I completed the manuscript.

During that time, restrictions imposed by the Langston Hughes Estate made it impossible for me to examine his full papers at Yale University's Beinecke Rare Book and Manuscript Library. It was necessary to wait for several collections containing other Hughes materials to be processed at the Moorland-Spingarn Research Center (formerly the Moorland-Spingarn Collection) at the Howard University Library, and in the Fisk University Library. There was an even longer wait while over seven hundred documents and records pertaining to Hughes were reviewed by the Justice Department for release under the Freedom of Information Act.

Langston Hughes: Before and Beyond Harlem is a biographical and critical narrative focusing on the major influences that shaped his life and career. It concentrates on his development before he moved to Harlem in the 1940s. An epilogue chapter highlights his later years. Special attention is given here to hitherto unknown facts about his life and the missing links in his autobiographical volumes, *The Big Sea* and *I Wonder as I Wander*. In the autobiographies Hughes exercised a certain literary license: he occasionally omitted significant personal data and obscured relevant facts. In *Langston Hughes* I have corrected the record or enlarged upon it. However, as I did not have access to his complete papers, this work is in no way intended as a definitive biography.

A primary objective of the book is to place in perspective the man of letters, for Hughes's legacy extends beyond the limited stereotype of him as the "bard of Harlem." *Langston Hughes: Before and Beyond Harlem* treats him in the context of his time—the poet, translator, essayist, novelist, dramatist, librettist, folklorist, short story writer, journalist, and world traveler, who made a lasting impact at home and abroad. Some of his militant writings which were not anthologized in *Good Morning, Revolution* are reproduced here in their biographical context.

Much of the information in this book derives from the secondary sources that Arna Bontemps suggested I seek out. Fortunately, I started early enough to reach as well some of the primary sources before their voices were stilled. The Acknowledgments include the names of some of those now deceased. The narrative is replete with the names of others who died while the manuscript was in preparation: Margaret Bonds, Ralph Bunche, Jacob Burck, Jasper Deeter, Michael Gold, Roland Hayes, Granville Hicks, Zell Ingram, Joe Louis, Clarence Muse, Paul Robeson, David Alfaro Siqueiros, (Neil) Homer Smith, Donald Ogden Stewart, William Grant Still, Leopold Stokowski, and Edmund Wilson.

This manuscript was tentatively entitled *The Darker Brother* when it was announced as a work in progress. The title was later changed to more clearly reflect the overall thrust of the text.

Most of all, this book is the story of one of the most prolific and versatile American writers of his generation, who gained an international reputation and sustained it, at great odds, over four decades. Throughout his career, he endured every possible hardship and never gave up. His spirit kept me going in the long search to find out what I could about his life and work. I hope that *Langston Hughes: Before and Beyond Harlem* is testament to all that he represented.

FAITH BERRY

Acknowledgments

The author gratefully acknowledges the help of the primary sources without whose personal recollections this manuscript would not be the same. Some of those individuals are now deceased. They live in my memory as much as in this book. I pay tribute to them with deep respect and gratitude: Katherine Garrison Chapin Biddle (Mrs. Francis Biddle), Arna Bontemps, Emerson Harper, Rayford Logan, William Patterson, Theodore Poston, Frank Reeves, Esq., Amy Spingarn (Mrs. Joel Spingarn), and Ella Winter (Mrs. Donald Ogden Stewart). The late Ralph Baird, Léon Damas, Benjamin Harrison Lehman, and John Sutton also provided helpful information.

For the valuable insights and information they shared with me, I owe equal appreciation to Raoul Abdul, Rudolph O. Aggrey, David Amran, Theodore S. Amussen, Gonzales Austin, George Bass, Dr. & Mrs. Edmund Randolph Biddle, Roy Blackburn, Sterling Brown, Virginia Roxborough Brownley, Henri Cartier-Bresson, Alice Childress, Mercer Cook, Matthew Crawford, John Hammond, Jean Blackwell Hutson, Si-Lan Chen Leyda, Maxim Lieber, Mr. & Mrs. Henry Lee Moon, Carlton Moss, Richard Bruce Nugent, Louise Thompson Patterson, Eulah Pharr, Saunders Redding, Bernard Rucker, Margaret Rullman, Marie Seton, John Short, Eva Sharp, Linda Tarpley, and Frances Wills (Mrs. Charles Thorpe).

For their generosity with documentation and various leads of one kind or another, I also thank Gail Bashein, Thomas Battle, John L. Brown, Dr. & Mrs. William Cheek, Charles Cooney, Charles Coppens, Sophy Cornwell, John DeWitt, Louis George Griffin, III, Milton Gustafson, Lorene Hawley, Lawrence Hill, Frances Knight, Miriam Matthews, Waldo Moore, George Murphy, Ethel Payne, Charlotte Price, Dorothy Porter Wesley, Estelle Rebec, Harold Rome, Constance Sayre, Ann Shockley, Peter Steffens, Cornelia Stokes, William Tribe, Michael Winston, and the late Barbara Watson and Luce Zea.

I am grateful, too, to the friends and colleagues whose comments and ideas from their own research were willingly offered and always helpful:

Arthur Davis, Theodore Hudson, Nathan Huggins, David L. Lewis, Hollis Lynch, Arnold Rampersad, James Spady, and Darwin Turner. For the relevance of their previously published studies on Hughes, I also thank Richard Barksdale, Donald Dickinson, James Emanuel, Milton Meltzer, Therman O'Daniel, and others.

I could not have completed parts of this manuscript without the important resources and helpful personnel at the Moorland-Spingarn Research Center, Howard University Library; Schomburg Center for Research in Black Culture, New York Public Library; Bancroft Library, University of California, Berkeley; Special Collections: Fisk University Library; the James Weldon Johnson Memorial Collection, Beinecke Rare Book and Manuscript Library, Yale University; the Carl Van Vechten Collection, New York Public Library (although the bulk of the Hughes-Van Vechten Correspondence there is sealed until 1999); the Manuscript Division, Library of Congress; the National Archives; the Langston Hughes Collection, Langston Hughes Memorial Library, Lincoln University (Pa.); the Houghton Library, Harvard University; the Kansas State Historical Society, and the University of Kansas Library. I thank Hughes's surviving literary executor-trustee, George Bass, for permission to quote from the poet's papers in some of those manuscript collections.

Relevant materials were also obtained through the Freedom of Information Act (FOIA), although I had to wait nearly a year for records pertaining to Langston Hughes to be processed. (Certain pages are still classified and withheld under a (b)(1) exemption pursuant to Executive Order 11652 and have not been released despite my written appeals since 1978.)

I am indebted to my sister, Gail, who helped me find an able secretary, Diane Tuininga, who typed most of the manuscript; to Dr. Gladys Forde, who extended me gracious hospitality in Nashville, Tennessee, while I completed research at the Fisk University Library; and to Dr. & Mrs. Ira McCown, Mr. & Mrs. Martin Arrington, and Joan Bunche, who offered me the comforts of home during my numerous trips to New York City. To my publisher, Lawrence Hill, and editor, Donald J. Davidson, go many thanks for their encouragement and help in making the book a reality. I could not have asked for a publisher with more integrity or a more knowledgable, dedicated, and considerate editor.

Last, but not least, I owe abiding appreciation to the persons to whom this book is dedicated: my parents who were a source of inspiration, support and assistance in many ways from beginning to end; and Saunders Redding, who read the first draft and made many helpful suggestions for the final narrative.

Whatever the inadequacies of the research or content of the text, I take the full responsibility for all.

F. B.

LANGSTON HUGHES
Before and Beyond Harlem

❧ I ❧

From These Roots

J AMES MERCER LANGSTON HUGHES[1]* was born in Joplin, Missouri, on
February 1, 1902, the second son of James Nathaniel Hughes and Carrie
Mercer Langston Hughes. Two years before, nearly to the day, his parents
had mourned the death of their first-born infant. They had buried him on a
snowy February 8, 1900, in a pauper's grave. Langston, as if marked from
birth to survive, would live to prove it. From the cradle to the grave, he
was destined to overcome the odds against him.

If his parents ever told him about the infant brother they had interred in
Joplin, Langston never mentioned it publicly. Whatever he really knew of
his sibling's death is as much speculation as history. But on his first and only
trip to Joplin as an adult, in 1958, he visited his brother's grave in the city's
Fairview Cemetery.[2]

Langston was the last child of his parents' star-crossed marriage. On the
branches of their unusual family tree, where pride ran as deep as the roots,
the mystery of his dead brother is not without social implications.

His mother, born to one of the most politically prominent and well-
educated Afro-American families of the nineteenth century, was twenty-six
when she eloped with James Nathaniel Hughes, an aspiring lawyer, two
years her senior. Their marriage, on April 30, 1899, in a civil ceremony in
Guthrie, Oklahoma Territory, with no friends or relatives present, caused
gossip for miles around. The couple quickly left for Joplin, but rumors of a
"shotgun wedding" spread.

James Nathaniel had been born in Charlestown, Indiana, in September 1871
to parents who were freed by the Emancipation Proclamation. His father,
who was also named James, had fought in the Civil War, and died in 1887,
when his son was sixteen. Both of James Nathaniel Hughes's male grandparents were white, his female grandparents black. On the paternal side, he was
descended from Sam Clay, a whiskey distiller of Scottish origin who lived

*Footnotes to the text will be found on pages 331–58.

I

in Henry County, Kentucky, and on the maternal side from Silas Cushen-
berry, a Jewish slave trader from Clark County, Kentucky.

Langston's mother, who preferred to be called Carolyn, had been born in
January 1873 on a farm near Lawrence, Kansas. Her paternal grandfather
was Ralph Quarles, a wealthy Louisa County, Virginia, planter, who had
attained the rank of captain in the Revolutionary War. Her grandmother,
Lucy Langston, was his half-Indian, half-Negro housekeeper. Carrie's father, Charles Howard Langston, was the second of three sons born to Ralph
and Lucy. The Louisa County court record shows that in 1806 Quarles
declared Lucy and her heirs, including a daughter Maria, free and "clear of
the claims of all persons whatsoever." The three sons grew up on their
father's Virginia plantation, and when he died in 1834—the year of Lucy's
death also—his will provided for their education and, upon reaching the age
of twenty-one, financial independence.

Shortly after Quarles's death, the three boys, shepherded by Gideon, the
eldest, moved to Ohio, where Charles, then seventeen, attended Oberlin
College for two years. Later he moved to Cleveland, where he taught
school and became secretary of the Ohio Anti-Slavery Society. For nearly
three decades, he was active in the abolitionist movement in Ohio, Illinois,
and Kansas. At an antislavery convention in Columbus in 1851, Charles
declared, "I have long since adopted as my God, the freedom of the colored
people of the United States, and my religion, to do anything that will effect
that object...."[3] One of the things he did to "effect that object" was to aid in
the escape to Canada of an alleged fugitive slave named John Price. For his
part in this affair, known historically as the *Oberlin-Wellington Rescue*, Charles
was sentenced to twenty days imprisonment and fined nearly one thousand
dollars.[4] At his trial, his eloquent and impassioned speech against the Fugitive Slave Law caused the judge to reduce his fine, even though the jail
sentence provoked widespread protest on his behalf.

That was in 1859, the year of John Brown's raid on Harpers Ferry. One of
the casualties of Brown's abortive foray against the slaveocracy was a black
man, Lewis Sheridan Leary. In 1869, Charles Langston married Leary's
widow, Mary, one of the first colored women to attend Oberlin College;[5]
and in 1870, the Langstons moved to Lawrence, Kansas, an abolitionist
bastion, where many flocked during the black migration westward following the Emancipation Proclamation. That same year, their first child, Nathaniel Turner Langston, named for the legendary leader of a slave revolt,
was born. Three years later, Mary gave birth to a daughter, Carrie. She
would become the mother of Langston Hughes.

Her childhood with her brother, Nat, and the Langstons' two other
children from previous marriages—Charles's teenage son, Dessalines (Deese)
Langston, and Mary's young daughter, Louise Leary Langston—offered

more family security than any that Carrie's own son would ever know. Growing up on the family farm in Lakeview near Lawrence, she came of age as her father became a prominent civic leader and later a Republican nominee for the state legislature in Douglas County. Although Langston Hughes would later write in his autobiography, *The Big Sea*, that his grandfather, Charles, "didn't much care about making money," the latter cared enough to make a controversial speech on August 1, 1879, admonishing black Kansans that the only way to get ahead was "to get and keep money."[6] He tried to follow his own economic advice in 1888, by opening a grocery store with a partner in Lawrence. But four years later, at age seventy-five, he was dead, leaving his family with more financial debts than accumulated wealth.[7]

At age nineteen when her father died, Carrie went to work as a clerk in the district courthouse to help support herself and her mother. Two years later, in 1894, she enrolled as a part-time student at the University of Kansas College of Arts to study German and English.

Her university experience lasted only a year. With the death of her father, the family's financial situation deteriorated rapidly, and it reached the poverty level when Carrie withdrew from the university in 1895.[8] That same year, the family house at 732 Alabama Street was mortgaged for debts. At age twenty-two, she began working as a grammar school teacher in Guthrie, which was then the capital of Oklahoma Territory. There she met James Nathaniel Hughes, a storekeeper ambitious to practice law.

James Hughes was living ten miles from Guthrie, in the township of Langston —which was named for Carrie's uncle, John Mercer Langston.[9] As lawyer, politician, Freedman's Bureau appointee, college administrator, diplomat and, in 1888, the first Afro-American Representative to Congress from Virginia, Langston had become a legend in his own time. The town of Langston, Oklahoma Territory, founded and named for him in 1890, seemed for the young Carrie Mercer Langston the ideal place to try to begin a life of her own. But her marriage to James Hughes in 1899 did not yield all that she had hoped.

The Oklahoma Territory, where thousands had rushed to establish homesteads, was no paradise, and no place for a young black man to practice law. For racial reasons, James Hughes was denied entry to law school in Oklahoma. Frustrated but determined, he studied law through correspondence courses from Chicago, but his application to take the Oklahoma Territory bar exam was rejected by all-white examiners. The coupled moved in the summer of 1899 to Joplin, Missouri, where they were soon joined by Carrie's mother, Mary Langston. But the lead-mining town of Joplin, where James Hughes worked as a stenographer and bookkeeper for a mining firm, proved little better than the place they had left. In their rented home at 1602 Missouri Avenue, where their first son died and their second son was born, there were financial difficulties. When James Hughes moved out to live alone—Langston was still an infant—Carrie moved in with her mother at 1046 Joplin Street. Petulant, hard-working, and driven by ambitions that racial prejudice denied fulfillment, Hughes, after four years of marriage and newly a father, made up his mind, in October 1903, to leave the United States. When Carrie, who really did not understand her husband, refused to accompany him, he left her. He would go first to Cuba, then to Mexico. Although he contributed to the support of his wife and young son, he would not see them again for four years.[10]

LANGSTON HUGHES's earliest impressions were of Lawrence, Kansas, where his mother took him to live with his maternal grandmother when he was slightly more than a year old.

> My grandmother raised me until I was twelve years old. Some-
> times I was with my mother, but not often. My mother and
> father were separated. And my mother, who worked, always
> traveled about a great deal, looking for a better job.[11]

The early separation of his parents, the frequent moving about from one place to another, the absence of a father, the presence of poverty and racial discrimination—each in its way marked him for life, but never made him bitter.

During his early years, he lived with his mother only briefly and at intervals. By the time he was twelve he had spent short periods of time in seven cities because of her frequent moving about. As he grew older, she demanded more of him emotionally than she gave, yet some of his earliest memories and influences are of what he learned from her.

Clearest among these memories were those of her giving dramatic recita- tions from plays and reading her original poetry at the Interstate Literary Association, which was organized in Lawrence by her father. Though she possessed an artistic bent and had a dramatic flair (she was one of the first of her generation to cut her hair short), her poetic talent did not match her son's. And if it had, it is unlikely that she would have developed it; she was pure dilettante. But her artistic interests and inclinations were part of Langston's heritage.

At the impressionable age of six and a half, he began school in Topeka, where his mother was working as a stenographer. He had difficulty enter- ing a white school there. Part of his memory of this experience was that "my mother, who was always ready to do battle for the rights of a free people, went directly to the school board, and got me into the Harrison Street School."

In Topeka, mother and son lived together in one room over a plumbing shop. Managing as best she could in the only circumstances she could afford financially, she attempted to compensate for the absence of a father, nurturing the boy in her free time in the things she liked—plays and books—interests he took hold of and never forgot. Years afterward, he wrote: "My mother used to take me to see all the plays that came to Topeka, like *Buster Brown*, *Under Two Flags*, and *Uncle Tom's Cabin*. We were very fond of books and plays. Once we heard *Faust*."

In Topeka, his mother also took him to what he remembered later as "the little vine-covered library." It was in this quiet atmosphere that, by the time he was in first grade, he had discovered in books a world of escape and security. Through books he created a fortress against the vicissitudes of childhood. Through his experiences at the Harrison Street School, he learned not only that he was a child without parents, unlike most other children, but also that, unlike those around him, he was black. And amidst the clamor that arose because of his attendance at the school, he learned also, that some white people—and they were both teachers and pupils—would come to his aid and stand up for him. It was this awareness at a tender age that later made him say: "I learned early not to hate *all* white people."

Before beginning his first full school year at the Harrison Street School, the young Hughes traveled to Mexico with his mother and grandmother. His father had sent for them. He had met his father once, hastily, the year before, during the first of James Hughes's three short sojourns in the United States. The second meeting, in 1908, of the then six-year-old boy with his father and the reconciliation between his parents in Mexico were of brief duration. As if to symbolize the family's disruption, an earthquake shook Mexico City.[12] Though the family escaped injury, Carrie Hughes was ready to leave Mexico as soon as the ground trembled. Though the language barrier had discouraged her, the earthquake produced a resolve to return to Kansas. Never of the same temperament as her husband, who was no less patient, but twice as determined as she, their marriage was all but legally terminated with the departure for Kansas. It was the last the boy would see of his father for eleven years.

❦ 2 ❦

Significant Moves

I N THE ABSENCE OF A FATHER, Langston Hughes spent his formative years, until the age of puberty, under matriarchal influence. When he entered second grade, he was again living with his grandmother, Mary Langston, in Lawrence. Until her death when he was twelve, he remained in her care, except for two summers—one in Kansas City and another in Colorado Springs, Colorado, which he spent with his mother. This matriarchal influence would later manifest itself in some of his fiction—most notably in his autobiographical first novel, *Not Without Laughter*. In the novel a small boy, Sandy, is reared by a grandmother; and women, rather than men, play the dominant role. In real life this influence was the source of a profound psychological development: a deep-seated self-protectiveness in his attitude toward women. It marked his adult years, and may explain why he never married, never formed any lasting relationship, except platonic, with a woman. It may also have been the source of his deeply ambivalent, yet respectful, feelings toward his mother, and why, even as an adult, he maintained a latent dependency upon a mother-figure. The only parent he really knew as a child was his mother, yet she was always just beyond his reach when he needed her most and he began early seeking maternal substitutes in teachers, family friends, and women he called his aunts. This search continued through his adulthood, and he never really abandoned it. His mother, lacking love and security in her own life, could never provide them to a growing son.

Among the deeply felt experiences of his youth, growing up with his grandmother was one of the most indelible. She provided him a home, but she was never a substitute for his parents. As he reflected upon his childhood:

> I was unhappy for a long time, and very lonesome living with my grandmother. Then it was that books began to happen to me, and I began to believe in books—where if people suffered, they suffered in beautiful language, not in monosyllables, as we did in Kansas. And where almost always the mortgage got paid. . . . [1]

6

During the years he spent with his grandmother, who was then in her seventies, they lived in a small house on Alabama Street near the University of Kansas. In order to meet her mortgage payments, she rented out rooms to families or to university students. Impoverished after her husband's death, she was too proud of the Langston name to borrow or beg from friends and too self-reliant to work for anyone. While her husband lived, the family income was derived from the Langstons' small farm and a grocery store which Charles Langston owned in partnership with an associate, Richard Burns. Although the family enjoyed a considerable social position throughout Charles's life, the prestige he earned in Lawrence as president of the colored Benevolent Society, grand master of the Negro Masons, founder of the Interstate Literary Association, and active participant in local politics did not supplement the family income.

Rather than accept the domestic service jobs that most colored women performed in Lawrence, Mary Langston frequently moved in with friends, taking her grandson with her, and renting all the rooms in her house to make ends meet. Mortgage payments sometimes deprived them of food. It embarrassed him to have little boys visit him at his grandmother's house.

> I remember one summer a friend of my mother's in Kansas City sent her son to pass a few weeks with me at my grandmother's home in Lawrence. But the little boy only stayed a few days, then wrote his mother that he wanted to leave, because we had nothing but salt pork and wild dandelions to eat. The boy was right. But being only eight or nine years old, I cried when he showed me the letter he was writing his mother. And I never wanted my mother to invite any more little boys to stay with me at my grandmother's house.

The adult Hughes remembered his grandmother as "Indian and proud," though one of his favorite jokes (and strong dislikes) became "Negroes who mention their Indian grandmothers more than once a week," an element of satire that was reflected more than once in his creative writing.[2] Mary Langston's grandmother had been a Cherokee, and she herself looked Indian. Copper-colored with high cheekbones, and long black hair that grayed as she grew older, she was small and delicate in appearance but tough in spirit.

In Lawrence she would often sit on the porch in a rocker with her grandson on her lap and tell him stories about the days of slavery. Hughes developed a sense of his racial heritage from her, though she had never been a slave, and she had traveled about at will with free papers in her native North Carolina. Her stories were about heroic people and events she re-

membered, and Hughes later recreated his impressions of her storytelling in
a long poem called "Aunt Sue's Stories":

> He knows that Aunt Sue
> Never got her stories out of any book at all.
> But that they came right out of her own life. . . .[3]

He was too young as a schoolboy to place in historical perspective some
of the events his grandmother related, but the remembrance of them remained with him. On one occasion she took him to Osawatomie, where
John Brown had lived; there, three years before she died, he saw her seated
on the speaker's platform with Theodore Roosevelt, honored as the last
surviving widow of John Brown's raid on Harpers Ferry.

Details that Hughes did not learn about Harpers Ferry and Lewis Sheridan Leary from his grandmother before her death, he learned many years
later from his friend and lawyer, Arthur B. Spingarn, an avid collector of
books and archives by and about Afro-Americans. In 1930, when he was
twenty-eight years old, Hughes wrote to Arthur Spingarn:

> I didn't know any of the things you told me about Sheridan
> Leary in your letter. I am mighty glad to have those facts, and it
> was surely good of you to look them up for me. I wish I had
> been old enough to learn more from my grandmother before she
> died.[4]

When his grandmother died in 1915, her house was reclaimed by the
mortgagee, and thirteen-year-old Langston went to live with family friends
known to him as Uncle and Auntie Reed. He did not cry at his grandmother's passing. Her austere tutelage had left no room for love. He shed
no tears because "something about my grandmother's stories (without
her ever having said so) taught me the uselessness of crying about anything."

His grandmother's death meant adjusting to another home. Years later
his fictional character Jesse B. Semple says what Hughes himself must have
felt as a child moving from one household to another:

> "I were a passed-around child. While my mother was not there
> and my father was not there and they was separated, I were left
> with whoever would take care of me when they was not there.
>
> "Nobody was mean to me, and I do not know why I had that
> left-out feeling, but I did, I guess because nobody ever said,
> 'You're mine,' and I really did not belong to nobody. . . ."[5]

During the months he lived with the Reeds, Langston had for the first
time a sense of what it meant to live with and belong to a family. "For me,"

he said about this couple that took him as a son into their home, "there have never been any better people in the world. I loved them very much."[6]

The Reeds owned a small house with a garden, cows, and chickens—a block from the Kaw River, not far from the Lawrence railroad station. Mr. Reed earned his living laying sewer pipes and digging ditches for the city, and Mrs. Reed sold milk and eggs to neighbors. Their simple but settled way of life gave Langston a sense of routine and security he had not known with either mother or grandmother. With the Reeds he became less the lonely, introspective boy who withdrew into a world of books. He helped them set the hens and drive the cows to pasture, and on Saturdays he attended football games at the University of Kansas. And he never went hungry at their table:

> My Auntie Reed cooked wonderful salt pork greens with corn dumplings. There were fresh peas and young onions right out of the garden and milk with cream on it. There were hoe-cake, and sorghum molasses, and apple dumplings with butter sauce. And she and Uncle Reed owned their own house without a mortgage on it, clear.

When his grandmother was alive, he had often seen her read her Bible, but she did not try to instill religion into him. Mrs. Reed, an ardent Christian, did. She demanded Langston's weekly attendance at Sunday school and church. On one occasion, at Auntie Reed's insistence, the youth attended a revival where the children of the congregation were asked to come forward and commit themselves to Christ. Langston, experiencing no great surge of spirituality, as he had been told he would, went forward simply to avoid being the only child who refused. Abed that night, feeling lost and deceitful, feeling let down by a Jesus who had not appeared, he buried his head beneath the covers and sobbed aloud, unable to stop.

The revival episode revealed an attitude, unconscious at the time, that did not change as Hughes grew older. Religion as an expression of piety impressed him not at all; yet, as a nonbeliever, his greatest doubts often brought him closest to faith. As an adult, he believed that organized religion had failed. He refused to join a church, and rarely entered one except to attend special programs or to listen to gospel music. The Negro spirituals haunted him and were echoed in some of his verse. But also echoed in his verse are the doubts, the questionings of the existence of a God, the strange, oppressive dichotomy of one who wants to believe and cannot. For instance, in 1925, he published this:

God to Hungry Child

Hungry child,
I didn't make this world for you.
You didn't buy any stock in my railroad.
You didn't invest in my corporation:

Where are your shares in standard oil?
I made the world for the rich
And the will-be-rich
And the have-always-been rich.
Not for you,
Hungry child.[7]

And two months later, he published this:

Prayer

I ask you this:
Which way to go?
I ask you this:
Which sin to bear?
Which crown to put upon my hair?
I do not know,
Lord God,
I do not know.[8]

By the early thirties Hughes had become a mocking, blasphemous, anti-Christian, caricaturing God as a weakling drunk, in the poem "A Christian Country," and Christ as a nigger and a "most holy bastard," in "Christ in Alabama," and as a willing tool of chauvinists and exploiters, in "Goodbye, Christ."

Over the years, the poet's attitude softened. In his gospel plays and certain of the poems written toward the end of his life, he could depict Christ as a martyr and a saviour. But he never lost his religious doubts.

But as he was growing up, other characteristics than his religious attitude separated him—made him "different"—from many children of his age. When most pre-teenage boys in Lawrence were playing ball, Langston Hughes was going alone to the theatre. The interest in plays, which he had acquired from his mother, soon developed into a favorite diversion. At age thirteen he began working after school and on Saturdays. This earned him money with which to do what he wanted to do. In the spring, he collected maple seeds and sold them to the seed store. For a brief time, he delivered newspapers and sold *The Saturday Evening Post* and *Appeal to Reason*, a radical tabloid which he was told by the editor of the local daily to stop selling lest it get Negroes into trouble. He got his first regular after-school job when he entered seventh grade. He cleaned the lobby and public bathrooms of a hotel for fifty cents a week. With the money he earned he went to the movies—Charlie Chaplin, Theda Bara, and Mary Pickford were his favorite stars—until the local theatre put up a sign No Colored Admitted. When theatrical shows came to town, he attended performances at the Opera House, usually sitting in the gallery (most often all alone), because it was the only place colored people were allowed to sit.

SHORTLY before he turned fourteen, Langston's mother sent for him to join her in Lincoln, Illinois. She was now Mrs. Carrie Clark.[9] Her second marriage, at the age of forty-three, seemed to promise greater stability than the first. Her new husband, Homer Clark, a chef cook with an infant son, was originally from Topeka. He was neither irascible nor particularly ambitious, and he accepted his new wife's son as readily as she accepted his. From the beginning, and for the remainder of his life, Langston referred to Gwyn, who was ten years his junior, as his brother "Kit." Having grown up without knowing his father and without brothers and sisters, Langston eagerly accepted his new situation as instant older brother and adopted stepson.

In *The Big Sea*, he reflected that "I liked my step-father a great deal, and my baby brother also; for I had been very lonesome growing up all by myself, the only child, with no father and no mother around." But for these same reasons he was psychologically unprepared for some of the developments. Langston's stepfather, like his mother, regularly traveled from place to place in search of a better job, and the family was separated more often than it was together. In his stepfather's absence, Langston's mother became increasingly more dependent upon her son than attentive toward him. The adolescent boy was treated less and less like a child and more and more like an adult. At a time when he needed parental guidance, he was forced to look inward, as he had through most of his childhood, to rely upon himself. But he quickly became attached to his stepfather. He wanted his recognition and attention. He never forgot that "the day I graduated from grammar school in Lincoln, Illinois, he had left my mother, and was not there to see me graduate."[10]

At his grammar school graduation in Lincoln, Illinois, the spring of 1916, fourteen-year-old Langston Hughes was elected class poet. Until his election he had never written a poem.

Up to that time I had never thought about being a poet and was rather surprised at being elected Class Poet. In fact, I hadn't expected it. But I guess the youngsters in my class felt I had some rhythm to give a poem. The teacher told us a poem had to have rhythm. And so suddenly a boy called out my name, Langston Hughes, and the whole class said "Ay," unanimously—and that's the way I became a poet. . . . [11]

With a sense of appreciation that was to become even more characteristic of him as he grew older, he dedicated a verse to all eight teachers in the school, though only three, Ethel Welch, Laura Armstrong, and Frances Dyer, had actually influenced and encouraged him. Ethel Welch, his favorite teacher, had told him she believed he had talent for writing and suggested books for him to read. "In a sense," he wrote, "I owe the beginning of my literary career to Ethel Welsh [sic]."[12]

Until he entered high school, he preferred fiction to poetry, and tried to read all the novels his mother brought home from the Lincoln Library. His favorite authors were Edna Ferber, Harold Bell Wright, and Zane Grey. The only poetry he then liked was the folk dialect verse of Paul Laurence Dunbar and Henry Wadsworth Longfellow's epic *Hiawatha*. Perhaps faint overtones of Dunbar's influence can be heard in a few of Hughes's early blues poems, but almost all of Dunbar's verses explore and expound themes quite different from those found in the work of the adult Hughes. Dunbar almost completely avoided the subject of racial injustice;[13] Hughes's work— poetry, prose, and drama—deals widely with it. There is no evidence, either, that *Hiawatha* influenced Hughes, though as a child he undoubtedly identified with the Ojibwa Indian boy, who was reared by the aging Nokomis, as Langston had been reared by his aging grandmother.

By the time Hughes entered high school in the autumn of 1916, his literary and social interests had changed greatly. At the end of the summer following his graduation from grammar school in Lincoln, his stepfather, now in Cleveland, sent for the family to join him. Cleveland would be the eighth city the young Hughes had moved to—but for most of the next four years, it would actually be a place to call home.

3

The Making of a Poet

THE MOVE TO Cleveland in 1916 opened up a whole new world for the young Langston Hughes and the members of his family. With World War I raging in Europe and European immigration temporarily on the wane, jobs in factories, steel mills, and munitions plants were opened up to Negroes. In the wave of the Great Migration (1914-1918), black Americans made a mass exodus from the South to the North, seeking new opportunities. Homer Clark had got a job in a steel mill, but unable to withstand the extreme heat of the furnaces, he held it only briefly. Yet his short stint in the mill had its effect, and undoubtedly Langston had this in mind when, a sophomore in high school, and newly influenced by Carl Sandburg, he wrote:

> The mills
> That grind and grind,
> That grind out steel
> And grind away the lives
> Of men—
> In the sunset their stacks
> Are great black silhouettes
> Against the sky.
> In the dawn
> They belch red fire.
> The mills—
> Grinding new steel,
> Old men.[1]

Hughes's mother, with her husband idle, and household expenses to meet, took a job as a maid. Clark at last was able to find work, first as a building caretaker, then as janitor of an apartment building. The family's income, like the income of most black people in the urban centers during

13

these years, went mostly to pay rent. "We always lived, during my high school years, either in an attic or a basement, and paid a lot for such inconvenient quarters," Hughes wrote later. Because of the continuing (and increasing) migration, it was difficult for black families to find a place to live in Cleveland. The Negro district was crowded to capacity, and on the east side of the city, whites were moving out of one-family houses, cutting them up into apartments, renting them for double and triple the rents they would have otherwise charged.

The Cleveland high school Hughes attended for the entire four years of his secondary schooling was Central High School, then predominantly white. Despite the huge urban migration of blacks from the South, the number of black students in the school was small. By the time Hughes graduated, his class contained ten Afro-Americans. Most of his classmates were sons and daughters of East European and Russian immigrants. He found these young people more democratic and less anti-Negro than native white Americans. Central, an institution dating from 1846, reflected Cleveland's social and economic changes during the early part of the twentieth century. Many years before, the school had been attended by the children of affluent white residents. As they moved to more remote sections of town, they were replaced by the foreign-born immigrants, many of whose children Hughes came to know. He began to understand that there were religious as well as racial differences in the school and in the nation. The Jewish-gentile split, which frequently occurred in the class and club elections, was all too apparent. On occasion, he considered this division the reason he won many class offices; a Negro, he was a compromise candidate.

Langston was popular with his classmates and his teachers. He was a good student with a place on the honor roll and an acknowledged leader in every activity he entered. During his four years at the school, he was elected student council representative, secretary of the French Club, treasurer of the Home Garden Club, and president of the American Civics Association (called during the war period the Americanism Club). It was at Central High School that young Hughes came into his own as a gregarious young man whose attitude about himself and others helped him make friends wherever he went. In this situation the feelings of insecurity and loneliness of his early childhood dissipated. He worked well at projects which required working alone, but he also cooperated well with others. Athletics was hardly his forté, but the relay team of which he was a member won two citywide championships.

At school his best friend was a Polish boy, Sartur Andrzejewski. His devout Catholic family made Langston feel welcome in their home. He also made numerous Jewish friends. They impressed him because they were "interested in more than basketball and glee club." From some of these students he borrowed books such as *The Gadfly*, Ethel Boole Voynich's novel about the reunification of Italy, and Romain Rolland's *Jean Christophe*, about a musician's personal struggle as an artist in an alien world. Many of them exchanged political ideas with him and lent him copies of *The Liberator* and *Socialist Call*, and took him to hear speeches by Socialist leader Eugene V. Debs, who opposed the war and America's entry into it. When the Russian Revolution occurred in 1917, young Hughes celebrated it with many of his classmates whose parents had lived under the czar, and who welcomed the coming to power of Lenin. The war years and the political ideas of many of his foreign-born or first-generation American friends made a deep impression upon him, at an age when he was beginning to form political preferences and convictions. He never forgot that he and his classmates were questioned by the principal about their loyalty to America and that the homes of some of his friends were raided by police, who took their books away. Hughes became president of Central's Americanism Club, which the principal organized, but the club lasted only briefly. Many of the students' ideas—their support of Debs, for instance—conflicted with the principal's ideas of what the club should aim to do.

After America's entry into the war in April 1917, compulsory military training was instituted at Central High School, and Langston became a lieutenant in the school's military corps. It was in part from this school and this atmosphere, from the war years and their aftermath, and from what he saw and learned of the plight of blacks during the Great Migration, that young Langston Hughes received his first education in radical politics. That education would begin to show in some of his poems as early as 1925, five years after his graduation from high school, and during the depression of the 1930s it would reach its peak.

IN ADDITION to his school activities, Langston took part in the arts program of a neighborhood community center. The Neighborhood Association, later known as Karamu House, had opened around the corner from his house the year he moved to Cleveland. It would prove everlastingly significant in Hughes's life. The organizers of this neighborhood settlement house were Russell and Rowena Jelliffe, a young couple who had come to Cleveland in 1915 at the invitation of the Second Presbyterian Church. They were both Oberlin graduates and social workers, interested in producing plays. Their community project, during the days when Hughes first took part in its activities, occupied two small cottages—in one of which the Jelliffes lived—where adults and children of the neighborhood could attend classes in arts and crafts. Other programs, chosen by the participants, were added from time to time. Langston Hughes came to know the Jelliffes well, becoming one of the first youngsters to go regularly to the Neighborhood

Association. He was then more interested in the graphic arts than in writing. This interest had developed through the art and painting classes of Miss Clara Dieke, one of his favorite teachers at Central High School.

During his freshman year he participated in the Neighborhood Association in the time he had free from school activities and an after-school job at a soda fountain on Central Avenue in the Negro district. At the end of that school year, after a long search for an employer willing to hire a Negro, he found full-time summer employment as a stock boy running a dumbwaiter at Halle's, one of Cleveland's large department stores.

His sophomore year marked the beginning of his serious interest in poetry and in writing. The strongest impetus came from his second-year English teacher, Miss Ethel Weimer, who introduced her class to the Chicago school of poets: Vachel Lindsay, Edgar Lee Masters, and—the poet Hughes admired most, and eventually his greatest influence in the matter of form—Carl Sandburg. Miss Weimer recognized Langston's talent and encouraged him. One of his high school poems was about Sandburg, whom he referred to as his "guiding light." At age fifteen, Hughes wrote:

> Carl Sandburg's poems
> Fall on the white pages of his books
> Like blood-clots of song
> From the wounds of humanity.
> I know a lover of life sings.
> I know a lover of all the living
> Sings then.[2]

The summer following his sophomore year Hughes spent in Chicago, the harsh industrial city whose impact upon Sandburg had inspired *Chicago Poems*, published in 1916. The city was then also considered the most important cultural and literary center in America, though no such reasons were cause for Hughes going there. He had gone to join his mother, who, again separated from his stepfather, was now working as a cook for a lady who owned an exclusive millinery shop in the Loop. He became the shop's delivery boy. During the sweltering summer months Langston, his mother, and Gwyn, now age six, lived in one small room on Wabash Street, next to an elevated railway in Chicago's crowded South Side. Nearby was South State Street, a teeming thoroughfare, "full of workers and gamblers, prostitutes and pimps, church folks and sinners." He would remember these people and one day bring them to life in his poetry.

But that summer in Chicago, working days and going home nights to the small, cramped quarters on Wabash Street, he wrote no poems. It was an unpleasant and difficult time for him, especially his relationship with his mother. Again, as happened each time Homer Clark went unpredictably his own way, Carrie Clark clung all the more tenaciously to Langston. When fall came, and he was ready to return to Cleveland for school, with the little money he had been able to save, she tried to make him remain in Chicago, quit school, and go to work to help her. It was a traumatic time for him. But now no longer a child without defenses, he argued that dropping out of school would lead him nowhere in life.

> My mother, as a great many poor mothers do, seemed to have the fixed idea that a son is born for the sole purpose of taking care of his parents as soon as possible. Even while I was still in high school, whenever my amiable but unpredictable stepfather would wander away, my mother would suggest that I quit school and get a job to help her.
>
> "But, Mama," I would say, "with no training, what kind of job can I get that would pay enough to make it worthwhile leaving school? At least if I get a little education, I'll be better able to help you afterwards."[3]

For the first time—and not the last—he asserted himself against her, going alone to Cleveland while she remained temporarily in Chicago. That autumn, he lived alone for a while in a rooming house. He prepared his own meals, which almost every evening consisted of hot dogs and rice, for he could not afford to eat out. By November, when the war ended, he was beginning to observe notable changes in Cleveland: the theatres and restaurants in the downtown area were beginning to refuse service and accommodations to blacks; rents were soaring; and as white soldiers returned from active duty, they were replacing blacks, who were discharged from their jobs. At Central High School, the talk was as much about the triumph of the Bolsheviks and the way they were ending race hatred and economic exploitation in Russia as about the armistice. Hughes became as conscious of the events in Russia as of what was happening in Cleveland: "The daily papers pictured the Bolsheviki as the greatest devils on earth, but I didn't see how they could be that bad if they had done away with race hatred and landlords—two evils that I knew well at first hand."[4]

Some months later, he read John Reed's account of the Bolshevik revolution, *Ten Days That Shook the World*, partly because almost all his friends at Central were reading it, partly because his reading range had widened to include almost everything he had time for, from fiction to philosophy. He still liked Edna Ferber, but he preferred Theodore Dreiser, and he was having a go at Schopenhauer and Nietzsche. He was a frequent visitor to the Cleveland Public Library, where he met and was encouraged in both his reading and his poetry writing by Miss Effie L. Power, the library's director of work with children. She would one day write the introduction to his book of verse, *The Dream Keeper.*

The poems he wrote at this time, often jotting them down quickly in a notebook as soon as they came into his head, he rarely showed to anyone. "I began to be afraid to show my poems to anybody, because they had become very serious and very much a part of me. And I was afraid other people might not like them or understand them," Hughes later confessed.[5] Several of his earliest poems were first drafted in his notebook during this period, and he began to send them to various magazines. These verses were promptly returned with rejection slips, though on one memorable occasion he received an encouraging word scribbled on a slip from the *Liberator.* His poems about Carl Sandburg and the steel mills were published in *The Belfry Owl,* Central's literary magazine.

Hughes was not at this time seriously trying to write short stories, but he wrote his first vignette as an English class assignment. Less than three hundred words, "Mary Winosky" was about a white immigrant scrubwoman who died and left $8,000. The idea for the story came from a newspaper clipping. The theme of human isolation foreshadowed the deep interest Hughes would take in the universal human problems of the masses, and it helps to explain the fact that much of his later work, both in poetry and prose, would be done to serve a social purpose.

The same year, 1918, he was reading Guy de Maupassant in French. In *The Big Sea,* he tells us: "I think it was de Maupassant who made me really want to be a writer and write stories about Negroes, so true that people in far-away lands would read them—even after I was dead." He was struck mainly by Maupassant's simplicity of language, the illusion of reality he created, and his focus upon *les petits bourgeois.* But the influence of the French author was neither total nor permanent. Not until some fifteen years later did Hughes begin to write short stories—by which time he was overwhelmingly influenced by D. H. Lawrence.

SOON after Hughes turned seventeen, he received a letter from his father. It came from Mexico in the spring of 1919, and it was laconic, typical of the father he had not seen for eleven years.

> MY DEAR LANGSTON:
>
> I am going to New York for a few days on a business trip in June. On the way back I will send you a wire to be ready to meet me as the train comes through Cleveland. You are to accompany me to Mexico for the summer.
>
> Affectionately,
your father,
JAMES N. HUGHES[6]

Langston's mother, who had reconciled with Homer Clark and returned to Cleveland, where she found work as a waitress, was upset by this letter. It aroused a fear that her son would choose to remain in Mexico and deprive her of a vital source of support. But Langston, curious about his father and anxious to see Mexico, refused to be persuaded by her arguments. Promising to return from Mexico at the end of the summer, he met his father in Cleveland—though in slightly different circumstances than they had arranged by letter—and journeyed with him by train to Toluca, where James Hughes lived.

The summer was a grave disappointment. Langston had constructed an idealized image of his father, who "represented for me the one stable factor in my life." The reality shattered the image. He did not like his father, whose devotion to material values, and his rigorous self-control in pursuit of them, ruled out all other passion. He had no human warmth, permitted himself no display of affection. Langston was outgoing and inclined to demonstrativeness. He had great sympathy for the downtrodden and the poor, including the Mexican Indians; his father despised them, just as he despised and hated American blacks. In the father's oft-spoken opinion, blacks had only themselves to blame for their dismal poverty and powerlessness. Like Mexican Indians, American Negroes to James Hughes were shiftless and stupid and given to senseless religious fervor they would be better off without.

In the fifteen years he had lived in Mexico, the elder Hughes had let nothing stand between him and his goal of becoming wealthy. When his son visited him that summer of 1919, he owned rental properties in Mexico City (most of them tenement dwellings), a ranch in the central highlands, and a house in Toluca. In Toluca, he was general manager of the Sultepec Electric Light and Power Company. He had also been admitted to the Mexican bar. His knowledge of the law, coupled with his business sense, had contributed to substantial earnings from money lending and mortgage foreclosures. But the wealthier he became, the more cheaply he lived and the less gracious the quality of his personal life. The difficulty with which he had obtained his fortune caused him to live as if in constant fear of losing it. Most of his property in Mexico had been acquired during the regime of dictator Porfirio Diaz—and in the years immediately following Diaz's fall, when the country was torn by bloody political and military strife.[7] Although he espoused the political ideas of the Mexican aristocracy and their recently fallen leader, he lived in Toluca in a style that was anything but aristocratic. Langston complained of the diet of meat and beans and, conspiring with the Mexican cook, managed to vary it by charging food to his father in the local shops when his father was away. He repeatedly drew his father's reprimand.

His father frequently traveled on business trips to Mexico City and to the ranch. He was gone for days at a time, and Langston saw little of him. The boy was lonely. Moreover, during the entire summer there was not a word from his mother to sustain a sense, however weak, of filial attachment. Bored with the study of bookkeeping and typing that his father had set him to, and depressed by his inability to establish a rewarding relationship with anyone—because he could not speak Spanish well enough to communicate— he suffered from a deepening malaise. With his weekly allowance of ten pesos, he went to the movies, which, after the (Catholic) church, was Toluca's foremost community center. The small town, not then the bustling Friday market tourist attraction it later became, offered Langston little that was exciting to do. Located at a high altitude in Central Mexico, Toluca was dry and cool, and most of the townsfolk made their living from agriculture or basket weaving.

Even if Langston had not been a stranger in Toluca, his limited knowledge of Spanish would still have permitted him no meaningful access to the scant social life the town afforded. His closest acquaintance was his father's *mozo*, Maximiliano, an Indian boy of about his own age, who taught him to ride horseback. Langston took long rides alone through the surrounding countryside and to nearby villages. But desolating loneliness drenched him like a deluge. He contemplated suicide, one day taking a loaded pistol from his father's desk drawer.

> I put the pistol to my head and held it there, loaded, a long time, and wondered if I would be any happier if I were to pull the trigger. But then, I began to think, if I do, I might miss something. I haven't been to the ranch yet, nor to the top of the volcano, nor to the bullfights in Mexico, nor graduated from high school, nor got married. So I put the pistol down and went back to my bookkeeping.[8]

In early August his father promised to take him to Mexico City, where he was going on a business trip. Langston looked forward to the visit, pressing and packing his clothes ten days ahead of the departure date. But on the morning they were to leave, he fell ill with what—years later—he diagnosed as an infectious hatred of his father. This psychosomatic illness was the first, but not the last, of his young manhood. It struck suddenly at breakfast with nausea and violent stomach pain. He could not travel, except back to bed, and his father left without him. Four days later, when his father returned, he was still abed; the nausea persisted, and his fever was dangerously high. A doctor ordered him hospitalized.

So he got to Mexico City after all, for the nearest hospital was there, and he went first class. "This time my father engaged seats in the parlor car and

took me to the American Hospital. . . ."9 Langston later remembered, acknowl-
edging it was contrary to his father's frugal inclination. "For two or three
weeks I got pushed around in a wheel chair in the charming gardens of the
American Hospital. When I learned that it was costing my father twenty
dollars a day to keep me there, I made no effort to get better. It pleased me
immensely to have him spending twenty dollars a day."10

By September he was well enough to return to Cleveland. He left Mexico
not having seen a bullfight, or the floating gardens of Xochimilco, or much
else he had hoped to see. But optimistic soul that he was, he had not
altogether given up on his father, nor abandoned his quest for a home.

LANGSTON journeyed from Mexico to the United States by train. Almost as
soon as he crossed the border the sort of personal affronts he had not
experienced in Mexico threatened, and he braced himself to meet or to
avoid them. At the railroad station in San Antonio he spoke Spanish and
pretended to be Mexican in order to buy sleeping-car accommodations to
St. Louis. The same evening, as he was sitting at a small table in the dining
car, a white man at the same table burst out, "You're a nigger, ain't you?"
At a refreshment stand in Union Station in St. Louis, where he had to
change trains, the clerk refused to serve him after asking if he was colored.
"I knew I was home in the U.S.A.," he wrote later.11

Having been in Mexico for three months, Langston was not aware that
1919 had been an unusually bad summer for race relations almost everywhere in the United States. The "truce" that had prevailed between blacks
and whites during the war was broken with the return of American troops
from Europe. Negro soldiers, it was said, learned things from the French
"that would render them social hazards when they returned to America."12
Racial animosities flared and blazed, causing major conflagrations in eight
cities in the "red summer" of 1919.

Back in Cleveland, the young Hughes showed scarcely any concern for
what W. E. B. Du Bois, the black scholar-leader and editor of *The Crisis*
described in an editorial as the Negro's "unbending battle against the forces
of hell."13 He was busily involved in the work of his senior year in high
school and engaged in a tug of war with his mother, who looked forward to
the day when at last he would graduate—since she could not break his
determination to do so—go to work, and, as she put it, "be of some use to
her." The tension between mother and son increased when she surmised
that he wanted to go to college; that letters from his father were urging him
to it (and inviting him to come again to Mexico); and that, indeed, his main
present effort was to sustain a scholastic average and compile an extracur-
ricular record tht would make him acceptable to a university. He managed
to keep a B average. He was elected editor of the yearbook as well as class

poet. His poems appeared more or less regularly in Central High's *Belfry Owl*, and one of them, "When Sue Wears Red," inspired by one of his few black classmates, was good enough to achieve publication in *The Crisis* three years later.

The resolution of the struggle with his mother was put off from day to day. Langston had already made up his mind that the best way to try to be on his own in some new place was to accept his father's offer to go to college, but he was reluctant to tell his mother this. Although he had no great love for either of his parents, he felt torn between them. Perplexing traits of his mother matched equally perplexing traits of his father: *Her* insensibility against *his* austerity, *his* taciturnity against *her* garrulity, *her* lack of discrimination against *his* snobbism, *his* harsh prudence against *her* indiscretion. Langston did not know whether to be more tolerant of his father's miserliness or his mother's and stepfather's extravagance (though something in his own nature made him more inclined to accept the latter).

> My mother and step-father were interested in making money, too. . . . But they were interested in making money to *spend*. And for fun. They were always buying victrolas and radios and watches and rings, and going to shows and drinking beer and playing cards, and trying to have a good time after working hours.[14]

During his senior year, much to Langston's surprised delight, his father raised his monthly allowance; while, much to his distress, all through his senior year, as in previous years, his mother nagged him to contribute to her support. He graduated with honors in June 1920, despite his problems at home. When finally the showdown came and he told his mother he was returning to Mexico and accepting the opportunity to go to college offered by his father, she reacted angrily, cruelly, disconsolately. Langston never forgot the scene his mother made, and he probably drew upon the memory of it for his one-act play, *Soul Gone Home*. The two main characters, mother and son, seem to speak straight out of Hughes's personal life.

> MOTHER (*Proudly*) Sure, I could of let you die, but I didn't. Naw, I kept you with me—off and on. And I lost the chance to marry many a good man, too—if it weren't for you. No man wants to take care o' nobody else's child. (*Self-pityingly*) You been a burden to me, Randolph.
>
> SON (*Angrily*) What did you have me for then, in the first place?
>
> MOTHER How could I help havin' you, you little bastard? Your father ruint me—and you's the result. And I been worried with you for sixteen years. (*Disgustedly*) Now, just when you

get big enough to work and do me some good, you have to go and die.[15]

So it was with no glad heart that Langston Hughes set out alone for Mexico in the summer of 1920. Indeed, he was miserable and—in a word that was just acquiring a new meaning—blue. The mood persisted. It generated some of his early published work. "I felt pretty bad when I got on the train," he wrote about this episode. "I felt bad for the next three or four years, to tell the truth, and those were the years when I wrote most of my poetry."[16]

In spite of his personal unhappiness, the summer in Mexico in 1920 was an altogether better summer than the one before. His father went out of his way to be agreeable. His father's new housekeeper, a German widow named Berta Schultz (whom the elder Hughes later married), and her ten-year-old daughter, Lotte, brought a sense of solid, enduring comfort to the household. They spoke neither English nor Spanish, but Langston picked up enough German from them and from his father, who was fluent in the language, to communicate with them. He enjoyed a freedom of movement and association he had been denied on his previous visit. In order to improve his Spanish, he began reading Spanish novels (the works of Vicente Blasco Ibáñez then interested him most). And though he was still shy about speaking the language, his increasing proficiency opened up to him the social life of Toluca. His mastery of riding so pleased his father that the latter took him for a weekend visit to the ranch.

During the trip, Mr. Hughes set forth his notions about his son's education. He wanted Langston to study in either Switzerland or Germany, become a mining engineer, and return to Mexico. There was, he said, a great future in the silver mines near the ranch. By a great future he meant making lots of money, and having lots of money in Mexico meant, as he told his son, he wouldn't have "to live like a nigger with niggers."

Langston demurred. He would not succeed at mining engineering. Besides, he really did not want to make money—not even a good deal of money—for the sake of making money. What he wanted most was to write, and Columbia University, he thought, could provide the learning and, since it was on the edge of Harlem, access to the atmosphere he felt he needed to absorb.

James Hughes thought his son's ambition foolish and that perhaps, if he kept him in Mexico, Langston would mature and come around to his father's point of view. It was understood, then, that at least for the time being, there would be no money for Langston's education, or even for his return to the United States.

Langston sublimated his disappointment and unhappiness in his writing.

He had been writing in inspired spurts from the day he left Cleveland. One of his best-known poems was written on the train ride to Mexico. It emerged in part from thoughts about his father, whose racial attitudes Langston found so different from his own. He jotted the poem down on the back of an envelope—his notebook not being handy—as the train crossed the Mississippi River to St. Louis.

The Negro Speaks of Rivers

I've known rivers:
I've known rivers ancient as the world and older than the
    flow of human blood in human veins.

My soul has grown deep like the rivers.

I bathed in the Euphrates when dawns were young.
I built my hut near the Congo and it lulled me to sleep.
I looked upon the Nile and raised the pyramids above it.
I heard the singing of the Mississippi when Abe Lincoln
    went down to New Orleans, and I've seen its muddy
    bosom turn all golden in the sunset.

I've known rivers:
Ancient, dusky rivers.

My soul has grown deep like the rivers.

The free form and the easy, simple language show the influence of Sandburg, but the subject matter and the emotional thrust are distinctively Hughes's. "The Negro Speaks of Rivers," which was published in June 1921, a year after it was composed, was the first poem of his literary maturity, and the first to be published in *The Crisis*, the official organ of the National Association for the Advancement of Colored People—the NAACP. The poem was followed a month later in *The Crisis* by "Aunt Sue's Stories," inspired by his relations with his grandmother. During the next three years Hughes's poems appeared almost solely in *The Crisis*.[17] He had begun reading the magazine regularly in Toluca, and subscribed to it while there. And from Mexico he submitted his first contributions to it. The editors had been impressed. During a period of fifteen months in Mexico, he wrote seven other poems, five prose sketches, and one one-act play. All appeared in 1921 in *The Brownies' Book*, which W. E. B. Du Bois, editor of *The Crisis*, had established for children.[18] None of the seven, mostly lyrical, poems Langston wrote in Mexico touch upon race, and all the prose sketches, except one entitled "Those Who Have No Turkey," reflect the youthful writer's Mexican experience: "Mexican Games," "In a Mexican City," "Up to the Crater of an Old Volcano," and "The Virgin of Guadalupe." His first one-act play, *The Gold Piece*, is set in an unnamed Mexican village. These juvenile selections, along with the two poems published in *The Crisis*, marked his first publication outside *The Belfry Owl*.

If Langston Hughes was unhappy during this time, as he tells us he was, it is not reflected in his work. He was not given to brooding; self-pity was scarcely a habit with him. Under the circumstances, he perhaps had a right to feel wronged by his father, but he did not indulge it. Neither then nor during the rest of his life was he able to bear grudges or to act decisively in terms of them. Although James Hughes refused to provide money for his son's return to the States (to say nothing about college) as the summer moved toward autumn, Langston harbored the belief that his father would relent: it was some months before the belief was justified.

Meantime, Langston went to work. For the next year he taught the English language in a Toluca business college in the mornings and in a private girls' school in the afternoons, in addition to private tutoring. Some of the money he saved toward college, some he sent to his mother, and the rest he spent going every weekend during the season to bullfights in Mexico City. Bullfighting was a great attraction for him. Later, after he had seen many bullfights and learned to admire the superb coordination, skill, and grace of good matadors, and to understand the rules that governed the activity in the bullring, and to appreciate the ceremony that attended it, he could write, "There's no sport in the world so lovely as a 'corrida de toros.'..."[19] But he never succeeded in writing about it. More than once— as he later admitted—"I tried to write about a bullfight, but could never capture it on paper." Its fascination for him was probably related to his obsession with the idea of death—an obsession that is evident in much of the poetry he wrote over the next three decades. Like his older contemporary, Ernest Hemingway, who had the same, though purer, obsession, Hughes attributed overwhelming symbolic significance to the *corrida*. "It is not a game or a sport," Hughes wrote. "It's life playing deliberately with death. Except that death is alive, too, taking an active part."

Throughout his adult life Hughes maintained a philosophical attitude about death. Significantly, during his young manhood, by strange twists of fate, he barely missed death twice. The first time was in Toluca. An elderly German brewer who lived in the town walked into the Hughes household one day intent on shooting Langston, believing the youth was keeping company with an eighteen-year-old German girl, Gerta Kraus, whom the brewer had hired as housekeeper. Langston had no romantic interest in the girl, but the brewer did. The old man, finding her in the Hughes house— where, with her mother, she was visiting Frau Schultz—shot the girl three times, wounded Frau Schultz, then went about the premises looking for Langston. Neither Langston nor his father was at home. The brewer turned himself in to the police, his pistol still loaded with two bullets. Langston returned home from one of his classes a half-hour after the shooting, just after an ambulance had rushed the women to the hospital.

During his remaining months in Mexico, most of Langston's time was taken up with teaching and writing. But he had time for social diversions, too, and he spent more than one fine evening with young men his own age watching the girls of Toluca as they promenaded in the town square.

There were also occasional weekends with his father at the ranch. By slow degrees father and son reached a kind of understanding. Perhaps each saw something of himself in the other—determination, personal integrity, and stubborn persistence in a course once chosen. Or perhaps there was between them a mute acceptance of the father-son relationship and what it traditionally committed them to and was supposed to mean. At any rate, they got on together and learned to like each other. Although James Hughes professed to believe writing a waste of time, he seemed to take pride in his son's talent; and although he continued to argue the benefits of a European education, he agreed at last to finance his son's studies at Columbia, beginning with the fall term of 1921.

The days could not pass too quickly for Langston. He was ready to leave some time before his September departure date, when he turned his English classes over to a woman from Arkansas, who had "never come across an educated Ne-gre before." When the day came, his father, whom he would never see again, accompanied him to Mexico City. There Langston took the train to Vera Cruz, and thence by boat through the Gulf of Mexico to the Caribbean and into the Atlantic. This first sea voyage stirred a latent wanderlust, which he suppressed at the time. New York was his immediate goal. Viewing the city skyline as his ship approached through the evening dusk, he was sure that "it was better to come to New York than to any other city in the world."[20]

❧ 4 ❧

Hail and Farewell

L ANGSTON HUGHES HAD A WEEK TO HIMSELF before classes began at Columbia University, and he spent it getting acquainted with Harlem.
The area was still a mixed racial community in 1921, but it was already
being called "the Negro capital of the world." At that time some seventy-
seven thousand black people—most of them recent arrivals from the southern states and the Caribbean—inhabited the area stretching from 130th
Street north to 145th, and from Fifth Avenue to Eighth Avenue. Along the
main avenues of Harlem, Jews ran a variety of small businesses, notably
grocery stores and pawnshops, and lived in quarters above them. There
were sizable numbers of Italians and Irish as well, and some of the more
elegant townhouses on the southern edge of Harlem near Central Park were
still occupied by prosperous whites. But blacks predominated. Langston
Hughes was fascinated: "I wanted to shake hands with them, speak to
them."[1] He was impressed, too, that within a short distance of the YMCA
on West 135th Street where he roomed, lived black writers, artists, and
prominent figures whom he had read about in the Negro press, and whom
he might chance to see on the street.

> It was Harlem's Golden Era, that of the twenties. I was nineteen
> when I first came up out of the Lenox Avenue subway one
> bright September afternoon and looked around in the happy
> sunlight to see if I saw Duke Ellington on the corner of 135th
> Street, or Bessie Smith passing by, or Bojangles Bill Robinson
> in front of the Lincoln Theatre, or maybe Paul Robeson or Bert
> Williams walking down the avenue. Had I been able to recog-
> nize any of them, it would have been only because I had read all
> about them in the Middle West, where I had gone to school, and
> I had dreamed of maybe someday seeing them. I hoped, too, I
> might see in New York some of the famous colored writers and
> editors whose names were known around the country....[2]

27

He didn't find Bojangles Bill Robinson in front of the Lincoln Theatre, but he enjoyed going there to listen to the blues and to black folk comedians. He also went to the Lafayette Theatre, a few blocks away on 132nd Street and Seventh Avenue, where a Negro stock company, starring Abbie Mitchell and Andrew Bishop, put on such popular melodramas as *Paid in Full, The Chocolate Soldier, Within the Law*, and *Madame X*. He found the popular nightclubs—the Cotton Club, Barron's, Leroy's and Small's—some of which, in the not distant future, would become the backdrop of many of his blues poems. In the Harlem branch of the New York Public Library, a few blocks from the YMCA, he discovered the just developing Schomburg Collection of Negro Literature and History—a resource he was to find indispensable throughout a long writing career. Churches and funeral parlors, night clubs and restaurants, shops and stores, newspaper offices and real estate firms, lawyers and doctors, fortunetellers and hairdressers were all a hop, skip and a jump from any place he happened to be.

At age nineteen, Hughes was as much taken with the myth of Harlem's exoticism as any white person during the nineteen twenties. His youthful impression of a gay, rollicking Harlem outweighed any realization that it was a community whose growing economic and social problems were causing it to emerge as a ghetto. But he learned.

> My youthful illusion that Harlem was a world unto itself did not
> last very long. It was not even an area that ran itself. The famous
> nightclubs were owned by whites, as were the theatres. Almost
> all the stores were owned by whites, and many at the time did
> not even (in the very middle of Harlem) employ Negro clerks. . . .[3]

But his first week was not spoiled by any such knowledge, and he was reluctant to move to Morningside Heights when Columbia opened.

There was difficulty from the start. The university's unstated policy was not to house Negro students in the dormitories, but there had been no hint of the racial identity of Langston Hughes in the application mailed from Mexico; and when he showed up at 111 Hartley Hall to claim the room he had been assigned, university authorities yielded it grudgingly. It was an unpleasant beginning to what turned out to be an unsatisfactory academic year. The science and math courses he was required to take bored him; his French class was too large for effective instruction. Only English literature came near to meeting his intellectual interests, but even this course did not give him the satisfaction he got from the noncredit lectures he attended in lower Manhattan at the Rand School of Social Science. A six-year-old institution founded by the American Socialist Society to offer courses in literature, the arts, and politics to the working class, the Rand faculty included such left-wing intellectuals as Norman Thomas, Scott Nearing, and

Ludwig Lewisohn. The school was part of the radical education of Langston Hughes.

Although he was accepted on the reportorial staff of the Columbia University newspaper, *The Spectator*, his assignment was an unpleasant joke, and he quickly withdrew. He was asked to cover the fraternity beat and social events, but Afro-Americans were not welcomed into fraternity houses or at social functions. Indeed, the whole university atmosphere was unfriendly. By the end of the first term, though, he had made a few acquaintances among "outsiders" like himself, including a Chinese classmate who often invited him to Chinatown. And during April and May 1922 several of his poems appeared in *The Spectator*, signed "Lang-Hu."[4] Sounding phonetically like Lang Who?, his pen name reflected the way Hughes felt as a Columbia student—unsure, unknown, and unwelcome.

Harlem held by far the greater attraction for Langston, and if he needed excuses to go there, he now had two. First, his mother, again separated from her husband, was living in Harlem (and Langston was helping to support her on the allowance from his father). And second, and more important, Harlem and its people and its throbbing tide of life were providing the inspiration for most of the poems he wrote during that academic year. Between January and December 1922, thirteen of his new poems appeared in *The Crisis*. Four of these—"Negro," "My People," "The South," and "Mother to Son"—are among the most famous; and "Negro," which later appeared as "Proem" in *The Weary Blues*, Hughes's first volume of poetry, is probably, after "The Negro Speaks of Rivers," the most often quoted. Like the earlier poem, "Negro" summarizes the history, reveals the racial pride, and suggests the depths of subterranean energy that are both the sources and the subjects of Afro-American expression.

Negro

> I am a Negro:
> > Black as the night is black,
> > Black like the depths of my Africa.
>
> I've been a slave:
> > Caesar told me to keep his door-steps clean.
> > I brushed the boots of Washington.
>
> I've been a worker:
> > Under my hand the pyramids arose.
> > I made mortar for the Woolworth Building.

I've been a singer:
  All the way from Africa to Georgia
  I carried my sorrow songs.
  I made ragtime.

I've been a victim:
  The Belgians cut off my hands in the Congo.
  They lynch me now in Texas.[5]

I am a Negro:
  Black as the night is black,
  Black like the depths of my Africa.

While "My People" is a paean of praise to the beauty of blackness, and "Mother to Son" strikes the ever-recurring theme of the Afro-American's endurance and enduring hope, "The South" is Hughes's first protest poem.

Not all of the poems written in this period can be called "racial," and not all of them were imitative of Sandburg's free verse form. One was a recapturing of a memory of Mexico, another a tribute to a dead friend. Three were nature poems, and two more were experiments in poetic forms: blues and "jazz rhythm" pieces of the type of "Song for a Banjo Dance" and "Danse Africaine."[6]

Submission of his work to *The Crisis* brought him an invitation. It came from Jessie Fauset, herself a poet and novelist, who was then literary editor of the magazine. Miss Fauset had written the young poet at least one encouraging letter while he was still in Mexico. Discovering from a change in the address of his subscription that he was now in New York City, she tracked him down and invited him to lunch at the Civic Club. The invitation upset him. He lacked self-assurance and social ease, except among his peers—and he did not consider himself a peer of *The Crisis* staff members.

I pictured the entire staff of the *Crisis* as very learned Negroes and very rich, in nose glasses and big cars. I had a tremendous admiration for Dr. W. E. B. Du Bois, whose *Souls of Black Folk* had stirred my youth, but I was flabbergasted at the thought of meeting him. What would I say? What should I do? How could I act—not to appear as dumb as I felt myself to be? So I didn't go near the *Crisis* until Jessie Fauset sent for me.[7]

He responded to Miss Fauset's invitation by asking if he could bring his mother along. His mother, if nothing else, was outgoing, and on such an occasion could be counted upon to do the talking. The luncheon went off better than he expected, for he found himself at ease with the gracious Miss Fauset.

Hughes's association with *The Crisis* staff, though sporadic, increased his determination to pursue eventually the literary life and introduced him to an aspect of it that, much later, would prove important in his career. Through an arrangement made by Augustus Granville Dill, business manager of *The Crisis*, the young poet gave a public reading of his works at Manhattan's Community Church—the first church in which he was invited to read his poems. In the future, he would devote several months a year to this activity, and it would later account for a large part of his income. In 1921-22, however, public reading brought in no money; and he could have used considerably more than his father sent him. "My father," he remembered, "kept wondering why I ran out of money so quickly. But I didn't have enough for college, my mother and me, too."[8]

Still, he managed even some of the things his frugal father would have undoubtedly labeled extravagant extras. The theatre had replaced the bull-fight as a prime interest to Langston, and he sometimes skimped on necessities to attend it. In the 1921-22 season he saw (and carefully noted) every major production on Broadway. These included *Rain* (John Colton's adaptation of Somerset Maugham's famous story "Sadie Thompson"); Eugene O'Neill's *Anna Christie* (which won the Pulitzer prize that year); *Hamlet*, with John Barrymore in the title role; *La Malquerida*, by Jacinto Benavente, the Spanish playwright who was awarded the Nobel prize in 1922; and Baileff's *Chauve Souris*, a widely acclaimed Russian musical novelty that Hughes saw twice. He was equally impressed with an American musical hit called *Shuffle Along*, by Nobel Sissle and Eubie Blake (who also performed in it). It was an all-Negro production, starring Florence Mills, and it knocked down the barriers that had kept Broadway an exclusive white preserve for many years.

As the end of the academic year drew near, Langston made a decision he had been pondering for some time: he would withdraw from the university. Although he failed physical education, his final marks were respectable—three Bs, a C, and an incomplete in mathematics—and grades were not the determining factor in his decision. He was not motivated to continue studying in order to become a mining engineer, and to have his father pay for his education in the expectation that he would was a kind of cheating. It was in essence the way he put it when he wrote to his father that, after a certain date, he need not send him any more money: he was quitting the university. He would go to work and make it on his own. James Hughes sent no more money. He did not bother to reply.

HIS EXAMS OVER and his education ended at least temporarily, Hughes moved to Harlem in early June. By this time his mother, once more reconciled with Homer Clark, had returned to Cleveland and was no longer a drain on his limited funds. Still, it was necessary for him to exercise great care in order for his money to last until he found a job. Day after day, he answered all the likely ads for busboys, waiters, handymen, clerks—anything he thought he could do. Soon he learned that unless the notices specified "colored" there was no need for him to apply. His father's warnings about living in the United States were not, after all, merely the rationalizations of a wrong-headed and embittered man. "Experience," Langston wrote later, "was proving my father right. On many sides, the color line barred your way from making a living in America."[9]

Finally, he got a job on a truck farm on Staten Island. He worked from dawn until dark six days a week and sometimes for a few hours on Sunday. "Only once during the whole summer did I go to New York," he later remembered, "and that was to see Rudolph Valentino in *Blood and Sand*, because I liked bullfights and I wanted to see if they had a real one in the picture."[10] For his job he was paid fifty dollars a month, plus bed and board (and his bed was a haystack). But he liked the work:

> There was something about such work that made you feel useful
> and important—sending off onions that *you* had planted and seen
> grow from a mere speck of green, and that *you* had tended and
> weeded, and pulled up and washed and even loaded on the wagon—
> seeing them go off to feed the great city of New York.[11]

Working at this common occupation made him feel spiritually close to Walt Whitman, whose *Leaves of Grass* he was reading and whose influence he was beginning to feel. Hughes was especially fond of "Calamus" and "Song of the Open Road." Like Whitman, Hughes wanted to be a writer without becoming—in Whitman's term—a "literatus." Like Whitman, Hughes wanted to share the common man's experiences, for he wanted to be a spokesman for the common man. Whitman, while still in his twenties, had written in his notebooks:

> I will not descend among professors and capitalists—
> I will turn the ends of my trousers around my boots,
> my cuffs back from the wrists, and go with drivers
> and boatmen and men that catch fish or work in the fields.[12]

This was Hughes's own spirit. And that spirit was troubled when his job ended after the harvest on the Staten Island farm and he returned to Manhattan.

Again, congenial and well-paid employment in New York City was hard to come by. Langston encountered many of the same problems of racial discrimination he had found during the summer. He grew despondent and fearful that he might not find work at all. His Harlem landlady—a strongly maternal, amiable, optimistic Negro woman named Mrs. Dorsey—could not reconcile him to his situation, but she encouraged him daily not to give up. In this period of acute but hardly rational emotional depression, he assuaged his feelings by writing poetry. It was at this time that he wrote "Mother to Son," a poem that was inspired by Mrs. Dorsey. It ends on a note that is widely taken as expressive of the folk spirit and wisdom of the Afro-American people. It is a note that Hughes struck many times:

> So boy, don't you turn back.
> Don't you set down on the steps
> 'Cause you finds it kinder hard.
> Don't you fall now—
> For I'se still goin', honey,
> I'se still climbin',
> And life for me ain't been no crystal stair.[13]

Hughes managed to get a job as delivery boy for a florist. The hours were long, the wages were low, and his employer was demanding and ill-tempered. Langston soon quit. Finding other employment that autumn was not easy. As he wrote later, "It seemed to me now that if I had to work for low wages at dull jobs, I might as well see the world, so I began to look for work on a ship."[14]

For three weeks he tramped the docks and in and out of shipping offices, and finally he was taken on as a mess boy on the S.S. *West Hassayampa*. He did not know it at the time, but the *West Hassayampa* wasn't going anywhere. Towed forty miles up the Hudson River to Jones Point, opposite Peekskill, it was moored there to serve as mother ship and quarters for a crew of mostly Swedes and Spaniards whose job it was to maintain a fleet of idle freighters that had been decommissioned shortly after World War I.

Langston liked his new job. The work was not difficult. It left him lots of time for writing and reading and listening to his shipmates' tales of distant seas and foreign ports. His contact with the Spanish-speaking crew members not only preserved his fluency in the language, but helped to revive an interest in Spanish literature that he had developed in Mexico. The Spanish author who involved him most that winter was Pio Baroja,[15] whose essays and novels he read avidly. Two of Baroja's great themes were vagabondage and adventure, both of which Hughes could identify with. He could also relate to the Spaniard's satire of a pretentious and exploitative aristocracy; it confirmed some of his own social attitudes about Mexico and America. His reading ranged wide, and included all he could find in the ship's library: Samuel Butler's *Way of All Flesh*, Joseph Conrad's *Heart of Darkness*, and

Gabriele D'Annunzio's *Flame of Life*, plus the volumes of Whitman, Nietzsche, and Baroja he had brought along with him. Only Whitman's work, however, seems to have influenced Hughes's own writing—and that only a little.[16] He was finding his special bent, speaking more and more in his own voice. In the five months of that winter and spring at Jones Point, he completed more than a dozen poems, eleven of which appeared in *The Crisis* that year—nine of them in the August issue.[17] Like "The Weary Blues," which he worked on, but did not complete—and which later became the title poem of his first volume of poetry—most of this output reflected his interest in Harlem specifically and Negro urban life generally. "Cabaret," "Jazzonia," "Poem," "Young Prostitute," and "Young Singer" were among these.

Because the river froze, going ashore was difficult, and Hughes left ship only twice. One of his poems, "Monotony," was perhaps written in response to those conditions.

> Today like yesterday
>   Tomorrow like today:
> The drip, drip, drip,
>   Of monotony
>
> Is wearing my life away:
> Today like yesterday
> Tomorrow like today.[18]

The two occasions he went ashore were mainly to go to the theatre and to visit Harlem. He saw *Chauve Souris* for the third time, the Moscow Art Players Production of *Salome*, and performances of *Romeo and Juliet* and *Will Shakespeare*.

Meanwhile, the poems in *The Crisis* had attracted the attention of Alain Locke, a scholar-critic-teacher on the faculty of Howard University. Locke, a Phi Beta Kappa graduate of Harvard and the first black Rhodes Scholar, was a bachelor in his late thirties who delighted in giving advice and encouragement to young men of talent and promise; he initiated a correspondence with Hughes in January 1923. The older man was thoroughly convinced that there were enough black writers, artists, and thinkers to generate a new and distinctive cultural movement. His first letters to young Hughes rang with this conviction. Indeed, he was already acting on it: he had begun editing material for a book expressive of his view on literature and culture, *The New Negro*. In subsequent letters he invited Hughes to contribute to it. The book would prove seminal, when published in 1925, to what became known as the Harlem Renaissance. The available evidence suggests that the poet did not respond to Locke's overtures immediately. Early in February, he wrote (from Jones Point):

> It is too bad I am not living in New York anymore. I am missing so many interesting people. I am chasing dreams up here, though, and that's an infinitely more delightful occupation even than living in New York, where all my old dreams had been realized: college (horrible place, but I wanted to go), Broadway and the theatres—delightful memories, Riverside Drive in the mists and Harlem. A whirling year in New York! Now I want to go to Europe, stay for a while in France, then live with the gypsies in Spain (wild dream, isn't it?) and see the bullfights in Seville. . . . [19]

Locke, of course, did not know of Hughes's shyness, his self-effacement, and nothing in this letter indicated it. But another letter later in the same month hinted that at the time the poet preferred the screen of letter writing to the exposure of face-to-face meeting. Their friendship in its early stages was sustained through correspondence; and the two men developed a relationship that on Hughes's part seems to have been filial, and that on Locke's part was made the instrument of considerable assistance to the poet's career. But in early 1923, the excuse Hughes gave for not meeting the older man—a request Locke coupled with a request for the poet's photograph—was frank, yet polite.

> It would be very inconvenient for you to come up to Jones Point and I can't come down to the city just now, so I am afraid we will have to postpone our meeting until some other time. This is a most out of the way place and our ship is at the very end of the fleet, a good half mile of slippery gang-planks and icy decks from the shore landing. And then at the end of your journey, you would find a very stupid person because I am always dumb in the presence of those whom I want to be friends with. You have written me such an understanding letter that I would like to know you, but I'd rather you wouldn't come up here to see me.
> I shall write you again soon. [20]

In succeeding months, Hughes sent Locke several new poems, some of which he asked the professor's advice concerning an outlet for publication.

By the late spring of 1923, something besides writing was on Langston Hughes's mind. The wanderlust that had seized him when he had sailed from Vera Cruz to New York nearly two years before stirred anew. Thanks to his life on the *West Hassayampa*, and the tales he had heard from the ship's crew, and the sea smell borne on the wind that swept her decks, the stirring grew to a surge, a tumult. He wanted to be on a vessel that was going somewhere. He decided to leave the fleet in May. The steward wrote a recommendation declaring the bearer, Langston Hughes, "competent, courteous, capable, trustworthy, and efficient."[21] Just before he left Jones Point, Hughes wrote Professor Locke ambivalently: "Please write to me soon as I shall not be here much longer. The hills are at their loveliest now and I do not like to go, but there are other rivers in the world to see besides the Hudson. And oh! so many dreams to chase!"[22]

In June, having found the S.S. *Malone*, a ship that needed a mess boy, he was on his way to Africa.

Africa and Europe

A BOARD THE S.S. MALONE OFF SANDY HOOK, Hughes threw overboard all the books he had accumulated since Toluca. It was a symbolic act of purgation. He had, he tells us, "believed in books more than people—which of course was wrong," and casting his books into the sea purged him of that belief and, indeed, of his need to read as an escape. The real world and the drama of real life would take precedence over the world of books. The adult Langston Hughes (he had just turned twenty-one in the spring of 1923) would read only enough to keep abreast of what was happening in the popular arts and of what the most reputable contemporary authors were doing in poetry and prose. Ridding himself of his youthful addiction to reading was a consequence less desirable than another.

> ...that night off Sandy Hook, they [his books] seemed like everything I had known in the past, like the attics and basements in Cleveland, like the lonely nights in Toluca, like the dormitory at Columbia, like the furnished room in Harlem, like too much reading all the time when I was a kid, like life isn't, as described in romantic prose;...It was like throwing a million bricks out of my heart—for it wasn't only the books that I wanted to throw away, but everything unpleasant and miserable out of my past....[1]

The S.S. *Malone* was a freighter with a crew of forty-two, and Hughes felt lucky to be aboard, especially since she was bound for Africa. His work in the officers' mess was not overly demanding. He rose at six, served breakfast, tidied the officers' quarters, served lunch, was generally free in the afternoon, and served dinner. There was time for writing, but he wrote little. During a voyage of nearly six months, Hughes wrote only one piece, "The Ships, Sea and Africa," and that, for all its prose-poem quality, showed scarcely a hint of the effective prose stylist he eventually became.[2] He spent much of his leisure time with the crew—a rowdy bunch of seamen given to drink and boisterous behavior—some of whom later served Hughes as models for fictional characters, and with whom he tried bravely to play the hail-fellow-well-met. It was not his habit to gamble or drink, and he did not run after women, but the crew apparently did not hold these abstinences against him.

Years later he would confess to one of his closest friends that, in the all-male atmosphere aboard ship, he was goaded toward his first homosexual experience. It is almost certain, too, that he used memories of that voyage four years later in creating the fictionalized character of the young sailor depicted in the short story "The Little Virgin," about whom he wrote: "The sailors called him the Little Virgin because they discovered that he had never known a woman and because of his polite manners."[3]

During the trip, he was too involved with his personal reactions to evaluate what he saw and felt, and too ardently storing up impressions to record them. His first sight of Africa was the beginning of an emotional experience that he was never to forget and that he would advert to time and again.

> When I saw the dust-green hills in the sunlight, something took
> hold of me inside. My Africa, Motherland of the Negro peoples!
> And me a Negro! Africa! The real thing, to be touched and seen,
> not merely read about in a book.[4]

Africa did much more than affect his senses. It was more than touch and sight and sound. As the S.S. *Malone* put into ports in Senegal, Guinea, the Gold Coast, Sierra Leone, Liberia, Nigeria—all along the west coast to Portuguese Angola—he became aware of Africa's colonialism, of white domination, of "white men with guns at their belts." He wrote bitterly of this some years later, when his experiences in the Caribbean further aroused his political consciousness.

> Black:
> Exploited, beaten and robbed,
> Shot and killed.
> Blood running into
> > Dollars
> > Pounds
> > Francs
> > Pesetas
> > Lire
> For the wealth of the exploiters—...[5]

The exploitation he saw in African ports seemed to cast a fog over the meaning of "civilization." He told dock workers on the Gold Coast what he later expressed in a poem: "You do not know the fog / We strange so civilized ones / Sail in always."[6] And he echoed the sentiment in a 1925 poem:

Liars

It is we who are liars:
The Pretenders-to-be who are not
And the Pretenders-not-to be who are.
It is we who use words
As screens for thoughts
And weave dark garments
To cover the naked body
Of the too white Truth
It is we with the civilized souls
    Who are liars.[7]

In Africa, Hughes saw Europeans Only signs, and was sharply reminded of the White Only signs of the American South. Yet he did not see the American black's weary sense of patience, of excessive gratitude for token advances. In Africa, Hughes heard much talk of Marcus Garvey, the Jamaican black nationalist leader, whose back-to-Africa movement and whose ideas for self-determination for black people were ridiculed by most Negroes in the United States. Garvey was taken seriously in Africa, where his ideas were having influence: Africans were beginning to see the white man's "mission" for what it was. Seventeen years later, referring generally to this colonial exploitation and specifically to the owners of the *Malone* and other ships in the African trade, Hughes complained that they "paid very little for the labor" and even less for the things they took away. "The white man dominates Africa," he wrote. "He takes produce, and lives, very much as he chooses. The yield of earth for Europe and America."[8]

Painful as this realization was, even more painful—probably because it was on a personal level—was Hughes's sense of being rejected by Africans.

[Africa] was the only place in the world where I've been called a white man. They looked at my copper-brown skin and straight black hair,... except a little curly—and they said: "You—white man."[9]

The memory of one small incident still brought a flash of pain long afterward. Walking one evening with an acquaintance in a Nigerian village, he expressed a wish to see a juju ceremony, and was informed, "White man never go see Ju-Ju." When he insisted that he was not a white man, he was told, "You no black man, neither." It was not until a year later that Hughes could write about it, and he did so in a piece entitled "Burutu Moon: An Evening in an African Village."[10] It was the first piece he wrote for money, and that perhaps had something to do with the sense of strain it generates. But it was several years before the whole experience of Africa and his personal reactions to it could be turned into fiction or poetry. Caustic verses such as the one quoted earlier and "Johannesburg Mines," "The English," and "Black Workers" are all a direct result of some of his early reactions to Africa.

The reactions he later turned into strong, often caustic words were not the reactions the youthful Hughes felt or expressed in some of his letters. His initial impressions of Africa make him seem—at twenty-one—insensitive to the effects of colonialism which, later, struck him with great force. A letter written from Dakar, Senegal, to his mother is especially revealing when compared with some of his published work on Africa.

> DEAREST MOTHER:
>   This morning I had my first sight of Africa. At sunrise we were running along the coast—a coast of long low hills and strange jagged rocks, and now and then the tall silhouette of a palm tree against the sun. We were close enough to see the strange white houses on the hills and the flags on the French forts. This is the state where Siki, the black French Boxer came from.
>   You should see the clothes they wear here. Everything from overcoats to nothing. I have laughed until I can't. No two people dress alike. Some have on capes, some shawls, some pants. Some wear blue cloths fastened around their necks and feet, blowing out like sails behind. . . . Some have on preacher's coats, others knee pants like bloomers with half hose and garters. It's a scream! But everybody's different and you can't tell a woman from a man. You ought to see them!. . .
>
>   Love, Love, Love
>   Langston[11]

Curiously enough, little of the African experience found its way into his prose fiction, and that which did, reworked by his imagination, has little significance as personal history. For instance, the Anglo-African protagonist in his short story, "African Morning," was not in reality a twelve-year-old boy in "a calico breech of faded flowers," and his African mother was not dead, and he did not live with his English banker father. Hughes's real-life model was a sixteen- or seventeen-year-old named Edward, who lived in Port Harcourt (Niger Delta) with his mother, who on her part had been deserted by her "master," Edward's banker father, when he returned to England. The real-life Edward wore British clothing, spoke the English language, and in general modeled himself on his father's people, who rejected him with the same passive indifference as the African people, who ostracized him. The only similarity between the fictional and the factual account is in the theme of the tragic mulatto.[12]

Other incidents related to the *Malone* voyage did find their way into Hughes's short stories, notably "Bodies in the Moonlight," "The Young Glory of Him," and "The Little Virgin," which appeared in *The Messenger* in 1927 as his first published short fiction. "Luani of the Jungles," which belies its title, was published in *Harlem* a year later. Although Wallace Thurman, who was editor of both magazines, bought the three stories for *The Messenger* at ten dollars each, he wrote Hughes "that they were very bad stories, but better than any others he could find, so he published them."[13]

It is also possible that the events described in "The Sailor and the Steward" are based on occurrences aboard the *Malone*. Though there is nothing in Hughes's autobiography alluding to the incidents presented in the story, and he did not cast himself as the Cuban sailor protagonist, the setting is a ship bound for Africa.[14]

Hughes's autobiography indicates that life aboard the *Malone* certainly provided enough material that could have been turned to fictional account. One such example is a racial incident in which Hughes was at odds with one of the ship's officers. Though he got along well with most of the crew, the third engineer, a Southerner, proved an unpleasant exception. Coming late to a meal while the ship was in port, the engineer found Hughes serving some African customs officials. Shouting, "I don't eat with niggers," the engineer ordered the Africans to leave the table. Hughes, blazing with anger, picked up a heavy tureen and told the engineer, "You get out of here yourself." The engineer withdrew. For reasons known only to himself, the officer did not bring this incident to the attention of the captain, and he never bothered Hughes again. Hughes, unlike most of the crew, presented no disciplinary problems to the captain. Indeed, the captain "never said a word to me the whole trip except, when money was being issued, the customary: 'How much?' " And Hughes invariably replied, "A pound, sir."

By the time the *Malone* left the coast of Africa, almost every sailor had acquired either a parrot or a monkey. (The purchase of a monkey figures in "Luani of the Jungles," and he claims to have paid three shillings, an old shirt, and a pair of shoes for a wild, red monkey he named Jocko that he bought in the Congo.) Autumnal storms plagued the vessel on the voyage home. During one such storm, dozens of parrots and monkeys escaped, chattering and squawking, creating untold havoc all over the ship. Persistent bad weather forced the creaking freighter off course and delayed her several days. Food shortages developed; the handful of passengers complained about the lack of fresh meat, fruit, bread, and milk. The passengers were no better fed than the officers or ordinary crew, who, while still over a week from home port, had only sardines and wormy oatmeal to eat. Mutiny threatened, but did not erupt. When the voyage ended in New York in early November, the entire crew was fired. This did not trouble Hughes. He took the subway to Harlem.

DESPITE its unhappy ending, the voyage of the S.S.*Malone* incited Hughes's lust for travel. He intended to stay ashore only long enough to buy some clothes and make a brief visit to McKeesport, Pennsylvania, where his mother, stepfather, and stepbrother were living. But in New York he discovered that the great Italian actress Eleonora Duse would be performing at the Metropolitan Opera House in Ibsen's *Lady from the Sea* in ten days, and he would not forgo the opportunity to see her. When he finally reached McKeesport, his funds were low. Instead of a planned gift of fifty dollars, he could offer his mother only some souvenirs he had brought from Africa— beads, brass trays, and slippers made of rhinoceros hide. Fortunately, for the moment, his family was not in dire need of money. Both his mother and her husband were working; Gwyn, Hughes's eleven-year-old stepbrother, was attending the local school, and the family was settled comfortably enough on the top floor of a house near the Monongahela River. They enjoyed a rare sense of stability, and for a few days Langston enjoyed it with them. It was the first time the four had been together in three years. But the sea soon beckoned him to anywhere, to everywhere.

Back in New York, in late November, Hughes signed on as mess boy on a freighter sailing to Constantinople and Odessa. It was to sail within the week, and Langston took his belongings and boarded ship at once. On his first night, all the money he had—only four dollars, but an important sum to him—was stolen while he slept. Two days later, the chief steward fell and broke his arm. His replacement preferred an all-white crew, and he told Langston, along with a Puerto Rican mess boy, that his services would not be required. The dismissal was a stroke of luck—at least for Langston Hughes. A month later the ship was sunk by a mine left over from World War I, and more than half the crew drowned. Hughes might have been among them, for he had never learned to swim. For the second time, he missed a rendezvous with death.

Meanwhile, Hughes took work on a weather-worn boat running between Hoboken and the West Indies, but quit before sailing when he discovered that his boss, the cook, was "a vicious old Negro from Barbados" who expected him not only "to act as general mess boy, but also peel potatoes, knead the bread, scrub the galley, wash the pots, empty the ashes, shine the brass—and wake him up in the morning as well, with a cup of coffee in hand...."[15]

While in Hoboken, he was hired on a freighter making regular runs between New York and Holland. The ship—coincidentally named the *McKeesport*—was a good one with a good crew, and Hughes felt quite at home. Except for rough winter seas and high winds during the twenty-day crossing to the Netherlands, the voyage was pleasant enough, and Hughes never forgot any of the details of the ten days he spent in Rotterdam over the Christmas season in 1923. He remembered Rotterdam's waterfront taverns gay with Yuletide excitement, the famous Schiedamschedyk quarter where sailors went to eat and drink, the walks along frozen canals, the picturesque corbie-step houses, and the warm generosity of a people he had half expected to be withdrawn and cold.[16] He especially remembered being invited, along with some of his shipmates, to the home of an old dock watchman, whose wife stuffed them with holiday cakes, and whose French son-in-law told stories of Paris that sparked Hughes's longing to go there. But he yearned to go many places, and this did not diminish in the weeks just ahead, when between one voyage and another early in 1924, Hughes was Countee Cullen's house guest in New York, and travel was a topic of conversation. But that was not all they talked about.

It was in fact their first meeting, after corresponding for nearly a year. Like their mutual friend, Alain Locke, Cullen had first read Hughes's poems in *The Crisis* and had begun writing to him at Jones Point. Letters were not all that Langston had received from Countee, who had also sent him a sensual poem inscribed "For L.H." and titled it "To a Brown Boy." (It was published in *The Bookman* in November 1923.) Hughes surely sensed the nuances in the poem. By then he knew, too, that there was between him and Locke and Cullen an attraction to their own sex.

Cullen, who had not yet been abroad, was as eager to hear about Hughes's travels as Hughes was to catch up on the news of Harlem. The two poets liked and respected each other, but were complete opposites in poetic style and approach. Cullen was a traditionalist, and drew inspiration from the English poets, especially Keats. Hughes was unconventional, inspired by the folk idioms, rhythms, and themes of his own people. They discussed poetry and talked about college. Cullen, a year younger than Hughes and a sophomore at New York University, was very soon to win second prize in the Witter Bynner poetry competition.[17] He was convinced that a formal education was the highroad to accomplishment. Hughes believed this, too, but he also believed that seeing the world offered special advantages, that travel was a valuable supplement to the library and the classroom. Travel or formal learning: Hughes did not know which to give the prior claim, and he must have thought about both a good deal during the few days of ship leave that January 1924. Had he remained in college, he would have been in his junior year; and if he put off returning much longer, he would be embarrassingly older than his classmates. On February 2, a day after his twenty-second birthday and three days before the *McKeesport* sailed again, Hughes wired Alain Locke in Washington, indicating a frantic effort to enter Howard University. But two days later he had changed his mind.

> DEAR FRIEND:
>
> Forgive me for the sudden and unexpected message I sent you. I'm sorry. I should have known that one couldn't begin in the middle of the term and that I wasn't ready to come anyway. But I had been reading all your letters that day and a sudden desire came over me to come to you then, right then, to stay with you and know you. I need to know you. But I am so stupid sometimes.
>
> However, I am coming to Howard and I want to see you and talk to you about it.
>
> I am sailing again tomorrow but you may write me in Holland....[18]

He had never had a crossing so difficult as the one that began on February 5. Three days out of New York, the chief engineer fell ill and died.[19] A frightful storm pounded the freighter as she rocked against high winds through bitter-cold seas. In mid-ocean the wireless operator went berserk, and the danger of colliding with another vessel rose tremendously. When the busboy in the officers' mess was severely scalded, Hughes took over his duties, slipping and sliding through passageways made all but impassable by monstrous waves crashing across the decks. But the greater the difficulties, the headier the challenge. In *The Big Sea* Hughes exulted that "the strength of a ship and the strength of water, and the strength of a handful of men going on through the storm, against distance and wind and waves until they get where they are going is thrilling...."

Nevertheless, when the *McKeesport* reached Rotterdam after Hughes's third passage aboard, he decided that he had had enough of the seaman's life for a while. Besides, he wanted to see Paris. His desire to go there was tantamount to a determination to leave ship, especially after an unpleasant incident with the *McKeesport* chef, as he later revealed in an unpublished manuscript:

> I quit my ship in Rotterdam because the chef wouldn't give me a piece of chicken one Sunday. All the officers were eating chicken. And I, the cabin boy, was only permitted to gaze upon the empty platters. There was chicken left in the oven, but the chef

said it wasn't intended for the members of the crew. We could eat stew. So I quit and went to Paris.[20]

He drew his pay and took the night train, arriving at the Gare du Nord the morning of February 23, 1924. He had seven dollars. He didn't know anybody in Paris, or for that matter, in all of Europe, "except the old Dutch watchman's family in Rotterdam."

Considering his financial and social situation, Hughes should have made finding a job his first concern, but the lure of Paris was irresistible. He chose to see the sights first. He checked his baggage and took a bus to the Place de l'Opéra, in the very center of the city. From there he walked the few blocks to the Place de la Concorde, where he got his first sight of the Avenue des Champs-Elysées and the Arc de Triomphe in the distance. It thrilled him: all of Paris thrilled him that first morning. He did not know where to turn, whether to walk up the Champs-Elysées or down beside the Seine, past the Jardin des Tuileries. "I took the river," he wrote in his autobiography, "hoping to see the bookstalls and Notre Dame. But I ended up in the Louvre. . . ."

That night he slept in Montmartre. In the course of his daytime wandering he had come across an Afro-American ("in a doorman's uniform") who told him that Montmartre was where a good many of his black countrymen lived. Many, as Hughes discovered, had come as soldiers and remained after World War I. Mostly musicians and entertainers, they worked in the theatres and nightclubs. Jazz, respected by sophisticated Frenchmen as a serious art form, was very popular, and black jazz musicians were in great demand. Hughes was told by a few whom he met in a Montmartre café that "less you can play or tap dance, you'd just as well go back home." And so it seemed, for no job materialized as soon as he had expected. He tried all the places where he felt a lack of fluency in French would not be a handicap— the American library, the American embassy, the English language newspapers. Nothing. Then he tried all the large nightclubs and hotels, hoping to be taken on as doorman or busboy or dishwasher; but he had no *carte d'identité*, and no money to obtain one. Besides, many Frenchmen were out of work, too. When Hughes sought employment as an unskilled laborer on a construction project, he was chased away with shouts of "*Salaud!*" and "*Sale étranger!*"

After more than a month of unrewarded searching, Hughes found it difficult to meet the expenses he shared with a Russian *danseuse* in a Montmartre hotel. Growing desperate, he wrote his mother and stepfather in McKeesport asking for a loan—the first he had ever asked of them. His reason for not making the request of his own father is worth noting, if only because it is both disingenuous and conscience-stricken.

> Before I would have written my own father for a penny, I would have died in Paris, because I knew his answer would be: "I told you you should have listened to me, and gone to Switzerland to study, as I asked you!" So I would not write my father, though hunger reduced me to a skeleton, and I died of malnutrition on the steps of the Louvre.[21]

Between father and son, correspondence had all but ceased, and Langston had no idea that James Hughes was even then also in Europe—a paralytic patient in a sanitarium in Kamenz, Germany. If the son ever learned of the fact, he seems never to have mentioned it.

The response from his mother deepened his depression. His stepfather, the letter said, was in the hospital with pneumonia; his stepbrother had been expelled from school; the river that ran by the house in McKeesport was threatening to flood them out. And to cap all, his mother did not have a job: there was no money. Shouldn't he, Langston, she wrote, come home, "instead of galavanting all over the world as a sailor, and writing from Paris for money?"

Finally, he found a job as doorman at a small Montmartre nightclub on the rue Fontaine. A blue cap with gold braid, which he purchased at the local *marché aux puces*—France's flea market—was his uniform. He got five francs a night, his dinner, and tips. It was not one of the fashionable cabarets frequented by *le beau monde*. Its patrons were ladies of the night and men who looked to be entertained by girls who were hired by the club for that purpose. There was professional jealousy and frequent fights occurred; Langston had not known he was "expected to be a bouncer as well as a doorman." "I didn't like the task of fight-stopping," he wrote later, "because the first fist fight I saw there was between ladies, who shattered champagne glasses on the edge of the table, then slashed at each other with the jagged stems. . . . For such a job, five francs was not enough, and the fights were too much, so I was glad when I found other work. . . .[22]

His next job, as dishwasher and second cook, then as waiter, was more congenial. It was at Le Grand Duc on rue Pigalle in the heart of Montmartre. When he went to work there in the early spring of 1924, the Grand Duc's popularity with celebrities, royalty, and affluent high society was at its peak, but when its featured entertainer, Florence Embry, a sultry singer from Harlem, left before the summer season to open her own night club, business declined. But not among the true aficionados of the new music or the black professionals of the entertainment world. The latter especially flocked to the Grand Duc in the wee hours after their work was done, and in what soon came to be called "jam sessions" experimented with jazz and cut musical capers for their own pleasure and edification. Hughes, who worked from eleven at night until seven in the morning, wrote "Jazz Band in a Parisian Cabaret" evoking these sessions. The poem appeared in *The Crisis* in December 1925, and was included in his second poetry collection, *Fine Clothes to the Jew*, in 1927.

"Jazz Band in a Parisian Cabaret" was one of several new poems Hughes worked on that spring, although his general mood was not right for the production of poetry. He claimed he wrote most when he was unhappy, and he was not generally unhappy in Paris. Writing days and working nights, he was happier than he had been for some time. Now living alone— his Russian friend having moved on to Le Havre—he had more time to devote to his poetry, though often he chose to see Paris instead. In May he wrote to Alain Locke: "I have been working hard for the last two weeks on my poetry. It's the first time within the last two years that I have really had time to do any continuous work on my stuff. When I'm finished with what I have now, I shall try not to write anything else this summer, as there are so many things to see in Paris....[23] His attic *chambre de bonne* at 15 rue Nollet was "right out of a book," he wrote later, "and I began to say to myself that I guess dreams do come true, and sometimes life makes its own books, because here I am living in a Paris garret, writing poems and having champagne for breakfast (because champagne is what we had for breakfast at the Grand Duc...)."[24]

Yet there were intervals of depression, and some of his poems of this time reflect it, speak out of it:

Song for a Suicide

Oh, the sea is deep
And a knife is sharp
And a poison acid burns;
But they all bring rest
In a deep, long sleep
For which the tired soul yearns—
They all bring rest in a nothingness
From where no road returns.[25]

And another he entitled "Poem":

Poem

> I am waiting for my mother.
> She is Death.
> Say it very softly.
> Say it very slowly if you choose.
> I am waiting for my mother,
> Death.[26]

Whether it was because he was waiting for Death, or for some other reason, Hughes was less than certain about his future, or even about planning for it. He was certain only that he did not wish to stay in Paris beyond autumn. In April he wrote to Locke inquiring about the chances for entering Howard University. He was doubtful even of saving his passage out of the fifteen francs he earned each night, but "I would like very much to come there next September," he wrote.[27] Then, in May, in a letter accompanying some of his new poems, he wrote again: "I want to leave in September. If not home to New York, then on to Spain and South America...."[28]

Professor Locke seems not to have reacted to his young acquaintance's uncertainty. What he did react to was the poems, one of which, "A Black Pierrot," he sent to René Maran, then editor of the French review *Les Continents*, which immediately published it, together with Hughes's poem "Negro" in its July issue that year.[29] Their appearance marked the young poet's first foreign publication. Locke wrote that he would be in Paris in July; he wanted to talk to Hughes about contributing to a special Harlem issue of *Survey Graphic*. One of the poems Hughes wrote that spring in Paris, he sent to Locke as well as to *The Crisis*, which published it in June:

Lament for Dark Peoples

> I was a red man one time,
> But the white men came.
> I was a black man, too,
> But the white men came.
>
> They drove me out of the forest.
> They took me away from the jungles.
> I lost my trees.
> I lost my silver moons.

Now they've caged me
In the circus of civilization.
Now I herd with the many—
Caged in the circus of civilization.

Like several similar poems Hughes wrote during this period—"The White
Ones," "Our Land," and "Afraid"—"Lament for Dark Peoples" was part of
his personal response to being nonwhite in the Western world. Seeing
Europe after his trip to Africa had a deepening impact upon his racial and
social consciousness, and the theme of being "caged in the circus of civilization" is recurrent in some of the poems he wrote in Paris.

But none of this precluded his enjoyment of a Parisian spring, which he
later described in his autobiography as being as "golden green a spring as I
have ever seen." Through the references and allusions in the letters and the
autobiography to his responses to the season, one understands why spring is
the dominant season in some of his fiction. But one also wonders why he
did not make even greater use of it—and of nature generally—in his imagi-
native writing as a whole. Here and there, and now and then, he uses nature
as imagery or theme, but scarcely enough to alter the over-all impression
that his imagination worked best with urban life, that he was preeminently
a poet of the people and the city. Perhaps some of the great delight he took
in the Parisian spring, in strolling through the Tuileries, the Jardin de Lux-
embourg, the Parc Monceau, and the forest of Versailles, was associated
with and derived from being in love.

What we know of the young lady he met that spring is what he tells us,
and that is precious little. In *The Big Sea*, he said her name was Mary,
though her actual name was Anne Coussey.[30] He met her through an American who had lived in Paris since the end of the war, but who regularly
received *The Crisis* and knew Hughes's poems: Rayford Logan, whom
Hughes would know better years later as a prominent Negro author and
professor of history. But on a personal level, he never forgot him as the
friend who helped him find a job at the Grand Duc, and introduced him to
Anne Coussey—the "charming and cultured, good-looking colored girl"
whom the poet took dancing and to the theatre that spring in Paris. Hughes
described Anne (alias Mary) in a poem that appeared in *The Crisis* in June of
that year:

Fascination

Her teeth are as white as the meat of
   an apple.
Her lips are like dark ripe plums.
I love her.

Her hair is a midnight mass, a dusky aurora.
I love her.
And because her skin is the brown of an
    oak leaf in autumn, but a softer color,
I want to kiss her.

Vivacious and pretty, she was of Anglo-African descent, and native to London. When Hughes met her, she was a student at Raymond Duncan's school for arts and crafts in Paris.[31] Their affair lasted no more than a month. It ended when Anne's father—believing she was earnestly considering marriage—cut off her allowance and demanded her return to London. She had indeed proposed to Hughes, and though he was perhaps as deeply infatuated with Anne as he would ever be with anyone, the seriousness of her devotion frightened him. At age twenty-two, he was hardly ready to cope with it. Nor did he seem to trust the feeling as more than fleeting. The experience, brief though it was, probably influenced his subsequent relations with women. A poem that he wrote after Anne's departure, "The Breath of a Rose," is symbolic of the way he felt about romantic love most of his life, and of the way he usually expressed it in the few love poems he wrote. Forever after his relationship with Anne, Langston Hughes seemed to believe that love between man and woman was as evanescent as "the breath of a rose," and he revealed it as such in poems like "Young Bride," "Passing Love," and "Spring for Lovers."

ANNE was already a fleeting memory by the time Alain Locke visited in July. The professor's unexpected early morning arrival could have been embarrassing for Hughes, who some days earlier had permitted a homeless and pathetic dope addict named Bob to share quarters with him on the rue Nollet. It was a quixotic gesture of compassion that, though typical of the poet, Locke might be hard put to understand. But one day after Locke's arrival, Hughes gave up the room to Bob and moved to the rue des Trois Frères. Apparently, the reason for the move was not mentioned between them, for Locke had other things to discuss with the poet at this their first real meeting. His ultimate destination that summer, after travels to Germany and England, was Italy, and he hoped to persuade his young friend to join him there when the Grand Duc closed for the season. But first he wanted to talk about his plans for the special issue of *Survey Graphic* he had been asked to edit. Locke put it bluntly—he was counting on the poet: would Hughes contribute to the special issue? The request was flattering, and Hughes happily responded yes, then shyly asked some questions of his own. Of the recent poems he had already sent him, were any suitable? "Youth," for instance?

> We have tomorrow
> Bright before us
> Like a flame.
>
> Yesterday
> A night-gone thing,
> A sun-down name...[33]

Locke liked it fine; he had already selected "Youth," "Our Land," and "Dream Variation" from the new poems Hughes had sent him, and he wanted still more. He also wanted to include them in *The New Negro*. Hughes agreed to write and submit others for the book and the special issue.[34]

His immediate business done, Professor Locke lingered on in Paris. He knew the city and its cultural and intellectual resources almost as well as he knew London and Berlin, both places where he had lived and studied. Through Locke, Hughes made his first serious acquaintance with European culture, and thanks to Locke, he also discovered artistic and cultural aspects of Paris he had not explored before. The professor took him to the Opera-Comique, where they heard *Manon*. He introduced him to René Maran and arranged for Hughes to meet the noted American collector of modern art, Albert C. Barnes, who invited the poet to lunch. The luncheon engagement, however, changed but slightly Hughes's knowledge and interest in modern art: "I ordered some *fraises de bois* and thought about Mary [Anne], away off in London, as I ate them, because I didn't know anything about modern art then, so my mind wandered."[35]

Alain Locke, Albert Barnes, and Paul Guillaume, art critic and French associate of the Barnes Foundation, had been contributors that spring to an African art issue of *Opportunity* magazine in which one of Hughes's Africa-inspired poems had appeared.[36] Later that summer Hughes met Paul Guillaume and saw his private collection of African art and learned a little about the growing influence of that art upon the Cubist painters—Picasso, Gris, and others living in Paris at the time.

Others with whom Hughes was later to become intimate friends—Louis Aragon, the poet and novelist, and Henri Cartier-Bresson, the photographer—were also in Paris, but Hughes did not meet them in 1924. Indeed, had he had the opportunity he might have rejected it. That year and for some time thereafter, Hughes reacted unhappily to the French: even his very pleasant association with Paul Guillaume did not change his opinion that Frenchmen were inhospitable and often unbearable. "French people (Mon Dieu!!) I can't ever love them," he wrote in one letter.[37] Nor did he come in contact with any of the expatriate Americans who were then in the French capital— Gertrude Stein, Ernest Hemingway, Donald Ogden Stewart, Margaret Anderson, and Sylvia Beach—with some of whom he was later associated. He certainly knew that one of their meeting places was Sylvia Beach's Shakespeare and Company, but he seems never to have gone to the bookstore. There he would have met Margaret Anderson and Jane Heap, editors of *The Little Review*. He admired the magazine but thought that his own verse was not "eccentric enough" for reception there.[38]

After Locke left Paris in July, Hughes's only "literary" contact abroad was through correspondence with the Jamaican-born poet, Claude McKay, who was then living in the south of France. None of the African or Caribbean writers whom Hughes was later to know, influence, and translate— Léopold Senghor, Aimé Césaire, Jacques Roumain, Léon Damas, and Birago Diop, among others—had yet reached Paris. Rather than the literati, Hughes preferred the entertainers, musicians, and service personnel at the Grand Duc. Among his favorite people at the club were the vocalist Ada Smith—destined for international fame as Bricktop—and two Italian employees, Luigi and Romeo, bartender and waiter, respectively, with whom he went to Italy when the Grand Duc closed for the August vacation.

Hughes did not let his uncertainty about the future mar his delight in the first few days in Italy. After spending a day with Luigi in Turin, Hughes and Romeo moved on to Desenzano, Romeo's home town. It was a "postcard village" on Lake Garda, and the villagers joined with Romeo's parents to make Hughes feel at home. He went to picnics and dances and on excursions to other towns around the lake. In one of several letters to Locke from Desenzano he wrote that "the kindness of the people here makes me very happy, though I have been forced to eat, drink and be entertained more than I really enjoy."[39] Gradually, as the future became the present and nothing was settled, Hughes's letters took on a different tone. His funds were running low, and he was not sure that he could go to Venice: could Locke come to Desenzano? From there "we could go to Verona for a few hours to see the tomb of Romeo and Juliette [sic] and the arena where Duse appeared...I wish you were here now. Your company in Paris has spoiled me for being alone."[40]

Plans for August were finally decided. After an overnight stop alone in Verona, so he might visit the Capulet's tomb, Hughes went on to Venice as Locke's guest. Natural teacher that he was, Locke lit up Venice with its ancient magnificence and brought it to life for Hughes through history and legend. Afoot, the two explored the Piazza San Marco, Venice's regal square, dominated by St. Mark's Basilica and the pink-and-white marble Doge's Palace. They took a gondola through the Grand Canal, along which Locke pointed out and recited the history of the most famous landmarks and palaces, including the Vendramin-Calergi Palace, where Richard Wagner died. Dr. Locke "knew who had painted all the pictures, and who had built all the old buildings"; and he seemed bent on acquainting the young poet with all of them, especially the works of Titian and Tintoretto in the Accademia Gallery, the School of San Rocco, and the Church of Santa Maria della Salute. But the graphic arts and architecture were not Hughes's great bent, and "before the week was up, I got a little tired of palaces and churches and famous paintings...I began to wonder if there were no back alleys in Venice and no poor people and no slums."[41] Hughes's social consciousness never slept for long, and before he and Locke left for Genoa, he "found that there were plenty of poor people in Venice and plenty of back alleys off canals."[42]

Hughes's account of his experiences in Genoa does not jibe with the facts that can be gleaned from the correspondence between him and Professor Locke. *The Big Sea* omits some revealing matters of substance, twists some, and imagines others. It does not say that Hughes and Locke journeyed together from Venice to Genoa (whence Locke sailed to the United States). What it does say is that Hughes set out alone to visit the writer Claude McKay, and that his money and passport were stolen, forcing him to interrupt his trip in the Italian port city. The truth, though, was something else again. He never got to the South of France to see McKay. Hughes wrote Locke (from Genoa):

> How much I hated to see you leave yesterday. We really were having a delightful time together. Certainly our week in Venice was as pleasant as anything I can ever remember.
> But I wish you could have seen the Albergo Populare before you left, then you wouldn't doubt me when I say that it's a wonder. For twenty-one lira a week one has one's own room, a baggage locker, [room] tax and service. And it's very clean....[43]

Hughes spent six weeks in Genoa, and he was not as down-and-out as the autobiography makes it seem. He wrote Locke that he had "found a restaurant where it's impossible to eat more than a five lira meal. And that's from soup to cheese. And lovely wine....So I'm good for at least a month here if nothing turns up."[44] He was not literally a beachcomber in Genoa, though in *The Big Sea* he says he was. But his funds dwindled at the end of a month, and he found himself forced to wait for a ship with a Negro crew or a steward who would sign him on: "Several American boats came into the harbor during my weeks in port and, one by one, the white boys were signed on. But they would not take a Negro in the crew." While waiting for passage, he did odd jobs around the harbor. One day he earned a little more than two dollars by helping to paint a ship, *City of Europa*. He acquired a few lira by selling his clock. He had time for reading. He wrote (and sent to Alain Locke) one of his best-known poems.

I, Too

I, too, sing America.

I am the darker brother.
They send me to eat in the kitchen
When company comes,
But I laugh,
And eat well,
And grow strong.

Tomorrow,
I'll be at the table
When company comes.
Nobody'll dare
Say to me,
"Eat in the kitchen,"
Then.

Besides,
They'll see how beautiful I am
And be ashamed,—

I, too, am America.[45]

He wrote at least one piece of prose, too—"Burutu Moon" about his experience in Africa—which he sent to *The Crisis*. He asked the editor "to please pay [him] twenty dollars for it, because [he] was stranded and starving in Italy—but would try to live until the money got there."[46]

By the time the money did reach Genoa, Hughes was on his way to New York. He had finally found a ship that permitted him passage. He was taken on as a workaway without pay.

Although most of the time was spent scrubbing decks and doing odd chores, the voyage was memorable. It took him along the Tyrrhenian coast to Leghorn (Livorno) and Naples, thence to Sicily, where he visited Catania, Messina, and Palermo. When the boat reached the Spanish coast, he went ashore and saw as much as he could see during stopovers in Valencia and Alicante. Hughes had been gone ten months when the ship docked in New York on November 10, 1924. He had exactly twenty-five cents. He took the subway to Harlem.

✤ 6 ✤

Spring Cannot Be Far Behind

HIS FIRST DAY BACK IN HARLEM Hughes spent as the guest of Countee
Cullen, and that evening they attended a dance given for the benefit
of the NAACP.[1] It was almost as if it were a benefit for Hughes. Editors from
The Crisis, the official organ of the NAACP, whom he had not seen in nearly
three years, greeted him with the welcome news that they had liked the
article he had submitted from Italy, and that the twenty dollars he had asked
for was waiting for him. They also informed him that his poem "Afraid"
was in the current issue of their magazine. If neither fact had any important
consequences for his career, Hughes was sensitive to the possibility that
some of the people he met that night could have. Walter White, an NAACP
official and the author of a new novel, *The Fire in the Flint*, introduced the
young writer to James Weldon Johnson and to Carl Van Vechten. Johnson,
whose work as poet, novelist, and librettist—and as executive secretary of
the NAACP—was widely known, would be one of the first to anthologize
Hughes's poems.[2] Van Vechten, white patron of the arts, writer, and critic,
would later advise Alfred A. Knopf to publish Hughes's first volume and,
later still, would become one of the black poet's close personal friends. But
in November 1924, nearly two years before Van Vechten's fifth novel,
Nigger Heaven, catapulted him to fame, he was as unknown to Hughes as
Hughes was to him. "Sometime during the course of the night," Van
Vechten later wrote, "Walter White asked me to meet two young
poets...Countee Cullen and Langston Hughes. Before that moment I had
never heard of either of them."[3] A few days later, at a literary gathering
where he had been invited to read his poetry, Hughes made the acquaintance of another person who was to play a significant role in his career as
friend and collaborator, Arna Bontemps. A native of Louisiana, but reared
in California, Bontemps had recently arrived in New York after graduating
from Pacific Union College. His first published verse had appeared that
summer in the same issue of *The Crisis* as Hughes's "Youth" and "Poem."

The meeting between the two young poets was the beginning of a friendship that lasted until Langston Hughes's death forty-three years later.

Hughes could only spend a few days in New York, and only then as a nonpaying guest. He could not afford even the inexpensive lodging in the YMCA. Furthermore, his mother, who had again separated from her husband, was urging him to join her in Washington, D.C., where she was living with relatives. He was reluctant, for it meant living at least partly on the generosity of people whom he scarcely knew. He was reluctant even after the relatives extended him a cordial invitation. They liked his poems, they said, and "would be pleased to have a writer in the house."[4] Quite aside from feeling a sense of duty toward his mother, he decided in the end to go because of a set of related circumstances: Alain Locke was in Washington, and so was Howard University, and he wanted to return to college. With what he had left of the twenty-dollar payment from *The Crisis*, Hughes bought a ticket for his first trip to the nation's capital.

Their pleasure at having a writer in the house should have forewarned Hughes about these relatives whom he had never seen. They lived in that section of Washington called Le Droit Park, where none but affluent blacks then lived, and they were disposed to boast of it. Themselves without distinction, they nevertheless laid claim to it. They were related to his great-uncle, John Mercer Langston, a Congressman of the post-Reconstruction era and the first dean of the Howard University law school. And after all, they could introduce their writer-cousin "as just back from Europe" without saying that he got back "by chipping decks on a freight ship"—a qualification that Langston Hughes himself thought essential. It would have helped explain his faded shirts and frayed trousers and the seaman's peajacket he wore in lieu of an overcoat. He was jobless and broke, and he made no pretense to the contrary. Failing to get a job as a page boy in the Library of Congress, he took work in a laundry, much to the mortification of his cousins and their friends. "Cultured Washington," he wrote later in *The Big Sea*, "I mean cultured colored Washington, who read my poems in the *Crisis*, did not find it fitting and proper that a poet should work in a wet wash laundry.... And since none of them had any better jobs to offer me, I stayed there. The laundry at least paid twelve dollars a week."[5]

But on such wages he could save nothing toward entering Howard University. Encouraged by Alain Locke, he looked into scholarship possibilities for the next academic year. Nothing. He refused to exploit the fact that he was the grand-nephew of John Mercer Langston. He refused, too, to have his mother suffer continuing humiliation at the hands of their relatives. So with mother and stepbrother he moved into two furnished but unheated rooms on Twelfth Street in northwest Washington not far from his place of work. His mother took a job as a domestic. Pooling their meagre wages, they moved three times and barely made ends meet through one of the bleakest winters any of them ever knew.[6] Nor did the Jim-Crowism of Washington help. The theatres, concert halls, and motion picture houses which offered the best entertainment were barred to blacks, who were frequently insulted even when they visited public tax-supported institutions such as the Smithsonian Institution, the Library of Congress, and the Washington Zoo.

Despondent, Hughes found an outlet in poetry. Many of the poems he wrote that winter and early spring were inspired by the experiences he had with the people he met along Washington's Seventh Street—the thoroughfare he later vividly described as "the long, old, dirty street, where the ordinary Negroes hang out, folks with practically no family tree at all, folks who draw no color line between mulattoes and deep dark-browns, folks who work hard for a living with their hands."[7] They were people he could identify with and learn from. He went to their storefront churches and listened to their singing of the gospels and spirituals. He went to the places they frequented and caught the pulse beat of their lives in such poems as "Hard Luck," "Railroad Avenue," and "Midwinter Blues." But if most of the poems he wrote during this period reflect the innermost feelings and down-and-out blues of the urban folk he met along Seventh Street, they reflect also his own feelings and concerns, for he felt as one with those whose "midwinter blues" he shared. Few of these poems appeared in print before 1926, and when most of them did appear at the height of the Harlem Renaissance in a collection titled *Fine Clothes to the Jew*, some influential black critics condemned them as "low-life" and as traducing black people.

The few new poems of Hughes's that appeared in magazines that winter of 1924-25 were hardly among his best. An objective appraisal of "Subway Face" and "Poppy Flower," which appeared in *The Crisis*, and "Troubled Woman," which was published in *Opportunity*, must rate them mediocre. Only one of the poems published that winter, "Song to a Negro Wash Woman," which appeared in the January *Crisis*, bears comparison with those he had written earlier in Europe, and there is good reason to doubt that this poem, despite its title, was actually drawn from his experience of work in a laundry. In a letter dated August 20, 1924, and sent from Italy, Hughes wrote Alain Locke that "the poems are being mailed today. Not 'Washer Woman.' I don't want it there."[8]

In March 1925, the poems solicited by Locke for the *Survey Graphic*—the year before—appeared in the special issue of that magazine, "Harlem: Mecca of the Negro." That spring Hughes also wrote and published various "mood" poems as well as those in the manner of the blues and jazz rhythms. "Liars," for instance, a subjective mood poem, was printed in *Opportunity*, and

"Negro Dancers," in jazz rhythm, was printed in *The Crisis*. Hughes's varied experiences in Washington were conducive to the varied poems he produced. "I didn't like my job, and I didn't know what was going to happen to me," he later wrote in his autobiography, "and I was cold and half-hungry, so I wrote a great many poems." In May, three highly personal poems appeared in *The Buccaneer*. One of these is worth noting for its similarity in imagery and mood to "Song for a Suicide," which he had written in Paris the year before.

Ways

A slash of the wrist,
A swallow of scalding acid,
The crash of a bullet through the brain—
And death comes like a mother
To hold you in her arms.

Of equal interest and probably of greater significance is the fact that Hughes composed several political poems—his first of this genre—which were printed in *The Workers Monthly* that spring.[9] For the rest of his career, his various moods—lyrical, dramatic, expository—were often interrupted by, or combined with, the need to be political. His deep sense of social consciousness was ever constant, even if at times not all of his poetry revealed it. During the months he spent in Washington, some of his poems were political for personal as well as for social reasons.

Park Benching

I've sat on the park benches in Paris
Hungry
I've sat on the park benches in New York
Hungry.
And I've said:
I want a job.
I want work.
And I've been told:
There are no jobs.
There is no work.
So I've sat on the park benches
Hungry.
Mid-winter,
Hungry days,
No jobs,
No work.[10]

But his hard-luck days in the nation's capital seemed to be coming to an end. Though he lost the job at the laundry, his family connections led, in March 1925, to his gaining work as personal assistant to Dr. Carter G. Woodson, the distinguished black scholar and founder of the Association for the Study of Negro Life and History.[11] The Association was then ten years old, but its staff was small, and Dr. Woodson had heavy responsibilities as editor of the quarterly *Journal of Negro History*. Being personal assistant to him was a rewarding, and demanding, experience, which Hughes later wrote about in an essay, "When I Worked for Dr. Woodson."[12] Besides opening the office, supervising the clerical staff, screening Dr. Woodson's callers, keeping lists and records of various kinds, sorting mail and reading proof, Hughes had to keep the office clean and tend the furnace, stoking it in the morning and banking it at night. But having a "position" rather than a job brought him again into social contact with "the best people," whom he was later to excoriate in "Our Wonderful Society: Washington."

> I began to meet some of the best people. The people themselves assured me they were the best people,—and they seemed to know. Never before, anywhere, had I seen persons of influence, —men with some money, women with some beauty, teachers with some education,—quite so audibly sure of their own importance and their high place in the community. So many pompous gentlemen never before did I meet. Nor so many ladies with chests swelled like pouter-pigeons whose mouths uttered formal sentences in frightfully correct English. I admit I was awed by these best people....[13]

Hughes was being ironical, of course, about being awed. Two years earlier, or even a year before, he might truly have been awed, but he was no longer the shy young man who spoke hesitantly and blushed as he had done in the presence of the editors of *The Crisis*. Now he could mock, and in Washington he had reason to mock, the conspicuous display and the pretensions of the "best people"—their parties, their fraternity pins, their furs and cars, their vaunted "background." He had established his values along quite other lines. He disdained the rigid class and color differences the "best people" drew between themselves and Afro-Americans of darker complexion, of smaller means and lesser formal education. He disdained, too, the cultural and intellectual shallowness of the class in which he steadfastly refused to claim membership. The "best people" knew nothing and cared less about the New Negro cultural awakening. If they knew of Jean Toomer, whose novel *Cane* Hughes admired, or Rudolph Fisher, whose short story "City of Refuge" had appeared in the *Atlantic Monthly*, they knew of these two Washingtonians only to resent them for not choosing to write about the "best" colored people. And as Hughes was to discover, the complaint was a common one among upper-class blacks all through the Harlem Renaissance:

> I understand these "best" colored folks when they say that little has been written about them. I am sorry and I wish some one would put them into a nice story or a nice novel. But I fear for them if ever a really powerful work is done about their lives. Such a story would show not only their excellencies but their pseudo-culture as well, their slavish devotion to Nordic standards, their snobbishness, their detachment from the Negro masses and their vast sense of importance to themselves. A book like that from a Negro writer, even though true and beautiful, would be more thoroughly disliked than the stories of low-class Negroes now being written....[14]

Hughes also discovered that publication of *The New Negro*, edited by Alain Locke, did not mollify upper-class Washington blacks. They did not see themselves represented in the poems, essays, stories, and illustrations in this collection published in May 1925. They thought that the lifestyles and the character types depicted in many of the selections would bring all black people the contempt of white America. The critical essays of Alain Locke, the "racial" stories of Zora Neale Hurston and the West Indian author Eric Walrond, and the poetry of Sterling Brown and Langston Hughes, among others, completely turned off blacks who considered themselves belonging to an elite class of society: *they* did not speak in dialect or use the urban ghetto idiom. For them *The New Negro* was no herald of high creative and cultural achievement and no bright promise of the future. But for Langston Hughes it was both. Indeed, the promise of the future was personally signalized for him in certain events and circumstances of that very month when *The New Negro* was published.

On May 1, at a presentation banquet at the elegant Fifth Avenue Restaurant in New York City, Hughes was awarded the highest prize for poetry in the first literary competition promoted by *Opportunity* magazine, the official publication of the National Urban League. The winning poem was "The Weary Blues," which he referred to as his "lucky poem":

> Droning a drowsy syncopated tune,
> Rocking back and forth to a mellow croon,
>   I heard a Negro play.
> Down on Lenox Avenue the other night
> By the pale dull pallor of an old gas light

> He did a lazy sway...
> He did a lazy sway...
> To the tune o' those Weary Blues.
> With his ebony hands on each ivory key
> He made that poor piano moan with melody.
> O Blues![15]

In addition to winning the first prize, Hughes tied for third place with second-prize winner Countee Cullen, and won honorable mention for two other poems. Hughes's third-place poem was "America," and "The Jester" and "Songs to the Dark Virgin" won honorable mention. The first prize was forty dollars, which an anonymous donor doubled.

Hughes had reason to remember the awards banquet. As the *New York Herald Tribune* pointed out in an article about the banquet—and apparently coining the term "Negro Renaissance," which appeared in the title—"White critics whom everybody knows [and] Negro writers whom nobody knew met on common ground."[16] But some of the Negro writers would not be unknown for long. Within months prize-winners Hughes, Cullen, and Walrond would have books out, swelling the tide of the Renaissance, and such names as Zora Neale Hurston, Rudolph Fisher, and Wallace Thurman, among others, would be mentioned wherever there was talk of the "New Negro." At the banquet Hughes met Miss Hurston, Eric Walrond, and numerous other black writers for the first time. He also met most of the judges of the literary competition—among them John Farrar, editor of *The Bookman*; James Weldon Johnson, whose acquaintance he renewed (it was Johnson who read the prize-winning poem to the guests), and Henry Goddard Leach, editor of *The Forum*, who asked permission to reprint the poem in his publication.[17] The only luminary missing was Walter White, absent because of a speaking engagement in Trenton, New Jersey.

Of greater consequence to the New Negro literary movement (and to Hughes's career) was his meeting *Opportunity* editor Charles S. Johnson at the banquet and renewing his acquaintance with Carl Van Vechten.[18] Johnson, along with Jessie Fauset and Alain Locke, Hughes declared later, was foremost among "the three people who mid-wifed the so-called New Negro literature into being." A sociologist and educator by training, the stately Charles Spurgeon Johnson was only nine years older than Hughes, but to the latter he always seemed much older and wiser. When they met in May 1925, Johnson was national director of the Department of Research and Investigation of the Urban League and the spirit behind its two-year-old monthly magazine, *Opportunity*. In March 1924 he had invited a group of promising young Afro-American poets and writers to an integrated literary symposium at New York's Civic Club. Langston, in Paris at the time, had missed that occasion, where some of his contemporaries met prominent white American intellectuals and literary personalities for the first time. But he heard all about the evening from Locke, for it was there he received the invitation from the editor of the *Survey Graphic* to compile the special issue on Harlem's emerging literati. That was largely due to Charles S. Johnson. All that caused Hughes to say later, "Mr. Johnson I believe, did more to encourage and develop Negro writers during the 1920's than anyone else in America. He wrote them sympathetic letters, pointing out the merits of their work. He brought them together to meet and know each other. He made the *Opportunity* contests sources of discovery and help."

Van Vechten shared Johnson's enthusiastic concern, particularly for the work of Langston Hughes. The night of the *Opportunity* banquet he urged Langston to send him enough poems to make a book, and he, Van Vechten, would submit them to his publisher. Less than three weeks later, Hughes's manuscript had been accepted by the publishing firm of Alfred A. Knopf.[19] Van Vechten pledged himself to write an introduction to the volume, which at his suggestion Hughes titled *The Weary Blues*. And very soon thereafter—again with Van Vechten's help—the sophisticated magazine *Vanity Fair* bought prepublication rights to several of the poems.[20]

Van Vechten's link with the Harlem movement was of a different persuasion than Charles S. Johnson's: rather than Van Vechten's influencing it—beyond his contacts with publishers and influential New Yorkers—the movement influenced him, especially that aspect of it described as exotic primitivism. It was an aspect and a quality he recognized in some of Hughes's early poems and which he strove to represent in his novel *Nigger Heaven*. He must have recognized, too, in the young poet's work the oscillating pattern of tragic irony and humor that is so characteristic of almost all Van Vechten fiction.

In August, Hughes returned again to New York, this time to receive the second prize for the essay and third prize for poetry in the first Amy Spingarn Contest in Literature and Art. The 1925 contest, offering fifteen prizes in five categories—poetry, fiction, drama, the essay, and illustration—was officially announced in the November 1924 issue of *The Crisis*. All manuscripts had to be submitted under a pseudonym by April 15, 1925. Hughes used the name "Raif Dickerson" for his essay, and "Ralph Anson" and "Jerry Biera" for his poems. Names of prizewinners were published in the July 1925 issue of *The Crisis*.

Altogether, there were over six hundred entries. Winning second place—thirty dollars—for his essay, "The Fascination of Cities," which recorded his impressions of Kansas City, Chicago, New York, Mexico City, and Paris, was important to Hughes. It gave him an incentive to go on developing his prose style, which he felt to be weak. But he must have been disappointed in the third prize—ten dollars—for poetry. He had entered six poems, and two of these, "Cross" and "Minstrel Man," were later to be among the most widely reprinted of all Hughes's poems.

Cross

My old man's a white man
And my old mother's black.
If I ever cursed my white old man
I take my curses back.

If ever I cursed my black old mother
And wished she were in hell,
I'm sorry for that evil wish
And now I wish her well.

My old man died in a fine big house.
My ma died in a shack.
I wonder where I'm gonna die,
Being neither white nor black?[21]

Minstrel Man

Because my mouth
Is wide with laughter
And my throat
Is deep with song,
You do not think
I suffer after
I have held my pain
So long.

Because my mouth
Is wide with laughter
You do not hear
My inner cry.
Because my feet
Are gay with dancing
You do not know
I die.[22]

These departed greatly from the subject and style of the poem by Countee Cullen that won first prize. Hughes must have guessed later that they offended the literary sensibilities of the chief poetry judge, William Stanley Braithwaite, a black poet who, like Cullen, wrote in the tradition of the English romanticists.

Hughes's acquaintance with the world of art was widened during his brief August visit to New York City. He met Aaron Douglas, whose drawings had illustrated *The New Negro*. At Eric Walrond's he was introduced to Miguel Covarrubias, the Mexican artist, who was fascinated with Harlem and who would do the dust jacket for *The Weary Blues*. Winold Reiss, the German–American painter who was one of the judges in the Spingarn contest, made a crayon drawing of Hughes that later appeared on the cover of *Opportunity*.[23]

Back in Washington, Hughes found welcome relief from the attentions of the "best people" through Mrs. Georgia Douglas Johnson, whose acquaintance he had first made at the *Opportunity* banquet in May. A poet highly respected by knowledgeable contemporaries, Mrs. Johnson had made her home into the literary center of Washington's black poets and writers. Beginning in early fall, Hughes missed scarcely one of the Saturday night literary salons, where the latest novels, plays, and poetry were served up, as it were, with homemade cake and wine. "My two years in Washington were unhappy years," Hughes wrote later, "except for poetry and the friends I made through poetry."[24] One of the friends he made—not at Mrs. Johnson's but through a meeting on a Washington streetcar—was Waring Cuney, a young poet who had attended Howard before transferring to Lincoln University. It was Cuney who persuaded Hughes to apply for admission to Lincoln, a black, all-male college in Pennsylvania that had been founded by the white Presbyterian Board of Missions before the Civil War.[25] Hughes had applied to Harvard under the influence of Locke, who had taken a Harvard doctorate nearly twenty years before, and Countee Cullen, who was in graduate school there. Lincoln, Cuney said, was a fine college; one found time to write there, because there was no demanding social life; and the costs were low. Listening to Cuney, Hughes was sure he would prefer Lincoln to Harvard.

But $225—the cost of Lincoln for the spring semester—seemed a quite considerable sum to Hughes. Literary prizes and the prospect of having his first book published did not put him "in the money." Nor did his review of a new novel called *Sailor's Return* in *The Crisis* that November help much financially either. Besides, he was no longer working for the Association for the Study of Negro Life and History. Having decided that his work there left him too little time for writing and that he preferred a "job" to a "position," he took employment as a bus boy in the Wardman Park Hotel.[26] His wages were hardly enough to pay his rent. Indeed, he managed only because meals were part of his compensation. Unless the public readings he was planning to give of his poetry brought in a goodly sum, or he lucked into a scholarship, the hope of entering Lincoln in February was very dim.

In late October, he wrote to Walter White, with whom he had been corresponding about literary matters for several months:

> I am working in a hotel....I am trying to get the funds for college (Lincoln) in February but I'm afraid I won't make it without help, so I've just written Mr. Johnson to see if he and the Garland Fund can't help me. What I want is this: A loan of

about three hundred dollars a year for the next three years, said money to be returned to the lender within three years after graduation. That would put me thru school. Some big hearted person ought to be interested enough in the development of talent to grant me that. . . .

My book of poems has gone to press. Now I'm working on my first book of prose which will perhaps be called *Scarlet Flowers: The Autobiography of a Young Negro Poet.* You think it's a good title?[27]

White told him some weeks later that he would try to help out on the scholarship, but that the title *Scarlet Flowers: The Autobiography of a Young Negro Poet* "doesn't exactly hit me between the eyes. . .it sounds like Louisa M. Alcott."[28] Hughes couldn't have agreed more. "The title for my prose book does sound sort of Louisa Alcottish, doesn't it?" he wrote back. "Glad you spoke of it."[29] But by then his mind was occupied with more than his prose book, and he abandoned the original title. In early December, an incident gave him heart and brought him a wave of unexpected publicity.

Vachel Lindsay, then perhaps the most famous poet in America, was a guest at the Wardman Park, where he was to read his poems in the hotel auditorium. Hughes, wishing to make Mr. Lindsay's acquaintance, lacked the audacity simply to approach him and introduce himself. Nor could he do it following the poetry reading, since blacks would not be admitted to it. Finally, Hughes hit upon an expedient. He placed three of his previously published poems—"Jazzonia," "Negro Dancers," and "The Weary Blues" —beside Mr. Lindsay's dinner plate "and went away, afraid to say anything to so famous a poet, except to tell him that I liked his poems and that these were poems of mine."[30]

That night Lindsay interrupted the reading of his poems to tell his audience that he had discovered a bus-boy poet and to read the poems Hughes had put beside his plate. The next day reporters and photographers besieged the hotel and lay in wait for the black poet. Pictures of Hughes and stories of his having been "discovered" by Vachel Lindsay appeared in many of the important newspapers nationwide, including, of course, the *Washington Evening Star.* Though Lindsay did not meet Hughes face to face until several days later, he did leave behind a letter of encouragement and advice written on the flyleaves of a set of Amy Lowell's biography of John Keats and had the hotel office deliver them to the young poet. "Do not let any lionizers stampede you," Lindsay wrote. "Hide and write and study and think."

But for the next several days there was no hiding and scarcely any writing. So many of the curious flocked to the Wardman Park to see the black bus-boy poet that Hughes's life was quite disorganized. As soon as payday came, he quit the hotel and went to New York. There he made final arrangements for the poetry readings that were to follow publication of *The Weary Blues* in February. There, too, at a party given by Carl Van Vechten in his honor, he met Arthur Spingarn, a prominent lawyer. Earlier that day, Hughes had at last accepted Mrs. Amy Spingarn's long-standing invitation to tea. From the moment he met Mrs. Spingarn and Arthur Spingarn, her brother-in-law, emotional ties were formed between Hughes and the Spingarn family that lasted for the rest of their lives. As Hughes's pro-bono attorney and personal friend for more than forty years, Arthur Spingarn made the poet's concerns his own and was unstinting in his public praise and admiration of Hughes.

Langston never quite warmed up as much to Arthur's brother, Joel Spingarn, a former Columbia University professor who was well known for his work with the NAACP. In 1914, as chairman of the NAACP board of directors, Joel had established the Spingarn Medal, which was to be awarded annually to an Afro-American of high achievement. Hughes liked and respected Joel, but found him aloof and cold, unlike his amiable wife, Amy. A woman of great personal wealth, inherited from her father, Amy Spingarn would become a secret benefactress of the poet and a source of enduring encouragement.[31] When he called upon her for the first time, he learned that she had not forgotten his letter of appreciation for the contest for which she had provided the prizes—a contest which, as she wrote in *The Crisis*, had been sponsored out of her "deep interest and faith in the contribution of the American Negro to American art and literature."[32] At this first meeting, Mrs. Spingarn encouraged Langston Hughes to talk, drew him out to speak with intimate candor of his background, his travels, his forthcoming book, and his future plans. He told her why he had left Columbia, and why he preferred to resume his studies at Lincoln instead of Harvard, although Harvard, he was quick to add, held out the possibility of a scholarship, which Lincoln did not. He expressed an attachment, a sympathy, a concern for others, as well as an earnestness about his own work and education, and Mrs. Spingarn, a mother of four, responded to him and all he said with warm understanding. Hughes wrote to her—somewhat incoherently—a few days later regarding his decision about college in a thank-you letter:

DEAR MRS. SPINGARN:

I enjoyed meeting you last week. I liked meeting your husband too, and seeing your daughter and that lovely painting that she made....Now I have good news about college. I may be able to get a private scholarship to Harvard, if I try hard enough, and if I choose to be "the splendid young man" the terms call for...I know that people are more interesting than books, and life, even a busboy's life out of school, more amusing than a professor's in school. But I do want to be able to earn a little time for my own work (which I haven't now) and a little money for travel. So maybe I'd better try Harvard....[33]

Mrs. Spingarn's immediate response was an offer to finance his education—at Lincoln if he preferred it to Harvard—until he received his baccalaureate. The offer, made during the Christmas season of 1925, was the happiest holiday gift Hughes had ever had. On December 29, he again wrote Mrs. Spingarn.

I have been thinking a long time about what to say to you and I don't know yet what it should be. But I believe this: That you do not want me to write to you the sort of things I would have to write to the [Harvard] scholarship people. I think you understand better than they the kind of person I am or surely you would not offer, in the quiet way you do, the wonderful thing you offer me. And if you were the scholarship people, although I might have to, I would not want to accept it. There would be too many conditions to fulfill and too many strange ideals to uphold. And somehow I don't believe you want me to be true to anything except myself. (Or you would ask questions and outline plans.) And that is all I want to do—be true to my own ideals. I hate pretending and I hate untruths. And it is so hard in other ways to pay the various little prices people attach to most of the things they offer or give.

And so I am happier now than I have been for a long time, more because you offer freely and with understanding, than because of the realization of the dreams which you make come true for me....I do want to go to Lincoln in February, but I had not expected to be able to do so. Strange that in the middle of a seemingly hopeless winter, you should be the person to make "trees grow all around me with branches full of dreams."[34] But that is what you have done. You are surely the spirit of Christmas....

If you ever wanted anything and then had stopped wanting it, because you were sure you wouldn't get it, then you may understand how glad I am, and how surprised....I'm happy. What can I say to you to make you understand how very happy.[35]

In February 1926 Langston Hughes enrolled as a student at Lincoln University, in a village of the same name in Pennsylvania.

❧ 7 ❧

A Temple for Tomorrow

Hughes's enrollment at Lincoln University coincided almost exactly with his twenty-fourth birthday and the publication of his first volume of poetry. He had no difficulty accepting the fact that he was nearly six years older than most of his classmates, but at a time when the Harlem Renaissance was beginning to peak, it was not so easy to meet the demands made upon a new and immediately popular poet. The demands conflicted with his studies. By early March, he was complaining to Alain Locke about a heavy schedule of poetry readings, "in Cleveland on April 16, Oberlin the following Sunday, . . . Indianapolis asks for the 4th but I'm afraid I can't take it. I wouldn't want to stay away from school two weeks. That is, I don't want to."[1]

After truck gardening, dishwashing, cooking, waiting on tables, and all the other things he had done in the years just past, he took to his studies with enthusiasm. He fell in love with Lincoln—with the geography of the area (just forty miles southeast of Philadelphia) and with the atmosphere of the University. In the letter just quoted he also wrote, partly in jest:

> I like Lincoln so much that I expect to be about six years in graduating. I don't ever want to leave. . . . Out here with the trees and rolling hills and open sky, in old clothes, and this do-as-you-please atmosphere, I rest content. This must be the freest of Negro schools. Professor Wright says it has always been the policy of Lincoln to let the men do as they choose, because then one is always likely to do right. . . . [2]

But as Hughes learned little by little during three and a half years there, all was not ideal at Lincoln, and Professor Wright's remark was a rationalization. Established in 1854 as the first college in the North for black men, the Lincoln of the nineteen twenties still had no Afro-Americans on its faculty, or on its administrative staff, or on the board of trustees. What at first seemed the "freest of Negro schools" would be perceived as something else again in the months ahead. The freedom was a function of the color line, as Hughes wrote in *The Big Sea*, "that cuts across American life, dividing the white from the non-white...the dark students on the campus, the white teachers in their houses across the road—meeting a few hours a day for classes, and that was just about all."

In his first term, though, Langston Hughes had little time to think about or even to observe the operation of the color line at the university. There were class assignments to pursue, "bull sessions" to take part in, and poetry-reading invitations to accept or reject. With the February publication of his book, such invitations poured in. The critical reception of *The Weary Blues* highlighted his spring and summer. Reviews in the *New York Times, Washington Post, Boston Transcript, New Orleans Picayune, The Independent, World Tomorrow, The New Republic*, and *Palms* were laudatory. The only derogatory review in a white publication appeared in the *Times* [London] *Literary Supplement* where Hughes was referred to as a "cabaret poet";[3] but many fewer Americans saw that review than saw DuBose Heyward's in the *New York Herald Tribune* a few days later. "Hughes," Heyward wrote, "has given us a 'first book' that marks the opening of a career well worth watching."[4]

Black critics, except for Jessie Fauset in *The Crisis* and Alain Locke in *Palms*, generally were somewhat less complimentary. Indeed, some of them heartily disliked the "jazz poems" that made up the first section of the book. Hughes's friend and fellow poet, Countee Cullen, wrote in the February 1926 issue of *Opportunity* that he considered the "jazz poems as interlopers in the company of the truly beautiful poems in other sections of the book," and he took exception to some of the poems in other sections on racial rather than esthetic grounds.

> Taken as a group the selections in this book seem one-sided to me. They tend to hurl this poet into the gaping pit that lies before all Negro writers, in the confines of which they become racial artists instead of artists pure and simple. There is too much emphasis here on strictly Negro themes; and this is probably an added reason for my coldness toward the jazz poems. . . .

Hughes's friendship with Countee, though enduring, was never quite the same afterward. There can be little doubt that he was referring to Cullen and responding to Cullen's criticism when he wrote, a few months later, in a piece for *The Nation*:

> One of the most promising of the young Negro poets said to me once, "I want to be a poet—not a Negro poet," meaning, "I want to write like a white poet"; meaning, subconsciously, "I would like to be a white poet"; meaning behind that "I would

like to be white." And I was sorry the young man said that, for
no great poet has ever been afraid of being himself. . . .[5]

"Most of my own poems," Hughes continued in defense of his jazz poems,
"are racial in theme and treatment, derived from the life I know. In many of
them I try to grasp and hold some of the meanings and rhythms of jazz . . . jazz
to me is one of the inherent expressions of Negro life in America".[6]

The Nation essay, which became a declaration of motives and intentions
for some of the younger artists and writers in the New Negro movement,
was one of the few things Hughes wrote in the spring (and summer) of
1926. Though more than thirty "new" poems appeared in various magazines that year, all save a few had been written prior to his enrollment at
Lincoln, and most of them would be included in his second volume, Fine
Clothes to the Jew, published in 1927.[7] There was almost literally no time and
little inclination for the concentrated effort of poetic composition. He was
busy with public poetry readings in New York, Philadelphia, Bordentown,
Trenton, Cleveland, and several other places. Besides, it was a relatively
happy period for him, and he wrote little when he was happy. Yet there
were days of introspection, of a need to be alone, of deliberation. The
subject of some of his pondering that spring was romantic love. At least one
poem, "A Letter to Anne," is believed to have been about Anne Coussey
(alias Mary), whom he had met in Paris two years before.

A Letter to Anne

Since I left you, Anne,
I have seen nothing but you.
Every day
· Has been your face,
And every night your hand,
And every road
Your voice calling me.
And every rock and every flower and tree
Has been a touch of you.
Nowhere
Have I seen anything else but you,
Anne.[8]

Two other love poems provide insights into what was to become his attitude toward the women who, smitten by his good looks and his reputation,
were already beginning to create for him a dilemma, if not a problem. The
first appeared in The Crisis in April.

The Ring

Love is a master of the ring
And life a circus tent.
What is this silly song you sing?
Love is the master of the ring.

I am afraid!
Afraid of love
And love's bitter whip!
Afraid,
Afraid of love
And love's sharp stinging whip.

What is this silly song you sing?
Love is the master of the ring.

A month later, the second appeared in *Opportunity*.

Love Song for Lucinda

Love
Is a ripe plum
Growing on a purple tree.
Taste it once
And the spell of its enchantment
Will never let you be.

Love
Is a bright star
Glowing in Southern skies.
Look too hard
And its burning flame
Will always hurt your eyes.

Love
Is a high mountain
Stark in a windy sky.
If you
Would never lose your breath
Do not climb too high.

Hughes seemed to fear any enduring, emotionally charged relations with women. He also seems to have made up his mind quite early that he could not write, travel, do the things he wanted to do, and have a serious love affair all at the same time. The record is quite clear on this point: he avoided serious romantic courtships during his college years and immediately thereafter. Gregarious and affable, though occasionally shy, he made friends easily among both men and women, but except in two notable instances—both of which would come later—his strongest friendships with women were those in which he could prove himself a devoted, loyal friend, not a lover.

Among the men at Lincoln, "Lank" was considered a "regular guy" in spite of the age difference. He took the "hazing" inflicted on all new students in the same good spirit he later took the rigors of being initiated into a college fraternity. He joined Omega Psi Phi fraternity and the Phi Lambda Sigma English Society. If his schedule and periods of introspection sometimes kept him from dormitory bull sessions, he did his share of participating when he did attend. Though he elected to live alone during his junior year, in his first term his room was a gathering place for fellow students and he let his books—newly acquired from authors and admirers—circulate freely. He wrote Locke that at Lincoln "one can use, wear, or borrow anything anyone else has. There's a fine spirit of comradeship and helpfulness here."[9] Hughes in turn added to the spirit of "comradeship and helpfulness" by contributing some of his unpublished poems to "The Poet's Corner" in the school's bi-monthly publication, the Lincoln News.[10]

In January, shortly before leaving Washington for Lincoln, Hughes had read his poetry to musical accompaniment before the Playwriter's Circle, presided over by Alain Locke. It was an experiment he wanted to try again, and when the Lincoln University glee club presented its annual spring concert, he departed from the traditional program (of spirituals and classical music) by reading blues poetry accompanied by blues on piano. It was a great success, adding to the popularity of his new book among Lincoln faculty and students. In appearances away from the campus he could not regularly have musical accompaniment for his poetry readings, but in years to come he would read his poems to blues and jazz whenever the opportunity arose.

As that spring wore on, he accepted fewer and fewer reading invitations, especially those that offered only to pay his travel expenses. His finances, as well as his class schedule, did not permit him much option. But there was another consideration. When his Aunt Sallie, his father's sister, who had not seem him since he was a baby, invited him to Indianapolis, he wrote Locke, "I didn't feel like going way out there now,—aunt or no aunt! This sun and earth and coming spring here is too good to me. When not even New York attracts how could any village in the hinterland prove amusing?"[11]

Even more illuminating—though somewhat misleading—is the fact that in that same letter to Locke, he wrote, "New York like to bored me to death last time." Although he had complained that "New York seemed rather dull," the word "bored" did not truly describe his reaction to the Harlem of the mid-twenties. The truth was that he was disenchanted with the image of Harlem as an exotic, hedonistic place that pleasure-seeking whites had been largely responsible for creating. The atmosphere was very pretentious. It was surface, and the surface was false. "Thousands of whites came to Harlem night after night," Hughes wrote later, "thinking the Negroes loved to have them there, and firmly believing that all Harlemites left their houses at sundown to sing and dance in cabarets, because most of the whites saw nothing but the cabarets, not the houses."[12] His disenchantment had been growing ever since his return from Europe, and two of his poems appearing in the December 1925 *Crisis* (one of which was "Minstrel Man") perhaps reflect the fact. Another, titled "Disillusion," reflects, too, a vague ambivalence.

Disillusion

I would be simple again,
Simple and clean
Like the earth,
Like the rain,
Nor ever know,
Dark Harlem,
The wild laughter
Of your mirth
Nor the salt tears
Of your pain.
Be kind to me,
Oh, great dark city.
Let me forget.
I will not come
To you again.

Disenchantment and disillusion were probably the overriding reasons why Hughes wrote to Locke as he did in May that "I'm going to Haiti and points south this summer if any boats run at all. I've been home too long."[13] But circumstances soon dictated that he scrap those plans. As he entered the final weeks of the semester, he realized that a trip to the Caribbean was more than he could afford. The money he had earned from poetry readings was exhausted, he was in debt to the village snack shops, and the fees he had expected to get from *Poetry* and the *New York Herald Tribune*, which had accepted some of his poems, had not arrived by late spring. It could have been that he was hinting when he wrote to Locke that "surely some '*Deus ex machina*' will step in from somewhere with at least railroad fare to New York. The fun comes in wondering just what God it will be."[14]

In June, *The Nation* solicited from Hughes his essay "The Negro Artist and the Racial Mountain," as a response to "The Negro Art-Hokum," by black satirist George Schuyler.[15] The essay, bought and published by the magazine the same month, provided Hughes with enough money for trainfare to New York, but he lingered at Lincoln a while longer. Apparently, work on what turned out to be his autobiographical first novel, *Not Without Laughter*, was going too well just then to be interrupted. He wrote Locke, "I'm doing 10 to 20 pages a day now and rather enjoy it."[16] When he did go to New York later in June, he took a room in a house on West 137th Street, in the heart of Harlem, where another aspiring young black writer, Wallace Thurman, was living at the time.

Thurman, a native of Salt Lake City and a graduate of the University of Southern California, had moved to New York the year before. Brilliant, restive, and facile, his superior talents later landed him a job with the Macaulay Company—the first black to be hired in an editorial capacity by a major publishing firm.[17] Later, too—largely because of Thurman's personality and his bohemian lifestyle—his home became a favorite gathering place for both white and black artists and writers. He had not yet written *Infants of the Spring*, the scurrilous novel that fictionalized so many characters of the Harlem Renaissance, including himself (as a character named Raymond). But he had the setting for "Niggeratti Manor," which he made famous as the fictional center for numerous fictionalized artists. In reality, Niggerati Manor was 267 West 136th Street, a Harlem rooming house as well known for all-night parties as for enlightened intellectual discussions. Formerly a tenement, it had been bought by a black businesswoman, Iolanthe Sydney, and converted into living quarters for impecunious writers and artists. She herself was fictionalized in Thurman's novel (as Euphoria Blake), and he was even less kind in his portrayal of her than he was of Hughes, whom he disguised as a poet named Tony Crews in *Infants of the Spring*:

> As time passed, others came in. Tony Crews, smiling and self-effacing, a mischievous boy, grateful for the chance to slip away from the backwoods college he attended. Raymond had never been able to analyze this young poet. His work was interesting and unusual. It was also spotty. Spasmodically he gave promise of developing into a first rate poet. Already he had published two volumes, prematurely, Raymond thought. Both had been excessively praised by whites and universally damned by Negroes. Considering the nature of his work this was to be ex-

pected. The only unknown quantity was the poet himself. Would
he or would he not fulfill the promise exemplified in some of his
work? Raymond had no way of knowing and even an intimate
friendship with Tony himself had failed to enlighten him. For
Tony was the most close-mouthed and cagey individual Raymond had ever known when it came to personal matters. He
fended off every attempt to probe into his inner self and did this
with such an unconscious and naïve air that the prober soon
came to one of two conclusions: Either Tony had no depth
whatsoever, or else he was too deep for plumbing by ordinary
mortals.

Hughes never let Thurman come too close, and the latter always resented
it, but when *Infants of the Spring* was published, Hughes must have recog-
nized himself as "Tony," along with their contemporaries Thurman sati-
rized, including Countee Cullen as DeWitt Clinton, Rudoph Fisher as Dr.
Manfred Trout, Eric Walrond as Cedric Williams, Zora Neale Hurston as
Sweetie May Carr, Alain Locke as Dr. A. L. Parkes, and Harold John
("Bunny") Stephanson as Stephen Jorgenson, who in real life was one of
Thurman's white lovers.

Hughes's relationship with Thurman began and continued amicably. Later,
some of their acquaintances would accept Thurman's boast that his association with Hughes was more than just friendly. But those who knew them
both knew better. One who did was Bruce Nugent, a struggling artist who,
to spare his family, used the pen name Richard Bruce. He had met Hughes
in Washington, where they became good friends. Encouraged to join the
Harlem Renaissance crowd in New York, Bruce lived with Thurman (at
267 West 136th Street) and later said of him: "Wallie had a fascination for
people that only the devil could have—an almost diabolical power. Langston
was the opposite; he couldn't touch anyone without making them better.
He brought out the good in everyone...he was not corrupted. He had the
toughness of absolute goodness, which Wallie never had."[18]

In the summer of 1926 Thurman was working as managing editor of *The
Messenger*. Before he took over, it had been a "radical" black magazine
guided for eight years by A. Philip Randolph, organizer of the Brotherhood
of Sleeping Car Porters. When his message of socialism finally failed to
catch on in Harlem, the magazine changed hands and opened its pages to the
new surge of artists and writers of the Harlem Renaissance. *The Messenger*'s
content soon became a cultural hodgepodge, which Hughes later described
as "God knows what." Thurman couldn't control the editorial decisions, so
in his spare time he organized a small circle of friends and acquaintances,
including Hughes, painter Aaron Douglas, and writers Zora Neale Hurston

and Gwendolyn Bennett, to plan a black quarterly of the arts. They chose to call it *Fire!!*—"the idea being," Hughes wrote in *The Big Sea*, "that it would burn up a lot of the old, dead conventional Negro-white ideas of the past, *épater le bourgeois* into a realization of the existence of the younger Negro writers and artists, and provide us with an outlet for publication not available in the limited pages of the small magazines then existing." The first issue was scheduled for the fall of 1926. Meanwhile, Hughes was still contributing to "small magazines," such as *Opportunity*, where five of his poems were accepted for the October issue, with illustrations by Aaron Douglas.

Hughes was involved in other projects as well. He had to pay his own way through the summer, and he did so by writing lyrics for a projected revue, *O Blues!* featuring black American folk music. Caroline Dudley (Reagan), the white producer who had taken *La Revue Nègre* to Paris the year before and helped launch Josephine Baker to stardom, wanted authenticity in her new revue, and she thought Hughes could provide it. She hoped to have Paul Robeson star. Hughes worked on the musical most of the summer, but in the end, production plans fell through. Robeson, already famous as a singer and actor, with dramatic performances in Eugene O'Neill's *Emperor Jones* and *All God's Chillun Got Wings*, accepted an invitation to star in the London production of *Showboat*.

As far as Hughes was concerned, working on the production was not wasted. Quite the contrary; it was rewarding. For one thing, he lived on what he earned, and for another, working on theatrical skits and writing lyric sequences tapped talents that he would call upon time after time in his long career. Though he did not then (or ever) know how to play a musical instrument, he knew that music was important to him. With a composer named Ford Dabney, he experimented that year with the libretto for a short dramatic musical which the two titled *Leaves*. Hughes was fond of opera, and he loved jazz, gospel music, and the blues. That summer he met Rosamond Johnson, the musically gifted younger brother of James Weldon Johnson. For amusement on several evenings they worked out musical settings for some of Hughes's poems.[19] That summer, Hughes also wrote lyrics for the voice and piano rendition of W. C. Handy's "Golden Brown Blues," and reviewing Handy's *Blues*, set forth his own creative and critical involvement with blues music:

> The folk blues are pictures of the life from which they come, the life of the levees, of the back alleys, of dissolute streets, the red light districts and the cabarets of those with not even a God to look to. They are a long ways removed from the expectancy and faith of the Spirituals. Their hopeless weariness mixed with an absurdly incongruous laughter makes them the most interesting

folk songs I have heard. Blues are sad songs sung to the most despondent rhythm in the world. . . .[20]

It was partly out of an interest in music that Hughes began attending Harlem "house-rent parties," which he claimed were "often more amusing than any nightclub."[21] That summer he went to one almost every Saturday night, and there met "ladies' maids and truck drivers, laundry workers and shoe shine boys, seamstresses and porters"; and he wrote "lots of poems about house-rent parties."[22] These poems, not evident in Hughes's published poetry of the period, were one-dimensional and superficial. He was not then ready to deal fully with the social significance of Harlem life, or to comment incisively, as he would do later, on the day-to-day struggle for existence of the average Harlem dweller.

His most serious poetic effort during those months centered upon the meaning of another social phenomenon. Almost since childhood, when one of his playmates in Lawrence was a golden-haired boy whose mother was colored and whose father was white, he had been "intrigued with the problem of those so-called 'Negroes' of immediate white-and-black blood. . . ."[23] This, the tragic mulatto theme, which had appeared earlier in the poem "Cross," was to engage him time and again for several years, and his second poetic treatment of it came that summer of 1926. The poem was "Mulatto." Referring to it in *The Big Sea* nearly fourteen years later, Hughes declared, "I worked harder on that poem than on any other that I have ever written."[24]

Hughes read the poem to much applause at a gathering of artists and writers in the home of the James Weldon Johnsons that August. There were many such gatherings, and the young poet attended his share of them, then and later, when he went fairly regularly to New York from Lincoln for weekends and holidays. In spite of his disenchantment with certain aspects of the city, he enjoyed New York. But he inveighed against and avoided the night clubs and restaurants that attracted so many of the wrong kind of white people and discriminated against blacks. For these reasons, he never went to the famous Cotton Club, for instance. Only twice that summer did he leave town—once to read his poems at an industrial workers camp in Erie, Pennsylvania, and once to spend a weekend with Joel and Amy Spingarn at Troutbeck, their country place in Amenia, New York. In a letter welcoming Professor Locke home from another summer in Europe, Hughes wrote, "New York is the nicest town in the world. I'm getting real provincial in that respect."[25]

If Hughes read other unpublished poems at social gatherings that summer and in the weeks that followed, there is no record of it. Literary entertainment was not standard at Harlem parties or at parties downtown to which the black literati were invited. Only Jessie Fauset's affairs, offering "much poetry but little to drink," were actual literary soirées. At Aaron and Alta Douglas's, where everyone brought food and liquor, the conversation was usually political. The Walter Whites encouraged the social talk of Harlem at their buffet suppers. Gatherings at Wallace Thurman's were bohemian, unlike those at A'Lelia Walker Robinson's, the "joy goddess," whose large apartment on West 136th Street, called the "Dark Tower," welcomed everyone from poets to racketeers.[26] Hughes recalled that A'Lelia's parties were as "crowded as the New York subway at the rush hour." The parties given by the novelist and ballet critic Carl Van Vechten and his wife, ballerina Fania Marinoff, were as exotic as the hosts themselves. Flamboyant and epicene, they seemed right out of Van Vechten's own fiction, with their guest list bringing together people as diverse as Bessie Smith and Salvador Dali, Helena Rubinstein and Somerset Maugham, and Bojangles Bill Robinson. Hughes never forgot them or the people he met there.

> Not only were there interesting Negroes at Carl Van Vechten's parties...but there were always many other celebrities of various colors and kinds, old ones and new ones from Hollywood, Broadway, London, Paris or Harlem. I remember one party when Chief Long Lance of the cinema did an Indian war dance, while Adelaide Hall of *Blackbirds* played the drums, and an international assemblage crowded around to cheer.[27]

Van Vechten's parties, and those he attended in Harlem, had supplied him with material for his novel *Nigger Heaven*, published that August.[28] For the forty-six-year-old Van Vechten, Afro-Americans were at one and the same time atavistic and exotic specimens and embodiments of bourgeois respectability. His novel reflected these characteristics, but Hughes saw more of the latter than the former, writing to Locke as soon as the novel appeared that "colored people can't help but like it. It sounds as if it were written by an NAACP official or Jessie Fauset. But it's good."[29] Hughes refused to join the critical chorus of blacks who condemned the novel as exploitative; instead he joined well-known black critics Charles S. Johnson, James Weldon Johnson, George Schuyler, and Wallace Thurman in defending it. In an article some months later in *The Pittsburgh Courier*, he wrote:

> It seems to me too bad that the discussions of Mr. Van Vechten's novel in the colored press finally became hysterical and absurd. ...Because it was considered obscene everybody wanted to read it...and more Negroes bought it than ever purchased a book by a Negro author. Which is all very fine because *Nigger Heaven* is not a bad book. It will do nice people good to read it and maybe

it will broaden their minds a bit.... The sincere, friendly and
helpful interest in things Negro of this sophisticated author as
shown in his published reviews and magazine articles, should at
least have commanded serious, rather than vulgar reviews of his
book....[30]

Indeed, when Van Vechten was threatened with a lawsuit for failing to
obtain permission to use certain blues songs in *Nigger Heaven*, Hughes came
to the novelist's aid. "As several such songs were quoted in the book," Van
Vechten later wrote, "my publisher and I decided to employ Langston
Hughes to replace these with original verse to exactly fill the spaces. I
telephoned him at Lincoln University...and he accepted the commission
with high good humor. He spent the ensuing weekend locked up in my
apartment and Monday morning his songs were ready for the printer. They
appeared in the seventh edition [sic] of the novel, but apparently nobody
noticed the change or commented on it."[31]

Hughes makes no mention of this in his autobiography. He was curiously
silent or disinclined to speak openly about various other people and incidents that figured in his literary career. Was there, for instance, a connection
between Van Vechten, Mabel Dodge Luhan, and Hughes's 1926 poem "A
House in Taos"? The poet had never been to Taos when he wrote the poem,
and he claimed later, "At that time, I had never heard Mrs. Luhan's name."[32]
It is pure speculation, but the poem may well have been indirectly inspired
by stories that Van Vechten and others had told Hughes about Mabel Dodge—
an old friend of the novelist's—and Tony Luhan, an Indian who happened
to be her fourth husband.[33] Hughes had also heard gossip about an affair
between Mabel and the mulatto Jean Toomer, whose recent trip to Fontainebleau, as a disciple of the Russian mystic Gurdjieff, she had helped to
finance. And if stories about them, why not stories about Mrs. Luhan and
D. H. Lawrence, whose liaison in Taos was equally well known to the New
York literati through the writer-critic Witter Bynner, who lived in nearby
Santa Fe, and had housed Lawrence and his wife, Frieda, during their first
night in New Mexico.[34] At any rate, as Hughes himself admitted, the poem
in four titled parts "was a strange poem for me to be writing in a period
when I was writing mostly blues and spirituals."

A House in Taos

RAIN

Thunder of the Rain God:
And we three
Smitten by beauty.

Thunder of the Rain God:
  And we three
  Weary, weary.

Thunder of the Rain God:
  And you, she and I
  Waiting for nothingness.

Do you understand the stillness
Of this house in Taos
Under the thunder of the Rain God?

SUN

That there should be a barren garden
About this house in Taos
Is not so strange,
But that there should be three barren hearts
In this one house in Taos—
Who carries ugly things to show the sun?

MOON

Did you ask for the beaten brass of the moon?
We can buy lovely things with money,
You, she and I,
Yet you seek,
As though you could keep,
This unbought loveliness of moon.

WIND

Touch our bodies, wind.
Our bodies are separate, individual things.
Touch our bodies, wind,
But blow quickly
Through the red, white, yellow skins
Of our bodies
To the terrible snarl,
Not mine,
Not yours,
Not hers,
But all one snarl of souls.
Blow quickly, wind,
Before we run back into the windlessness—
With our bodies—
Into the windlessness
Of our house in Taos.

Competing with some six hundred entries, "A House in Taos" won a first prize of $150 in the Witter Bynner Undergraduate Poetry Contest for 1926.[35] Bynner, who was associated with the Poetry Society of America and the magazine *Palms*, and is believed to have encouraged Hughes to submit the poem, was assisted in judging the contest by two other poet-judges. One of them was Vachel Lindsay, who must have been pleased (and perhaps surprised) that the bus-boy poet he had "discovered" less than a year before should prove himself so soon in so important a contest. By 1927, Hughes would also receive the John Keats Prize of twenty-five dollars from *Palms* for "A House in Taos." Meanwhile, in the autumn of 1926 Hughes was himself a judge, with Babette Deutsch and James Weldon Johnson, of the second Amy Spingarn Contest in Literature and Art, and he went to New York City, where the first prize in poetry was awarded to Arna Bontemps and the second to Countee Cullen, both his close friends.

But the golden days of the Harlem Renaissance were sometimes clouded with disappointment and failure. *Fire!!*, the quarterly to which Hughes, Thurman, and other organizers had contributed much time and talent, and in which Cullen and Bontemps were represented, was a critical fiasco. The first and only number was issued in November, and except for a short favorable review that month in *The Bookman*, the journal went unnoticed by most of the white periodicals, and the black press, except for *Opportunity*, condemned it bluntly and vigorously. The reviewer for the influential *Baltimore Afro-American* began his scorching notice, "I have just tossed the first issue of *Fire* into the fire." Of Hughes's two poetic contributions, "Elevator Boy" and "Railroad Avenue," he remarked, "Langston Hughes displays his usual ability to say nothing in many words."[36] Most black critics objected to what they considered the sensational, ribald contents of *Fire!!* Alain Locke was somewhat more sympathetic. Writing in *The Survey* nine months after the quarterly appeared, he declared:

> The bold, arresting red and black of its jacket is not accidental— this is left-wing literary modernism with deliberate intent: *The Little Review, This Quarter,* and *The Quill* are obvious artistic cousins. Indeed one's first impression is that *Fire* is more charac- teristic as an exhibit of unifying affinities in the psychology of contemporary youth than of any differentiating traits of a new Negro literary school. A good deal of it is reflected Sherwood Anderson, Sinclair Lewis, Dreiser, Joyce and Cummings, recast in the context of Negro life and experience....For the present the racialism of this interesting young group is more a drive than an arrival, more of an experiment than a discovery....[37]

The sales of *Fire!!* were very disappointing. Stacks of the issue were stored. In an irony like no other, a fire reportedly destroyed them all, leaving the sponsors with a printer's debt of more than a thousand dollars.

But a letter attributed to Hughes and allegedly sent to Wallace Thurman tells a different story.

> FIRE!!! which I now hear wasn't burnt up at all in anybody's cellar but is in the possession of Service Bell...FIRE that I thought was in smoke, but which is now a la casa de Service Bell, after Locke said that you said they all got burnt up at 267.[38]

"Service Bell" was the actual, though somewhat curious, name of a black actor-singer who lived briefly in the infamous bohemian apartment house at 267 West 136th Street. When Bell moved out, it was said he took with him the unsold copies of *Fire!!* and stored them in a basement elsewhere in Harlem. Though none of the *Fire!!* contributors could ever prove it, the rumor persisted. Hughes purportedly complained to Thurman:

> Service Bell...therefore holds the whole younger generation in his grasp, and in 2650 when we're the prey of research experts...his heirs will receive a tremendous sum for the lot, all first and last editions of original copies containing source material on the whole Negro Renaissance....[39]

But Thurman and the group decided to let the fire die down. So many heated arguments had spread about *Fire!!* that they thought another would only fan the flames of critics. Enough was enough. Fire or no fire.

Langston Hughes had armed himself against the adverse critical reaction to *Fire!!* In "The Negro Artist and the Racial Mountain" he had written, "We younger Negro artists who create now intend to express our individual dark-skinned selves without fear or shame. If white people are pleased we are glad. If they are not, it doesn't matter.... If colored people are pleased we are glad. If they are not, their displeasure doesn't matter either."

If this was his conviction and his abiding creed—and his subsequent writings suggest that it truly was—it served him when his second volume of verse was published in February 1927. *Fine Clothes to the Jew* contained some of his most controversial (but not his best) poems. The volume displeased most black critics for some of the same reasons as *Nigger Heaven* and *Fire!!* had, and some white critics, in contrast to the reception given *The Weary Blues*, found it easy to restrain their enthusiasm. DuBose Heyward wrote, "In *Fine Clothes to the Jew* we are given a volume more even in quality, but because it lacks the 'high spots' of *The Weary Blues*, by no means as unforgettable as the first book."[40] The *New York Times Book Review* critic, indulging in the white paternalism that was characteristic of the period, remarked that "Langston Hughes belongs to the colored race and it is therefore impossible to estimate him beside, say, Humbert Wolfe or Richard Aldington."[41] And the *Boston Transcript* commented—somewhat inaccurately—that the poet "is using the same things which brought him first into notice, but that he is doing it consciously rather than from his heart."[42] Babette Deutsch, noting that the dialect poems showed "craftsmanship of high order,"[43] was somewhat less laudatory than Julia Peterkin, who found "the prayers and shouts...turned into poetry with art and skill."[44]

In Afro-American publications, only the reviewers for *The Crisis, Opportunity, The Chicago Defender, The Washington Eagle* were sympathetic. *The Crisis* called it "the outstanding book of the month" in a March "What to Read" column. The reviewer in *Opportunity* referred to Hughes as a "Proletarian Poet," noting that "'Railroad Avenue,' 'Brass Spittoons,' 'Prize Fighter,' 'Elevator Boy,' 'Porter,' 'Saturday Night,' and songs from the Georgia Roads, all have their roots deep in the lives of workers."[45] Though *Fine Clothes to the Jew* differed considerably from the proletarian poems Hughes would write during the 1930s—and it is the only volume of poetry in which he does not mention Harlem—his effort was to recapture, through the use of folk-blues forms, the lives and scenes of Washington's Seventh Street. Dewey Jones quoted the poet as having intended to give "an interpretation of the so-called 'lower classes,' the ones to whom life is least kind...to catch the hurt of their lives, the monotony of their 'jobs,' the veiled weariness of their songs."[46]

But most black critics missed this, or ignored it. They dubbed Hughes the "poet lowrate of Harlem" and a "sewer dweller," and described his poems as "trash."[47] They saw Hughes's homeless, jobless men, his mistreated working women, his betrayed and deserted lovers, his young prostitutes, as vignettes of racial stereotypes they wanted to deny and forget. These figures and these themes were to recur time and again in Hughes's later work, in both poetry and prose, for he had a deep sense of their reality, and especially of the reality of black women—traceable in part to his awareness of the experience of his own mother—and he entered their minds and hearts more fully than did any other black American poet. His critic and friend, Alain Locke, recognized the significance of the poems then—and later. So did Charles S. Johnson, who claimed that "no Negro writer so completely symbolizes the emancipation of the Negro mind."[48] Locke thought *Fine Clothes to the Jew* "notable as an achievement in poetic realism, in addition to its particular value as a folk study in verse of Negro life."[49] Walter White added that "when he leaves the more confining form of the blues, Mr. Hughes evokes magnificently stirring emotions from the life of Negro porters and prostitutes and others of humble estate."[50]

Although Hughes did publish a nine-point reply to his critics, for the most part he took both the good and the bad criticism in stride.[51] He certainly did not believe his book was "a disgrace to the race" and a "return to the dialect tradition...parading...racial defects before the public." He actually considered this book of poems better than his first, because it said more about other people than about himself. With good-natured humor he wrote to Professor Locke, "'Fine Clothes' is still getting grand reviews—all the way from 'He's a great poet' to 'He's a low-down hound.' How they do vary!"[52] He was less good-natured some months later when an Afro-American sociologist-teacher, Allison Davis, charged that the book had been influenced by the author of *Nigger Heaven*, who had "misdirected a genuine poet."[53] Hughes's response was spirited:

> I do not know what facts Mr. Davis himself may possess as to how, where, or when I have been misdirected by Mr. Van Vechten, but since I happen to be the person who wrote the material...I would like herewith to state and declare that many of the poems in said book were written before I made the acquaintance of Mr. Van Vechten....Those poems which were written after my acquaintance with Mr. Van Vechten were certainly not about him, not misdirected by him, some of them not liked by him, nor, so far as I know, do they in any way bear his poetic influence.
>
> My second book is what I personally desired it to be and if the poems which it contains are low-down, jazzy, cabaret-ish, sensational, and utterly uncouth in the eyes of Mr. Davis the fault is mine,—not Mr. Van Vechten's....[54]

And thirteen years later, in *The Big Sea*, Hughes wrote, "What Carl Van Vechten did for me was to submit my first book of poems to Alfred A. Knopf, put me in contact with the editors of *Vanity Fair*, who bought my first poems sold to a magazine, caused me to meet many editors and writers who were friendly and helpful to me...and otherwise aided in making life for me more profitable and entertaining."

The only thing he regretted about *Fine Clothes to the Jew* after its publication was the title: It offended some Jews, but people like the Spingarns and those he had known since high school accepted his explanation and remained his friends and admirers. As Hughes later explained the title: "I called it *Fine Clothes to the Jew*, because the first poem, 'Hard Luck,' a blues, was about a man who was often so broke he had no recourse but to pawn his clothes—to take them, as the Negroes say, to 'the Jew's' or to 'Uncle's.'"[55]

Paradoxically, during the spring and summer of 1927, after publication of *Fine Clothes to the Jew* and long before the criticism died down, none of Hughes's poems that appeared in periodicals touched upon the racial theme. They were about love ("Passing Love" and "Tapestry"), or they were memorialist ("Lincoln Monument"), or about imaginary visions ("For an Indian Screen"), or, like one entitled "Day," about death (a theme that became of such importance to him that he devoted half a volume to it in 1931).

Day

Where most surely comes a day
When all the sweets you've gorged
Will turn your stomach sick
And all the friends you've loved
Will go away
And every gold swift hour
Will be an hour of pain
And every sun-filled cloud
A cloud of rain
And even the withered flowers
Will lose their long-held faint perfume
And you alone will be with you
In that last room—
Only your single selves together
Facing a single doom.[56]

Racial themes were very much present in his prose, however. He wrote two articles on the theme for The Pittsburgh Courier in April, and that same month the first of his short stories with an African setting, "Bodies in the Moonlight," appeared in the The Messenger. Indeed, it was during this period that he gave sustained attention to stories based on his African journey and his experiences as a crewman on the S. S. Malone.[57] Besides, the May Crisis carried his long, six-part autobiographical prose-poem, "The Childhood of Jimmy," the most revealing personal account he was to write before The Big Sea. The next month the same magazine published his substantial religious poem, "Ma Lord," partly written in dialect and presenting the folk-created image of an anthropomorphic God. Sensitive black critics undoubtedly found it more acceptable than the folk-inspired "gospel shouts" of Fine Clothes to the Jew.

Although his principal energies, when he was not studying, went into writing, including contributions to the Lincoln University student publication, he also read his poetry at places not distant from the university. "I've been invited to read my poems at Walt Whitman's House in Camden on March 1st," Hughes wrote Walter White. "Invitation came from Walt Whitman Foundation, and because I admire his work so much it seems a great honor for me to read my humble poems in the house where he lived and worked...."[58] At another engagement, a YMCA conference at Franklin and Marshall College in nearby Lancaster, he roiled the waters. In his autobiography he said, "Since then, I've discovered a lot of hooey revolves around interracial conferences in this country." At the time, he wrote to Locke on a postcard, "I've seemingly disturbed the calm of this nice student's YMCA conference by making a speech asking what they are doing about colleges like this one...where 'Negroes are not encouraged to attend.' They really stopped discussing religion awhile."[59] What he did not tell Locke, but later quoted in *The Big Sea*, was the response of the white director of the conference: "There are some things in this world we must leave to Jesus, friends. Let us pray!"

DURING that spring of 1927 Hughes made frequent weekend visits to New York, where he often joined Alain Locke, who made the trip from Washington. The latter, pleased with the success of *The New Negro*, then in its second printing, had recently edited another volume, *Four Negro Poets*, in which Hughes was represented by twenty-one poems.[60] Meanwhile, Charles S. Johnson was including an unpublished Hughes poem in *Ebony and Topaz: A Collectanea*, published in 1927 by *Opportunity*. Eleven of his poems were also anthologized that year in *Caroling Dusk* by his friend Countee Cullen, and three more appeared in *Portraits in Color*, written by Mary White Ovington, a social worker, writer, and founding member of the NAACP.

Things "Negro" were the vogue, and many wealthy whites, especially in New York City, followed the vogue. One of these was Mrs. Charlotte Mason, an influential arts patron. She was the wealthy widow of a noted surgeon and acknowledged authority in the field of parapsychology and therapeutic hypnotism. Having married in her early thirties, she was the second wife of Dr. Rufus Osgood Mason, who, nearly twice her age, had died in 1903. She still shared the views her husband had expressed in such monographs as "Telepathy and the Subliminal Self," and "Hypnotism and Suggestion in Therapeutics, Education and Reform," and she subscribed to his belief that the most significant manifestations of the spiritual were found in "primitive," "child races," such as Indians and peoples of African descent, whose creative energies, Mrs. Mason believed, had their source in the unconscious. As Hughes wrote later, "Concerning Negroes, she felt that they were America's great link with the primitive...that there was mystery and mysticism and spontaneous harmony in their souls...that we had a deep well of the spirit within us and that we should keep it pure and deep."[61]

Mrs. Mason was particularly attracted to the work of Professor Locke and his philosophy of "the New Negro." In turn, her money and influence seem to have hypnotized him. Like a courtier before a queen, he presented to her at her Park Avenue apartment the most promising artists and writers of the Harlem Renaissance, including Hughes, Zora Neale Hurston, and Aaron Douglas. Locke's postulate in the introductory essay of *The New Negro* that Negroes must free themselves from the patronizing and the philanthropy of whites was one he himself ignored when it came to Mrs. Mason. He agreed with her that one must encourage young black artists to stress African origins in their work. This was the side of the professor that Wallace Thurman later satirized in *Infants of the Spring*, disguising Locke in the character of Dr. Parkes, whose message to Harlem Renaissance writers and artists was: "Let me suggest your going back to your racial roots, and cultivating a healthy paganism based on African traditions." Nevertheless, among the artists and writers Locke presented to Mrs. Mason, Hughes was one of those who most impressed her, whose talent she wanted to "protect," and whose "great link with the primitive" (according to her beliefs) she wanted to remain strong. For his part, Hughes found Mrs. Mason "instantly one of the most delightful women I had ever met, witty and charming, kind and sympathetic, very old and white-haired [she was then in her seventies] but amazingly modern in her ideas, in her knowledge of books and the theater, of Harlem, and of everything then taking place in the world."[62] Hughes was ultimately to outlive this "very old and white-haired" woman by only twenty-one years.[63] But beginning in the spring of 1927, and for three and a half years thereafter, she was his principal patron, and she fastened upon him a grip that only the gradual reassertion of his personal and creative integrity permitted him to break.

The Spingarns' patronage made no demands, and he expected none from Mrs. Mason, who, childless, requested that her young protégés call her "Godmother" and stipulated that she not be revealed as their benefactress.[64] Her request that he write her several times a week, about everything he was doing, he found rather flattering—at least at the time. When in the late spring he was scheduled to give a poetry reading during commencement week at Fisk University in Nashville, Tennessee, and at a YMCA conference in Texas the following week, it did not seem demanding of his new patron to suggest that afterward he join Zora Neale Hurston, another of her protégés, in New Orleans, and that they journey by car back to New York together, gathering black folk material on the way. And of course Mrs. Mason would have no objection if, incidental to meeting Zora Hurston in New Orleans, he made a brief visit to Cuba. Perhaps he could find a black Cuban composer to collaborate with him on a black-oriented opera she would be happy to subsidize.

The summer passed much as Langston projected it, though not in every detail. At Fisk, where he began to sense he had become a public figure, though not a celebrity—an image he refused to project throughout his public career—and where he was made to realize that his contribution to

Afro-American literature was not unimportant, he was received with great warmth. From Nashville he went to Memphis to see Beale Street and to relax. Beale Street disappointed him, and it was not until several years later, when he visited it with W. C. Handy, whose "Beale Street Blues" made it famous, that he got over his disappointment. A great flooding of the Mississippi River forced the cancellation of his trip to Texas and delayed his progress to New Orleans. By way of Vicksburg he went to Baton Rouge, where he talked to refugees from the flood, and was angered by the distinction the American Red Cross made between black and white. The treatment accorded blacks, he said later, was "a classic example of Dixie" prejudice. The incident was perhaps the beginning of an enduring animosity Hughes held toward the American Red Cross. In later years he refused to contribute to the organization because of its one-time policy of separating the blood of black and white donors.[65]

He reached New Orleans at the end of the third week in June and stayed until mid-July, living in the old French Quarter, which, he wrote Arthur Spingarn, he found "so lovely I'd almost like to stay here all the time."[66]

But Cuba beckoned, and he signed on a freighter, the S.S. Nardo, as a mess boy to Havana and back, just, it seems, for the fun of it. A postcard from Havana informed the Spingarns, "I've a job with the most mixed-up crew imaginable—Spaniards, Chinese, German, on a trip to Cuba for sugar— am having a great time."[67]

Back in New Orleans, he met Zora Hurston, just as their mutual patron had arranged for them to do. Writing of this episode in The Big Sea, Hughes honored his pledge to protect Mrs. Mason's anonymity, and he made meeting Miss Hurston seem an accident of fate. He "ran into Zora Hurston," he wrote, who was "on a collector's trip for one of the folklore societies"; in fact, she was there through the financing of Mrs. Mason—and so was Hughes.[68] But unknown to Godmother, Zora was also being financed at the time by the Association for the Study of Negro Life and History to collect research materials for Columbia University anthropologist Franz Boas. To support her field trip through the South, the association's director (and Hughes's former employer), Dr. Carter G. Woodson, granted her a six-month fellowship of $1400. Neither Boas, Woodson, nor Hughes knew at the time that Zora had spent a few days of her Florida expedition on a honeymoon, after eloping secretly in May with her fiancé of six years.[69]

Zora would, in fact, soon have a written contract with Mrs. Mason, as a result of the 1927 trip through the South. That contract, which would also affect Hughes indirectly, was but one example of the control Mrs. Mason exerted over Zora, who willingly accepted the arrangement, spelled out in the following text:

This agreement made and entered into this 1st day of December, 1927, by and between Charlotte L. Mason, of New York City, first party, and Zora Hurston, of the same place, second party;

WITNESSETH:

Whereas said first party, Charlotte L. Mason is desirous of obtaining and compiling certain data relating to the music, folk-lore, poetry, voodoo, conjure, manifestations of art, and kindred matters existing among American Negroes but is unable because of the pressure of other matters to undertake the collecting of this information in person and,

Whereas, said second party, Zora Hurston, has represented to said first party that she is capable of performing said work of collection and compilation, and is ready and willing to do so. . . .

In consideration of said services, the first party hereby agrees to pay the second party the sum of *Two Thousand Four Hundred* dollars ($2,400.00), payable in equal monthly installments of Two Hundred ($200.00) on or about the first day of each month during the continuance of this agreement, and further to furnish second party with one moving picture camera and one Ford automobile for the personal use of said second party in this connection. . . .

This agreement shall continue for a period of one year from the date hereof.[70]

A year older than Hughes,[71] Zora Hurston had studied at Howard University and Barnard College, and was interested in anthropology and black folklore (later becoming one of Franz Boas's graduate students). She had grown up in Florida and knew the South well, and she spent the rest of the summer of 1927 (sans husband) introducing Hughes to towns and plantations in Alabama and Georgia as they made their way to New York. "Blind guitar players, conjur men, and former slaves were her quarry, small town jooks and plantation churches, her haunts," Hughes wrote later.[72] Besides, he thought her a great wit, "a perfect book of entertainment in herself," and except that he was perhaps a bit embarrassed because he could not help with the driving (he never learned to drive), the motor trip was a great success.

The journey was very much on his mind when he returned to Lincoln, but he wrote no poems about it or about the South immediately. This might have been because his spontaneity was thwarted by Charlotte Mason. His concern was with the living realities of the unromanticized and unfabled South, while Mrs. Mason thought his themes should be its mythic black folklore and its "exotic," "primitive" music. He wrote Locke, "I loved the South,—but I'm afraid I loved it for all the wrong things, instead of the right ones. It seemed rather shameless to be colored and poor and happy down there at the same time. But most of the Negroes seemed to be having a grand time and one couldn't help but like them. I'm sick of being unhappy anyway."[73]

The ambivalence of the tragicomic theme suggested in this statement had already found expression time after time in such poems as "The Jester," "Minstrel Man," and "Laughers," and would repeat itself in such poems as "Black Dancers" and "Black Clown." It is no accident that one of his favorite symbols was the clown, the "Pierrot," and the titles of some of his most representative works of fiction, *Not Without Laughter* and *Laughing to Keep from Crying*, are not just happenstance symbolic. Yet there was an emotional and intellectual problem that he never resolved or altogether accommodated himself to—that joy was truly a virtue, a saving grace for his people derived from a folk wisdom which the white world ridiculed and misunderstood. Alluding to this in "Laughers," Langston referred to his people as "Loud-mouthed laughers in the hands of Fate." It expressed a sense he would voice again, most notably in *Not Without Laughter*, where the protagonist, Sandy, ponders the question of Negro poverty. Were Negroes "poor, because they were dancers, jazzers, clowns?...The other way round would be better: dancers because of their poverty; singers because they suffered; laughing all the time because they must forget."

Hughes was not prepared to write about the South after his first trip: it was only during and after his second trip several years later that he was ready. Though he was very much a poet of spontaneity, quite often some of the experiences and impressions he turned into poetry required time to crystallize in his mind before he put them on paper. For example, the poems he published that fall of 1927, "Montmartre Beggar Woman" and "I Thought It Was Tangiers I Wanted," reflected experiences he had had abroad, and the short story "The Little Virgin" was creatively related to his trip to Africa. And it was perhaps only as a result of impressions gained from experiences in Africa and Europe, as well as America, that he could write the poem that appeared that October:

Being Old

It's because you are so young—
You do not understand.
But we are old
As the jungle trees
That bloomed forever,

Old as the forgotten rivers
That flowed into earth.
Surely we know what you do not know:
Joy of living,
Uselessness of things.
You are too young to understand yet.
Build another skyscraper
Touching the stars.
We sit with our backs against a tree
And watch skyscrapers tumble
And stars forget.
Solomon built a temple
And it must have fallen down.
It isn't here now.
We know some things, being old,
You do not understand.[74]

All in all, he wrote very little during his junior year in college, and he curtailed his poetry-reading appearances. And if he studied hard instead, he also spent more weekends in New York, where he passed as much of his time on Park Avenue as in Harlem. Mrs. Mason, who fancied herself as his Godmother-guardian, was quite demanding, and her generous subsidies put him under an obligation. Only very slowly did Hughes begin to realize that some of her requests, such as writing letters to her almost daily (unmentioned in his autobiography), were in the nature of demands. She chose the books he read, the music he listened to, and the plays he saw. Though he later declared that all he needed to do was say "when and where I wished to go and my patron's secretary would have tickets for me," the truth is that he went where Mrs. Mason chose, and she frequently went with him. There was no dearth of places and programs that, she felt, fostered the "inner direction" she intended he follow. He saw the Heywards' dramatic adaptation of *Porgy*[75] and *Simba*, a motion picture depicting life in the African bush. He read *Congaree Sketches* and *African Saga*. How a gift of Sandburg's *Lincoln*, which Mrs. Mason gave Hughes for his twenty-sixth birthday, fitted into her scheme for her protégé's literary and cultural development is impossible to say. She knew he was an ardent admirer of Sandburg. One may speculate that the gift was meant to create a restorative psychological diversion and to weaken the impression that she really intended to make him into the person she wanted to make him into; yet secretly she wished to make him responsive only to what she thought black people should be responsive to: Bessie Smith rather than Eleonora Duse; blues, jazz, and spirituals rather than the German lieder of Roland Hayes or the symphony concerts of the New York Philharmonic Society.[76] And Hughes was responsive to the subtle manner she had of directing him. "She has her victrola now," he wrote Locke early in the academic year, "and a great collection of records, all of Paul Robeson, I believe, and almost all the best blues. She loves the 'Soft Pedal' and even the 'Yellow Dog.' And they sound marvellous on her machine."[77]

Hughes did not know then that Paul Robeson, an older and more self-assured artist, had refused Mrs. Mason's patronage and guidance. The young poet had accepted her as a surrogate mother, whose interest in him was entirely unselfish and altogether motivated by maternal love. "No one else," he wrote later, "had ever been so thoughtful of me or so interested in the things I wanted to do, or so kind and generous toward me."[78] She relieved him of all financial worries. Moreover, employing her usual shrewdness and the façade of anonymity, she agreed to send Hughes's foster brother, Gwyn, to school in Springfield, Massachusetts, where he would board with a black family. The arrangements were made through Alain Locke, to whom Langston, at the direction of Mrs. Mason, sent the following:

> Godmother wishes you to have a memorandum of the facts about Gwyn. Here goes:
> 13 years old
> Sixth grade
> Tendency to colds
> Needs good food
> Family where there are other children desirable
> Also New England preferred because of schools
> Change him if possible around end of Jan when the school term ends.
> In no case mention her or myself. Bills to be paid through you.
> Write Godmother as soon as you have a place. . . .[79]

Hughes responded to his patron like a doting son, though he "felt bad sometimes because I couldn't share my new-found comfort as fully as I might have wished with my mother, who was working as a cook in a rest home in Atlantic City."[80]

Meanwhile, Hughes was seeing very little of Locke, who was a visiting lecturer at Fisk University in the second semester of that academic year, 1927-28. They kept up a regular and lengthy correspondence, but the tone of Hughes's letters had changed. The tone was now simply dutifully grateful. Referring to Locke's role in geting Gwyn satisfactorily placed in Springfield, Hughes wrote, "I'm very glad about it and deeply appreciative for what you've done."[81] But his gratitude was not so deep as to earn mention in *The Big Sea* of Locke's role in this and certain other personal matters on his behalf, including the introduction to Charlotte Mason. Only time would tell all the reasons why.

With no financial worries, Hughes was content during those months. But happy-go-lucky, even when he was not always happy, was the impression he gave even to those who knew him best. In keeping with the pattern of not writing when he did not feel blue, he wrote little and in general slighted the literary life. It was ultimately to lead to a weakening of his relationship with his patron. That semester he published only three poems and a book review and gave two poetry readings.[82] As the guest of Anne Spencer, a noted black poet, he gave a public reading in Lynchburg, Virginia;[83] and a month later, at the behest of the Lincoln University Glee Club, he read at Princeton University. But the highlight of his spring was the April 9 wedding of Countee Cullen and Yolande Du Bois, whose father, after more than a quarter of a century, was still the most distinguished Afro-American leader and spokesman. Hughes was a member of the wedding party, as were other young and talented friends of the couple. In both the social and the artistic sense, the occasion came at the height of the Harlem Renaissance (which would soon decline precipitously). The wedding was a pageant performed before three thousand witnesses in Harlem's Salem Methodist Episcopal Church, pastored by Cullen's adoptive father. In rented attire (though Mrs. Mason would undoubtedly have bought him the formal outfit), Hughes escorted the bride's mother down the aisle. He was embarrassed to accompany Mrs. Du Bois in a hired suit that was fading, but he made a joke of it. All this was more easily forgotten than another aspect of the wedding. There were disturbing rumors that his fellow poet Cullen was more deeply in love with his handsome best man, Harold Jackman, than with the bride. The marriage lasted less than two years, and during that time husband and wife were longer apart than together.[84] "Countee should never have married," Hughes told a close friend, "for some of the same reasons I should never marry." And so far as Hughes was concerned, that was that.

The wedding and the events surrounding it—Cullen and Jackman's sailing off to France together in June, without Yolande—were talked about for months, but the new novels by black authors aroused almost as much talk in Harlem literary-social circles. *Quicksand* by Nella Larsen, *Plum Bun* by Jessie Fauset, *Walls of Jericho* by Rudolph Fisher, and *Home to Harlem* by Claude McKay were all published in 1928. The first two were highly praised by older black critics, and *Walls of Jericho* only a little less so. But for Hughes and a few other younger critics, *Home to Harlem* was the novel of the season. Hughes praised it publicly and privately. "Just finished Claude's *Home to Harlem* and am wild about it," he wrote Locke. "It ought to be named *Nigger Hell*, but I guess the colored papers will have even greater spasms than before anyhow. It is the best low-life novel I've ever read. Puts Francis Carco and Pio Baroja—even Gorki in the shade—for that kind of thing.[85] Up till now, it strikes me that *Home to Harlem* must be the flower of the Negro Renaissance—even if it is no lovely lilly."[86]

Hughes's own novel, *Not Without Laughter*, was to be quite different from this, or any other that he had read, and he settled down to work on it seriously in June in the Lincoln dormitory, where he remained most of that summer. Fortunately for him, Mrs. Mason was spending the summer in Europe, and there were no interruptions from that source. But the writing was not easy. He wanted it to be autobiographical, to reconstruct his own boyhood through the character of "Sandy" growing up in a "typical Negro family" in a small town in Kansas. But Hughes's own family was far from typical; the members of it led atypical lives. So did his beloved Uncle and Auntie Reed, with whom he had lived for a time (and who in no way resemble the aunt and uncle whom Sandy briefly lives with after the death of his grandmother). Hughes could draw upon the memory of his stepfather, "who was a wanderer," in creating the character Jimboy, Sandy's father, and he could draw a few parallels between Anjee, Sandy's mother, and his own mother; he could also make fictional use of the cyclone that had blown his grandmother's front porch away. But he could not, as he intended, use his own grandmother, Mary Langston, as a model for Sandy's Aunt Hager, whom he conceived of as "typically" making her living as a laundress, speaking in dialect, and spending Sundays "wasshippin' de Lawd" in a fundamentalist Baptist church. In short, as he brought the story to life, his "autobiographical" novel was turning out to be almost entirely a work of his creative imagination. Even Sandy, who was supposed to be the protagonist at the very center of the action, growing up from age nine to sixteen, was poorly focused. Sandy at home, at school, at his job after school, did little to advance the plot, but functioned as a kind of chorus commenting on the doings of Aunt Hager and her three daughters—Tempy, who marries a postal clerk, rises above her class, and rejects everything "niggerish"; Anjee, a domestic, married to Sandy's footloose and wastrel father; and Harriett, the youngest, who becomes a showgirl and prostitute. Only toward the end do Sandy's experiences (and his character) begin to relate to those of his creator, when his mother tries to persuade him to abandon his education and go to work to help support her. (When published in 1930, *Not Without Laughter* would be criticized as structurally defective and inadequately developed.)

In mid-August, Hughes put the draft of his novel aside and went to Cape Cod for a brief vacation.

WHEN he returned to Lincoln that fall, Hughes was determined that his senior year would be his best year academically. This had nothing to do with the fact that greater restrictions on class cuts had been laid down, or that he had been known as a frequent "cutter." His reputation, not to speak of his importance to the prestige of the university, would have exempted him from classes when he found it necessary. But that year he wanted to make the most of all Lincoln had to offer; to prepare himself, as he indicated when he applied, to be a good teacher, and "to be of more use to my race and America." He had since had second thoughts about a professional teaching career, after Joel Spingarn advised him not to become an academician if he wanted to be a poet-writer. Nevertheless, Hughes wanted all that his professors (most of whom were Princeton-trained) could offer him in the liberal arts program, and to maintain the over-all B average he had accumulated in literature, history, philosophy, languages, and the sciences. He even scheduled Saturday classes, thus giving up his weekends. To fulfill the requirements of a course in education, he practiced teaching in a public school near the campus. What little time he spared himself, he worked on his novel and wrote a few poems,[87] and having discovered poetic talent in some of his fellow students, he projected the idea of editing a volume of verses by Lincoln University poets.[88] He felt stimulated, challenged.

Yet something that he had overlooked before began to bother him, vex him. At a university with an all-black student body there were no courses supportive of black racial pride; no course offerings of the contributions of black people to literature or history or to American, African, or Caribbean civilizations; no black professors. Hughes was convinced that this was a glaring, intolerable deficiency, and the attitude of the majority of students toward it compounded his distress. Moreover, he was dismayed by the students' attitude toward having an all-white faculty. "Over and over," he wrote, "I heard many students agree that it was better so, that there was something inherently superior in white teachers that Negro teachers did not have. I wanted to prove that the students believing this were wrong, and that Lincoln was fostering—unwittingly, perhaps—an inferiority complex in the very men it wished to train as leaders of the Negro race. I wanted to show that the color line is not good on campus or off."[89]

For his senior project in sociology, Hughes decided to study the Lincoln campus—its academic goals and standards, its social atmosphere, and its student-faculty relations. Though he enlisted the help of two other students to make a needed survey among 129 upper-classmen, the resulting twenty-six-page paper was Hughes's own. It was forthright. Given the times, it was bold. Hughes passionately deplored the finding that 63 percent of the Lincoln juniors and seniors preferred an all-white faculty. He attacked the (unstated) policy that opposed employing even such outstanding black scholar-professors as Charles S. Johnson, Charles H. Wesley, and Alain Locke. He lashed out at a faculty-student relationship that was confined to classroom contact. The results of the survey created a furor at Lincoln—and elsewhere. The *Afro-American* newspaper carried a banner headline on April 27, 1929: "Lincoln's Sensational Survey Made Public." Several black institutions wrote the University that they would not employ Lincoln graduates on their faculties, since Lincoln students had so little pride that they did not deem blacks capable of teaching blacks. These and kindred matters were still on Hughes's mind some years later, when he again criticized the social attitudes that prevailed at Lincoln in his student days.

> Why did a large number of the students at my own Lincoln University, when I made a survey there in 1929, declare that they were opposed to having teachers of their own race on the faculty? And why did they then (and probably still do) allow themselves to be segregated in the little moving picture theatre in the nearby village of Oxford, when there is no Jim-Crow law in Pennsylvania—and they are some four hundred strong? And why did a basketball team and their coach walk docilely out of a cafe in Philadelphia that refused to serve them because of color? One of the players explained later, "The coach didn't want to make a fuss."
>
> Yet Lincoln's motto is to turn out leaders! But can there be leaders who don't want to make a fuss?[90]

Yet there was one strange, incongruous note to Hughes's Lincoln survey paper. It appeared in the foreword, and it is not farfetched to surmise that it was added at the insistence of Mrs. Charlotte Mason, who demanded to see *everything* Hughes wrote. The foreword is strikingly similar to the introduction and to certain passages of *The Indians' Book*, which Mrs. Mason influenced Natalie Curtis to write.[91] Moreover, Hughes himself hints that his patron influenced the writing of the foreword: "After I had finished my survey, I added a kind of poetic foreword. . . . A poetic foreword has no place in a sociological survey, but, nevertheless, I put it there as a kind of extra flourish." The apologetic tone is revealing. The foreword reads:

> In the primitive world, where people live closer to the earth and much nearer to the stars, every inner and outer act combines to form the single harmony, life. Not just the tribal lore then, but every movement of life becomes a part of their education. They do not, as many civilized people do, neglect the truth of the physical for the sake of the mind. Nor do they teach with speech alone, but rather with all the acts of life. There are no books, so the barrier between words and reality is not so great as with us. The earth is right under their feet. The stars are never far away.

The strength of the surest dream is the strength of the primitive
world.[92]

In the context of the study-survey itself, the foreword is preposterous. But
not until much later did he fully perceive that this was a subtle instance in
which his patron manipulated him. But even then his perceptivity was
developing—and not only in regard to Mrs. Mason. Indeed, on his Commencement Day, June 4, 1929, he gained some insight—and in a certain
sense lost some of his compassion—when one of the university's most
prominent alumni, reprimanding him for his sociological study, remarked,
"Suppose I told the truth to white folks. I never could have built the great
institution I've built for my race." Although Hughes tried to see the best in
everybody, this comment marked him indelibly. This influential black
educator was probably the model for a character in a satirical short story,
"Dr. Brown's Decision," published some six years later.[93] Hughes's portrait
of T. Walton Brown (a character whose initials are anagrammatic for
Booker T. Washington[94]—about whom Hughes was distressed and ambivalent all his life) was trenchant. Referring to the Commencement Day encounter a decade later, he wrote, "I had never thought much before about
the nature of compromise. For bread how much of the spirit must one give
away?"

MEANTIME, following commencement, he continued to accept a generous,
regular allowance from his patron. There were surely days when he wished
he hadn't. Mrs. Mason's demand that he send her progress reports on his
novel had an effect on his nerves. It was probably one reason why, that
summer, he began taking neurophosphates. Furthermore, he began to realize that her suggestion he cease answering any letters except hers was another subtle way of controlling him. In July she wrote:

> DEAR LANGSTON:
> ...First, that you have closed the door to an intrusion on your
> spirit by not answering letters is a comfort to me because it
> leaves your living untouched except by Sandy and the people of
> your novel.
> About your taking neurophosphates now: Don't misunder-
> stand me, Langston, but you are still young enough to use the
> truth of your creative instinct to keep your nervous system quiet
> and steady, as you have nailed down a regular physical life for
> each day. Dear Heart, the strain of your nerves comes from the
> urge that burns and flames in you to push the novel through as
> fast as you can. ... Think of the nervous condition as stored
> energy. With that take deep breathing, take deep breaths, will-

ing yourself mentally to keep the spiritual urge throbbing and complete relaxation of the nervous system at the same time. My child, this is the only way that Godmother still walks on this planet. . . . [95]

He did not then know that Mrs. Mason had been seriously ill that spring and had kept the news from him, as she had from Zora, to whom she confessed in August, "In May, Zora, I was very ill, and we didn't know whether I would pull through or not, but I have made it a rule when children are at a distance not to have them alarmed."[96] A strange, debilitating illness had begun to show itself, and only her iron will controlled it. Unable to write legibly, she dictated all her correspondence through a close family friend—a young sculptress, Cornelia Chapin, and her older sister, Katherine Garrison Chapin Biddle. Thanks to them, she kept in close touch with her "godchildren."

That summer, whenever Hughes sent her manuscript pages of his novel, she responded—often at considerable length—with critical suggestions and advice. "I think your rearrangement of the chapters is very good," she declared in one letter. "But about the title. . . *So Moves This Swift World* is not characteristic enough of you and your writing, which is always original and arresting."[97] Needless to say, no more was heard of *So Moves This Swift World*. Hughes changed the title to *Not Without Laughter*.

He spent most of the summer at Lincoln working on his novel, and the rest of it as the only black passenger on a vacation journey up the Saguenay River in Canada. Midway there he left the boat in protest against its segregated dining room, and finished the Canadian trip by train. He was well supplied with money. Nothing in his personal world then foreshadowed the stockmarket crash soon to come in October. Returning to Pennsylvania in the early fall, he spent several weeks in Moylan Rose Valley, at the Hedgerow Theatre, working on a play he had been considering. As several of his poems attest, the theme of the tragic mulatto had been on his mind for a long time. Now he intended a deeper exploration of it through the medium of the drama, which, second only to poetry, was his favorite genre. As early as 1926 he had declared, "We have an honest American Negro literature already with us. Now I wait the rise of the Negro theater."[98] He meant to contribute to that rise. Of the dozen or so plays with Afro-American themes that appeared on Broadway during the Harlem Renaissance, only three were written by black authors.[99] Those written by whites were stereotypical. Hughes, believing the black playwright had not been given his due on the Broadway stage, and that variations on the tragic mulatto theme, such as Ridgely Torrence's *Granny Maumee* and DuBose Heyward's *Mamba's Daughters*, told only part of the story, decided to undertake the writing of a contemporary tragedy in two acts, titled *Mulatto*, about miscegenation in the Deep South.

Later that autumn, however, he shelved the play temporarily to resume work on *Not Without Laughter*. By this time he had settled in Westfield, New Jersey, some thirty miles from Manhattan, where Zora Neale Hurston was also living in the same boarding house. Their mutual patron had insisted on this move from New York to Westfield. She contended that the social life of Harlem would be a distraction from writing, especially for Hughes, who insisted—over Mrs. Mason's objection—that his novel needed extensive revisions. "It seemed so bad"—he wrote later—"it made me sick. . . . I couldn't bear to have the people I had grown to love locked up in long pages of uncomfortable words, awkward sentences and drawn-out passages. I began to cut and rewrite, page after page."[100] Mrs. Mason, pressing Hughes to complete the novel, hired a stenographer for him. Louise Thompson—a young woman recommended by Alain Locke—commuted between New York City and Westfield.

Having Louise as a stenographer turned out to be a blessing for Hughes—in more ways than one. He had already met her in Harlem, but beginning that autumn of 1929 they developed a strong friendship that would grow even stronger later. Kindred spirits they were, and in their backgrounds there were certain parallels. Six months his senior, Louise had been born in Chicago and reared in the West, and had spent her early youth in as many different cities as he. She, too, had a stepfather, a chef cook who had traveled about from place to place, always thinking the grass was greener elsewhere. Her mother, like Hughes's own, by force of circumstance had also worked as a domestic. Louise had graduated from the University of California at Berkeley in 1923, with a major in economics and business administration and a minor in Spanish. Fair enough to pass for white, she had briefly passed as a Mexican to work as a Girl Friday in a San Francisco office, after finding all such employment opportunities closed to "colored" applicants.

Too proud of her race not to be a part of it, Louise Thompson had come to Harlem in 1928, by way of graduate school in Chicago and a teaching position at a black college in Pine Bluff, Arkansas, and at Hampton Institute in Virginia, where she had supported a student strike against the school's paternalistic policies. Like Hughes, she had a great admiration for W. E. B. Du Bois, whom she had heard speak at Berkeley, and she had gravitated toward the "Harlem Renaissance" that he had helped to launch. Beautiful and brilliant, she had quickly become a popular figure on the Harlem social scene. Wallace Thurman, the leading bohemian intellectual, proposed to her almost as soon as they met. They were married in August 1928—and separated within six months. By the time Charlotte Mason hired her as a stenographer for Hughes, Louise had recently completed study at the New York School of Social Work on an Urban League fellowship. She was looking for a more permanent job, but she willingly accepted the assignment to help Langston. And he was glad she did. He finished the revisions on *Not Without Laughter* early in the winter, and Knopf accepted the novel for publication. With a long and worrisome job of creation behind him, he was relieved. But not for long.

In February 1930, at a dinner party given by Taylor Gordon in New York City, he met Theresa Helburn, one of the founders of the Theatre Guild.[101] He mentioned his play, *Mulatto*, to Miss Helburn, but she was not interested. All the plays by or about Negroes offered to the Guild were serious problem dramas, she complained. She suggested he write a comedy.[102] Though Hughes was far from enthusiastic at first, he took the suggestion to Zora Hurston and proposed that they collaborate.

Miss Hurston jumped at the idea. She suggested they could use one of her folk tales about a Negro striking another over the head with a mule bone in a quarrel over a turkey. According to the tale, the aggressor is brought to trial before the congregation of the church and found guilty by the preacher-judge, who holds that a mule bone is a more dangerous weapon than the jawbone of an ass, with which the Biblical Samson had slain ten thousand Philistines. The culprit, the preacher decides, should be run out of town.

Hughes suggested modifications. The quarrel between the men—long-time friends—would take place in front of the village store over a girl who had just come to town. The arrest would split the black community along denominational lines, Baptist and Methodist. The church trial would be an absolutely hilarious climax involving Baptists on one side and Methodists on the other, but resulting in the decision the preacher-judge rendered in Miss Hurston's version. The dramatic resolution would come in a scene in which the exiled man is approached by his former buddy, who wants to forgive and forget. The girl reappears, and the two men, reconciled only moments before, try to outdo each other in a proposing contest (Miss Hurston's suggestion). She accepts one of the suitors, and promises to get him a steady job with the white folks for whom she works. Work! This is far from what the men think married life is all about, and they leave the girl behind as they shuffle off, singing and dancing, down the road.

Miss Hurston thought Hughes's modifications and his idea that the play should be developed in three acts fine. It was agreed that Hughes would construct the plot and develop the characters, while she would work on the dialogue, giving it its authentic Southern tone and nuance.

Employing the stenographic assistance of Louise Thompson, the collaborators got started in late March and within a month had completed drafts of the first and third acts and a partial draft of a part of the second. In May,

Miss Hurston went South, taking with her copies of the work they had done and the notes, including the outline for the second act, which she pledged to finish during her absence.

Hughes, meantime, decided to work on *Mulatto*, at the Hedgerow again for a few weeks that summer, and since *Mule Bone*—the title they had decided on—was a first venture at commercial theatre for him and Miss Hurston, they agreed it might be a good idea to let Jasper Deeter, the director of the Hedgerow Theatre, have a look at it and give advice. Deeter was one of the few people privy to the exact nature of their collaboration (except Miss Thompson and Mrs. Mason). Both Hughes and Zora had decided that since the play was to be the first black folk comedy written by blacks, they would say as little publicly about it as possible until it was completed. Even their mutual friend Carl Van Vechten, whom they bade bon voyage when he sailed for a brief trip to Europe that spring, was told only that they were working on something: they would, they said, surprise him with it when he returned.

Toward the end of the summer, Miss Hurston wrote to Hughes that she would stay South until November, and he put all thought of *Mule Bone* aside. Even work on *Mulatto* was suspended. Other concerns occupied him. *Not Without Laughter* was published in July 1930, and its critical reception was mixed, to say the least. The *New York Times* and the *New York Herald Tribune*, pointing to the novel's defects, reviewed it with faint praise; and so did *The Nation* and *Saturday Review*.[103] By fall, Sterling Brown in *Opportunity*, Walt Carmon in *New Masses*, and the reviewer in the London *Times* all had written laudatory reviews,[104] but these did not assuage the disappointment Hughes felt when he "went to Far Rockaway that summer, and felt bad" that the novel was not all he had hoped it would be. The judgment that the novel was incompletely realized does not seem unfair in view of the finished product. Still, *Not Without Laughter* eventually became his most widely translated work. There was no indication of that then, except perhaps in the sales, for despite the increasing severity of the economic depression and the waning of the Harlem Renaissance, sales of the novel soon outstripped the combined sales of his two volumes of poetry.

The effects of the depression were seen everywhere. Eviction notices were almost as common as work-wanted ads. Hundreds of the homeless slept in doorways and subway stations. Breadlines formed before dawn and stretched for blocks. Hughes "got so [he] didn't like to go to dinner on luxurious Park Avenue—and come out and see people hungry on the streets.... I knew I could very easily and quickly be there, too," he wrote, "hungry and homeless on a cold floor, anytime Park Avenue got tired of supporting me."[105] Partly to escape these dismal scenes and partly to satisfy the enduring whim of his patron to find a black Cuban to write the music for a black opera libretto she wanted Hughes to write, he had gone to Cuba again in early March 1930 for a few weeks.[106] He had not found a composer. Mrs. Mason was exasperated. She expected her protégés to do what she demanded of them and to be what she wanted them to be. Miguel Covarrubias, the Mexican painter, whom she had sent to Bali, had returned without accomplishing the mission she had sent him on. Now Hughes. But he was beginning to resent the fact that "she possessed the power to control people's lives—pick them up and put them down when and where she wished."[107] He was increasingly aware of the hazard to his personal and artistic integrity in accepting her patronage.

In addition, he was something more than miffed with Zora Hurston when she returned to New York in November. So far as he could tell, she had not done the promised work on *Mule Bone*, and seemed reluctant even to discuss it. Every time they were supposed to get together to resume work on the play, Miss Hurston found some excuse. Obviously, too, he noticed Mrs. Mason favored her "Goddaughter." She set her up in an apartment on West 66th Street. Zora played up to her in ways Langston could not bring himself to do. She amused and flattered Mrs. Mason by calling herself "Godmother's primitive child" and "dumb darky." But Zora was anything but dumb. She had mastered the dumb darky role a long time ago. By playing it for white people, she had managed to work her way out of a background of familial and economic insecurity. She entertained her patron. She led her to believe that she, too, had an interest in psychic phenomena. If Mrs. Mason believed—as she claimed she did—that she could "read" some of her young protégés' minds, Zora would not disillusion her: sometimes Zora seemed to believe it herself. For instance, she wrote, "My relations with Godmother were curious...there was and is a psychic bond between us. She could read my mind, not only when I was in her presence, but thousands of miles away."[108]

Though they lived only blocks apart, she frequently wrote to Godmother in this vein.

> I know that you will know that I felt your radiating spiritual self, before this letter arrives. I am writing it as a confirmation. I am here, Godmother, receiving from you and sending to you.
>
> With that peculiar understanding of me that you have, I know that you understand this letter in a way that no one else can. It is a message that only Zora could send to Godmother alone of all the millions upon this earth and be understood. I am meeting you at the altar places and I am acquiescent. Yes, Godmother, I don't get all the words that you are stretching out to me, and if I

have not been strong enough to send my answer through the
ether, this stumbling letter will have to do until I can gain more
strength....[109]

Zora was a faker and a performer par excellence. (Wallace Thurman exposed these attributes of hers in the character of Sweetie May Carr in
Infants of the Spring.) Hughes was incapable of such sycophancy and deception. He had to be himself, whether or not he pleased his patron. He had to
write out of himself and not out of the character Mrs. Mason tried to
impose upon him. "She wanted me to be primitive and know and feel the
intuitions of the primitive," he later wrote. "But, unfortunately, I did not
feel the rhythms of the primitive surging through me, and so I could not live
and write as though I did. I was only an American Negro—who had loved
the surface of Africa and the rhythms of Africa—but I was not Africa."[110]
The one poem he published about Africa in 1930 obliquely expressed this
sentiment.

Afro-American Fragment

So long,
So far away
Is Africa.
Not even memories alive
Save those that history books create,
Save those that songs
Beat back into the blood—
Beat out of blood with words sad-sung
In strange un-Negro tongue—
So long,
So far away
Is Africa.

Subdued and time-lost
Are the drums—and yet
Through some vast mist of race
There comes this song
I do not understand,
This song of atavistic land,
Of bitter yearnings lost
Without a place—
So long,
So far away
Is Africa's
Dark face.[111]

Although he remarked later that when his novel went to press, he "didn't feel like writing anything else then, so I didn't," and that this contributed to dissension with his patron, he actually wrote several poems. Five appeared that summer in *The Crisis*, two others in *Opportunity*, and one on the cover of the *Tuskeegee Messenger*.[112] They were the first new poems he had published since 1929, when "Silhouette," a poem about lynching, was printed in the *Anthology of Revolutionary Poetry*. The new poems had nothing to do with primitivism. As a whole, they were about love and death and spiritual awakening, and the longest, "Advertisement for the Waldorf-Astoria," was political.

> In the midst of that depression, the Waldorf-Astoria opened. On the way to my friend's home on Park Avenue I frequently passed it, a mighty towering structure looming proud above the street, in a city where thousands were poor and unemployed. So I wrote a poem about it called "Advertisement for the Waldorf-Astoria," modeled after an ad in *Vanity Fair* announcing the opening of New York's greatest hotel. (Where no Negroes worked and none were admitted as guests.)[113]

He showed parts of the poem to his patron, who had no difficulty restraining her enthusiasm then—or later, presuming she ever read *New Masses*, where the complete poem was published one year later. "It's a powerful poem!" she told him. "But it's not you." It is doubtful whether Hughes actually showed her the poem's last lines (which he later omitted from *The Big Sea*):

> Listen Mary, Mother of God, wrap your new born babe in
> the red flag of Revolution: the Waldorf-Astoria's
> the best manger we've got. For reservations: Telephone EL. 5-3000.[114]

Although he hinted that the poem contributed to the discord with his patron, the account may have been a smokescreen on his part. The break between them took place in late 1930; the Waldorf-Astoria opened its doors in October 1931; the poem was published in December 1931. Not everything adds up exactly as he presented it.

Nevertheless, it was Charlotte Mason's view that the expression of political opinions should be left to white people, like herself. Her own political opinions, however, never extended much beyond holding forth during drawing-room conversation. She "had been devoted in a mild way to the advancement of the Negro," but she never joined the NAACP. She did not even hire black servants. The "advancement" she was most interested in for Afro-Americans was limited to her belief in an image of cultural exoticism and in supporting black artists whom she thought would foster it, not in encouraging their political consciousness. Hughes's poems, by that autumn, were increasingly political. "Negro Servant," "Black Seed," "Merry Christmas," and "Pride"—all of them social protest verses published by December—must have hit her where it hurt. Especially "Pride":

Pride

Let all who will
Eat quietly the bread of shame.
I cannot,
Without complaining loud and long,
Tasting its bitterness in my throat,
And feeling to my very soul
Its wrong.
For honest work
You proffer me poor pay.
For honest dreams
Your spit is in my face,
And so my fist is clenched
Today—
To strike your face.[115]

Hughes does not mention his political poems in *The Big Sea*, except "Advertisement for the Waldorf-Astoria," or say that they were a contributing factor in the rupture with his patron. Her objection, he claimed, was that he was not writing enough. The facts, however, reveal that it was not what he *did not* write that displeased her, but what he *did* write. And her insistence that she see everything he wrote did not help matters on either side. Hughes's displeasure with this demand resulted in the writing of one poem which he never showed her and did not publish until nine years later:

Poet to Patron

What right has anyone to say
That I
Must throw out pieces of my heart
For pay?

For bread that helps to make
My heart beat true,
I must sell myself
To you?

A factory shift's better,
A week's meagre pay,
Than a perfumed note asking
What poems today?[116]

Hughes's pride and his developing social consciousness brought about the final break with his patron, which came on a wintry day in December 1930. His autobiographical account of the end of their relationship is more anguished than angry. "I asked kindly to be released from any further obligations to her, and that she give me no more money, but simply let me retain her friendship...." Somewhat naively, he had believed the latter entirely possible, never realizing that her interest did not extend to any relationship in which she could not exert control over him, "But there must have been only the one thread binding us together," he confessed later. "When that thread broke, it was the end." She lectured him on the limitations of his talent, reminded him of all the things she had done for him. But for her he would never have written his novel. But for her his foster brother would not have had the privilege of attending a New England school. She predicted that, lacking her support, Hughes would fail. "That beautiful room," he wrote years afterwards, "that had been so full of light and help...for me, suddenly became like a trap closing in, faster and faster, the room darker and darker, until the light went out with a sudden crash in the dark.... Physically, my stomach began to turn over and over—and then over again. I fought against bewilderment and anger, fought hard, and didn't say anything. I just sat there in the high Park Avenue drawing-room and didn't say anything. I sat there and listened to all she told me, closed my mouth hard and didn't say anything."[117]

The unpleasant goodbye was traumatic for Hughes and irrevocable for both concerned. Suppressing his anger toward his patron, he became violently ill, as he had eleven years earlier when he suddenly hated his father. For several days he visited one physician after another, seeking relief from severe abdominal pain. He was given laboratory tests; he was x-rayed. One physician diagnosed a tapeworm; another said he had none. "And, of course, all the while, I knew what was the matter," he admitted later, "but couldn't say it, for if I did, the world started to float away."[118] He was suffering a psychosomatic illness. But even after it had passed and his spirit quieted, he could not really come to grips with his painful experience, nor to a true comprehension of the character of Charlotte Mason. His subsequent account and summing up of the episode is a gloss. "I had loved very much that gentle woman who had been my patron and I wanted to understand what had happened to us that she had sent me away as she did...I thought she liked *me*.... But I guess she only liked my writing, and not even that any more."[119]

His spirits were abysmally low when he left New York to spend the Christmas holidays in Cleveland, where his mother and stepfather, again reconciled, were living.

BUT NOT ONLY was his relation to his patron and her financial support at an end. With the onslaught of the economic depression, the Harlem Renaissance was at an end, too. As Hughes wrote later, "Some Harlemites thought the millenium had come" with the onset of the Renaissance. "They thought the race problem had been solved through Art...I don't know what made any Negroes think that—except that they were mostly intellectuals doing the thinking. The ordinary Negroes hadn't heard of the Negro Renaissance." Hughes admitted, "I had a swell time while it lasted. But I thought it wouldn't last long....how could a large and enthusiastic number of people be crazy about Negroes forever?"[120]

The break with his patron, coinciding with the close of the Renaissance, was a blessing, although in terrifying guise. His early career was over; he could move in a significant new direction unencumbered by the past. The jazz and blues poems he had written—so appropriate to the Jazz Age—were no longer a literary concern. He had already made a new beginning and signalized it in the December *New Masses* with an open letter, "Greetings to Soviet Workers," and with a poem :

Merry Christmas

Merry Christmas, China,
From the gunboats in the river,
Ten-inch shells for Christmas gifts
And peace on earth forever.

Merry Christmas, India,
To Gandhi in his cell,
From righteous Christian England,
Ring out, bright Christmas bell!

Ring Merry Christmas, Africa,
From Cairo to the Cape!
Ring Hallelujah! Praise the Lord!
(For murder and for rape.)

Ring Merry Christmas, Haiti!
(And drown the voodoo drums—
We'll rob you to the Christmas hymns
Until the next Christ comes.)

Ring Merry Christmas, Cuba!
(While Yankee domination
Keeps a nice fat president
In a little half-starved nation.)

And to you down-and-outers,
("Due to economic laws")
Oh, eat, drink and be merry
With a bread-line Santa Claus—

While all the world hails Christmas
While all the church bells sway!
While, better still, the Christian guns
Proclaim this joyous day!

While Holy steel that makes us strong
Spits forth a mighty Yuletide song:
SHOOT Merry Christmas everywhere!
Let Merry Christmas GAS the air!

The political voice of Langston Hughes was beginning to speak loud and clear.

❧ 8 ❧

A Bone of Contention

ALTHOUGH HUGHES'S RETURN TO CLEVELAND separated him from his political contacts in New York, his affiliation with *New Masses* as a contributing editor kept him in touch with Michael Gold, the magazine's editor, and others in the literary world. *New Masses*, which had begun in May 1926 as a radical monthly on literature and politics, had advanced steadily leftward at almost the same time Hughes's own career was moving in that direction. His first publication in the magazine, in December 1926, had been five blues poems. They had appeared when the magazine's masthead still read like a Who's Who of Literary America, with such names as Sherwood Anderson, John Dos Passos, Eugene O'Neill, Carl Sandburg, Upton Sinclair, Louis Untermeyer, and Edmund Wilson, as well as Harlem Renaissance writers Claude McKay, Jean Toomer, Eric Waldron, and Walter White listed as contributing editors. Not until September 1930, when the magazine became a vanguard voice for revolutionary writers did Hughes's name go on the masthead.[1] Then and later he knew that *New Masses* was under the editorial control of Communist intellectuals such as Michael Gold, whom he respected as a poet, social critic, and champion of the working class. He also had agreed with Gold's 1926 *New Masses* essay declaring that "poetry must become dangerous again. Let's have poems thundering like 10-ton trucks and aeroplanes."[2] Hughes had "thundered" into 1931 with four new poems that he wrote soon after he arrived in Cleveland: "To Certain Negro Leaders," "Tired," "A Christian Country," and "Call to Creation," which he submitted for a February *New Masses* issue.

In Cleveland, unable to afford immediate surgery for the tonsillitis that kept him bedridden for most of the Christmas holidays, Hughes completed a translation of Gustavo Urrutia's article "Negro Tourists and Cuba" for a February issue of *The Crisis*. He was in financial straits. He was down to nearly the last penny he had received from his former patron, and he would get no more from that source. He could not count on much from book royalties; his contributing editorship carried no salary; and finding a wage-earning job was next to impossible. The economic depression was as severe in Cleveland as in the rest of the country. Hughes's foster brother, no longer in school in New England, moved in with relatives so that Langston could live with his mother and stepfather in their three basement rooms on Carnegie Avenue.

In early January Hughes received some news that, though hardly pleasant, made him glad he had come to Cleveland. Russell and Rowena Jelliffe, husband and wife co-directors of Karamu House, where Langston had been active as a high school student, informed him that their theatre group was about to obtain production rights to a Negro folk comedy which they hoped to stage in February. The play, one they had first learned of in mid-December from the Samuel French theatrical agency in New York, was *Mule Bone*; the author was Zora Neale Hurston. Hughes knew immediately that it had to be the play he and Zora, swearing each other to secrecy, had collaborated on some time back. Now she was claiming the play was hers alone.

Hughes was aghast, and so were the Jelliffes. Mrs. Jelliffe immediately got in touch with Barrett Clark, a representative of the Samuel French theatrical agency from whom she had obtained production rights; and Hughes, to protect his rights, sent for his own drafts of the script—which he had left in Westfield—and wrote Miss Hurston for an explanation. Meantime, though, the script had arrived from the agency, and it was easy to see why the New York Theatre Guild, to which it was first offered, had turned it down. Zora Hurston had made changes that weakened the dramatic structure of the first act; the second act, which she had written alone—though using the notes prepared by Hughes—simply proved that she was no playwright; and the third act was submitted in two versions: the original that she and Hughes had written together, and another based on the original.

Although it was true that Barrett Clark, representing the French theatrical agency, as well as the New York Theatre Guild, had not received the play directly from Miss Hurston, and although—as she declared in a long-distance telephone conversation with Hughes—she did not know it had been submitted to the Theatre Guild and then to the Jelliffes, it was nevertheless true that she had passed the script on to Carl Van Vechten without revealing that the play was a collaboration. Van Vechten had passed it on to the theatrical agency. Moreover, although Hughes did not know it then (and only too late did he learn) Miss Hurston had secretly copyrighted the play in her own name under the title *De Turkey and De Law*.[3] But angered by the deception he did know about, Hughes wrote Van Vechten the whole story. A few days later Hughes received a strange letter from Zora, finally responding to the two he had written her. She had marketed the play under her own name, she wrote, because she objected to his proposal that Louise

Thompson, their secretary-stenographer, share in the royalties. Hughes had shown, she said, more interest in Miss Thompson's welfare than in hers. "Not that I care what you give of yourself and your things....But I do object to having my work hi-jacked."[4]

Hughes responded to this with a threat to bring legal suit. But he also got in touch with Louise Thompson, who, having broken with Charlotte Mason in the autumn of 1930 for reasons not unlike his own, had become assistant to the director of the Congregational Education Society. Miss Thompson had not seen Zora for months, had no idea of what had happened, and was dismayed that Zora had tried to involve her. She would gladly come to Cleveland for a day, she wrote, and explain what she knew about the collaboration to the Jelliffes and their theatre group, the Gilpin Players.[5]

As strange as Miss Hurston's earlier letter was, a second letter, post-marked January 20—crossing Hughes's letter threatening litigation—was even stranger. She now implied that her reason for marketing the play under her own name was her emotional attachment to him; and after de-ploring this, that, and the other, she wrote—referring to why she had interrupted their collaboration in Westfield to go south:

> Langston, please believe me when I say that my thoughts were too painful to me for me to talk to you. I couldn't bear myself saying certain unpleasant phrases to you. So I just went off to myself and tried to resolve to have no more friendships. Tears unceasing have poured down inside me.
>
> So I just went off to work the play out alone—carefully not using what was yours. Please believe me when I say the money doesn't matter. You can have anything I have at any time.[6]

On the same day she posted this letter, Miss Hurston wired the Jelliffes that she would not authorize the production of *Mule Bone*, and asked them to return the script. They did so at once. But the next day two telegrams arrived contradicting the first: "O.K.," read one; and "Proceed. Good Luck," read the other. Both were signed Zora Neale Hurston.

Half convinced that Zora was losing her mind, and persuaded by Carl Van Vechten's expressed hope that he and Miss Hurston would settle their differences in order to go ahead with the production of the play that Van Vechten thought had great possibilities, Hughes wrote a placating "Zo Darling" letter. He was no longer thinking of bringing a legal suit. He had applied for copyright of the original play in both their names; and also (in a twelve-page letter) he had asked his lawyer-friend, Arthur Spingarn, to represent him in working out an agreement with Miss Hurston. "If you feel that the major part of *Mule Bone* is yours," Hughes wrote, "I am quite willing that you have two-thirds of all incomes, myself accepting one-third, and have so informed Mr. Spingarn."[7]

Although Miss Hurston, whose collaboration was nominal at best, did not deserve so generous a settlement, Hughes made the offer to assure the Cleveland production of the play. Mrs. Jelliffe wanted a written agreement as quickly as possible, and since she was willing to pay a substantial royalty, Hughes hoped Miss Hurston would accept his offer at once. He had use for the money. He was ill and needed medical care, and besides, the controversy over *Mule Bone* was exhausting. But Zora was perverse. She interpreted Langston's bringing in Arthur Spingarn as intermediary as a move against her, and when she met with the lawyer on January 24, Zora used Langston's passing mention of possible litigation as an excuse for not settling until she had consulted her own agent. Nor was she appeased by the letter that Mr. Spingarn dictated to Langston in her presence: "Litigation is the last thing either of you should think of if it can possibly be avoided, not only for your own sakes, but for the sake of the group."[8]

"The group," of course, was the Gilpin Players, which, under Rowena Jelliffe's direction, had already begun rehearsal. The Players were going ahead on the warrant of Zora Hurston's earlier wires telling them to proceed, and on the further warrant of her affirmative telephone conversation with an official of the *Cleveland Plain Dealer*, the newspaper under whose auspices the play was to be produced at the Theater of Nations. However, on January 27, there was another wire from Zora Hurston to Rowena Jelliffe: all future communications should be directed to Miss Hurston's literary agent, Elizabeth Marbury. As a matter of fact, the agent was already involved. A letter had come from Miss Marbury the day before requiring the Jelliffes to bear half the cost of Zora's train fare to Cleveland; Miss Hurston had told Spingarn that she wanted to go there "to discuss the whole situation face to face in a friendly manner."[9] The Jelliffes agreed. Their contract proposal would pay half Miss Hurston's railway fare to Cleveland for a production which would include her name jointly with that of Langston Hughes. Meanwhile, Hughes had revised the first and third acts and rewritten the second act in order to bring the play into conformity with the original version. He had also written to inform Miss Marbury that copies of the script and all details relevant to it could be obtained from Arthur Spingarn. But when no further word came from either Zora or her agent, Mrs. Jelliffe wrote Mr. Spingarn.

> It seems to me that Miss Hurston has behaved very strangely. I know from Louise Thompson, who worked with them on the typing of the play, that Langston Hughes did the construction of the play and that it was understood between [them] from the

beginning that they were to be co-authors of the play. Moreover, I have seen and examined in detail the worknotes for the
entire play in Mr. Hughes's own handwriting. I can see, comparing his script with hers, that she has made changes in an
attempt perhaps to claim that she has re-written the play. But
there's no question that it is the same play—and the changes are
feeble.

   Believing as I do, that Langston Hughes has rights in the
matter, I will not produce it under her name alone. I think she
has treated him very badly....

   I am wondering whether she is not really too unreliable a
person to deal with....

   Would you care to have Louise Thompson's angle on the
affair?...I know Miss Thompson and believe implicitly in her
integrity.[10]

On Monday morning, February 2, Miss Hurston telephoned. She had
arrived in Cleveland the night before, she informed Mrs. Jelliffe, and was
ready for a conference. On the very evening of Miss Hurston's arrival, the
Gilpin Players had decided not to go on with the production of *Mule Bone*,
but Mrs. Jelliffe, believing they might reconsider, arranged for Zora and
Langston to meet with her that afternoon. Sensitive to the personal difficulties between the two writers, Rowena Jelliffe left them alone to talk at
first—in the hope that these difficulties could be resolved. It was probably a
mistake. Zora was as adamant as ever. After arguing that the story, the
dialogue, and the humor were hers, even if Langston had put them all
together, that it was *her* play and she should have top billing, she brought
up her grievance against Louise Thompson, who, Zora professed to think,
was hoping for a share in the royalties. She declared that by marketing the
play on her own she was protecting them from Miss Thompson. This was
not an argument Langston was willing to accept. He had great respect for
and loyalty to Louise Thompson, the first person he had turned to following the harrowing break with Charlotte Mason, their quondam patron.[11] He
pointed out that Miss Thompson had been paid for her secretarial assistance
and neither wished nor expected anything more. But Zora was not molli-
fied. Little by little, he began to understand that what Zora really resented
was Miss Thompson's scorn of Zora's fawning behavior toward Mrs. Mason,
and that she also resented the mulatto woman's beauty, which, she presumed—however erroneously—was a trap for Langston's affections. But
Langston also realized the scope of Zora's literary and pecuniary ambition.
He was not surprised to have her end the conversation by saying, "The show
must go on." She would sign the agreement for the Cleveland production,

and she would meet with him, Rowena Jelliffe, and the Players the next evening.

By now, he was not surprised by Zora's unpredictability either. Sometime during the evening of February 2, she learned that Louise Thompson had been in Cleveland the previous week. In a blaze of anger, she called Rowena the next morning, accused her of acting only on Hughes's behalf, and cancelled the meeting with the Gilpin Players. She would never, she sneered, allow her name to be linked with Hughes's on *Mule Bone* or any other play. Responding to this outburst as calmly as she could, Mrs. Jelliffe proposed another meeting of the two writers and herself for that evening. This time their conference was held in Langston's bedroom, where, under doctor's orders, he was confined. His infected tonsils threatened a severe illness. (Although he said in *The Big Sea* that he had had a tonsillectomy when he and Zora had their last "literary quarrel" on *Mule Bone*, he had not.[12])

The meeting was a failure, a fiasco. Zora let no one get a word in edgewise. She cast scorn upon Mrs. Jelliffe, Langston, and the absent Miss Thompson. There was more than a touch of irony. The playwrights had once considered calling the play *A Bone of Contention*, and their last conference was not unlike a scene in a play itself. It ended with the cancellation of the Cleveland production. *Mule Bone*, Miss Hurston avouched, would never be produced.[13] Following her decision, she immediately telegraphed Charlotte Mason in New York: "Darling Godmother / Arrived safely / Have put the person on the run / Play stopped / Louise Thompson had been sent for to bolster case and I smashed them all / Be home by weekend / All my love / Zora"[14]

Informed of the whole matter, Spingarn wrote Hughes later that since the play was not to be produced, no legal steps would be taken; but in the event that Miss Hurston planned to produce it at some future time, he would obtain an injunction.

THE *Mule Bone* AFFAIR probably would have done more emotional damage to Langston had it not been for the welcome news he received a few days before the final quarrel. He had been awarded the Harmon Gold Medal, carrying a cash prize of $400, for *Not Without Laughter*. "Congratulations on Harmon. But what more do you want writing," Locke wired.[15] Hughes's reaction to Dr. Locke's wire would have been more appreciative had he not known that some days before it was sent, Locke had told Arthur Spingarn that Langston was wrong and Miss Hurston was right in the *Mule Bone* controversy. Langston wired Locke: "Please put me straight on Zora's attitude and your knowledge of matter by return wire collect. I am afraid I don't understand."[16]

Langston was unaware that Locke's congratulatory telegram about the

Harmon Gold Award was sent the same day the professor wrote the following letter to Charlotte Mason:

> Langston [won] the first prize in literature—gold medal and $400. This is a tribute to *Not Without Laughter* and the spirit it represents—which is yours. But the tragedy is the credit will go to swell the false egotism that at present denies its own best insight.
>
> Yesterday I received the enclosed telegram from Cleveland. It shows what you say about jews—Spingarn couldn't have written unless he wrote Sunday night—there has been too short an interval.
>
> I telegraphed [to Langston] "You say you don't understand; it's I who cannot understand you—writing congratulations on your Harmon award..." I don't think I should write the Cleveland people [Jelliffes]—but just send Z[ora's] introduction, showing absolute confidence in her....[17]

Hughes would have been distressed by the content of the letter, for more reasons than one. Alain Locke, six months before, had written to the Harmon Foundation to nominate Hughes for the literature prize.[18] Moreover, Locke's willingness to embrace the doctrinaire anti-Semitism of Mrs. Mason would have added to the poet's disillusionment and disappointment with the critic-professor (and Rhodes Scholar) he had once trusted as a friend. Locke's remark to her—"it shows what you say about jews"—was meant to cast an aspersion on Arthur Spingarn, whom the professor resented for wiring him that Langston had justifiable rights in *Mule Bone.*

And there was more Hughes did not understand about Locke, including not only the latter's siding with Zora, but siding against him when he broke with Mrs. Mason. Though Hughes was reluctant to think the professor had bartered his soul for the patronage of Charlotte Mason, he now tended to believe it. A letter to Arthur Spingarn was at least half vindictive:

> I do not understand Dr. Locke's zeal in upholding Miss Hurston's position—except that they are both employed by the same patron. Miss Hurston has probably claimed "Mule Bone" as entirely her own before Dr. Locke and their patron; and Dr. Locke, knowing only one side of the story, chooses to back Miss Hurston. So far as I can recall, I have never spoken to Dr. Locke about our comedy, nor was I aware until I heard from you, that he even knew Miss Hurston and I had worked on a play together....[19]

And there was another thing, too. Langston's reasons for not telling Locke about the play went further than his agreement with Zora to keep

Mule Bone a secret. For one deeply personal reason that the professor was well aware of, the poet had stopped confiding in him on most matters. Over a period of time, letters like the following had contributed to Hughes's increasing alienation from Locke:

> LANGSTON HUGHES,
>
> At increasing cost,—for pride is my master-sin, I have opened my arms three times to you, closed my eyes in confidence,—and waited. And three times, I have embraced thin air and blinked and then stared at disillusionment. Shades of my ancestors,—what whoredom is this!
>
> I know that you are the same person, I feel that you are the right person. I realize that you were nearer this time than ever before, and that perhaps for the first and last time you really wanted to,—but I will be too cheapened to say 'come' again....
>
> I cannot describe what I have been going through—it has felt like death—but out of this death and burial of pride and self there has suddenly come a resurrection of hope and love.
>
> Langston![20]

The tone of this was not unusual. Locke's frequent overtures put Hughes off, but it was Locke's stand on the *Mule Bone* affair that finally marked the end of Hughes's friendship with the older man. Even after the professor's death in 1954, Hughes, though entirely without malice, could not forget or forgive.

As for Miss Hurston, an ineradicable streak of obstinacy made her continue to press the issue of the play, which Langston would rather have ignored. Spingarn wrote in early March, "Miss Hurston was in to see me this morning. She tells me that there is no possible chance of her ever collaborating with you on the play and that she wants to eliminate all parts...in which you claim collaboration, and make a new play in which you will have no interest, and she wants a release from you of your rights in the play."[21] Hughes replied that he thought "it would be just as well to let Miss Hurston have the play...or at least her part of it?"[22] And some months later, when he did relinquish his rights, Miss Hurston, as willful and unpredictable as ever, wrote her patron that "it is one of the most unworthy things he ever did."[23]

By mid-March, when Hughes finally had a tonsillectomy, he had finished his own play *Mulatto* and prepared the volume of poems *Dear Lovely Death*[24] for publication. He wrote Arthur Spingarn that he expected to be in New York before the end of March. From New York, where there were loose ends to tighten, and where he would put *Mulatto* in the hands of a literary agent, he would set out for Florida and the Caribbean. Zell Ingram, a young artist from Cleveland, who was to design the cover of *Dear Lovely Death*, would travel with him. The two young men pooled their meagre resources, borrowed a car from Ingram's mother, and were off on March 22. Hughes did not tell his friends in New York how long he would be gone. He himself did not know. But he was glad to leave his recent unhappy experiences behind him and to escape the tragic reminders that the economic depression was deepening.

❧ 9 ❧

South of the Border

D RIVING TOWARD THE FLORIDA COAST, Hughes and Ingram's glad escape
from the New York winter was blurred by headline news as they
sped toward Daytona Beach. On March 25, nine black youths, accused of
raping two white women on a freight train passing through Alabama, had
barely escaped a lynch mob before they were jailed in the town of Scottsboro.
The news brought to Hughes's mind his first anti-lynching poem, which
had been published less than a year before.

Flight

Plant your toes in the cool swamp mud;
Step and leave no track.
Hurry, sweating runner!
The hounds are at your back.

No I didn't touch her.
White flesh ain't for me.

Hurry! Black boy, hurry!
Or they'll swing you to a tree![1]

He would write poems about the Scottsboro case, which within a few
months would become an international *cause célèbre*. But in Daytona Beach,
at Bethune-Cookman College, where he was a guest for two days, his own
immediate future and his own career were uppermost in his mind. In spite
of the fine critical acclaim of his poetry, and the prizes it had won, in spite
of its being translated into several foreign languages and included in more
than twenty anthologies, he could not live on earnings from it. At the age of
twenty-nine, the author of two highly acclaimed volumes of poetry and one
novel, Hughes had barely been able to eke out a living except by working at
menial jobs or by depending on the largesse of a patron. His predicament

embittered him, and many years later when he wrote of it, a touch of bitterness remained.

> The magazines used very few stories with Negro themes, since Negro themes were considered exotic, in a class with Chinese or East Indian features. Editorial offices then never hired Negro writers to read manuscripts or employed them to work on their staffs. Almost all the young white writers I'd known in New York in the 'twenties had gotten good jobs with publishers or magazines as a result of their creative work. White friends of mine in Manhattan, whose first novels had received reviews nowhere nearly so good as my own, had been called to Hollywood, or were doing scripts for the radio. Poets whose poetry sold hardly at all had been offered jobs on smart New York magazines. But they were white. I was colored.[2]

Mary McLeod Bethune,[3] the president of Bethune-Cookman College, was a warm admirer and friend of Hughes's. She had first met him at Columbia University, where she delivered an address while he was a student there. Now she suggested that he could tour the South and support himself by reading his poetry before college audiences. "Thousands of Negro students," she told him, "would be proud and inspired by seeing and hearing you." Although her suggestion seemed a hopeful prospect, it was not a solution to his basic dilemma: how he, a black poet, best known for blues and jazz poems that pleased the fancy of "established" publishers, could earn a living from the radical works he had been contributing to journals such as *New Masses*. Indeed, his first publisher, Alfred A. Knopf, had cautioned him that, as a black radical poet, he would find no large following in America.

But this was certainly not the case in Cuba—his first stop in the Caribbean that spring of 1931—where he was inspired to write a long poem excoriating American and European imperialism. The poem was "To the Little Fort of San Lazaro," published in *New Masses* one month later. After two previous visits, Hughes was no stranger in Cuba, and some of his works had already been translated into Spanish and published there. Now the island's oldest newspaper, *Diario de la Marina*, welcomed him enthusiastically with the headline: "EL POETA LANGSTON HUGHES NOS VISITA DE NUEVO"[4] —"The Poet Langston Hughes Visits Us Again." This time his visit would last long enough to seal lifelong friendships with those he had met before, including the journalist and diplomat José Antonio Fernández de Castro, and Nicolás Guillén, who would one day become Cuba's national poet.

The year before, during his two-week stay in Cuba, at Charlotte Mason's request—to find an Afro-Cuban composer—Hughes had been the subject of articles by both Fernández de Cástro and Guillén. Hughes had deeply influenced the poetry of Guillén, whose first volume, *Motivos de Son*, was published shortly after they first met. It was Guillén, who, incidentally, had conducted the first newspaper interview Hughes ever attempted in Spanish.[5] Fernández de Castro, who had been the first Cuban to translate Hughes into Spanish, as early as 1928, had introduced him to the Havana literati in 1930 with an essay, "Presentación de Langston Hughes," for *Revista de la Habana*.[6] Through Fernández de Castro, Hughes had immediately come to the attention not only of Guillén but also of the revolutionary Cuban poets Regino Pedroso, Pablo de la Torriente-Brau, and the influential editor of *Diario de la Marina*, Gustavo Urrutia. It was literary history in the making, for Hughes not only translated these Cuban writers into English, he also was destined to cross their paths again elsewhere on the globe.

The Cuban journalists and poets made Hughes's 1931 return to Havana a celebration. He had brought with him English translations of their work, some of which was scheduled that very spring for publication in American journals: Guillén's poem "Madrigal" in the March issue of *Opportunity*, Gustavo Urrutia's article "Students of Yesterday" in the April *Crisis*, and Regino Pedroso's poem "Alarm Clock" in the spring issue of *Poetry Quarterly*.

His Cuban friends entertained him and Ingram with parties, suppers, and nightclub galas, almost from the time they arrived until they departed five days later. And although Hughes appreciated the absence of an official color line, he realized that social class divisions in Havana were based at least in part on color. On that subject, he was to write later that "the darker a man is, the richer and more celebrated he has to be to crash those [class] divisions." And, indeed, he found it was color prejudice which caused him and Ingram difficulty when a white American attendant barred them entrance to a farewell beach party in their honor. When Ingram threatened a fight, both he and Hughes were arrested briefly. But their Cuban friends, embarrassed and angry beyond measure, tried to make it up to them with a more festive bon voyage party at one of Havana's most famous restaurants, El Baturro. "We left Cuba with the rhumba throbbing in our ears," Hughes said later. The next day, the two travelers were on a boat for Haiti.

THE WINDWARD PASSAGE to Haiti was for Hughes a dream fulfilled. Since childhood, he had wanted to see the world's first black republic, whose legendary history he had learned from his grandmother. She had told him how the slaves in the early 1790s had revolted against the French for twelve years and finally, after defeating Napoleon Bonaparte's expedition, won their independence. The black Haitian generals, Toussaint L'Ouverture, Jean Jacques Dessalines, and Henri Christophe remained Hughes's heroes even as an adult, and he was especially proud that his own great-uncle, John

Mercer Langston, had twice served in an independent Haiti as American consul general during the nineteenth century.

But the glorious images of Haiti's heroes and history were tarnished by the realities of 1931. In the capital, Port-au-Prince, the racial and social caste system angered him. It seemed more obvious and far worse than in Havana—and for different reasons. "It was in Haiti," he wrote later, "that I first realized how class lines may cut across color lines within a race, and how dark people of the same nationality may scorn those below them." It distressed him to see black Haitians illiterate, barefoot, and poor while the educated mulatto upper class wore fine clothes and lived in hilltop villas. He described the situation as "a surge of black peasants who live on the land, and the foam of the cultured élite in Port-au-Prince who live on the peasants."

He was equally provoked by the presence of American Marines, who, after a sixteen-year occupation of Haiti, seemed to walk around as if they owned it. In an essay, "White Shadows in a Black Land," he complained:

> Before you can go ashore, a white American marine has been on board ship to examine your passport, and maybe you will see a gunboat at anchor in the harbor. Ashore, you are likely to soon run into groups of marines in the little cafes, talking in "Cracker" accents, and drinking in the usual boisterous American manner. You will discover that the Banque d'Haiti with its Negro cashiers and tellers, is really under control of the National City Bank of New York. You will become informed that all the money collected by the Haitian customs passes through the hands of an American comptroller. And regretfully, you will gradually learn that most of the larger stores with their colored clerks are really owned by Frenchmen, Germans, or Assyrian Jews. And if you read the Haitian newspapers, you will soon realize from the heated complaints there, that even in the Chamber of Deputies, the strings of government are pulled by white politicians in far-off Washington—and that the American marines are kept in the country through an illegal treaty thrust upon Haiti by force and never yet ratified by the United States Senate. The dark-skinned little Republic then has its hair caught in the white fingers of unsympathetic foreigners, and the Haitian people live today under a sort of military dictatorship backed by American guns. They are not free.[7]

In Port-au-Prince, where Hughes and Ingram spent one week seeing the city, they stayed in "a distinctly non-tourist hotel near the port, patronized entirely by Haitians." Ignoring letters of introduction to the Haitian élite given him by Arthur Spingarn, Walter White, and James Weldon Johnson,

Hughes chose to become acquainted with the "People Without Shoes," a title he gave an essay which *New Masses* published that October. Even if he had had unlimited funds, he would not have socialized with well-to-do Haitians when he arrived. He preferred to ignore them. He wrote that "in Haiti of all places—with its thrilling history of the slaves who drove the French into the ocean and freed themselves—to find people divided by the lightness or darkness of one's skin, and whether or not one was able to afford shoes—well, I personally preferred the people without shoes." And in a postcard to *New Masses*, which the magazine published that July as "A Letter from Haiti," he wrote:

> Haiti is a hot, tropical little country, all mountains and sea; a lot of marines, mulatto politicians, and a world of black people without shoes—who catch hell.
>
> The Citadel, twenty miles away on a mountaintop, is a splendid, lovely monument to the genius of a black king—Christophe. Stronger, vaster, more beautiful than you could imagine, it stands in futile ruin now, the iron cannon rusting, the bronze one turning green, the great passages and deep stairways alive with bats, while the planes of the United States Marines hum daily overhead.

The trip to Cap Haitien from Port-au-Prince, which should have taken Hughes and Ingram twelve hours by bus, took them almost a month. It was a near-fiasco which Langston endured with good humor but which Zell did not suffer gladly. "He was tired, hungry, wet, homesick and mad when we reached Cap Haitien," Hughes said. Midway there, torrential rains had washed out the only road, forcing the bus to a standstill near St. Marc, where they spent three weeks. Their next vehicle, an open-air bus loaded with farmers, pigs, rice, and bananas, ran out of gas in the mountains, and they spent a cold, unsheltered night before reaching Cap Haitien in a tropical downpour. Once there, they vowed to travel no further than the Citadel, twenty miles away, for the rest of the summer.

Their stay in Le Cap—as residents called historic Cap Haitien—proved worth it. For twenty-five dollars a month, they found an ocean-front hotel room with a large balcony where Zell could paint and Hughes could write. When not working or sleeping, they went sightseeing, played dominoes with the dockhands, and drank in the hotel bar. Hughes made much to-do of the fact that Ingram was a ladies' man whose time was taken up by a local Haitian beauty named Coloma, while, he, Hughes, was entertained by her friend, Clezie-Anne. (Years later, friends who knew both men would say it was Hughes's subtle way of protecting Zell, whose interest in men was greater than his interest in women.)

When the rains in Cap Haitien finally ceased in mid-June, Hughes took

advantage of the splendid weather and made three pilgrimages to the Citadel. Towering three thousand feet above the sea, the great fortress with its
mighty staircases, great chambers, and dark dungeons was an impressive
relic of a glorious past, the early days of which were dominated by Dessalines,
the former slave who declared himself emperor and had the fortress constructed as his symbol.

That summer Hughes began writing about Dessalines, in whose life he
saw all the elements of a tragic drama. Le Cap itself seemed possessed by the
ghost of Dessalines, the "bravest of the brave" of Toussaint's generals, who
had withstood Cap Haitien's last attack by the French in 1803. But he was
so despotic as emperor that he was murdered within two years of his
coronation. Hughes, however, romanticized Dessalines. Writing to the sound
of distant drums throbbing across the bay, he titled the drama he wrote in
Cap Haitien *Drums of Haiti*. A few years later he would revise and rename it
Emperor of Haiti, only to rework it again as the libretto for his opera *Troubled
Island*.

So far as Hughes and Ingram were concerned, Haiti was indeed a "troubled island" that summer of 1931. Its social and color barriers seemed
especially onerous in Cap Haitien. Their hotel manager complained that
they were the only guests who socialized with the common people and that
"gentlemen" did not do such things. But Hughes did what he pleased. He
associated with the laborers and peasants, visited their homes, attended
voodoo rites and conga dances. "I tried to tell the hotel manager that one
can drink champagne and talk about Proust or Gide in New York," Hughes
said, "but one cannot see a conga dance there."

The one drink of which Hughes had too many in Haiti was not champagne but the potent spirit he later called "the famous drink we never see in
America." He recorded the experience in "Absinthe," a chapter written for *I
Wonder as I Wander* but never published. "Only once in my life," he confessed there, "have I been drunk to the point of utter irresponsibility. That
memorable occasion for me took place in Haiti one midweek night when it
was hot and very quiet in the dark streets of the Cap."

It happened in a bar patronized by American Marines and where persons
of color were not admitted until curfew time forced the white Marines back
to their quarters. "When I got to the door," Hughes wrote, "it seemed to
me enormously amusing to sit on the floor right in the doorway and not let
anyone else pass in or out. So I leaned back against the door jamb and put
my feet high in front of me on the opposite jamb of the door. It tickled me
no end seeing people trying to get over my upraised and outstretched legs. I
laughed fit to kill. And all the while, I knew just what I was doing."[8]

But there is some doubt that he knew what he was doing when later that
night he tried to scale his hotel garden wall instead of walking in through

the door; or when he went for a midnight swim alone and, fortunately for him, collapsed on the beach. In his inebriated state, to have survived the rough ocean currents would have been as unlikely as walking on the water. He had never learned to stay afloat even in a swimming pool, and that night, had he tried the ocean, he would not have lived to write about it.

But taken all in all, that summer he found himself and the inner strength to survive as a writer. The slow pace of life in the sun helped him come to grips with what he called "the cold and confusion of a bewildering New York winter." He might have stayed longer in the Caribbean had his Harmon Gold Prize money not dwindled as quickly as the summer itself. Ingram, believing he could stay as long as he continued writing to his mother in Cleveland for money, was disabused of that belief when she sent the last fifty dollars with a message that "enough was enough." So with just enough money for passage, Zell and Langston left Cap Haitien at the end of July as deck passengers on a Dutch freighter bound for Santiago de Cuba, via three Haitian ports.

When the boat stopped for one day in Port-au-Prince, Hughes disembarked and finally used one of his letters of introduction to the Haitian élite. He called upon Jacques Roumain, a young poet and ethnologist, then working in the Ministry of Information. Despite any reluctance Hughes may have had to contact him, he was later glad they met, and he would describe Roumain as "one of the few cultured Haitians who appreciated native folklore, and who became a friend of the people without shoes." The two poets chatted for an hour that July afternoon, and later that evening, Roumain surprised him with an official Haitian delegation at the boat. Hughes and Ingram could not have looked more like "people without shoes." They sat shirtless and shoeless on the deck, eating a meal of sausage and cheese, when Roumain introduced Hughes as "the greatest Negro poet who had ever come to honor Haitian soil."

Roumain, who was five years Hughes's junior, could not have been more similar to him in outlook, background, physical appearance, or social commitment. The two poets had an instant affinity for one another, which Roumain reflected in a poem published that year in the Haiti-Journal.[9] "Langston Hughes" was a tribute to the American Roumain never forgot. Nor would Hughes ever forget him, though they were destined to meet only twice again during Roumain's short lifetime.

AFTER STOPPING BRIEFLY in Leogane and Jérémie along the Haitian coast, Hughes and Ingram reached Cuba again by way of the Windward Passage. Except for a storm that forced them to spend the night in a hot, crowded shelter room, the trip was without mishap. By then they were accustomed to the heat, the discomfort, the inconvenience, and the tribulation of travel-

ing as deck passengers, but they were not quite ready for what they encountered when they landed in Cuba.

"At Santiago de Cuba," Hughes wrote, "the immigration authorities did
not know what to make of two American Negroes traveling on the open
deck, unable to display between them as much as fifty dollars. They argued
that only sugar cane workers traveled in that fashion. Therefore, since we
had no working permits, they refused to allow us on Cuban soil until we
posted bonds." Transferred to an immigration station, they spent three
days—to quote Hughes—in "a jail-like fortress in the harbor, zooming with
mosquitos, crawling with bedbugs, and alive with fleas."

Nine years before he published those words in *I Wonder as I Wander*, he
unfolded a slightly different version of his difficulties in Santiago de Cuba in
"My Adventures as a Social Poet." In this essay he attributed his problems
to politics and the Cuban dictator, Gerardo Machado,[10] whose secret police
had little sympathy for social reform or for poets who advocated it. Some of
Hughes's reformist poetry had appeared in liberal sections of the Cuban
press, and Hughes was convinced it had not escaped Machado's attention.

> Perhaps someone called his attention to these poems and transla-
> tions because, when I came back from Haiti weeks later, I was
> not allowed to land in Cuba, but was detained by the immigra-
> tion authorities at Santiago and put on an island until the Ameri-
> can consul came, after three days, to get me off with the provision
> that I cross the country to Havana and leave Cuban soil at once.[11]

In Havana, where Ingram's illness obliged Hughes to stay two days, he
was followed by Cuba's secret police and other authorities wherever he
went. He not only told this to José Antonio Fernández de Castro, his
Cuban journalist friend, but drew upon their conversation about it for a
short story, "Little Old Spy," which was published in *Esquire* three years
later. The opening lines seem straight from Hughes's own life: "A number
of years ago, toward the end of one of Cuba's reactionary regimes, on the
evening of my second day in Havana, I realized I was being followed."
Moreover, in the story Hughes's protagonist complains to a Cuban newspaper editor of being followed to a restaurant by a strange man. The fictional Cuban newspaper editor replies exactly as Fernández de Castro
allegedly replied when Hughes told him about the Havana restaurant on-
looker: "Maybe he thinks you're a Communist.... That's what they are
afraid of here."

The episode in Cuba was not the last in which Hughes would be harassed
and followed out of reactionary fears that he was a Communist. Within a
decade, he would be followed and reported on by informants for the Federal Bureau of Investigation (FBI) wherever he traveled.[12]

Arriving in Key West, Hughes and Ingram found the tires of their car flat, and to replace a tire and four tubes they had to pawn most their belongings before they journeyed to Daytona Beach. There Mrs. Bethune joined them on the ride to New York City. She reminded Hughes again to "go all over the South with his poetry" when they stopped at Coulter Academy, in Cheraw, South Carolina, and students urged him to recite his poems on the campus.

Arriving jobless and penniless in New York that August definitely influenced Hughes to follow Mrs. Bethune's suggestion that he apply to the Rosenwald Fund to finance his poetry tour south. He knew he could count on her to help him, and he was encouraged by her warm interest and concern for his career. In her own way, she also helped fulfill his need for a strong maternal figure. But as much as he admired and respected Mrs. Bethune, she could not take the place of an old family friend in New York, Mrs. Ethel Dudley Harper, whom he affectionately called "Aunt Toy."[13] She had grown up with his mother in Kansas, the first of twelve children, and she treated Langston like a member of her own family.

Married to a musician closer to Langston's age than her own (she was then forty-four), "Toy" Harper earned her living as a Harlem couturière, designing costumes for theatrical productions. Known as "Toy" for her diminutive size, she was anything but a toy in spirit. Having run away from home in her teens to begin a show business career as a singer and dancer, she had taken her first job as a snake charmer in a circus. Langston's friends, who believed she controlled rather than consoled him, and did not understand the bond between them, laughingly referred to her as "the snake charmer." But she treated him like a son, and he doted upon it.

"You have to understand Aunt Toy," he told friends who insisted she was domineering and who seemed not to understand the curious *ménage à trois* of Toy, her young husband, Emerson, and Langston, their "nephew," who moved in with them that summer of 1931 because his financial situation left him little choice.

Hughes's friendship with the Harpers, whose marriage lasted until Toy's death thirty-seven more years later, was a subject he never wrote about— perhaps because it was too emotionally complicated and involved for him and for them. It certainly was strong beyond breaking—especially with Toy, who shared nearly every problem Hughes had. She listened enough to his plight about Zora Neale Hurston over *Mule Bone*[14] to accompany him to the office of Miss Hurston's literary agent that summer. Zora, learning of their meeting with her agent, wrote angrily to Charlotte Mason:

Langston is back in town. I received an announcement that he was to lecture on the West Indies, or his travels to be exact,

under the auspices of *The Crisis*. He went down to my agent's
with a long line of the most malicious lies in an effort to prejudice them against me. He took along some woman whom he
introduced as his aunt to help him talk. All he got for his trouble
was to be called a vicious liar to his face, a sneak and a weakling.
The woman was asked what she was doing there and to keep her
mouth shut or get out of the office....[15]

Although he learned from her agent that Zora Neale Hurston had copyrighted *Mule Bone* in her own name, he did not try to get directly in touch
with her while he was in New York. Arthur Spingarn reminded him that he
could get an injunction to prohibit Zora from producing it, and that settled
the matter so far as Hughes was concerned. He wanted no further association with Zora Hurston, nor, indeed, with Mrs. Mason.

His decision freed him of any additional contact with the peripatetic
Zora, who was still dangling like a puppet from Charlotte Mason's pursestrings.
His former patron, who had raised an eyebrow at his protest poem, "Advertisement for the Waldorf Astoria," was now giving Zora the nod to
stage her folklore in the cabarets of fashionable New York hotels such as the
Waldorf. "Please see me with your vision, waving a fan gaily,"[16] Zora had
written to—in her words—her "guard mother" during the *Mule Bone* debacle. Even as the economic depression deepened, Zora was still having such
grandiose visions of fame and fortune. But her "guard mother" was more
deeply concerned about her protégée's literary contract and financial de-
pendence, and she reminded her of them in harsh terms:

> Make no use whatsoever of my name, whether in print or orally,
> in any future production....Finally, it is understood that the
> other data and material which you have collected on the mission
> for which I sent you shall not be used for any purpose without
> further permission from me, particularly that dealing with the
> conjure ceremony and rituals....[17]

By September 1932, Zora's financial ties to 399 Park Avenue would be
cut completely, a move which, even if not of her own choosing, freed her to
write some of the best novels of her generation. Mrs. Mason had never
financed her to write fiction or to publish or produce folklore material for
any purpose without her permission. Only too late did Hughes realize that
Zora's bizarre behavior about *Mule Bone* was the result in part of her need to
stay in Godmother's good graces and on her payroll as long as possible. But
they both knew that Zora had violated the restrictions of her written contract. In a 1929 letter describing material they might use in the play—which
she first wanted to entitle *Jook*—Zora had told Langston: "G[odmother]

would never consent for me to do so, so you will have to take it all in your name."[18] Hughes had not wanted or ever tried to gain solo credit, and his hope that they might be co-authors of the first folk comedy by Afro-Americans made him a victim of Zora's falsehoods and excuses. Her later claim that he "stole her play" only further exasperated him, ending in a broken friendship over a play that was never produced.

Abandoning *Mule Bone* spared Hughes the charade that Zora endured for the next year as she continued to compromise her integrity, signing her letters to Mrs. Mason, "Devotedly your pickaninny, Zora," "Darling My Mother God," and "Dear, dear Godmother, it is blessed to be loved by you."[19]

Hughes was also freed from having to play the diplomat with Alain Locke, who was still receiving money from Godmother and, of course, dutifully corresponding with her. But Mrs. Mason could not have been too pleased when "her dear brown boy"—as she called Locke—became critical of Zora's folklore concerts and wrote Godmother, who sponsored them: "It does seem as if all the young Negroes had completely lost their heads. In spite of all this crisis, they seem to be jig dancing as if nothing serious was going on."[20]

But Locke himself avoided anything as "serious" as the Scottsboro case, which was a major issue when Hughes returned to New York. It had been taken up by the Negro press, the liberal-to-left white press, and many well-known artists, black and white. Hughes's contacts on the staff of *New Masses* and in the Communist-oriented International Labor Defense (ILD) compared the Scottsboro case with the Sacco-Vanzetti case of the 1920s as an example of class struggle and ethnic or racial oppression.

Professor Locke, who still thought of himself as a spokesman for the New Negro, made no public statement on Scottsboro, but he kept Mrs. Mason informed of the involvement of Hughes and Louise Thompson, whose independence of thought and feeling Locke resented. After hearing Miss Thompson speak in Harlem on "The Significance of the Scottsboro Case," Locke wrote Mrs. Mason that the speech was a "masked harangue mixed with social service and lynching statistics and weak Communist platitudes about the solidarity of black and white labor."[21] On Hughes's political writings and speeches, he sent her everything he could find to justify their mutual hope that somewhere, somehow, he might hang himself. "He'll have a long rope," Locke wrote Charlotte Mason, "but eventually it will pull taut."[22]

Little did Hughes know of the professor's attitude when he wrote him some time later requesting one of Locke's original, signed manuscripts for an auction supporting the Scottsboro Defense Fund.[23] Hughes devoted much of his time during the autumn of 1931 to writing about the Scottsboro case.

By then, nearly six months had passed since eight of the defendants had been tried and found guilty and sentenced to death by all-white juries in three separate trials in Alabama. A mistrial had been declared in the case of the youngest defendant, Leroy (Roy) Wright, who was thirteen years old. But the case was far from over. Even the white *Birmingham Age-Herald* called the convictions "without parallel in the history of the nation."[24] Hughes wrote of the injustice in "Scottsboro"—a poem for the December 1931 issue of *Opportunity*:

> 8 Black Boys in a Southern Jail.
> World, turn pale!
>
> 8 black boys and one white lie.
> Is it much to die?. . . .[25]

Equally disturbing to Hughes was the acrimonious rivalry developing between the NAACP and the International Labor Defense (ILD) over which should have the opportunity to represent the Scottsboro youths in the courts. While he then remained politically to the left of his friend W. E. B. Du Bois and other officials of the NAACP, he personally objected to the Communist *Daily Worker* referring to them as "bourgeois reformists." Ostensibly, Hughes stayed clear of writing about this ideological dispute, but he also cautiously avoided sending any of his Scottsboro pieces to *The Crisis*, the NAACP's official publication. And whereas Du Bois's writings in *The Crisis* —of which he was still editor—were nowhere close to those of the Communist Party (which he would join some thirty years later), Hughes's 1931 play, *Scottsboro Limited*, ended with a scene in which the Scottsboro defendants join hands with the white proletariat and raise a great flag to the strains of the Communist anthem, "The Internationale."

While some people insisted that Hughes's play might have been "Communist-inspired," they could say the same of some of the writings of Theodore Dreiser, Lincoln Steffens, John Dos Passos, H. G. Wells and Thomas Mann. These writers were also expressing outrage and signing petitions circulated by the International Labor Defense. The ILD, believing the masses could best aid the Scottsboro defense through direct, nonviolent action and protest, constantly referred to the case as a "legal lynching," while the NAACP argued that it should be settled through the courts.

Though Hughes had friends in the ILD fold, and he supported the 1932 Communist candidate for Vice President of the United States, James Ford, a black man, he did not then or ever become a member of the Communist Party. His left-minded friends understood and respected his views, even if some found it an ironic contradiction when he applied to—in their words—

the "bourgeois, capitalist" Rosenwald Fund for financial assistance to take his poetry south. It was a contradiction that Hughes himself never explained in print, though he told friends he had little choice. He was broke when he applied to the Rosenwald Fund for financial assistance and to Southern educational, religious, and social institutions for poetry-reading bookings.

Two white students at the University of North Carolina, Milton Abernathy and Anthony Buttitta, learning of the possibility of Hughes's arrival there, wrote to him to request some of his work for publication in their biweekly, *Contempo*. He did not try to hide his feelings and thoughts on black-white relations, as, for instance, when he sent Abernathy and Butitta this poem:

White Shadows

I'm looking for a house
In the world
Where white shadows
Will not fall.

There is no such house,
Dark Brother
No such house
At all.

It was published immediately in the September 15 issue of *Contempo*. Why Hughes sent the two white student editors "White Shadows" is uncertain, for it was actually less reflective of his attitude toward race relations than "Union," which *New Masses* published that September 1931, shortly before his departure for the South.

Union

Not me alone
I know now
But all the whole oppressed
Poor world,
White and black,
Must put their hands with mine
To shake the pillars of those temples
Wherein the false gods dwell
And the worn out altars stand
Too well defended.[26]

Both "White Shadows" and "Union" were quite unlike another poem
which he published that October 1931 and which later became one of his
most widely reprinted poems: his conciliatory "October 16," commemorat-
ing John Brown's 1859 raid on Harpers Ferry. But at the time he wrote it,
he was not really concerned, as he would be later, with whether his poetry
appealed to both blacks and whites, to young and old, to rich and poor. In
1931–32, he was inclined—perhaps more than he ever would be again—to
put his career on the line, to write as he pleased. However, he was not
invariably "political," as some of his other poems published that autumn
show. "God," "Sailor," and "Lover's Return," in *Poetry* magazine, and
"Dying Beast," in *Literary Digest*, revealed the versatility that characterized
his poetry throughout his career.

Hughes could count more of his poems and books in print in 1931 than he
could count his dollars in the bank. More than twenty of his previously
published poems were circulating in American anthologies, and nearly a
dozen others were in foreign publications, including three translated into
Spanish by the eminent Argentinean writer, Jorge Luis Borges. He was as
proud of all that as he was of *Dear Lovely Death*, which Mrs. Amy Spingarn
had printed privately in a limited edition with illustrations by Zell Ingram.

But he still needed cash more than he needed anything else. That is one
reason why, late that summer, he began another playwriting collaboration—
this time with a Swedish writer, Kai Gynt. She had written a musical folk
drama, *Cock o' the World*, and she asked Hughes to write lyrics for it.
Having been burned by Zora Neale Hurston, Hughes consulted with Arthur Spingarn before signing any agreements with Kai Gynt. There was
added reason for caution, because Gynt had Paul Robeson in mind for the
starring role. Remembering that he had collaborated in 1926 on a musical,
O Blues!, which had never reached the stage with Robeson, Hughes doubted
that the world-famous singer, who was in even greater demand than
before, would be interested in *Cock o' the World*. By 1931 Robeson was
internationally acclaimed as an actor and singer; and that year after a four-
month concert tour in the United States, he hurried to England to perform
in his third O'Neill drama, *The Hairy Ape*.

Moreover, Hughes had heard the rumors, then rampant in Harlem, that
Robeson's marriage was on the rocks because, against his wishes, his wife
Eslanda had published a controversial biography, *Paul Robeson, Negro*. That
he might appear in *Cock o' the World*—when he had more important things
to consider—seemed unlikely to Hughes, but he thought it worth enough
of a try to spend part of the summer working with Kai Gynt on the script.

Meanwhile, Hughes continued with plans for a lecture tour, outlining his
itinerary, scheduling his lectures, and writing *The Negro Mother and Other
Dramatic Recitations*. When favorable responses came from several colleges

in late September, along with a letter from the Rosenwald Fund offering him a thousand dollars to read his poems, he was all but ready to go south. Ironically, only a few days before the news arrived, he had written a long ballad called "Broke" to include with five other dramatic recitations in *The Negro Mother* booklet. For his tour, a young Greenwich Village artist, Prentiss Taylor, designed and illustrated all six selections as a booklet to sell for a quarter. "Since Prentiss Taylor was white, a Southerner from Virginia," Hughes wrote later, "I thought maybe such a book, evidence in itself of interracial collaboration and good will, might help democracy a little in the South where it seemed so hard for people to be friends across the color line."

Final preparations for his trip forced him to put aside everything, including *Cock o' the World*. "Miss Gynt and I have been struggling night and day with the play," he advised Arthur Spingarn in a departing note.[27] It was not the last he would see of the play, but it was the last he would see of New York for a long while. His brief in-transit stay in New York City that summer and autumn of 1931 marked the end of his part in what remained of the "Harlem Renaissance." In his view, the Renaissance had ended when the stock market crashed and the Great Depression began. "By the time the thirties came," he wrote later, "the voltage of the Negro Renaissance of the twenties had nearly run its course. . . . The chain of influences that had begun in Renaissance days ended in the thirties when the Great Depression drastically cut down on migrations, literary or otherwise."[28]

His adieu to the Harlem literati that October 1931 was like a final farewell to an era. When he set out to carry his blues south, his literary journey of the thirties was just beginning.

❧ 10 ❧

On the Cross of the South

ALTHOUGH HE DID NOT KNOW HOW TO DRIVE, Hughes bought an inexpensive car for his lecture tour. He did not intend to ride Jim Crow trains south. As driver he engaged a former Lincoln University classmate, Radcliffe Lucas, who would serve as business manager as well. Packing the car full of copies of Hughes's published poems, including the new booklet, *The Negro Mother*, the two men left New York at dawn in late October on a tour that was scheduled to last eight months. The date marked a turning point in Hughes's career.

Having overcome the shyness of his youth, when he had often asked Countee Cullen to substitute for him at poetry readings, he was more than ready to face his first audience that autumn at a YMCA in Camden, New Jersey. He would benefit from his experience of having read his poetry to fraternity gatherings, the NAACP, the Urban League, the Walt Whitman Foundation, the Black Opals Society, and numerous churches and schools. But lecturing before one audience after another, day after day, city after city, was another story, as he soon discovered.

His first week went well. There were successful programs in Downington, Pennsylvania, then at Morgan State College in Baltimore, Howard University in Washington, D.C., and Virginia State College in Petersburg, Virginia (of which, incidentally, his great-uncle, John Mercer Langston, had been the first president). Not until November 7 at Hampton Institute, in Virginia, did he experience what he later described as "the beginning of my realization that I was in the South, the troubled Jim Crow South of ever present danger for Negroes."[1]

The weekend he arrived, a double tragedy had occurred. A former Hampton athlete, en route to a football game, had been beaten to death by a white mob. A few hours later, learning that Juliette Derricotte, the black dean of women at Fisk University, had died from an automobile accident after being refused emergency treatment by a white hospital in Georgia, Hughes agreed to speak at a student protest meeting. But the elderly white and

Negro heads of the Institute would not allow such a meeting to be held. "That is not Hampton's way," they told him. "We educate, not protest."

In an essay titled "Cowards from the Colleges," published in *The Crisis*, Hughes was still protesting the Hampton incident three years later. The more he saw of black colleges during his tour, the more convinced he became that the white hierarchy he had seen at Lincoln existed in all of them. Worse still, some black administrators seemed to outdo themselves trying to keep their students unaware and passive. When he wrote "Cowards from the Colleges," he was convinced that "many of our institutions apparently are not trying to make men and women of their students at all—they are doing their best to produce spineless Uncle Toms, uninformed, and full of mental and moral evasions."

Those thoughts must have weighed upon him when, en route to North Carolina, he composed a terse, satiric poem to include in his booklet *Scottsboro Limited*:

Justice

That justice is a blind goddess
Is a thing to which we blacks are wise.
Her bandage hides two festering sores
That once perhaps were eyes.

Much of November was spent in North Carolina. He could not have asked for more "protest" than he found there—and he was the subject of most of it. Some of the most dramatic incidents of his tour occurred at the all-white state university in Chapel Hill. Even before his scheduled lecture appearance on the campus, he was as controversial as the Scottsboro case. The December 1 issue of the campus tabloid, *Contempo*, featuring one of his most indignant works about Scottsboro on the front page, set off a furor in nearby towns. The Charlotte *Southern Textile Bulletin*, incensed over his *Contempo* essay, which was titled "Southern Gentlemen, White Prostitutes, Mill Owners and Negroes,"[2] accused him of "participating in the Communist effort to create interest in nine Alabama Negroes convicted of assaulting two white girls."

Contempo's student editors, Milton Abernathy and Anthony Buttitta, who had solicited Hughes's essay and a poem that appeared in the same issue, could not have been more delighted with all the commotion. Hughes took it all in stride, although he was uncertain at first whether his *Contempo* essay calling "Dixie justice blind and syphilitic" or his poem calling Christ a nigger and a bastard had created the most uproar. But as the controversy swelled, he discovered that it was the poem:

Christ in Alabama

Christ is a Nigger
Beaten and black—
O, bare your back.

Mary is his Mother—
*Mammy of the South
Silence your mouth.*

God's His Father—
*White master above
Grant us your love.*

Most holy bastard
Of the bleeding mouth:
*Nigger Christ
On the cross of the South.*

Outraged by the poem, some Chapel Hill citizens demanded that Hughes be run out of town. Later, he gave much of the credit for his protection to playwright Paul Green, the university's writer-in-residence, and to Guy Johnson, a professor of sociology. He did not mention Frank Porter Graham, a strong civil rights advocate, who was then in his first year as president of the University of North Carolina, and who certainly must have assumed much of the responsibility for Hughes's safety. The night the poet spoke at the campus theater, the building was packed to overflowing and vibrant with tension, and he was protected by a special police unit. Hughes may have been protecting Graham by never mentioning that the young university president had risked his own career to defend him.

Among the poems Hughes read that night was "The Negro Mother," which brought him a standing ovation. His twenty-five-cent booklet *The Negro Mother*, containing the title poem and others, proved so popular that it sold out in a small bookshop which Abernathy and Buttitta ran near the campus. The two enterprising students, who had invited him to be their guest when the local inn refused to lodge him, also gave a farewell dinner for Hughes "in defiance of Southern custom" at a restaurant on the city's main street. "If they were willing to go through with dinner in a public restaurant in the tense atmosphere of that small town, I was willing, too," Hughes said later. The dinner went off without incident, and his first extended tour of the South did not again expose him to the potential of dangerous or controversial consequences in a white university. "Poetry," he wrote later, "took me into the hearts and homes of colored people all over the South. But it took me into no more white colleges after Chapel Hill, and into very few white homes."

Nevertheless, the deeper he traveled into Dixie, the greater seemed the distance between the races. Julia Peterkin, the white author who had won a Pulitzer Prize with her "Negro" novel, *Scarlet Sister Mary*, and who had chatted with Hughes effusively at Manhattan cocktail parties, and reviewed his book *Fine Clothes to the Jew*, refused even to see him on the porch of her home in South Carolina. In Columbia, South Carolina, he encountered still another form of "southern hospitality" at the home of Dr. Everett Clarkson Leverett Adams, a white physician-author who had made a name for himself with such books as *Nigger to Nigger* and *Congaree Sketches*.[3] Hughes should have been forewarned: he had first heard about Dr. Adams from Godmother Charlotte Mason. When the elderly doctor, who had attended the poetry reading at Benedict College, invited him to his home, Hughes should not have expected the invitation to include his host, a local black physician, and he should not have been surprised when Dr. Adams's field hands and house servants were brought in to entertain him. The scenario typified what he was to describe later as "the great social and cultural gulf between the races" in the South.

Gradually and painfully, Hughes came to understand the patterns of bigotry and paternalism which operated in so many ways in the southern states. Warm, intelligent, and understanding white acquaintances were exceedingly rare. One was the poet Will Alexander Percy, who considered it a privilege to introduce Hughes to the audience of an Afro-American church in Greenville, Mississippi, and who became the poet's life-long acquaintance.[4] "I met less than half a dozen such gentlemanly Southerners on my winter-long tour," he confessed later in *I Wonder as I Wander*. Comparing the South with the North, he claimed he "had never known such uncompromising prejudices," when indeed he had.

One of those incidents of "uncompromising prejudice" in the North became the subject of Hughes's essay, "My Most Humiliating Jim Crow Experience"—an incident which occurred not in Dixie but in downtown Cleveland. As a high school teenager, trying to have a fifty-cent lunch in Bedford's Cafeteria, he had been billed $8.65 by a white cashier who deliberately overcharged him. "That's what it costs if you want to eat! Pay your check or else put down your tray and leave it," she had told him. Langston put down his tray and left.[5]

During his tour of the South, he was often treated with deliberate rudeness, and he faced it much the same way he had in Cleveland. He was rarely aggressive and outspoken except on paper. In a Savannah railway station, where he went to buy a Sunday *New York Times*, he was told by a white policeman that he could not exit from a waiting room door for "whites only."

In order to get out of the Savannah station with the *New York Times* that day, I had to go through the train gates and follow the railroad tracks to the nearest crossing to reach the street. I had never experienced anything so absurd before. The seriousness of that white policeman and the utter stupidity of being at a door, but not permitted to go through it, made me burst out laughing as I walked along with my paper from Manhattan.

Laughing to keep from crying was one of the ways Hughes survived the South. And later still, *Laughing to Keep from Crying* was more than a symbolic title for a volume of his short stories.

BY MID-WINTER, Hughes and Lucas, his tour-manager-companion, had devised a means that not only spared them humiliation but assured a profit from the tour. Hughes's standard lecture fee was one hundred dollars, plus board and lodging, but Lucas's letters to sponsors qualified this by offering a lower cash figure of seventy-five dollars, sometimes adding, "since we would be in the vicinity, anyhow, as a *special* concession, Langston Hughes would come for fifty dollars." But in those Depression days, when some sponsoring institutions could not afford fifty dollars, Langston spoke for twenty-five dollars, and when they could afford nothing, he spoke for free. In this way, he said, "I introduced my poetry to every major city, town and campus in the South that year. No matter how small a dot on the map a town was, we did not scorn it, and my audience ranged all the way from college students to cotton pickers to kindergarten children to the inmates of old folks homes."

Besides the bookings which Lucas secured, an ad in *Opportunity* magazine elicited other engagements.

THE NEGRO POET
Langston Hughes
Reading
His Own Poems

Now booking for his first
tour of the South. Schools,
lodges, churches, clubs.

For terms and dates, write:
Business Manager
OPPORTUNITY MAGAZINE

Accompanied by Lucas, Hughes crisscrossed some states two and three times before Christmas. There was scarcely a day's rest between programs.

He was in Georgia twice, and back again in North Carolina before heading for Florida, and then to Alabama for the holidays.

In Huntsville, Alabama, where Hughes had accepted an invitation to lecture at Oakwood Junior College on January 2, he was the guest of Arna Bontemps, who was on the faculty there. Greeting the 1932 New Year with Arna, his wife, and children was like being with his own family after a long absence. Though the two poets had become close friends in New York soon after they met in late 1924, they had seen each other infrequently during the next seven years. Arna's early marriage, the birth of his children, and his lack of interest in the bohemian circles and gatherings of "Niggerati Manor" on West 136th Street, had made him something of an anomaly among his contemporaries of the Harlem Renaissance. Unlike some of his talented literary friends who had taken to the bottle or to Gurdjieff or to homosexual liaisons, Bontemps had gone his way, living in upper Harlem, trying to make ends meet without the support of a patron. As Sterling Brown, a fellow poet, would later write: "He [Bontemps] was a sober, austere, melancholy, meditative, meticulous Christian gentleman, who was far from the hedonism blatant in the 'Harlem Renaissance' credo."[6]

Hughes saw Arna as a brother, and as one as stable as a tree withstanding storm and strife. Bontemps had written children's literature, won several prizes for his poetry, and in 1931 had published his first novel, *God Sends Sunday*. But unable to support his wife and two children during the Depression on his income from writing, he had accepted a teaching post at Oakwood Junior College. Now Hughes, officially a guest of the college, was the guest of the Bontemps. It was like old times, and made more remarkable by the resumption of a collaboration they had discussed in New York the previous summer—a juvenile book about Haitian children that had been prompted by Hughes's trip to the Caribbean.

Before Hughes left Huntsville for Miami that January, he discussed the juvenile book, chapter by chapter, with Arna, providing the background descriptions that were needed to write the text. They decided it would be a travel story, based on events in the lives of a Haitian brother and sister, Popo and Fifina. An outline, submitted to Macmillan by Bontemps, was accepted almost immediately, and the book was scheduled for publication later that same year.

Hughes returned to Alabama in February, but this time his commitment was to Tuskeegee Institute, and at Tuskeegee he was bitterly disillusioned. What he learned during his two-day visit mocked the adulation he had expressed for Booker T. Washington, the institute's founder, whom he had memorialized two years earlier in a poem for the cover of the *Tuskeegee Messenger*:

Alabama Earth

Deep in Alabama earth
His buried body lies—
But higher than the swinging pines
And taller than the skies
And out of Alabama earth
To all the world there goes
The truth a simple heart has held
And the strength a strong hand knows,
While over Alabama earth
These words are gently spoken:
Serve—and hate will die unborn.
Love—and chains are broken.[7]

Experience at the rural institute founded in 1881 by Booker T. Washington all but shattered the poet's childhood memories of the "national Negro leader" he had once heard speak in Kansas. His youthful reading of "Of Mr. Booker T. Washington and Others" in *The Souls of Black Folk* had already taught him that W. E. B. Du Bois had reservations about Washington's philosophy. Hughes's own unresolved questions as a young man about Washington's segregationist policies were answered on the Tuskegee campus. There he found that Washington had really meant what he said in his famous "Atlanta Compromise" speech about the races being "separate as the five fingers": keep the races separate; teach Negroes trades and crafts so that they could engage in the "common occupations of life"; teach them to avoid politics, in which only whites should be involved. The policies and practices of Tuskegee Institute were proof of his philosophy. There were, for instance, no courses in the liberal arts or the higher theoretical sciences. White guests of the institute were accommodated in a spacious guest house, whereas Negro guests were put up in a student dormitory or, if distinguished enough, in the president's home. (Hughes was housed in a dormitory.)

Except for a visit through the laboratory of the eminent black scientist George Washington Carver, Hughes's trip to Tuskegee filled him with gloom and discouragement, and a rage that rekindled his militancy. Some three months later he expressed all this in a poem:

Red Flag on Tuskeegee

White workers of the South:
Miners,
Farmers,

Mechanics,
Mill hands,
Shop girls,
Railway men,
Servants,
Tobacco workers,
Share croppers,
GREETINGS!
I am the black worker
  Listen:
That the land might be ours,
And the mines and the factories and
the office towers
At Harlan, Richmond, Gastonia,
Atlanta, New Orleans:
That the plants and the roads and
  the tools of power
Be ours:
Let us forget what Booker T. said:
"Separate as the fingers."
He knew he lied.
Let us become instead, you and I,
One single hand
That can united rise
To smash the old dead dogmas of
  the past—
To kill the lies of color
That keep the rich enthroned
And drive us to the time-clock and
  the plow
Helpless, stupid, scattered, and alone
  —as now—
Race against race,
Because one is black
Another white of face.
Let us new lessons learn,
All workers,
New life-ways make,
One union form;
Until the future burns out
Every past mistake
Let us get together, say:

"You are my brother, black or white.
You my sister—now—today!"
For me, no more, the great migration
   to the North.
Instead: Migration into force and
   power—
Tuskeegee with a red flag on the
   tower!
On every lynching tree, a poster crying FREE
Because, O poor white workers,
You have linked your hands with me.

We did not know that we were brothers.
Now we know!
That we were strong.
Now we see
In union lies our strength.
Let union be
The force that breaks the time-clock,
Smashes misery,
Takes land,
Takes factories,
Takes office towers,
Takes tools and banks and mines,
Railroads, ships and dams,
Until the forces of the world
Are ours!

White worker,
Here is my hand.

Today,
We're Man to Man.[8]

In the *Afro-American* newspaper, "Red Flag on Tuskeegee" appeared on the same page with an article that quoted Hughes as saying, "If the Communists don't awaken the Negroes of the South, who will? Certainly not the race leaders whose schools and jobs depend on white philanthropy and who preach 'be nice' and keep quiet."[9] While no Communist, Hughes had been radicalized by his journey South, and made ever more sympathetic to communism. Added to his disillusion with Tuskeegee was the uninterest he found there in the Scottsboro case. "Over Alabama that winter," he wrote later, "lay the shadow of Scottsboro. But I heard no discussion whatsoever of the case at Tuskeegee, although at nearby Kilby eight of the nine Negro boys involved were in the death house where I went to see them."

No visit he made on his long journey through the Deep South was as difficult for him as a Sunday visit to the Scottsboro boys in Kilby Prison in Montgomery. In a dismal prison corridor, separated by bars from the eight Scottsboro inmates, he read them his humorous verse. They appeared to have abandoned all hope. They didn't know who Hughes was, and his reading made no more impression on them than the prayers of the local black minister who accompanied him. He expressed to them his "hope that their appeals would end well and that they would soon be free."

Only one youth came up to prison bars and shook hands with Hughes. And to this young man, Clarence Norris, who three times would be sentenced to die in the electric chair but ultimately end up the only Scottsboro survivor, Hughes dedicated a poem seven years later:

August 19th...
A Poem for Clarence Norris

What flag will fly for me
When I die?
What flag of red and white and
    blue,
Half-mast, against the sky?
I'm not the President,
Nor the Honorable So-and-So.
But only one of the
Scottsboro Boys
Doomed "by law" to go.
August 19th is the date.
Put it in your book.
The date that I must keep with
    death.
Would you like to come and look?
You will see a black boy die.
Would you like to come and cry?
Maybe tears politely shed
Help the dead.
Or better still, they may help you—
For if you let the "law" kill me.
Are you free?
August 19th is the date.
Clarence Norris is my name.

The sentence, against me,
Against you, the same.
August 19th is the date.
Thunder in the sky.
In Alabama
A young black boy will die.
August 19th is the date.
Judges in high places
Still preserve their dignity
And dispose of cases.
August 19th is the date.
Rich people sit and fan
And sip cool drinks and do no
    work—
Yet they rule the land.
August 19th is the date.
The electric chair.
Swimmers on cool beaches
With their bodies bare.
August 19th is the date.
European tours.
Summer camps for the kids
If they are yours.
Me, I never had no kids.
I never had no wife.
August 19th is the date
To take my life.
August 19th is the date.
Will your church bells ring?
August 19th is the date.
Will the choir sing?
August 19th is the date.
Will the ball games stop?
August 19th is the date.
Will the jazz bands play?
August 19th is the date
When I go away.
August 19th is the date
Thunder in the sky.
August 19th is the date.
Scottsboro Boy must die.
August 19th is the date.

Judges in high places—
August 19th is the date—
Still dispose of cases.
August 19th is the date.
Rich people sit and fan.
August 19th is the date.
Who shall rule our land?
August 19th is the date.
Swimmers on cool beaches.
August 19th is the date.

World!
Stop *all the leeches*
That suck your life away and mine,
        World!
Stop *all the leeches*
That use their power to strangle
        hope,
That make of the law a lyncher's
        rope,
That drop their bombs on China
        and Spain,
That have no pity for hunger or
        pain,
That always, forever, close the door
Against the likes of me, the poor.
AUGUST 19th IS THE DATE.
What flag will fly for me?
AUGUST 19th IS THE DATE.
So deep my grave will be.
AUGUST 19th IS THE DATE.
I'm not the honorable So-and-So.
AUGUST 19th IS THE DATE.
Just a poor boy doomed to go.
AUGUST 19th IS THE DATE.

AUGUST 19th IS THE DATE.
Can you make death wait?
AUGUST 19th IS THE DATE.
Will you let me die?
AUGUST 19th IS THE DATE.
Can we make death wait?
AUGUST 19th IS THE DATE.

> *Will you let me die?*
> AUGUST 19th IS THE DATE.
> AUGUST 19th IS THE DATE.
> AUGUST 19th... AUGUST 19th...
> AUGUST 19th... AUGUST 19th...
> AUGUST 19th...[10]

Hughes's lecture tour forced him to forgo a meeting with the youngest Scottsboro prisoner, then fourteen-year-old Roy Wright, who was behind bars in Birmingham, spared the death penalty but not a life sentence.

Distressed that "not one Alabama Negro school" had sent visitors or even held a protest meeting in the state, he had said as much when he visited Arna Bontemps at Oakwood Junior College. There he was dissuaded from trying to interview Ruby Bates, one of the white plaintiffs who under oath had recanted her original testimony and allied herself with the International Labor Defense in an effort to gain freedom for the Scottsboro Boys:

> I wanted to interview Ruby Bates in Huntsville, but the Negro teachers at Oakwood thought I must be crazy. They would take no part in helping me locate her, and none of them would ac-company me to see her. Finally, they dissuaded me from the attempt, on the grounds that I would be taking my life in my hands, as well as endangering the college.

He took some consolation from the fact that he had sent four of his poems and his play *Scottsboro Limited* to New York to be published as an illustrated booklet, the proceeds from the sale of which would go to the Scottsboro Defense Fund. In February, he also wrote an essay, "Brown America in Jail: Kilby," and sent it to *Opportunity*. As far as he was concerned, his readers must not forget that Kilby Prison was symbolic, and that within its confines "all of Brown America was locked up."

BY MARCH 1, 1932, when Hughes and Lucas reached St. Louis, after a month spent between Mississippi, Arkansas, Louisiana, and Tennessee, they were relieved to head westward. Hughes had seen enough of the Deep South to feel deeply what he wrote over a decade later in the poem "One-Way Ticket":

> I am fed up
> With Jim Crow laws,
> People who are cruel
> And afraid,
> Who lynch and run,
> Who are scared of me
> And me of them.

> I pick up my life
> And take it away
> On a one-way ticket—
> Gone up North,
> Gone out West,
> Gone!

After a lecture at the State University of Iowa in Iowa City, he moved on to the University of Kansas in Lawrence, where a special welcome awaited him. The university campus, of course, had changed, and so had the city after eighteen years, but memories of his childhood spent there with his grandmother overwhelmed him. His return to Kansas proved to him that he had not overcome the memories expressed in a stream-of-consciousness essay written five years earlier:

> My grandmother died on Thursday. Grandmother. I didn't want her to die on Thursday. Every Thursday I sold papers and I missed selling papers because she died on Thursday. Somebody woke me up at three o'clock in the morning because my grandmother was dead. I went outdoors looking for my grandmother. She wasn't there. The moon was there, cold and ugly, but no ghost of my Grandmother. They wrapped her up in sheets and sent her away to the undertaker's. I didn't sell any papers on Thursday. I missed my grandmother. We moved away to another town. I went to another school. I didn't sell any more papers on Thursdays. I went to work in a big hotel. I missed my grandmother.[11]

His memories were stirred again a few days later when he spoke at Langston University in Langston, Oklahoma, where the town and the school were named for his great-uncle, John Mercer Langston. It was the same town where his parents had met some thirty-four years before. Having turned thirty just weeks before visiting Oklahoma, Hughes had told Bontemps that the older he grew, the more distant he felt from both his parents. His father, who still lived in Mexico, he had not seen for a decade. His mother he saw—or tried to see—at least once a year, and between times, when he could afford to, he sent her money. She expected it, for her circumstances had not changed much; she was still living in Cleveland and working as a domestic.

Heading eastward from Oklahoma, he entertained thoughts of seeing his mother on the way to New York, where he returned at Easter. But other matters took precedence, including arrangements for a poetry reading tour of Texas. In an unpublished manuscript, Hughes explained how he got to the Lone Star State:

> After Easter, I came near not getting to Texas in time for my programs. On the spur of the moment, Raddie decided to remain in New York and get married. His fiancée did not want him to go away again, so he got married. I had to find a new driver for my Southwestern and Pacific Coast tour. With Raddie's help by phone, we located in Philadelphia another classmate of ours, Ronald Derry. Derry said he'd love to go to California where he'd never been. . . . The only fly in the ointment of his enthusiasm —and my delight in finding another congenial driver—was that Derry could not drive!. . . Finally we located still another class-mate, George Lee, who could drive. . . . On Easter Monday, Lee, Derry and I headed for Texas. Lee was to share in the tour profits, but Derry just went along for the ride. Lee I called my Tour Manager, Derry I christened my personal secretary. As-tonished college students in Texas thought a poet must be very rich indeed to be traveling with both a Manager and a Secretary. [12]

Hughes, accompanied by his "manager" and his "secretary," gave readings in Dallas, Prairie View, Tyler, Beaumont, Houston, San Antonio and El Paso—before heading farther West.

In New Mexico and Arizona, where the three weary travelers hoped to see none of the Colored and White signs they had seen in Texas, they heard "We don't serve you folks here" in most restaurants and hotels, but in late April they received a warm welcome in Los Angeles, especially Hughes himself, who was the guest of a long-time friend from Kansas, Loren Miller.

A lawyer and editor of the state's oldest black newspaper, *The California Eagle*, Miller was only one year younger than Hughes. He had been born in Nebraska and reared in Kansas, where he attended college and law school. They had mutual friends and had kept in touch through them. In Los Angeles, Loren introduced Hughes to a standing-room-only audience as "the first Negro poet in America to span the continent, coast to coast, with his poetry." In response to all the publicity in *The California Eagle*, more invitations came than Hughes could accept. He was already booked solid, but when the local John Reed Club invited him to speak on the "Social Implications of Current Negro Literature," he could not refuse.

On this his first trip to the Golden State, he also wanted to visit friends and relatives, including his cousin, Flora Coates, and an uncle, John S. P. Hughes. From all Langston had heard since childhood, his uncle John's reputation aroused in him as much curiosity as his own father's exile in

Mexico. In recent years he had come to understand why relatives called his father and uncle the "gold dust twins." Though certainly not twins, both had migrated west in the late 1890s to purchase land in Oklahoma Territory during the Homestead Settlement. John Hughes, bidding everything he had on a piece of property, had struck oil, leased his land, moved to Los Angeles and acquired more real estate and more money. He had never married. His sister Sallie once remarked to Langston, "Your Uncle John is a strange, quiet man, but he's nothing like your father."

Langston could not have agreed with her more. When he visited his uncle's modest home in Los Angeles, he found little resemblance—except in size and color—between his uncle and his father. Beneath his uncle's aloof smile, there was a warmth which belied the reticent, cool manner. He listened with obvious interest when Langston talked, and when he bade goodbye, he pressed a hundred-dollar bill into his nephew's hand.

If meeting his uncle John had its rewards, so did a letter the poet received from San Francisco. It came from Noel Sullivan, who would eventually become as close a friend as any relative Hughes ever had. The two men had begun exchanging letters some six weeks before, after the poet's visit to Arkansas, where relatives of Eulah Pharr, Sullivan's housekeeper, had characterized Sullivan as "almost like a saint, . . . witty and wise, rich and kind—and not only has a colored staff in his home, but many colored friends in Paris, London, New York, everywhere." Mrs. Pharr herself was "colored" and, doubtless, prompted by her interest and concern, Sullivan's invitations to Hughes to be his houseguest had followed the poet to Texas and on to California, where poetry readings were scheduled in Oakland, San Jose, San Francisco, and Carmel.

Hughes accepted Sullivan's invitation and told him he would arrive in San Francisco by May 15. Derry and Lee decided to remain in Los Angeles for the summer Olympics, and Hughes drove north with Loren Miller. In San Francisco, at 2323 Hyde Street, high atop Russian Hill, they could not have been treated more royally. Sullivan's congenial staff, his spacious mansion, with its sweeping view of the bay, provided the poet, as well as other guests, with all the luxuries of a vacation. Hughes recalled it all vividly:

> After a long winter of touring across the whole country, I was more weary than I realized. To sink into a marvelously comfortable bed with sea breezes blowing in the window and be awakened the next morning by fresh orange juice and steaming coffee, then breakfast on the flowered terrace, with a car at my disposal later if I wished to see the city—all this exceeded any dreams of comfort I had ever had. There was even a secretary to whom I might dictate letters if I chose, and two gardeners who would

cut whatever flowers a guest might wish for his bedroom vases.
This well-ordered house that I was invited to use became my
base during my month of lecturing on the Coast.

Sullivan, who was born to wealth, suffered no economic deprivations
during the Depression. If anything, his inheritance had increased in 1930,
when his father, Frank J. Sullivan, and an uncle, Senator James D. Phelan,
died within three months of each other, leaving him the bulk of their
estates. Sullivan's mansion, once owned by the Scottish author Robert
Louis Stevenson, had been in the family since the early 1900s, when Noel's
mother, Alice Phelan Sullivan, purchased it as a home for Carmelite nuns.
After the death of his father, Noel had turned the house into a kind of
cultural center, where he frequently entertained artists and writers. While
Hughes was a guest, the motion picture actor Nelson Eddy spent one
weekend; distinguished international visitors dined there regularly. As Hughes
wrote later, "Everyday there were new guests for meals."

Eight years Hughes's senior, Sullivan was a bachelor, and an aspiring
concert singer, whose deep interest in the arts and humane causes was
expressed in generous gifts of time and money. He had studied music
abroad for some years and, living in France during the First World War, he
had volunteered as an ambulance driver for the American Friends Service.
Like his sister, Ada, who became a nun, he sought spiritual quests and
devoted himself not only to the arts and artists but to organizations such as
the California Committee of the American League to Abolish Capital Pun-
ishment. The man and all he stood for endeared him to Hughes, and for a
quarter of a century he was the poet's most trusted confidant—in some
instances even more so than Arna Bontemps.

Within a few months of their meeting, sensing that Sullivan, like himself,
was a homosexual—a fact never publicly expressed—Hughes wrote to him:
"I think, Noel, that life has given us the same loneliness."[13] Whether or not
they shared the same loneliness, they certainly shared the same virtues of
generosity, thoughtfulness, and gratitude. Few men more similar in temperament ever became better friends. They filled their lives with people;
they remembered birthdays and other special occasions; they wrote long
letters. Yet neither would ever fill the void of loneliness or overcome the
fear of being rejected, which resulted in reaching out to everyone, but
making a close, emotional commitment to no one.

Hughes, the very private man, who could be the public figure and still
keep a distance, was content and at ease on Hyde Street. He found much to
laugh and talk about with both houseguests and staff. Some time later, in an
unpublished draft of *I Wonder as I Wander*, Hughes wrote:

One night my host turned the house over to Eulah Pharr, and her husband so that they might give a party for me.... The house rocked with music and dancing until after midnight. It was a wonderfully jolly party, and among the guests was the promising young baritone, Kenneth Spencer. Noel Sullivan was a guest too.[14]

Eulah Pharr arranged for Hughes to speak at the local Negro settlement house. Word had spread about the success of his readings at the University of California at Berkeley, and in Oakland, San Jose, Fresno, and Bakersfield; and the night of his program at the Negro settlement house, black and white, rich and poor, the known and unknown gathered before the doors opened. This had happened before in other places, and it would happen again.

Ramon Navarro, soon to be famous for his role with Greta Garbo in *Mata Hari*, was in the audience when Hughes read at San Francisco's plush Women's City Club, and the first meeting between the poet and the actor there was said not to have been their last. Years later, rumors about them would spread—they were seen together here and there; they were more than friends; they shared living quarters in New York. But whether the rumors were true or false, no one seemed to know. When Navarro, who was three years Hughes's senior, met his death in 1968 in a *crime passionnel* at the hands of a male lover, gossip had linked him "romantically" with almost every man he knew.

A few days later, before he was scheduled to give a reading in Carmel, California, Hughes made a quick trip to speak in Portland and Seattle. There he was the guest of Horace Cayton—then a local policeman, but later a social worker in Chicago, and the co-author of an important study of urban life, *Black Metropolis*—one of the many people whose path would cross Hughes's again in years to come.

When he returned to Sullivan's, a telegram awaited him. It was from Louise Thompson in New York. A small group of Afro-Americans was being organized to make a film in Russia for Meschrabpom Film of the Worker's International Relief. Would he agree to write the English dialogue for the screenplay? The group would sail from New York by mid-June.

Hughes responded affirmatively. Louise, as volunteer executive secretary of the Co-operating Committee on Production of a Soviet Film on Negro Life, had already written him in March about the possibility of his being part of the interracial sponsoring committee. He had wired her from Kansas City:

> Happy be on Committee and consider possibility going to
> Russia...Am awaiting your letter. I shall probably be New
> York Easter. But on to Texas and California for April lecture
> dates. Will see you soon. But keep it quiet as have promised
> devote all New York time to play [Cock o' the World].[15]

Later he explained, "I thought if I were ever to work in motion pictures
or learn about them, it would have to be abroad." He knew that Hollywood
was closed to black scenarists, except as ghost writers of B-grade movies.
He did not want to put himself in Wallace Thurman's position, by writing
such scripts. The opportunity to work in films was one he might never find
at home, and his California friends Loren Miller and Matthew Crawford,
who had also been invited to participate, urged him to accept. Hughes
wrote Louise that he, Miller, and Crawford would be journeying east in his
car, in time for the New York sailing date. "Hold that boat, cause it's an ark
to me," he wired Louise on June 6.[16]

The last days of Hughes's California trip were spent at Carmel-by-the-
Sea, where he lectured in late May to the local John Reed Club and signed
his name to a petition supporting the Communist Party's 1932 presidential
candidates, William Z. Foster and James W. Ford. In signing the petition,
he joined a group of writers that included Sherwood Anderson, Malcolm
Cowley, John Dos Passos, Granville Hicks, Edmund Wilson, and two of
the most famous Carmel residents, Lincoln Steffens and Ella Winter, who
declared the major political parties "hopelessly bankrupt."

Steffens and Winter, who had divorced each other but were living together in Carmel that summer, had more than enough stories and advice for
Hughes about the Soviet Union. Ella, who was then completing her book
Red Virtue: Human Relationships in the New Russia, gave glowing reports of
collective experiments under the Bolsheviks. Steffens was more humorous
and less enthusiastic. He told Hughes to "be sure to take soap and toilet
paper for yourself—don't part with it!—and lipsticks and silk stockings for
the girls." Having listened to Steffens advise him "to be prepared *not* to like
anything in the Soviet Union—except what he called 'its potential,' " Hughes
remembered what the famous muckraker had remarked on his return from
Russia in the 1920s: "I've seen the future and it works."

"As I left him on the steps of his home within earshot of the Pacific surf,"
Hughes wrote later, "the frail little old journalist with the white goatee and
the twinkling eyes stretched out his hand in the misty Carmel sunlight and
wished me well."

So much had to be done so fast in preparation for his Russian trip that
Hughes hardly had time to tell his mother goodbye when he stopped in
Cleveland for a day in June before he set sail from New York. In "Coast to

Coast," an unpublished manuscript, he summed up the trip he had begun in October 1931:

> I had been nine months on the road, reading poetry almost nightly from Harlem to Houston, Miami, to Seattle, I had interpreted my poems from huge institutes like Tuskeegee and Hampton to little backwoods schools whose names I had never before heard. I had given lectures at the University of California at Berkeley, Tougaloo College in Mississippi, at the University of North Carolina in Chapel Hill, and the New African Methodist Church in Beaumont, Texas. I had met thousands of people, eaten hundreds of southern chicken dinners, attended dozens of receptions, drunk gallons of corn licker at parties, and driven some 36,000 miles over all kinds of roads from the sticky clay of Georgia to the gray-black mud of the Panhandle. I was tired. I looked forward to a long restful boat trip across the Atlantic.[17]

He came close to missing the boat's June 14 midnight sailing from the North German Line pier in New York. "The ship's gangplank was already two feet in the air when I reached it," he wrote later. "They lowered it to let me aboard."[18] Huffing and puffing with two suitcases, a trunk, a victrola, a box of phonograph records, and a typewriter, he made it aboard as the ship was signaling her departure with the horns blowing.

By the time he caught his breath, the S.S. *Europa* was steaming through the harbor, heading toward the open sea.

❧ I I ❧

Black and White

Hughes's hope for a "long restful boat trip across the Atlantic" was unfulfilled. His claim that "the voyage was fun," and that he "practiced German, studied Russian, played deck games and danced," was hardly the whole truth. The rest of it, like so much he omitted from I Wonder as I Wander, was another story. If life can sometimes be stranger than fiction, it had all the elements of being so that June on the S.S. Europa.

Among the characters omitted from the poet's account of that drama on the high seas was his erstwhile friend Alain Locke. He was probably the last person Hughes wanted to see, but he was very much there, making trouble as usual. Bound for his annual summer vacation abroad, after having suffered a mild heart attack that May, Locke was going to a European spa to recover. Having learned a week before the sailing date that he might encounter his friendly enemies, Langston and Louise, on the Europa, he had tried frantically to change his own travel arrangements.

Charlotte Mason, of course, had to be consulted before he could make any move. "The Russian picture party, headed by Langston and Louise, sails on the same boat with me June 15th," he wrote her. "What do you think of that?"[1] "I see nothing at present to do but go ahead...but I will keep the matter open until I can see you and get your judgment and advice as to which is the lesser of the two evils."[2]

At age forty-six Locke was more emotionally dependent on Godmother than he was at forty, when he met her, and it was on her advice that he finally decided to sail first class instead of second. "Won't they construe my changing class as weakness and fear of them," he wrote her plaintively.[3] He considered changing to the S.S. Bremen until he learned the group might also make the change.[4] But he found they were all in the same boat. He could not have been in more of a quandary than when he penned his first note to Godmother from the Europa:

> I wonder what's the use of calculating after all. This world had a
> way of playing jokes all the time. Instead of my changing, they

changed. . . . I stayed on deck until the boat sailed at 12:30 AM—
and then saw a wild crowd of young Negroes on the riverside
end of the pier. I went to bed convinced something was wrong.[5]

Aboard ship, Locke's desire to avoid what he called his "Langston eclipse"
hardly stopped him from following the poet around like a gull hawking a
fish. In letters composed like fiction—a talent he might have developed had
he given it the same time and energy he gave his correspondence—he wrote
of his every move to Godmother.

> Yesterday morning was up earlier than usual (before breakfast)
> asking for the passenger list. . . . The Russian Negro party is in
> third class. . . . This afternoon, after lunch, finally got permission
> to go over. . . . Langston came by the open door on the way to
> the bath—just getting up at 3 PM. He looked surprised for a
> moment, then suddenly glum—I merely said "Hello Langston"
> and he "ah hello there" in a mock jaunty tone—no handshake. "I
> was on my way to the bath."
> "So I see. Having a nice trip I hope."
> "Sure."[6]

Such encounters might have been innocent enough if Locke had not tried
to pit certain members of the film group against one another. Having
discovered among them two former Howard students, Leonard Hill and
Henry Lee Moon, he used them as informants, noting in his journals and
letters nearly everything they told him. The barriers protecting the privacy
of first-class passengers could have kept Locke separated from the party of
twenty-two young Afro-Americans in third class, had he really wanted to
be separated from them. But every day he went down to third class and
associated with the Hughes-Thompson group. Learning there was political
dissension in their ranks, he capitalized on it, spreading the word to his
fellow first-class passengers, including Ralph Bunche and others who had
read of the group's mission in the newspapers, which had been covering the
story for weeks.

The mission, sponsored by an interracial and international committee—
the Co-operating Committee for Production of a Soviet Film on Negro
Life—was to make a "realistic and historical" moving picture about the
Negro in America.[7] Chairman of the committee was militant Jamaican
socialist W. A. Domingo, whose name had been well known in Harlem for
over a decade. A one-time supporter of black nationalist leader Marcus
Garvey, whom he later denounced as a "Black Barnum," Domingo had
spared no words in making public statements about the relevance of the
Black and White film. In a letter inviting friends of the committee to a
bon-voyage party for the cast, he had announced:

The Committee believes that a pictorial event of great artistic
and social significance is heralded by the completion of its plans.
The American Negro has never been portrayed on screen or
stage in his true character, and this film, *Black and White*, to be
produced by the Meschrabpom Film Company of Moscow,
will be the first departure from the traditional pattern. It will
trace the development of the Negro people in America, their
work, their play, their progress, their difficulties—devoid of
sentimentality as well as of buffoonery. Meanwhile, Hollywood
producers continue to manufacture sentimental and banal pictures, and particularly cling to traditional types in portraying the
Negro. We therefore believe that *Black and White*, produced under
the best technical and artistic experience of Russia, will be welcomed by discriminating patrons of the cinema and those people
sincerely interested in the Negro. . . .[8]

When the group of twenty-two participants set sail, they included—Hughes
wrote later—"an art student just out of Hampton, a teacher, a girl elocution-
ist from Seattle, three would-be writers other than myself, a very pretty
divorcée who traveled on alimony, a female swimming instructor, and
various clerks and stenographers—all distinctly from the white collar and
student classes."[9]

Few of them were acquainted before the trip, and only two were professional performers: Wayland Rudd, who had appeared in *Porgy*, and Sylvia
Garner, who had played a minor role in *Scarlet Sister Mary*. But with jobs
difficult to find in America during the Depression, members of the film
group had jumped at the opportunity to travel with all expenses paid,
except for their boat fare from New York. As Hughes said afterward:

That most of our group were not actors seems to have been due
to the fact that very few professional theatre people were willing
to pay their own fares to travel all the way to Russia to sign
contracts they had never seen. Only a band of eager and adven-
turous young students, teachers, writers and would be actors
were willing to do that, looking forward to the fun and wonder
of a foreign land as much as to film-making.[10]

Those seeking "fun and wonder" were, as it turned out, the ones least
interested in leftist politics or the Soviet Union. Coming from California,
Minnesota, Virginia, Washington state, Washington, D.C., the West Indies, and New York, they represented varying opinions on the subject of
communism. It created a drama only too soon. The group had not reached
the middle of the Atlantic before the members began to argue and split into

opposing political camps. Their first day at sea, only a minority would vote with Langston, Louise Thompson, and Loren Miller to send a cable in support of the mother of two of the Scottsboro Boys, Mrs. Ada Wright, who was then on a European speaking tour for the Scottsboro Defense. A few days later, the three were voted down again when they suggested that their group be called the "Negro Film Workers Guild."

Only Allen McKenzie, the group leader, was a member of the Communist Party, and while he openly said so, he was not so vocal about Communist causes as Langston, Louise, and Loren. All three sent their names off individually that summer to *The New York Amsterdam News* and the *Daily Worker* in support of the Communist presidential slate of Foster and Ford. Their opponents in the group, who called them the "L-raising Trio," seemed not to bother them in the least. The more Langston, Louise, and Loren stood their ground, the more followers they won. Meanwhile, those who opposed them were spending more time with Alain Locke, who was daily writing to Godmother about how he was trying to remain "neutral" through it all.

The professor, for all his curious interest in the group, had no desire to associate with them publicly on the ship. When Ralph Bunche, a Howard University colleague, asked for an introduction to Hughes, Locke obliged after trying to avoid it. And when, at last, he introduced them, he hurried off, leaving the two men standing on the deck. Locke had an even more difficult time making excuses the day he took Bunche to the third-class social hall, then tried to dash off to avoid being photographed with the group. Godmother got the whole story as soon as he fled to his cabin.

> We went in—and they came forward effusively—took us on deck and said you have just come in time for the picture the ship's photographer is making of the group. For a moment my blood ran cold. . . . Bunche fortunately had his camera along—so I said oh, that gives us a chance to get one too. So we stood back of the photographer while they shifted and posed—and waited for stragglers. Langston was the one of the last to come—in light gray flannels, a striped jersey sweater with a rose in his buttonhole. Louise, who had been on the scene and had left—came back, and sat on the deck in the front row. As she passed up to the photographer with some directions—she caught my eye— and then said "How do you do, Dr. Locke—I heard you were on board." I said "How do you do Louise. I knew you were on board."[11]

The professor was no less reluctant to give his European address to group members than he was to be photographed with them. When he disembarked at Cherbourg, two days before they landed at Bremerhaven, he told his two young informants in the group to write him in care of his travel agency, Thomas Cook & Sons. "I cut my bridges with my mail," he wrote Charlotte Mason, "for I do not want to have several homeless and penniless derelicts on my hands."[12]

IN BERLIN, where the film party stayed two days before continuing by rail to Stettin, thence to Helsinki by steamer, they encountered what Langston later called "the first of our experiences with the famous Russian red tape." Visas had been impossible to obtain in New York, because no diplomatic relations then existed between the United States and the Soviet Union, and the Soviet visas, which Meschrabpom Film officials thought they had arranged to be picked up at the Russian Embassy in Berlin, were not there. "In fact," Hughes said later, "it seemed the Russian consulate had not been alerted as to our coming at all." Meanwhile, the group missed the travel connections to Leningrad via Finland. They spent the night in Berlin, at the time one of the entertainment capitals of Europe.

But one night there was more than enough for Hughes. "In spite of racial freedom," he wrote later, "Berlin seemed to me a wretched city. . . . The streets nearby teemed with prostitutes, pimps, panderers and vendors of dirty pictures. Some of the young men in our group got acquainted for the first time with what Americans in the pre-Kinsey era termed 'perversions.' " In that cosmopolitan city of five million, throbbing with as much decadence as creative energy, and still trying to heal the wounds of defeat from World War I, Hughes could see the writing on the wall—the end of the Weimar Republic several months before Hitler and his Nazis took over.

In Leningrad, where the film group arrived by rail a few days later, the atmosphere was quite different. Both culturally and economically the Soviet Union proved full of surprises. The twenty-two Americans had brought with them certain things they thought were unobtainable in Russia—canned goods, sugar, coffee, soap, toilet paper—but they were mistaken. Anything they wished for in the way of commodities, their Soviet hosts made available to their "American Negro worker comrades." In Leningrad, they were banqueted at the October Hotel with a meal which Hughes described later as running "all the way from soup on through roast chicken and vegetables right down to ice cream and black coffee."[13] In Moscow, they were officially greeted and photographed at the Nikolayevsky Railway Station before being hurried off to the Grand Hotel through streets full of cheering Muscovites.

But their appearance caused concerned whispers at the Meschrabpom Film studio. The German director, Karl Yunghans, did not know how a creditable film about exploited American Negro workers (to be called *Black and White*) could be made with a cast that looked more white than black, did not know Negro work songs, and, ranging in age from twenty-two to thirty-two, had not a tired, aging worker in it. Years later Hughes noted:

> I had traversed the South once, but many in our group had never crossed the Mason-Dixon line. They had little feeling for folk rhythms, and liking for the idiom. Being city people, college-trained, they were too intellectual for such old-time songs, which to them smacked of bandannas and stereotypes. However, in order to become movie stars, they were willing to try to learn "All God's Chillun Got Shoes," "Didn't My Lord Deliver Daniel?" or the "Hammer Song."

Nevertheless, every member of the group, including Hughes, signed contracts providing each of them 400 rubles per month, accommodations at the Grand Hotel, and ration books to shop in the stores. In the meantime they were at leisure until a script could be completed, and they spent many an afternoon skinny-dipping with Muscovites in the Park of Rest and Culture, and many evenings at the Meyerhold Theatre, the Bolshoi Opera House, the Moscow Art Theatre, and the Hotel Metropole Bar. As Hughes said later, "The reception accorded us twenty-two Negroes who came to make a movie—and whom the Muscovites took to be artists—could not have been more cordial had we been a Theatre Guild company starring the Lunts." They were invited to receptions, museums, factories, schools. The press hailed them with front-page photographs and stories. Hughes was interviewed on the radio. Negro residents of Moscow invited them to their homes, and the great Russian film director, Sergei Eisenstein, gave a party in their honor.

Eisenstein, world renowned for his films, *Strike, Potemkin,* and *October,* was not connected with *Black and White,* though Hughes must have wished he were when the script finally appeared. Written by a Russian who had never been to America, it seemed "foreign" to Hughes even in English translation; and revising it, which Hughes was called upon to do, seemed nearly impossible. He found the script "so interwoven with major and minor impossibilities and improbabilities that it would have seemed like a burlesque on the screen."

Set in Birmingham, the story presented what Hughes later described as a "trade union version of the Civil War." The protagonists were Negro workers, and although the leading white character was a progressive labor organizer, the villains were reactionary whites. The story line was credible enough, but many incidents in the plot were unbelievable. For instance, a scene suggesting that Red Army soldiers would join and rescue black workers in a riot against whites struck Hughes as ludicrously fantastic:

At first I was astonished at what I read. Then I laughed until I cried. And I wasn't crying really because the script was funny. I was crying because the writer meant well, but knew so little about his subject and the result was a pathetic hodgepodge of good intentions and faulty facts.

In conference after conference with Pudovkin, Ekk, and other Russian cinema experts, Hughes pointed out scenes, incidents, and dialogue that he considered either absurd or false, but aware that Lovett Forte-Whiteman— one of the Harlem organizers of the American Communist Party and then resident in Moscow—had contributed to the script, and that it had been approved by the Comintern, Hughes was reluctant to be too critical.

Rehearsing Negro spirituals and folk songs only added to the chaos. "The first rehearsal of the music," Hughes said later, "was funnier than anything in the script." Except for Sylvia Garner, most of the cast couldn't carry a tune. Moreover, the director Karl Yunghans spoke so little English that he could hardly make himself understood to the cast. Invited from Berlin by Meschrabpom especially for the production, he had recently completed an African travelogue, but that hardly prepared him for the dilemmas of *Black and White*. Concerned about delays in the picture, which Meschrabpom intended to be the first racial epic of its kind, Yunghans was also apprehensive about the choice of the leading white actor for the film.

John Bovington, an American dancer in Moscow, had been chosen to play the role of the progressive labor leader. "When Mr. Bovington showed up at the studio," Hughes wrote, "we did not think he looked like an labor organizer." A dévoté of the school of modern interpretive dancing, he had come to Moscow seeking "artistic freedom" (like Isadora Duncan), and he no more had the appearance of a "worker" than the rest of the cast. Although convinced that poor Yunghans was ready to jump in the Moscow River because of "an absurd scenario, tone deaf Negroes, and for a labor organizer, a dancer," Hughes saw even worse problems brewing in the film group.

Some members, knowing they had not come to Moscow just to sing spirituals every day, began to act up. "The days were long," Hughes said later, "and at night public places closed down too early to exhaust the energies of a group of lively Harlemites." Ignoring the advice of their executive secretary, Louise Thompson, "to uphold the honor of our race," they began to behave as tempestuously as movie stars on a Hollywood set. One female member attempted a dramatic suicide by swallowing poison in her canopied bed at the Grand Hotel. Several others refused overtures to attend a huge rally for the Scottsboro Boys in the Park of Rest and Culture, claiming they had not come to Moscow to act like Communists.

For Hughes, attending a Scottsboro rally in Moscow that July was nothing he would not have done in the United States, where his booklet *Scottsboro Limited* was being distributed in his absence. When offers came to translate it into Russian that summer, he requested that any proceeds from sales be sent to the Scottsboro Defense Fund. His presence in the Soviet Union was simply further evidence of his steady move toward the left. He had been moving in that direction for several years, and in 1932 he wanted the world to know it. He reflected it in the poems and essays he sent from the Soviet Union. One of his prose-poems, which appeared in *The Afro-American* that July 30, endorsed the American Communist Party Presidential candidates, Foster and Ford, and was a panegyric to the Soviet form of government:

> Arise, ye prisoners of starvation, you workers in the cotton fields of the South, and vote (but can you vote in a democracy?) for Foster and Ford.
>
> Arise, ye wretched of the earth, you black ones everywhere— hungry, underpaid, ragged in Cleveland, Detroit, Atlanta, Los Angeles—denied the rights of man—give your vote to Foster and Ford. For justice thunders condemnation. Karl Marx said it could not last forever—the brutality and stupidity of capitalism. It can't. Nobody can oppress, and oppress and oppress, without the hands of the new world rising to strike them down—in America, Ford and Foster are those hands.
>
> A better world's in birth! Look at Russia—nobody hungry, no racial differences, no color line, nobody poor. Listen to Foster and Ford....

That was not the half of it. By September he had come forth even more strongly in *New Masses* with his long poem, "Good Morning, Revolution." Like lightning bolt on bolt, he struck again in the September/October issue of *The Negro Worker*, where "The Same" and "Goodbye, Christ," two of his longest and most controversial poems, were published for the first time.

Uppermost in his mind when writing for publications such as *The Negro Worker* (an organ of the German-based International Trade Unions Committee) was the need to reach the working class. He knew he had already reached foreign intellectuals through *International Literature*, the central organ of the Union of Revolutionary Writers—some of whose members, incidentally, he met that summer before he left Moscow for Odessa. One was the poet Julian Anissimov, who translated some of Hughes's poems and introduced him to the Soviet literary critic Lydia Filatova. His name well known among the Russian literati, Hughes found himself compared with his literary contemporary, Claude McKay, who had been in Russia in 1922–23 and was admired there until he later turned anti-Soviet. But Hughes's own star could not have shone brighter in foreign literary circles. As Lydia Filatova pointed out a few months later:

> Hughes is one of the important poets of America today, and so far is the only established Negro writer whose work tends to leave the beaten track of petty-bourgeois and bourgeois Negro literature. Hughes has been for a number of years a contributor to *New Masses* and the revolutionary press of the U.S.A. In his poems of 1931–32, he is a revolutionary poet who uses his writing as a weapon in the struggle against capitalism, for the emancipation of toiling Negroes and toiling humanity in all countries.
>
> Yet before arriving at such poems as "Good Morning, Revolution," "Goodbye, Christ," and the play "Scottsboro Limited," Hughes had to go through numerous stages of gradual transition in shaking off the beliefs, moods, and illusions foisted on the Negro by centuries of oppression, in overcoming and eschewing the petty-bourgeois radicalism which is still upheld by many of his contemporaries, even such as Claude McKay, who once was near the revolutionary movement.... [14]

Hughes's clout with Meschrabpom Film, while heavy enough, still had not given him much influence over the *Black and White* script by that August. Meschrabpom was not an agency of the Soviet government, but of the Berlin-based Worker's International Relief (WIR). It had its own directors, even if they were quite obviously working with the Communist International (or Comintern). Hughes was uncertain which decisions came from the directors of the WIR and which came from the Comintern. So far as he knew and told the cast, only the Comintern, Meschrabpom, Yunghans, the scenarist, and a few others beside himself had seen the script. Told that "certain changes still have to be made," he and the rest of the cast were sent down to Odessa on the Black Sea, where filming was scheduled to begin August 16. They left Moscow on August 3.

Cruising down the Black Sea coast to Batumi must have had its pleasures, but neither the Caucasus Mountains nor the sandy beaches nor the exquisite Hotel Londres in Odessa was enough to mollify a group of disgruntled travelers who saw no sign of the Meschrabpom Film executives or crew when they reached Odessa. Having been in Russia for over a month, some members in the group grumbled that the cruise was a ruse, and all they had really rehearsed was a mob scene, where they had learned to shout:

> Let us unite, Brothers,
> Brothers in black
> Brothers in white
> Let us unite.

Moreover, the group was anything but united. After weeks of being told by Allen McKenzie, nominally the leader, and Louise Thompson, who tried to keep them organized, that the film would soon be underway, some complained that "the Soviets were deliberately giving them the run-around." With Henry Lee Moon and Leonard Hill both left behind ill in Moscow—but not too ill to continue writing complaints to Locke—the dissidents were led by Theodore Poston, a reporter, like Moon, for the Negro newspaper, *The New York Amsterdam News.* Jokingly referred to as "Daddy Long Legs" for his antics on the dance floor at Moscow's Hotel Metropole, Poston had been accused by others in the group of coming to the U.S.S.R. only to have fun and make trouble. Defiant of these opponents, Poston encouraged his faction to prance nude on the white sands of Odessa. If nude bathing was done in Moscow at the Park of Rest and Culture, they mocked, why not along the Black Sea beaches. Although he was not amused at the time, Hughes later wrote amusingly of Poston's beach antics:

> In spite of the pleas of our group leader, that summer thousands of astonished citizens from all over the Soviet Union, dressed in their best bathing suits, would suddenly see streaking down the Odessa sands a dark amazon pursued by two or three of the darkest, tallest and most giraffe-like males they had ever seen—all as naked as birds and as frolicsome as Virginia hounds, diving like porpoises into the surf, or playing leapfrog nude all over the place.

Such pranks, while alienating members of the group from one another, were only a prelude to confrontations to come. All hell finally broke loose when Henry Lee Moon, hastening to Odessa's Hotel Londres from his sickbed in Moscow, called the group together for a meeting to announce, "Comrades, we've been screwed!" Telling them the *Black and White* film had been cancelled, he showed them the August 12 European edition of the *New York Herald (Tribune)*, with a front-page story: "SOVIET CALLS OFF FILM ON U. S. NEGROES; FEAR OF AMERICAN REACTION IS CAUSE."

The unsigned newspaper story had been dispatched by Eugene Lyons, the United Press correspondent in Moscow. Never sympathetic to the Soviet Union, Lyons would later become known as author of a scurrilous book, *Red Decade.* His opinions did not irritate the film group so much as Moon's claim that the film cancellation rumors began four days after the group left for Odessa. More than that, Moon boasted that the manager of Meschrabpom Film Corporation, Otto Katz, had all but confessed to him on August 8 that the film was off for "technical" reasons. But Moon insisted to the group that the reasons were political, boasting that he had sent a radiogram with that information to *The New York Amsterdam News.*

The group needed only that spark to ignite tinder that had been gathering between them for weeks. Now it was in full blaze, and the hysteria and violent name-calling could be heard above and beyond the roaring surf in Odessa. Arguments about why the film was cancelled became what Hughes later referred to as "son-of-a-bitch" meetings. The Moon-Hill-Poston faction, joined by a former American Communist Party member of the group, Thurston McNary Lewis, shouted "Red Betrayal" and "we told you so" to the McKenzie-Thompson-Hughes-Miller faction, who demanded to know how Moon and Hill, supposedly immobilized in Moscow, had talked from their sickbeds to "reliable sources." *They* and their "reliable sources" were the "betrayers," their opponents claimed; they had given the story to the *New York Herald (Tribune)*, because *they* wanted the whole film venture to fail.

The angry recriminations only increased when Boris Babitsky, director of the Meschrabpom Film Corporation, met with the group in Odessa on August 16. He gave four reasons why production had been postponed: One, the scenario was unsatisfactory; two, some members of the cast were unsuitable; three, a Negroid-looking national group in Soviet Turkestan that was to be used in mass scenes had yet to be trained; and four, Meschrabpom lacked the technical facilities for the project. But even assurances that Meschrabpom would pay them their salaries as stipulated in the contract, which did not expire until October, and in the meantime give them a tour of the Soviet Union, or if they preferred, immediate transportation back to the United States, via Berlin or Paris or London, did not satisfy every member of the group.

Back in Moscow, where all had arrived by August 20, a few members of the group sought access to the Kremlin—to Stalin himself. Of course, they were refused, much to the satisfaction of those who had accepted the cancellation of the production with good grace. But now "the group" was really divided into two factions and a feud quickened between them. Moon, Hill, and Poston, fresh from talks with "reliable sources," told their colleagues that Stalin himself had made them all pawns in international politics. They said that an American engineer, Colonel Hugh Cooper, who had recently started construction of the Dnieprostroi Dam (the largest electrical power station in the world) had told Stalin, through V. M. Molotov, chairman of the Council of People's Commissars, that if he did not halt the production of *Black and White*, he, Cooper, would halt the construction of the dam. They also said they suspected that Colonel Cooper had the support of Ivy Lee, the Rockefellers' public relations consultant. Lee was a frequent visitor to Moscow, and was believed to be on retainer to the Soviet government as a "publicity director" to hasten official diplomatic recognition by the United States government.

Another of their "reliable sources," they said, was Raymond Robbins, an American who warned them in the Hotel Metropole Bar, weeks before, to dissociate themselves from the "anti-American" film. Robbins was in Moscow to negotiate with Stalin on the establishment of diplomatic relations between the two countries, and production of the film was a detriment to those negotiations. Robbins told them that *Black and White* would be stopped. The group split further apart, into what Lenin would have termed "infantile disorder." A few members marched on Meschrabpom, denouncing the studio executives and Yunghans as "lackeys" and "opportunists," causing pandemonium. Others, uncertain what to do, turned their anger ever more violently on one another. Langston Hughes was called a "Communist Uncle Tom." Louise Thompson was referred to as "Madame Moscow." Loren Miller was a "would-be-red-black-poet." The "L-raisers" in turn blasted their accusers as "informants of American imperialists." Arguing loud and long in Moscow's Mininskaya Hotel, they all agreed to go together to the Comintern. They went, but not as a united front—and not speaking with one voice. Hughes later explained:

> After several days it was agreed by unanimous vote that we would present our case to the Comintern, which was said to be, next to the Kremlin itself, the last word on international affairs. So a delegation, including myself, was chosen to go to the Comintern. There we were received by several old Bolsheviks sitting at a long table in a gloomy room. Some of our delegation arose and denounced Meschrabpom, Communism and "the Soviet betrayal of the Negro race" in no uncertain terms. I took the position that it was regrettable no film was to be produced, but since the script had been so mistakenly conceived, it seemed to me wise to make none. . . .

While the Comintern "promised to take the whole matter under immediate consideration," four members of the film group rushed to the *New York Herald (Tribune)* correspondent, charging "betrayal of the Negro workers of the United States and the world's proletariat and with sabotage against world revolution." Sounding like revolutionary Trotskyites in the August 24 international edition of the newspaper, the four angry young men were Henry Moon, Thurston McNary Lewis, Theodore Poston, and Lawrence Alberga, who were anything but revolutionaries.

To deny the charges of the four men, and the *Herald (Tribune)*'s assertion that eighteen others had *abstained* from the protest, fifteen members of the group signed a counterstatement prepared by Langston and Loren Miller. The statement said they supported Langston's view that no decent film could have been made from the scenario. These remarks were ignored by the American press, except for the *Daily Worker, New Masses,* and a few black publications. This oversight was not inadvertent. Louise Thompson, who cabled the statement to the Crusader News Service, wrote later:

> In the current issue of *The Crisis*, I notice a statement of your not having seen any satisfactory explanation of the postponement of the film "Black and White," for the making of which a group of twenty-two Negroes was invited to the Soviet Union last June.
>
> It is quite true that such statements have not been given such publicity in the white capitalist press of America as have the false allegations of complete abandonment of the picture for political reasons. The reason must be obvious to you, knowing as you do the attitude of this press to the Negro, as well as to the Soviet Union. Many statements have been issued collectively and individually by the majority of our group and have been steadily ignored by the representatives of the press through whom adverse statements were released. Eugene Lyons, the United Press correspondent in Moscow, refused to send out the statement signed by fifteen members of our group repudiating the charges of four of our number which he had readily cabled over the wires of the United Press Service.[15]

Yet news of what Hughes later called "the bitter end" would spread for months with the charges and countercharges, the denials and counterdenials, which began late that August. Moon, Poston, Lewis, and others left Moscow as quickly as they could and gave their version of events to Alain Locke, who reported to Godmother (in part):

> Before leaving Moscow they were threatened—one of the party was shot at, (at night as he was returning to his hotel) and another called out of a telephone booth and knocked unconscious by a man he as yet hasn't seen. They said they will expose the whole situation in the white and Negro press when they reach New York.[16]

No such incidents were reported in the *New York Herald (Tribune)*, which would have considered the provocations news had they actually happened. Nor were they contained in the long political communiqué cabled from Berlin by Moon and Poston to the *Amsterdam News* that October and published under a banner headline: AMSTERDAM NEWS REPORTERS TELL WHY SOVIET RUSSIA DROPPED FILM. Nor were they printed in the *New York Times*, which saw "fit to print" much of the Moon-Poston dispatch. Hughes, still touring the Soviet Union with a dozen others in the group, received none of the same attention when he offered a personal communiqué. Only the *Daily Worker* picked it up:

The film "Black and White," postponed on account of scenario difficulties, will be made in the Spring. Newspaper reports that I and other members of the Negro film group are adrift in Moscow without funds are absolutely untrue. Our contracts and salaries with Meschrabpom continue to October 26. The return passage to the United States is guaranteed. Several members of the group intend to remain in the Soviet Union. Many have already secured positions here. I plan to use the next few months to make a study of one of the Soviet National Republics.[17]

By October, so slanted did American press coverage of the film episode appear that the League of Struggle for Negro Rights—of which Hughes would become president in 1933—sent a protest delegation to *The New York Amsterdam News*. In the delegation was Communist candidate for lieutenant governor of New York, Henry Shepard. He argued that "the failure of *The New York Amsterdam News* to publish the statement of the majority group of Negroes, after it had published the charges by Moon and Poston, was deliberately done so as to turn Negro workers from the Communist Party."[18] Fearing loss of the black vote in the November election, Communist Vice-Presidential candidate James Ford also branded as false the "rumors spread by the capitalist press."[19]

Moon and Poston, having arrived in New York City by mid-October, only intensified the arguments with more articles and a rumor that "plans were underway" for an independent *Black and White* film in the United States.[20] The *Daily Worker* had already branded them in an October 6 editorial as "those who betray the Negro people."

Meanwhile, Meschrabpom, fuming over "patently ridiculous slanders" by Moon and Poston that "the film was abandoned for fear it might offend American sensibilities and interfere with the movement for the recognition of the Soviet government," issued a press release defending its past productions. As evidence that it had never hesitated to expose class oppression or offend sensibilities, it proudly cited its production of Pudovkin's *Storm Over Asia*, attacking American and British imperialism; *Black Sea Mutiny*, challenging French imperialism in the Near East; *Sniper*, summoning the international proletariat to arms against the ruling class; and its most recent picture, *The Deserter*, urging the German people to overthrow Hitler and fascism. With such a "list of uncompromising films," stated the press release issued through the Workers Film and Photo League of New York, Meschrabpom was "not worried about ruffling the sensibilities of the capitalist world."[21]

If Meschrabpom had no reservations about ruffling the sensibilities of the capitalist world in 1932, someone else did: Yosif Vissarionovich Dzhugashvili, known to the world as Stalin—"man of steel." And steel he was. Convinced, like Lenin, that "capitalism had grown into a world system of colonial oppression and financial strangulation," Stalin believed it had to be challenged. The challenge presented a paradox. To equal American industrial production, which was the ultimate goal of Stalin's Five Year Plan, it was necessary to employ American technical experts. And Stalin did. Among them was Hugh L. Cooper, the engineer in charge of constructing the Dnieprostroi Dam, and of blocking the production of *Black and White*. That the accusation of his interference with the film is grounded in truth is made clear in a "confidential" memo dated August 30, 1932, from the American consul general in Berlin, George S. Messersmith, to the U.S. Secretary of State.

No. 928
AMERICAN CONSULATE GENERAL
Berlin, Germany, August 30, 1932.
SUBJECT: Report of conversations with Colonel Hugh L. Cooper, concerning his visit to Russia.
The Honorable
The Secretary of State,
Washington.

Sir:

I have the honor to report that Col. Hugh L. Cooper of New York, returned from Russia several days ago and gave the Consulate General certain information with reference to conditions in Russia. Col. Cooper has been particularly agitated over the reception and kindly treatment which American negroes have had in Russia. It appears that recently a German film producer went to Central Africa where the suggestion occurred to him that a film could be produced exhibiting the negro as an object of barter and trade and subject to social humiliations which the white race were supposed to have heaped upon him. It appears that the production of this film did not interest German producers and that the promoter eventually found his way to Russia where the matter was favorably considered and, according to Col. Cooper, where plans were eventually started for the production of this film in Russia. The American negroes there resident were to take part in the film; but it was found that American negroes did not suit the parts which it was intended to portray and that certain difficulties arose with regard to the production. These facts came to the attention of Col. Cooper, according to his report, and he had an interview with Molotov regarding the whole subject of American negroes in Russia. The Russian Government, it appears, was disposed to listen to the objections made by Col. Cooper and called a meeting of certain responsible officials to consider the whole question. The project of producing the film came also before responsible members of the Government and an investigation took place which resulted in the scheme being entirely forbidden. Col. Cooper reports in fact that Russian officials had no sympathy whatever with the idea and drastically disapproved it. This gave an opportunity to make certain representations to the Russian authorities regarding the schooling of American negroes in Soviet Russia, in communist doctrine, etc., and it appears that in view of the strong stand in the matter taken by Col. Cooper, this procedure has now been entirely abandoned. Col. Cooper reports that about twenty-five negroes of American nationality are resident in Moscow and that they have received favorable treatment heretofore but that now their position has been entirely reversed. The result of the action of the Soviet Government was to throw these negroes into an embarrassing position and they appealed to the Third International to foster their interests and ambitions. In this connection Col. Cooper stated that the Third International appears to be at a very low ebb and that the Russian Government is giving it very little countenance and support. With regard to the negroes, Col. Cooper says he has the assurance of responsible Russian officials that negroes will not be allowed in the future to enter Russia. What disposition is to be made of those now there is not known, but Col. Cooper believes that the negro venture in Russia is totally at an end. . . .

Col. Cooper informed that he was returning to Russia next month to attend the opening of the great dam which his firm has just finished on the Dnieper river. He also informed that the Russians are considering another engineering project of importance concerning which his advice is being sought.

The foregoing is a report of the statements made by Col. Cooper to Consul Geist in a conversation yesterday, Col. Cooper having just returned from Russia.

In this connection the Department will be interested to know that on his passing through Berlin to Russia on this trip Col. Cooper called at the Consulate General and in a conversation with me showed that he was much exercised over the much advertised film which was to be taken in Russia to show the ill treatment of negroes in various parts of the world, particularly

in the United States. He spoke at the time of this film as being a
very ill advised venture. While Col. Cooper was in Russia I was
informed by a well-known and quite responsible newspaper man
in Berlin who has lived in Russia at various times and who has
intimate contact with sources of Russian information, that on
Col. Cooper's arrival in Russia he took up this matter of the
negro film with the authorities and emphasized to them the
desirability of not producing it. Meeting considerable resistance
the newspaper man states that Col. Cooper frankly informed the
Soviet authorities that he was so much chagrined over this film
project that it was his intention not to proceed to the formal
opening of the dam which represented his principal engineering
project so far in Russia. The newspaper man stated that it was
obviously through the influence of Col. Cooper that the project
of the film was abandoned.

Respectfully yours,

George S. Messersmith,
American Consul General.[22]

That Cooper deluded himself that "Negroes in the future will not be
allowed to visit Russia" or that "the Negro venture is totally at an end" is
made even clearer by subsequent events and circumstances.

Those members of the film group who, like Hughes, accepted an invitation from the theatrical section of the Soviet Trade Union to tour the
U.S.S.R., journeyed as far as Turkmenistan, which foreigners were usually
forbidden to visit. Afterward, some returned to stay in Moscow, as Hughes
later explained in an essay for *International Literature*, "Moscow and Me."

> When I came back to Moscow in the winter [of 1933], those of
> our group who had remained, seven in all, had settled down
> comfortably to life in the Soviet capital. Dorothy West was
> writing, Mildred Jones was taking screen tests for a new picture.
> Long, tall [Lloyd] Patterson who paints houses had married a
> girl who paints pictures, and together they have executed some
> of the finest decorations for the May Day celebration. Wayland
> Rudd, was studying singing, fencing and dancing, and taking a
> role in a new Meyerhold play. [Allen] McKenzie stayed in the
> films, working for Meschrabpom. And Homer Smith, as a spe-
> cial consultant in the Central Post Office, was supervising the
> installation of an American special delivery for Moscow mail. So
> the Negroes made themselves at home.

Of the group, only Homer Smith, for reasons never explained in his autobiography, *Black Man in Red Russia*, completely dissociated himself from (in his words) "the Black and White film fiasco." Having come with the film group to Russia, he would eventually stay fifteen years, only to claim later that he "met" the cast in Moscow.

Louise Thompson, who might have remained in the U.S.S.R. had she not had to depart that November to care for her ill mother in New York, told *The New York Amsterdam News* that "Russia today is the only country in the world that's really fit to live in. I'd live there any time in preference to America."[23]

Loren Miller, who, before returning to his California newspaper, wrote a series of articles for the *Daily Worker* on "How the U.S.S.R. Wiped Out Oppression," issued a farewell statement saying that "the Soviet Union is the best friend of the Negro and all oppressed people."[24]

Both Louise and Loren had said their farewells to Langston in Soviet Central Asia, where he would remain for nearly five more months. He was traveling there when news of the *Black and White* film and reviews of his latest book, *The Dream Keeper*, appeared in the United States, and he was little concerned that a critic for the *Saturday Review* wrote, "Langston Hughes is not a first-rate poet, even among those of his race."[25] That was less important to him than what he had been through in the past few months and what he hoped to do in the future. From Central Asia, where he sent a postcard with a poem to his mother, his message must have summed up all he felt after the debacle of *Black and White*. The words were from *The Dream Keeper*:

> Hold fast to dreams
> For if dreams die,
> Life is a broken winged bird
> That cannot fly.

He had left Moscow holding fast to the dream that *Black and White* might still be made in the spring. It was one of his dreams that never came true.

❦ 12 ❦

Dust and Rainbows

JOURNEYING THROUGH SOVIET CENTRAL ASIA that autumn, crossing paths once trekked by Alexander the Great, Arab potentates, Genghis Khan, and Tamerlane, Hughes was in a legendary region known as "White Gold." That vast expanse south of Western Siberia and east of the Caspian Sea was the Soviet Union's rich cotton belt, and Hughes wanted to compare it with the American South. There, too, were the dark-skinned Asiatics he intended to write a book about, the people once subjugated by the beys, emirs, and czars of Imperial Russia. He wanted to see how the Revolution had changed their lives and to compare their history with that of his own people. His quest would take him to two remote republics of Soviet Central Asia: Uzbekistan and the even more desolate Turkmenistan.

Because Soviet guidebooks declared Turkmenistan off limits to most foreigners, he had taken precautions before leaving Moscow. Through the help of Constantine Oumansky, a Soviet press attaché—and later ambassador to the United States—who had been squiring around a pretty member of the *Black and White* film group, the poet had finagled a six-month press card, contracts from *Izvestia*, and letters of introduction from the Writers Union.

In Uzbekistan, in company with a dozen members of the film group and a Soviet guide in Samarkand, Bokhara, and Tashkent, he saw something of the Middle Ages in the twentieth century. In those legendary cities, where camel caravans were as much a part of the traffic as street cars and automobiles, historic landmarks—mosques and mausoleums—hundreds of years old contrasted with new schools, apartments, and factories. In these ancient centers of textile trade between Russia and the East, progress and history unfolded before his eyes that 1932, especially in Uzbekistan.

Fifteen years after the Revolution, the dark Uzbeks, once known as the "Golden Horde," were administering Uzbekistan. Hughes never forgot the impression they made upon him. Later, in an essay, "Going South in Russia," he described how he met "a man almost as brown as I am who was the mayor of Bokhara," and he made a mental note: "in the Soviet Union dark men are also the mayors of cities"; to which he added another note while traveling from Uzbekistan to Turkmenistan on the Transcaspian Railroad: "write home to the Negro papers: 'There is no Jim Crow on the trains of the Soviet Union.' "[1] He saw and heard enough to know that such integration had not always been a reality.

> When I was in Tashkent, the regional capital of Soviet Central Asia, there were funny little old street cars running, about the size of the cable cars in San Francisco. I noticed a partition at the center of these streetcars and asked a brownskin Uzbek friend why it was there. He explained to me that in the old Tzarist days, that partition separated the Europeans from the Asiatics. . . .
> He said, "Yes, before the Revolution, we would have to sit in the back. But now everybody sits anywhere."[2]

When Hughes finally waved goodbye to his *Black and White* film companions, who accompanied him by train as far as Ashkhabad, the regional capital of Turkmenistan, he was at the edge of the Kara Kum Desert. Eighty percent of Turkmenistan was desert, and he could not have looked more strange when he stepped off the train, loaded down with two suitcases, a duffle bag, a typewriter, a victrola, and a big box of phonograph records.

Ashkhabad was then a dusty town and desert outpost for Russian soldiers and government officials working on the Five Year Plan. Its population was forty thousand. With occasional donkey carts passing by huge billboards of Lenin and Stalin, it did not resemble a bustling crossroads of world history. "In contrast to Tashkent and Samarkand," he said later, "it was a sleepy old town."

To this remote corner of the world often known as Turkestan, he had come in search of the majority population—the dark, nomadic Turkomans. Not a place frequented by tourists, Ashkhabad had no hotel, and Hughes was accommodated in the only local *dom sovietov*, or guesthouse, available. While it was quiet enough to do some writing, it was not a place to write home about. "Water was out in the yard somewhere," he wrote in *I Wonder as I Wander*. "The toilets were far out in the back yard."

With not one Ashkhabad resident speaking English, and no interpreter, any other American might have been lost. But not Hughes. In spite of the language barrier, which he quickly scaled, his room in the *dom sovietov* was soon a gathering place. It was there that, a few weeks later, he met the Hungarian journalist, Arthur Koestler, then working for a Berlin newspaper (and in a state of acute depression). As Koestler reported in his autobiography:

I heard the sound of a gramophone in the next room. The record was cracked, and it played the then popular tear-jerker sung by Sophie Tucker, "My Yiddishe Momma." It sounded eerie in the *dom sovietov* of Ashkhabad, and I got up to find out who my neighbor was. I knocked at his door and found a young American Negro squatting in front of a portable gramophone in a bare room similar to mine, and in a state of gloom similar to mine. He turned out to be the poet Langston Hughes, whose "Shoeshine Boy" [sic][3] I had read in Berlin and greatly admired. It was difficult not to say "Dr. Livingstone, I presume."[4]

Koestler had found, he said, "unexpected and pleasant company for the remainder of [his] journey in Central Asia."[5] He was in Turkestan for his own reasons. A member of the German Communist Party, he was a Hungarian Jew whose search for personal identity was not incidental to his Soviet journey. As he later admitted in his autobiography, "West Turkestan between the Caspian and the Pamir, is also the 'Turanian Basin' and is supposedly the place of origin of the Hungarian people. As a child I had learnt to regard the expression 'Turanian' as synonymous with 'Hungarian,' so in a sense I had come home."[6]

If he had gone to Turkestan in search of home, he discovered little there which pleased him. He was then twenty-seven; rootless and restless, he had studied at the University of Vienna and traveled widely in Europe, Palestine, and the Arctic. Before coming to Russia, he had lived in Berlin, writing for German publications. With the rise of Nazism, his association with one of the most important satirical journals, *Die Weltbühne*, was soon to end as abruptly as it would for Bertolt Brecht, Heinrich Mann, Ernst Toller, and Stefan Zweig, all of whom Hitler would drive into exile or suicide. When he met Hughes, Koestler was still testing his intellectual wings and claiming to be an avowed Communist (which he would later all but refute in *Darkness at Noon* and *The God That Failed*). He seemed to the poet a disenchanted intellectual who "wore his sadness on his sleeve." Describing him years later, Hughes wrote, "I have known a great many writers in my time, . . . some of them were very much like Koestler—always something not quite right in the world around them."[7]

Of writers sympathetic to the Soviet cause, no two could have been more different in temperament, especially in their reactions to Soviet Central Asia. For Koestler, Turkoman customs and attitudes did not reflect his idea of the Russian Revolution. Ashkhabad depressed him. The local tradition of sharing *khok-chai* tea by passing the cup from person to person displeased him. The drab accommodations in the *dom sovietov* distressed him. Everything was too communal, too unsanitary, too uncomfortable, for his Teutonic sense of individualism and order. With his interest in ideas deeper than his faith in the masses, he could not have disagreed less with Lenin's dictum that "the heart of the matter lies not in administrations nor in new decrees but in people."[8] For Hughes, who would have agreed with Lenin, Koestler seemed a paradox for a man who claimed to be a Communist. "To Koestler, Turkmenistan was simply a *primitive* land moving into twentieth-century civilization," he wrote. "To me, it was a colored land moving into orbits hitherto reserved for whites."

He attempted several different drafts of the pages he finally published about Koestler in *I Wonder as I Wander*, deleting some of the more cryptic passages.[9] Both politically and emotionally he felt estranged from the Hungarian writer, who must have been aware of it during their Russian sojourn. In *The Invisible Writing*, Koestler penned an accurate description of Langston Hughes:

> ...behind the warm smile of his dark eyes there was a grave dignity, and a polite reserve which communicated itself at once. He was very likeable and easy to get on with, but at the same time one felt an impenetrable, elusive remoteness which warded off all undue familiarity.

Before Koestler's arrival, Hughes had been dawdling in Ashkhabad, playing his victrola, using his room as a social center, and not writing much. But he changed all that after they met. "A writer must write," Koestler told him one night over a meal of camel sausage and vodka. Hughes, more accustomed to putting his thoughts into poetry than collecting material for prose, had gathered none of the facts and statistics Koestler asked him about Turkmenistan. The young journalist could hardly have been impressed that the poet couldn't pronounce the names of some of the people he had met in Ashkhabad. Least of all did he know how to spell them correctly. The president of the Turkoman Writers Federation, Shaarieh Kikilov, Hughes called "Charlie"—since "his first name sounded like a cross between Cherie and Charlie." Trying to pronounce the name of a local Red Army officer, he said, "I never did get his name straight, but it sounded like Yeah Tlang, or Yaddle-oang, or Ya-Gekiang...I finally settled for a nickname of my own coining, *Yeah Man*."

For Arthur Koestler, who didn't suffer nicknames or fools gladly, the spelling of his own name phonetically by Hughes as "Kessler" must have caused a raised eyebrow. The Hungarian, three years younger than Hughes, was all seriousness, and if he lacked a sense of humor, he lacked no sense of discipline. In *Arrow in the Blue*, he would explain how he overcame the hedonistic excesses he was sometimes prone to. "Work became my therapy and my drug," he said, "my compromise with a guilt-ridden ego, and a sacrificial offering to the ghosts of the past."

In Ashkhabad, he was soon leading Hughes to trade union councils, cotton mills, factories, schools and town hall meetings, and encouraging him to take notes and write the names of all the people they met. "So it was Koestler, really," Hughes admitted later—not without some resentment— "who started me to work in Ashkhabad. He wasn't happy unless he was doing something useful—if happy then."

Hughes, happy with any discovery of the old order having been replaced by the new, thought he had found that to be the case in Ashkhabad.

> In a museum in Ashkhabad, capital of Turkmenia, I saw signs on the wall as curiosities for the school kids to look at: SARTS KEEP OUT, in both the Turkoman and Russian language. I was told that in the old days these signs were at the entrances of the big beautiful public park in the heart of Ashkhabad. In Tzarist times that park was only for Europeans—white people, not for the native peoples whom the whites contemptuously termed 'sarts,' a word equivalent to our worst anti-negro terms.[10]

The European-born Koestler, unfamiliar with racial segregation, was looking at a different world. Although he romanticized the Turkomans in their "colorful national costumes," he was disgruntled with nearly everything else. After attending what he later called "the first great show trial in Central Asia," the Atta Kurdov Trial, in which a group of Turkomans was accused of crimes against the state, Koestler's mood darkened noticeably. The trial seemed to him a mockery, and many years later, Hughes, recalling his traveling companion's reaction, speculated that the trial was the beginning of *Darkness at Noon*.

But if Hughes thought Koestler's reaction to the Atta Kurdov trial was exaggerated, he knew that Koestler's subsequent account of the *Black and White* film-making mission was distorted. According to Koestler, after it was decided not to do the film and the rest of the troupe "was sent home with polite smiles and expressions of regret," Hughes, "who because of his great reputation in America, could not be got rid of in such a summary manner," was living in Central Asia as a "pensionnaire" writing a book which Soviet officials proposed that he write.[11] The truth is that Hughes took it upon himself to travel and write in Russia, and he expected Meschrabpom to meet its contractual financial obligations to him through October. When they did not, Hughes was "stranded," according to Koestler.

Indignant at the treatment of Hughes, I sent, unknown to him, a
long telegram to the Comintern, explaining his predicament and
the repercussions to be expected in America if it were to leak out
that its leading Negro poet had been lured under false pretenses
to Central Asia and simply forgotten there. It had an unexpected
effect: Hughes's money arrived a few days later.[12]

By all accounts it is true that the Hungarian writer and the American poet
left Ashkhabad together that October and headed south toward the Persian
border. They were joined by Shaarieh Kikilov, the president of the Turkoman
Writers Federation, and Kolya Shagurin, a Ukrainian writer. During an
overnight train ride across the desert to the ancient city of Merv, in the heart
of the cotton belt, they organized a "Writers Brigade."

THE CITY OF MERV was a great disappointment to Hughes. Known historically as the capital of ancient Persia, where Moslem, Hindu, and Christian
legends hold the Garden of Eden sprang, Merv was "as drab and ugly a city
as [he] had ever seen, and even more dust-covered than Ashkhabad." Moreover, Hughes and Koestler were not permitted to visit the ruins of the
ancient city, where some vestiges of lost glory remained, probably because—
to quote Koestler's questionable opinion—"the District Party Committee. . .
thought that it was a waste of time and petrol to indulge in the bourgois
romantic whim to look at the ruins of the by-gone past."[13] Instead, Hughes,
Koestler, and other members of the Writers Brigade were whisked off to
Kolkhoz Aitakov, the huge cotton collective in the Merv oasis.

Though Koestler reviled the persistence of traditional practices in the
Turkoman's Islamic culture on the huge collective—and especially the in-
conceivable, complete exploitation of women there—which were in total
contradiction to official Communist policies, programs and regulations,
Hughes said little more than he did later in his autobiography. But he had
his quarrels with Islam and its traditions, and he expressed them in three
important pieces: "Farewell to Mahomet," "In an Emir's Harem," and
"The Soviet Union and Women."

Traveling in Uzbekistan, he had championed the cause of Islamic women
who were fighting the traditions that literally enslaved them. One of these
women was Jahan Abinova, whom Hughes came to know very well, and
whose struggle—as Hughes sketches it—was typical of women of her age
and class:

She was born of poor peasants in a Kazakhstan village, she said.
When she was eleven years old, she was sold for one hundred
and fifty rubles as the fourth wife of a rich bey. He was not kind

to her. On the eve of the 1917 revolution, her husband moved
with his four wives to Tashkent. In October, Lenin and the
Bolsheviks triumphed in far-away St. Petersburg and Moscow.
Abinova learned that the Tzar had fallen and that soldiers and
beys would no longer rule Central Asia. Sensing the unrest of
the times, she ran away from her husband and never came back.[14]

When Hughes met her, she was thirty-five and vice-president of the Uzbek
Socialist Soviet Republic.

Having seen Abinova and other Uzbek women triumph over the harem,
he was convinced that Lenin's cautionary words—"every housewife must
learn to rule the state"[15]—were prophetic of the not distant future. And his
conviction was strengthened when, after the kolkhoz, he visited Permetyab,
another collective farm near the Afghan border. "Why such an excursion
was suggested to Koestler and me is still a mystery," he wrote later, although it should have been obvious that some Russian officials had wanted
them to see that the Revolution had even stretched across a scorching desert
to "a distant outpost of hell." "Just to get to Permetyab," Hughes wrote,
"would try the soul of the devil himself." Wading across desert gulches,
pushing their car out of sand drifts and getting drinking water from their
overheated car radiator, they finally reached what Hughes said was "the
most Godforsaken place I have ever seen, the dirtiest and the hottest." He
never forgot that village of mud huts and sheepskin tents. Fourteen years
later he wrote of the farm and his reaction to it:

> The farm was way down in the heart of Asia near the Afghani-
> stan border, not far from where the northernmost tip of India
> almost touches Soviet territory. Over the Soviet borders there
> was a steady trickle of immigrants from Afghanistan and India,
> mostly poor peasants from Beluchistan. These immigrants had
> heard that in the Soviet Union no beys or emirs or princes or
> colonial overlords robbed the poor of the fruits of their labor.
> They had heard that there the irrigation ditches were not con-
> trolled by the rich, and that no man had to till another man's
> fields in order to have the use of a little water for his own. The
> collective farm that Koestler and I visited was peopled entirely
> by turbaned Beluchi tribesmen.
>
> The men and women there were as brown as I am—in other
> words, a definitely colored people. The only white person on
> that farm—in fact, the only European for miles around—was a
> young and quite beautiful Russian nurse. She was in charge of
> the clinic and all of the health work for these Indian peasant
> farmers. She delivered their babies, nursed their sick, cured ma-

laria, and fought inherited venereal disease. She taught them that modern science and hygiene are better than old customs and superstitions—such as putting an axe under the bed to hasten child-birth, or washing newborn babies in sand. I was deeply impressed with the efforts such as this which the Soviet Government was making everywhere I went to care for the health of even the most backward of its peoples. . . . [16]

On the other hand, Koestler's implication was clear when he remarked, "If the Revolution had only occurred in Germany, at least it would have been a clean one." En route to Bokhara, Hughes twitted him jokingly that they would both be dead of cholera before leaving Central Asia. He had no way of knowing how close to death he himself would be in a few weeks. When Koestler left him in Bokhara for a brief trip to Samarkand, all Hughes wanted were "a few days of just not having to do anything" and of being free of his sometimes irritating companion. Weak from too many meals of melon, camel sausage, and a hard, indigestible bread called *lepioshkas*, which he often drank with green tea, he was already suffering stomach pains when he met Koestler in Tashkent.

Hearing Koestler complain that "here in Tashkent the jails are full of people, the Atta Kurdovs of Asia," and having to explain to him for the umpteenth time why he, Hughes, would not join the Communist Party, the poet looked forward with relief to his companion's departure for Moscow the next day. As for not joining the Communist Party, "I told him," Hughes said later, "I did not believe political directives could be applied to creative writing." But whether he joined the Party or not, he sympathized with it more than Koestler. The night they said goodbye, Hughes had only the vaguest sense of Koestler's own political commitment, or his heart and mind. Later—much later—he wrote in *I Wonder as I Wander*:

> I had shared with Koestler the Atta Kurdov trials in Ashkhabad, then Permetyab in the desert, and now Tashkent—traveling with him through the heart of Asia along the old caravan trails at the crossroads of the East. Were I a socio-literary historian, I might hazard a guess that here in 1932 were Koestler's crossroads, too—his turning point from left to right that was to culminate a few years later in his bitter attacks on communism.

Within a day or two after Koestler left, Hughes's severe abdominal pain forced him to seek the help of a physician, whose prescription, which contained arsenic, only made the pain worse. Acquaintances got him to bed, and when word of his severe illness reached government circles in Tashkent, the personal physician to the president of Uzbekistan was rushed to his bedside. All through his convalescence that cold November, members of the Uzbek Writers Union and others who befriended him were in constant attendance. They saw to it that he had living quarters which were warm, clean, and comfortable. They brought him food. And finally, when he was pronounced out of danger, they told him that *The Weary Blues* had been translated into Uzbek. It was a great compliment, and it influenced him to decide to remain in Central Asia, to learn as much as he could of the language, and to see as much as he could of the Uzbek Republic before his travel visa expired in January.

If he had been close to death, he had survived it full of high spirits. The spirit of survival was quintessential Hughes. No rainbows without a little rain. "God of dust and rainbows," he would write later in his career, "Help us to see / That without the dust / The rainbow would not be."[17] What he had learned in the desert of Central Asia inspired him to translate (with some assistance) from the Uzbek a long poem, "On the Turksib Roads," by Gafur Gulam.[18] It expressed all he felt about the people who helped him through his convalescence and made him feel at home away from home.

Having acquired a sufficient command of the Uzbek by studying it while he was bedridden, Hughes spent most of December fulfilling his literary commitments to *Izvestia*. Flush with sixty thousand rubles that the State Publishers paid him for *The Weary Blues*, and supplied with letters of introduction and authorization by the Uzbek Writers Union, he visited every site, facility, and institution in Uzbekistan he cared to, including citizens' youth clubs, schools, and cooperative farms. What impressed him most, however—probably because of his own creative interest—was the Uzbek regional theater. There he found poetry, music, and dance had been combined to create theater where none existed before the Revolution. One of his first articles for *Izvestia* was "Soviet Theater in Central Asia."

He was especially taken by the presentation of *Farhar Va Shirin*, a dance-drama, and the performance of its star, Tamara Khanum, as the heroine Shirin.

> Tamara Kanum... was the first unveiled female Uzbek dancer
> to dance on stage in the late 1920s. This was such an innovation
> in cities like Bokhara and Samarkand that the State had to supply
> a company of soldiers to guard her to keep the reactionary men
> folk from tearing her off the stage.[19]

Hughes interviewed her and later wrote to Noel Sullivan: "She was grand to me, and sent for the oldest drummers and reed blowers so that I could hear the folk music of the land. She did for me many of the subtle dance patterns that include movements of the eyes and fingers too delicate to be seen when performed on the stage."[20] His interview resulted in a long article later published in *Theatre Arts*—"Tamara Khanum: Soviet Asia's Greatest Dancer."

One of his last ventures in the Uzbek Republic, a visit to an experimental farm, was somewhat disappointing. If he had hoped to compare the cotton farms of the American South with those of the Soviet Union, he found the comparison in ways he had not expected. Accompanied by Bernard Powers, a black American engineer then living in the U.S.S.R., he arrived there on Christmas Eve, the invited guest of a group of Americans workers.

> There were about a dozen American Negroes attached to this cotton experimental farm, most of them from the South. Some were agricultural chemists, graduates of Tuskeegee or Hampton, others were from Northern colleges, and some were just plain cotton farmers from Dixie, whose job it was in Soviet Asia to help introduce American methods of cultivating cotton. Some worked in laboratories at the collective, testing the quality of seeds and the strength of cotton fibers, and some worked in the fields just as they had at home. It was an oddly assorted group of educated and uneducated Negroes a long way from Dixie—and most of them not liking it very well. Conditions of the Soviet collective, while a great change for the better for the Uzbeks were for Negroes from America more primitive than most of them had known at home, especially for the younger college people who, when they got dressed up for Christmas in the middle of Central Asia, still looked exactly like American undergraduates.

When he boarded the train for Moscow in early January, he had in his luggage at least fifteen pounds of notes and photographs for his projected book. He left behind his victrola and many jazz records only for the sake of traveling light. "I wouldn't give up jazz for a world revolution," he told Soviets who claimed jazz was "decadent bourgeois music." For though he had, in his words, "found the whole human meaning of the Soviet Union and its material and spiritual significance to the world of tomorrow,"[21] he could not and would not forfeit, deny, or neglect his own heritage to embrace that "whole human meaning." Yet his own meaning of not "giving up jazz for a world revolution" would later be distorted by critics who believed he was more "jazz poet" than revolutionary. Nevertheless, from Tashkent to Moscow that early winter of 1933, he was known as "Comrade Hughes"—a poet who had made a name for himself in the U.S.S.R. as well as in the U.S.A.

❧ 13 ❧

Zero Hour

WHEN HUGHES ARRIVED IN MOSCOW, his permit to travel in Russia had expired, and although he liked the capital city, he felt impeded—despite "nearly a half-suitcase full of rubles that had almost no value without the proper papers. It took a food card to get food, a residence permit to get a hotel room, and a travel permit to travel."[1] But when he finally settled in at the New Moscow Hotel, after staying a month with Walt Carmon, editor of the English-language edition of *International Literature*, he was ready to prolong his visit. He stayed five more months. He wrote to Noel Sullivan, "This is the only place I've ever made enough to live from writing. Poets and writers in the Soviet Union are highly regarded and paid awfully well as a class, I judge, the best cared for literary people in the world."[2]

Moreover, he appreciated the absence of Jim Crow. One of the articles he wrote, "Negroes in Moscow," suggests his appreciation.

> There are among the permanent foreign working residents of Moscow, perhaps two dozen Negroes, several of whom I have not met, as there is no Negro colony; and colored people mix so thoroughly in the life of the big capital, that you cannot find them merely by seeking out their color. Like the Indians and the Uzbeks and the Chinese, the Negro workers are so well absorbed by Soviet life that most of them seldom remember they are Negroes in the oppressive sense that black people are always forced to be conscious of in America.[3]

Witnessing people of color participating freely in the life of the Soviet Union renewed memories of the racial oppression he had suffered at home, and inspired him to write "Ballad of the Landlord," a poem which was first published that 1933 in the Russian journal *Krasnaya Nov* (Red Virgin Soil).[4] The same attitude inspired him to write "A New Song," a poem which *Opportunity*, the American journal that published it, called "bitter and defiant."[5] While no less defiant than Hughes's other writings of that period, "A

New Song" sang a different tune than the one he had chanted on race relations in the United States. Five years later, when he included the poem in a small collection issued by the International Workers Order, the bitterness was toned down. In the later version, gone were such closing lines as "Black World / Against the wall, / Open your eyes— / The long white snake of greed has struck to kill! / Be wary and be wise! / Before / The darker world / The future lies." By 1938, he would change all that to read:

> Revolt! Arise!
>
> The Black
> And White World
> Shall be one!
> The Workers World!
>
> The past is done!
>
> A new dream flames
> Against the
> Sun!

But in early 1933 he was still a most defiant Langston Hughes. "The time has passed," he told Homer Smith in February, "for us to sit by and bemoan our fate. We need now an art and a literature which will arouse us to our fate. Already we have had too much literature in the vein of the spirituals, lamenting our fate and bemoaning our condition, but suggesting no remedy except humbleness and docility."

Smith, who had left the *Black and White* cast to become a postal agent and free-lance writer in Moscow, published Hughes's statement in *The Afro-American* that winter. His reference to "Comrade Hughes" could only have perplexed those black American readers who tried to identify the poet with his two most recent books: *The Dream Keeper* and *Popo and Fifina*. Both were published in the United States in 1932 while Hughes was in Russia. They were hardly reflective of his new stance, but because they were released by commercial publishers they were better known than his 25¢ booklet *Scottsboro Limited*. Yet even *that* booklet was tame compared to some of his writing done in the Soviet Union.

Alain Locke, in an annual *Opportunity* review of important Negro books of the year, tried to sum up Hughes's work for 1932. It must have made the poet chuckle:

> Meanwhile, as the folk-school tradition deepens, Langston Hughes,
> formerly its chief exponent, turns more and more in the direc-

tion of social protest and propaganda; since *Scottsboro Ltd.* repre-
sents his latest moods, although *The Dream Keeper* and *Popo and
Fifina* are also recent publications. The latter is a flimsy sketch, a
local-color story of Haitian child life, done in collaboration with
Arna Bontemps, while *The Dream Keeper* is really a collection of
the more lyrical of the poems in his first two volumes of verse,
supplemented by a few unprinted poems—all designed to be of
special appeal to child readers. The book is a delightful lyrical
echo of the older Hughes, who sang of his people as "walkers
with the dawn and morning," "loud-mouthed laughers in the
hands of fate." But the poet of *Scottsboro Ltd.* is a militant and
indignant proletarian reformer, proclaiming

> *"The voice of the red world*
> *Is our voice, too.*
> *The voice of the red world is you!*
> *With all the workers,*
> *Black or white,*
> *We'll go forward*
> *Out of the night."*[6]

Hughes must have expected as much from Locke. As bitter toward Hughes
as ever, the professor was watching him from afar and reporting regularly
to Mrs. Mason. Yet even she must have grown weary of Locke's repetitions
of how Langston was "trying to be the great red black poet" in Russia.[7] Of
far deeper concern to Hughes than the professor's opinions were the pieces
he was writing for *Izvestia, Krasnaya Nov,* and *International Literature,* which
were paying him the rubles he was living on.

What was uppermost in his mind that winter before he was to leave
Russia was his relationship with a beautiful Oriental ballerina, Si-lan Chen,
who was also known as "Sylvia." They had met in Moscow before he left
for Central Asia, and the romance had blossomed. "Si-lan was the girl I was
in love with that winter," he confessed later in *I Wonder as I Wander.* Three
years his junior, she was the first woman he came close to having any deep
emotional feeling for. But even that, as Si-lan herself soon saw, did not
mean he was ready for any deep commitment. His having reached age
thirty-one that February seemed to make little difference. "He wasn't an
easy person to know," she would say years later, "and he wasn't straight-
forward. He was the last person in the world that I would have ever thought
would get married. He was a serious person who found his outlet in his
work, not in committed, physical emotion."[8]

For those and other reasons, she thought Langston was fantasizing when, months after they met, she wrote him that she dreamed of having a baby and he responded—"ours." She wrote him back, "What do you mean 'ours'? No one ever thought of babies, except how not to have one. I'm trying hard, dear, to be a great dancer."[9]

Si-lan had her sights set on her career as much as Langston had on his. She had made her debut at the Bolshoi in 1929, after only two years in Moscow, and was one of the most promising young ballerinas on the Russian stage. Of Chinese descent, she had been born in Trinidad, and had spent part of her youth there and in China, where her father had been Minister of Foreign Affairs in the Provisional Republic of Sun Yat-sen. When the Chinese counterrevolution of 1927 forced the family to flee to Russia, family connections had led her to the renowned Russian choreographer, Kassiane Golieowsky. A solo dance performance in 1930 at the Moscow Conservatory had brought her raves, followed by concerts at the Theatre Vakhtangov and appearances throughout the Soviet Union.

Hughes never saw her dance, but he had been enchanted by her from the moment they met. "Si-lan, I found a delicate, flower-like girl, beautiful in a reedy, golden-skinned sort of way, in her long tight, high-necked dresses with a little slit at the side showing a very pretty leg." He forgot all about his short stature when he stood next to her. They could not have looked more as if they had been meant for each other. Langston, with his olive skin and black hair, was handsome, and his flirtatious smile belied a quiet reserve. Si-lan, who was his height on her tiptoes, looked and carried herself like a Mandarin princess.

Traveling in Uzbekistan in December, he had missed her last Moscow concert of the season, and when they met again in January—while she was preparing for a tour of the Crimea—they made the most of their time together. Her residence in the Hotel Metropole was within walking distance of his own in the Hotel New Moscow, and the snow never stopped him. She was "a winter's delight," he wrote, "serving me tea and cakes in her lovely room overlooking the Bolshoi Square on snowy afternoons, and telling me dramatic tales of the Chinese Revolution and the family flight over the Gobi Desert into Turkestan when the counter-revolution took over."

If Langston was in love with her, Si-lan was the last person to understand his way of showing it. Even when he appeared romantic, it was difficult to know his deepest feelings. The more affectionate he tried to be, the more confused he seemed. At age thirty-one, he had lost his battle against homosexuality, but it was not easy for him to accept defeat. He knew that his most intense emotional attachment had been not to a woman but to a man, whom he identified as "F.S." in a dedicatory poem in *The Weary Blues*:

Poem

I loved my friend.
He went away from me.
There's nothing more to say.
The poem ends,
Soft as it began,—
I loved my friend.[10]

The blame for his fear of the opposite sex rightly lay with his mother, whose emotional demands had made wounds that his father's indifference perhaps had deepened. Langston could not tell Si-lan any of this—if indeed, he himself knew what troubled him and why. Their brief love affair—if such it was—offered no promise of fulfillment to Si-lan and no more promise of spring to either of them than a sad poem Hughes had written three years before:

Spring for Lovers

Desire weaves its fantasy of dreams,
And all the world becomes a garden close
In which we wander, you and I together,
Believing in the symbol of the rose,
Believing only in the heart's bright flower—
Forgetting—flowers wither in an hour.[11]

Langston behaved as if he believed love to be as ephemeral as a flower, and Si-lan, hurt and baffled, soon left for the Crimea. But not before the desk clerk at the Hotel Metropole gave her a sealed envelope containing a poem Hughes had addressed to her:

I was so sad over half a kiss
That with half a pencil—
I write this.
Love,
Langston[12]

And from the Crimea, she responded with a poem of her own composition:

Like birds in flight we passed our way
We spent together a glorious day.
But we had to part, what for I don't know.
Because I liked you—I liked you so![13]

Along with her own verse, she sent a slightly revised version of Robert
Burns's "Red, Red Rose":

> My love is like a red, red, rose
> That's newly born in June.
> My love is like a melody
> That's sweetly played in tune.
> And do I love you? Dear, I think so deep in love am I
> That I would come to you my dear, though t'were
> Ten thousand miles.

Hughes's affair with Si-lan, about whom he wrote so little, was far
deeper than his "Moscow romance" with a young Soviet actress he called
"Natasha," who filled half a dozen pages in *I Wonder as I Wander*. Their
relationship, much less serious than it was complicated, caused Hughes
enough guilt to describe most of the details. Natasha, whom he met at a
rehearsal at the Meyerhold Theatre and soon found himself escorting to a
party, was married. Not more than a month passed before she was ready to
seek a divorce and follow the poet to America. He had hardly encouraged it,
but unwittingly had gotten more than he bargained for when he used her
help to renew his American passport in Latvia and to obtain necessary
documents to travel home through the Pacific.

Thinking her marital status freed him to send her home to her husband,
he invited her to his room—and that was another mistake. "She got into the
habit of coming to the hotel more and more often," he said later, "which
eventually got to be annoying." Although he intended it to be a brief affair,
some of his friends got quite another impression. John Sutton, an Afro-
American then living in the Soviet Union, would remember Hughes escorting a Tblisi-born actress whom he introduced to friends as "someone special."
Years later, Sutton, meeting Hughes in Harlem, asked the poet if he had
married the actress. Obviously startled and perhaps a bit chagrined, Hughes
responded "yes and no"—in a tone that indicated a reluctance to talk about
it.[14] His reticence about certain aspects of his personal life was legendary.
But although he tried to hide it, this much is clear: he was ambivalent about
women, and his tolerance of those who demanded affectionate attention
was low. Referring to his Russian actress friend in his autobiography, he
tells us he "did not want to be bothered with an almost nightly female
visitor." In Natasha's case, the excuse he gave was his writing and "D. H.
Lawrence Between Us."

HUGHES had never read D. H. Lawrence until that February 1933, when
he met at the New Moscow Hotel the British author Marie Seton, who lent
him her copy of short stories, *The Lovely Lady*.[15] The title story hooked

him. "The possessive, terrifying elderly woman in 'The Lovely Lady,' " he said, "seemed in some ways so much like my former Park Avenue patron that I could hardly bear to read the story, yet I could not put the book down." A few nights later, instead of writing an article for *Izvestia*, he began writing a short story.

The controversial Lawrence, who had been dead three years when Hughes first read his stories, influenced him—indeed, inspired him more emotionally than stylistically. In style, tone, and structure, his own prose bears little resemblance to the Englishman's. Moreover, Lawrence's reactionary political views, and even his frequent diatribes against women, might have alienated Hughes had he read any further than *The Lovely Lady*. But by late spring, his reading of Lawrence's stories had inspired him to write three of his own, one of which, "Boy on the Block," he sent to Blanche Knopf.

He wanted to write a book of short stories, he told her; but meantime she was turning down the idea of his Russian travelogue, *Dark People of the Soviet*.[16] "I can't see readers awaiting just a nice book about Russia from *your* pen," she wrote, and he was hurt when Knopf accepted a German author's manuscript on Turkmenistan and Uzbekistan.[17] But Hughes had grown accustomed to her subtle hints and demands, even if he was no longer influenced by them. The two had differed about publication of *The Dream Keeper*; when he chose Prentiss Taylor to illustrate it, she had engaged someone else. It was probably the reason why, that 1933, he wrote her that he wanted to be represented by a literary agent, Maxim Lieber, then one of the best in New York and highly respected in progressive political circles.

Although the Knopfs had discouraged Hughes's revolutionary verses, he didn't stop writing them. One of his best appeared in *International Literature* that spring.

Letter to the Academy

The gentlemen who have got to be classics and are now old with beards
    (or dead and in their graves) will kindly come forward and
    speak upon the subject

Of the Revolution. I mean the gentlemen who wrote lovely books about
    the defeat of the flesh and the triumph of the spirit that
    sold in the hundreds of thousands and are studied in the
    high schools and read by the best people will kindly come
    forward and

Speak about the Revolution—where the flesh triumphs (as well as the
    spirit) and the hungry belly eats, and there are no best
    people, and the poor are mighty and no longer poor, and the

young by the hundreds of thousands are free from hunger to
grow and study and love and propagate, bodies and souls unchained
without My Lord saying a commoner shall never marry
my daughter or the Rabbi crying cursed be the mating of Jews
and Gentiles or Kipling writing never the twain shall meet—

For the twain have met. But please—all you gentlemen with beards who
are so wise and old and who write better than we do and whose
souls have triumphed (in spite of hungers and wars and
the evils about you) and whose books have soared in calmness and
beauty aloof from the struggle to the library shelves and the
desks of students and who are now classics—come forward and
speak upon

The subject of the Revolution.

We want to know what in the hell you'd say?

If Hughes's claim that he was most prolific when he was unhappy was
true, his months in Moscow were not his happiest, for they were among the
most productive of his literary career. Paradoxically enough, they were also
the most rewarding financially. "I made more from writing in Moscow in
terms of buying power than I have ever earned anywhere," he said later.
Much of the writing he did in Moscow was about the U.S.S.R. One of his
essays was even entitled "About the U.S.S.R.," and others—published in
Izvestia in Russian and in English—bore such titles as "Youth and Learning
in Turkmenistan," "New People," and "White Gold in Soviet Asia."

Those American critics who claimed he followed a "party line," that he
wrote what was expected of him and not what he felt, failed to see the
whole picture. For more than a decade thereafter he defended the Soviet
Union, even into the dawn of the McCarthy era, when he was paid not a
ruble to do it. One recurring theme was the condition of the darker races in
Russia compared with those in America, and a paradigm of it was his 1935
article "Minority Peoples in Two Worlds" in *New Masses*.

Nor did the poetry he translated from the Russian follow a "party line,"
though it sometimes seemed to border on it.

He translated Boris Pasternak and Vladimir Mayakovsky, two opposites
if there ever were any.[18] Mayakovsky, who had committed suicide in 1930
and been given a hero's burial, was still very much a hero in 1933, officially
enshrined as the "Poet of Communism." Even though Lenin had referred to
his style as "hooligan," Mayakovsky was praised and honored by Soviet
officials. They had much less praise for Pasternak, even two decades before
his controversial novel *Doctor Zhivago* was awarded the Nobel Prize. "Ev-

eryone in Moscow seemed to think that Pasternak might fall into political disgrace at any time," Hughes wrote. Yet he found him a "gentle likable man, cultured in appearance and shy with strangers," and he translated Pasternak's poem "Beloved" in *I Wonder as I Wander.*

Soviet remarks to the effect that "Pasternak did not produce a lyric line about the Five Year Plan" led Hughes to another famous poet who did: Louis Aragon, the French Surrealist turned militant Communist. Hearing Aragon recite his long, revolutionary poem "Magnitogorsk" in Moscow that spring inspired Hughes to translate it from the French, and his translation appeared in *International Literature* that year.[19]

Aragon and his wife, the poet Elsa Triolet, were only two of many "foreigners" Hughes met in Moscow. Among others of whom he was to hear much again were Marie Seton, who would become the biographer of Sergei Eisenstein and, later, Paul Robeson; John Hope, president of Atlanta University, where Langston would one day be poet-in-residence; and William Patterson, lawyer and executive secretary of the International Labor Defense, which defended the Scottsboro Boys. (Seven years later Patterson would become the husband of Louise Thompson, the woman Hughes's mother had hoped Langston himself might marry.) Though Hughes had no inkling of it then, the lives of some of his Soviet friends would end in tragedy. Karl Radek, an editor of *Izvestia*, would disappear in a purge. The Soviet dramatist Sergei Tretiakov, whose play *Roar, China* inspired the title for one of Hughes's poems, would be shot dead—"liquidated," to use the poet's own word—in 1938.

Hughes could not have foreseen in the spring of 1933 that Soviet domestic policy would take a sharp turn in December 1934, when Sergei Kirov, a rising Soviet official, was assassinated. It was then that Stalin's infamous purges began. But in 1933, the same year that Franklin D. Roosevelt offered official United States diplomatic recognition to Russia, Hughes had written to Ella Winter and Lincoln Steffens that he himself had "seen the future and it worked." Even the weather seemed a promise of brighter things. Winter was gone, the ice had melted on the Moscow River, and the trees and shrubs around the Kremlin Wall were blossoming under an azure sky. But it was time to leave. He had never intended to remain indefinitely. Nevertheless, he was apprehensive about traveling home via Germany, where reports about the rise of fascism and Hitler were ominous. That February the Nazis had set fire to the Reichstag, blamed the Communists, and, a month later, given Hitler abolute power for four years.

Hughes was determined to travel home via the Orient. He had dreams of seeing Peking and had already applied for his exit visa and tickets on the Trans-Siberian Express when the American author Agnes Smedley arrived from China saying that the situation there was grave. The dark clouds over the East had seemed at most only a distant threat, although the Japanese had occupied Manchuria and set up the puppet state of Manchukuo. They had invaded the international section of Shanghai and bombed Chapei.

The official Soviet travel bureau, Intourist, seemed "determined" to make an enemy of Hughes. He was thrown into depression by Intourist's delays in securing tickets and reservations, though the rest of official Russia indulged, respected, and paid him the singular honor of providing him a choice seat from which to view the May Day ceremonial parade.

His spirits lifted when Intourist, after making excuses and changes for several weeks, finally confirmed his reservations to leave Russia by the first of June. He knew it was then or never, for news that the Japanese had cut the Chinese railway at the Siberian border meant he had no time to lose.

Following a surprise farewell party, he was given a grand send-off at the Moscow railway station, where the atmosphere was "like that of a New York pier when a big liner is sailing." For his departure on June 7, the members of the Soviet Writers Union, the Meyerhold Theater troupe, and practically all the American colony were there.

Even Natasha, whom he had missed seeing in the crowd, was waving on the platform. A few days before, irate over his imminent departure, she had caused a big scene at his hotel. He had barely settled into his seat on the Trans-Siberian Express when the door of the compartment burst open—and there Natasha stood. She was, she said, going with him to Vladivostok. Taken aback, Hughes tried to reason with her, but she was adamant and began to cry. After several hours of talk, Natasha was persuaded to go back to Moscow. Bidding him a teary farewell, she got off at a small wayside station to take another train. He had begged her to do just that, and—he wrote later—"when she got off alone in the dark, I felt unkind, ungallant, embarrassed and unhappy...I felt very sad, very bad—yet very glad she didn't go any further." She had left behind gifts—a notebook for him and a Russian cashmere shawl for his mother. On the last page of the notebook she had written in French: "Comfort yourself—if there is a sin, it's my sin. Love me."

After ten days on the longest railroad in the world, he arrived in Vladivostok on the Bay of the Golden Horn. It signaled the end of a year-long journey through the Soviet Union, a part of the world he would never see again.

❧ 14 ❧

Chains of the East

VLADIVOSTOK SEEMED TO HUGHES more like the end of the world than the end of the Trans-Siberian Railroad. It was a dreary city on a peninsula, the site of a Russian naval base, and most of the area around it was marked off limits to tourists. He stayed only one day there before setting sail for Japan.

En route to Tokyo by boat, his first glimpse of the Orient was during a one-day stopover in Seishin, Korea, followed by a night in Kyoto, the Imperial City of Japan, where he was treated to an evening with the world famous "geisha girls." Kyoto seemed to him to be the most beautiful of Japanese cities, but as "impersonal as a Technicolor movie."

If it was a more personal touch he wanted, he got it in Tokyo, especially at the Tsukiji Theater—a progressive theatre where *Porgy* had been performed—and where he was hailed by the cast as the first black American writer to see one of the troupe's performances. From Moscow, Seki Sano, a former director of the Tsukiji, had written the cast to expect Hughes, whose poetry had already been translated into Japanese.

"Before reaching Tokyo," he wrote later, "I had made up my mind—come what may, and even if I went broke doing it—to stay at the much talked of Imperial Hotel built by Frank Lloyd Wright."[1] When the local newspapers discovered he was staying at Tokyo's Imperial Hotel, "from then on for the next two weeks, my time was not my own," he wrote later. "I was interviewed, photographed, shown the town, the temples, the theaters, the parks, the university; wined, dined and entertained most interestingly and energetically but finally to the point where I wished I'd remained anonymous a little longer."

But by the time he was seen at the Tsukiji Theater and in the presence of left-wing Japanese writers, he was no longer anonymous to the Japanese police. "I did not realize the Tsukiji was under a political cloud," he remembered afterwards. "But I learned later that it was considered a center of left-wing activities, pacifist, and opposed to the current Japanese invasion of China."

Nor did he know that he was being shadowed when he sailed for China aboard the *Empress of Canada* on July 1, or that the Tokyo Metropolitan Police Board had warned the Japanese consulate in Shanghai to track his every move when he arrived there.

JAPAN, pushing hard its invasion of China that summer of 1933, had not yet besieged Shanghai, the largest city. Shanghai would not be captured by Japan for four years, but it was already under foreign domination. With Shanghai's International Settlement still occupied by American and foreign powers—they had been there since the 1842 Treaty of Nanking—Shanghai seemed anything but Chinese to Hughes. "I was constantly amazed in Shanghai at the impudence of white foreigners drawing a color line against the Chinese, *in China itself,*" he wrote afterward. Worse, he found that "the Japanese were quicker to slap a Chinese coolie than the white colonial overlords."

Only weeks before he arrived, the Japanese had bombed Chapei, one of the Chinese sections of Shanghai, and Japanese guards were everywhere. Appalled to see that they had done nothing to try to stop the heavy traffic in narcotics and prostitution so long tolerated in the International Settlement, he later complained in *I Wonder as I Wander* that "cruelty and violence, corruption and graft, were written all over the face of Shanghai the summer I was there."

An enormous, sprawling place inhabited by four million people, Shanghai's International Settlement was separated from its Chinese sections by barbed wire fences and police patrols. Trying to see all the city was like trying to catch a dragon by the tail. His three-week stay was a delusive nightmare. Racial discrimination, poverty, vice, and drug racketeering put it on the map as the worst city Hughes had ever seen. None of the leading hotels in the International Settlement accepted Afro-American guests, though many were readily accepted as performers in Shanghai nightclubs. But it was not his intention to see only the cafes and clubs, and such tourist attractions as the Bubbling Well Road, the amusement park, the gambling casinos, and the race tracks. In search of the real China, which most tourists never saw, he ventured into the textile factories, where agents sold children into slave labor, and into the crowded back streets of the Chinese sections of town.

> Despite the warnings by Occidentals not to go outside the International Settlements alone at night nor wander too far even by day into the Chinese districts of Shanghai, I did so many times just to see what would happen. Nothing happened. I had been told, too, not to trust rickshaw boys outside the Settlement

boundaries—they might lead the unwary stranger into traps.
None did. The rickshaw men waited patiently for me if I chose
to descend from their cabs and walk around in the teeming,
odd-smelling exotic streets or go into the shops. So I came to the
conclusion that perhaps these well-meant warnings . . . might have
some validity for white foreigners—not much liked by the Shanghai masses in spite of years of missionary charities.

What Hughes saw in Shanghai resulted in his long, revolutionary poem,
"Roar, China," urging the Chinese masses to break the chains of foreign
domination. But he was certain the chains would not be broken under the
Chinese Nationalist flag of Chiang Kai-shek. Six years earlier, Chiang had
formed a right-wing government at Nanking in opposition to the left-wing
Kuomintang movement and all who did not support him. Hughes remembered the stories of Si-lan Chen, whose family had fled China to escape
Chiang's retribution, and he knew that neither the Nationalists nor the
Japanese puppet regime in China offered any hope for real reform. Moreover, Chiang's forces were fighting not only the Chinese Communists but
the Japanese. In Hughes's eyes, it all seemed to mean protracted war, with
no peace in sight.

He was as convinced as some of the Chinese intellectuals, whom he met
at private gatherings, that the nation's only hope seemed to be with the
Communists. One Chinese author who seemed certain of it was Lu Hsün,
also known as Chou Shu-jen, then the most famous literary figure in modern China. Hughes remembered him in *I Wonder as I Wander* as "under a
political cloud for his 'dangerous thoughts,' " perhaps never knowing that
the writer died of mysterious causes at age fifty-five—three years after they
met.

Hughes's meeting in China with people such as Lu Hsün and Soong
Ching-ling, better known as Madame Sun Yat-sen, caused Hughes trouble
with the Japanese police. Not only did they know that he had dined at the
Shanghai home of Madame Sun Yat-sen, they also knew he had traveled by
train to Nanking to visit the tomb of her late husband, the founder of the
Republic of China in 1911. To the Japanese, it was political heresy to revere
the memory of a man who, before his death in 1925, had agreed to work
with the Chinese Communists and had accepted help from the Russians.

The Japanese police must have told Hughes as much when they interro-
gated him aboard the N.Y.K. Line vessel, *Taiyo Maru*, en route from
Shanghai to Yokohama. He had almost missed the boat in Shanghai—as
usual, he was the last passenger aboard—but the Japanese police and port
authorities were waiting for him the next day in Kobe. When he sought to
go ashore for one day as an in-transit passenger, officials there pushed and

shoved him until, protesting loudly, he made a scene. In Yokohama, while the ship loaded cargo during a three-day layover, he disembarked, only to be harassed by more officials asking why he had gone to China, why he had visited Madame Sun Yat-sen, who happened to be not only the wife of the founder of the Republic of China but also the sister-in-law of Chiang Kai-shek.

Having reserved space on the *Taiyo Maru* for a July 25 sailing date to San Francisco, Hughes was allowed by police to disembark for a few days' layover in Tokyo, where he again stayed at the Imperial Hotel. The barriers of racial segregation had barred him from such luxury hotels in the United States, but not even the absence of the color bar in Tokyo meant he could come and go there as he pleased. The Japanese police saw to that.

One day into his Tokyo layover, he was placed in detention before he could even attend a farewell luncheon given in his honor by the leftist Central Committee of the Japanese League of Writers. Taken to the Tokyo Metro-politan Police Board for questioning, he was held for six hours and forced to make "official" statements about what he had done in Russia and China, what he had discussed with Madame Sun Yat-sen, what organizations he belonged to, and what his intentions were in Japan. Saying anything contrary to what the Japanese officials believed only made matters worse. "I realized that the Tokyo police had an almost complete dossier on everything I had done in both Tokyo and Shanghai," he wrote later. "I was amazed as well as flattered that my activities had been so closely watched."

He would not have been flattered, though, had he ever known that the foreign police in Shanghai's International Settlement had titled their report, "Movements of James Langston Hughes, American *Nigger* Writer in Japan." Nor would he have been pleased that their documents, along with statements to the Tokyo police, were exchanged in confidential memos between the American consul general in Shanghai and the U.S. State Department.[2]

Although he had threatened to contact American consulate representatives in Tokyo when he was detained, he never did—perhaps because he anticipated that they would have been in no position to intervene on behalf of the Japanese writers jailed for attending a luncheon in his honor. Ordered by Japanese authorities to have no further communication with Japanese citizens in Tokyo, Hughes was asked to leave the country within two days on the *Taiyo Maru*—on which he had already booked passage—and not to return to Japan again.

Before leaving the country, he gave his story to a sympathetic *New York Times* reporter, Stanley Wood. He told Wood how, after being inconvenienced by the Tokyo police, Japanese detectives had accompanied him to his hotel, searched his belongings, and examined every letter and document in his possession. However, the *New York Times* did not use Wood's version of the story—if he filed one; it printed an Associated Press dispatch, datelined Tokyo, Tuesday, July 25, 1933:

AUTHOR TO LEAVE JAPAN
J. L. Hughes Will Depart
After Questioning
As To Communism

James Langston Hughes, American Negro author, engaged passage on the steamer Taiyo Maru from Yokohama today for San Francisco after six hours of questioning by Tokyo police yesterday.

The police suspected Hughes of communicating with the Japanese Communist movement, which is being vigorously suppressed. This was not proved, but the police "suggested" that Hughes leave Japan immediately.

He arrived here Sunday from Shanghai after a recent visit to Russia. Eleven Japanese visitors in Hughes's hotel also were questioned as suspected of communism, but they were later released.[3]

The day he left Tokyo for Yokohama to board the *Taiyo Maru*, the daily *Japan Times and Mail* alleged that he was being deported. Sailing for the United States through the Pacific via Honolulu, he had plenty of time to read translations of everything the Japanese language newspapers printed about him. One of the charges infuriated him, and twenty-three years later it still rankled:

In Honolulu, I was shown, too, an alleged interview with me before I departed from Tokyo in which I was quoted by the Tokyo *Nichi Nichi* as saying that Japan was the destined savior of the darker races of the world, the leader of Asia, and a great stabilizing force in those areas of backward China where the armies of the Rising Sun were spreading culture. Apparently what had happened after I sailed from Japan was that the Japanese police had composed and released to the press a purported "interview" with me in which words were put into my mouth affirming all the pro-war attitudes I had heard expressed at the

Metropolitan Police Headquarters by my interrogators, but to which I did not subscribe. In the Japanese-language papers, I was pictured, on sailing, as praising Japan's imperialism to the highest. This fake interview seemed to me a most dastardly and contemptible thing to impose upon a visitor.

Hughes would have been equally perturbed had he ever seen the statements he was alleged to have made to the Tokyo police during his interrogation on July 23. But he never saw that report, which was kept classified in the confidential files of the U.S. State Department's Division of Far Eastern Affairs, and not declassified until after his death. He never knew what was lost in translation or changed by Japanese authorities in a report that had him saying the following:

> My name is James Langston Hughes, age 31, born in Missouri, U.S.A. . . . My parents are niggers and they were divorced when I was a child. . . . I am connected with the following organizations:
> International Revolutionary Writers League
> International Revolutionary Plot Writers League
> Authors League
> Dramatist Guild
> National Association for Advancement of Colored People
> Laborers Cultural League
> Being a Negro I have been struggling for the emancipation of the Negroes and of the oppressed masses and will continue my struggle forever. Communism aims at the emancipation of the oppressed masses but I still doubt whether or not complete freedom can be secured through the realization of Communism. I do not claim to be a Communist but I do not object to be regarded as a sympathizer because I sympathize with and support all Communist movements and also all oppressed people. After all, I am a liberalist who is interested in Communism and the struggles for the emancipation of the oppressed. . . . [4]

Terms such as "nigger" and "liberalist"—as translated by the Japanese— were hardly vintage Hughes. Nor was the tone of his remarks to the Tokyo police the same tone in which he described his Japanese experience in *I Wonder as I Wander*. Published in 1956, during the McCarthy "red-baiting" era, the autobiography muted any sympathies for Communism, but his earlier writings on the subject had been quite explicit.

But by the time *I Wonder as I Wander* was published, hindsight had made clear an incident he had not fully understood in 1933: why an agent from the Bureau of Investigation had shown up in Honolulu that summer not "to greet" him but "to meet" him. The Bureau, not known officially as the Federal Bureau of Investigation until 1935, had been controlled since May 10, 1924, by its director: his name was J. Edgar Hoover, and until his death nearly half a century later his rule was absolute. Under his anticommunist and anti-Negro rule, the FBI kept a file on Langston Hughes, and it remained classified until after the poet's death.

Hughes had no knowledge of those developments on the sunny August morning the *Taiyo Maru* sailed through the Golden Gate and docked in San Francisco. Noel Sullivan, whom he had written in advance, was waiting to greet him. After fourteen months, it was a welcome ending to a long voyage around the world. The economic depression had not come to an end when he arrived that summer of 1933, but "depression or no depression," he admitted later, "I was glad to be in my own land again."

❧ 15 ❧

Blood on the Fields

IN SAN FRANCISCO, HUGHES GOT A ROYAL WELCOME at Sullivan's Hyde Street mansion, where he arrived in style in his host's chauffeur-driven car. After an absence of fifteen months, no luxury was spared for him, and he joked later that "safely housed on Russian Hill above the Golden Gate, it was fun to get back to Capitalism." Eulah Pharr and her husband, who were still members of the household staff, saw to his comfort, and Sullivan, with festive luncheons and dinner parties, made Langston the toast of the town.

For at least a week, guests streamed in and out of the house eager to hear of the poet's travel adventures, leaving him little time for anything else. "The prelude to work at Hyde Street was delightful," he remembered later, "for, as before when I was there, fascinating guests were coming and going daily."[1] Among them were two Afro-American concert singers then better known to audiences in Europe than the United States: Marian Anderson, the contralto who had received raves that year in over a hundred concerts in Scandinavia; and tenor Roland Hayes, whose Fisk Jubilee Singer-trained voice Hughes remembered Godmother Mason as saying was better suited to Negro spirituals than "European music." Hughes would remember that years later when he wrote "most people thought of Negro vocalists only in connection with Spirituals. Roland Hayes and Marian Anderson were the first to become famous enough to break this stereotype."[2]

But the conversations that August 1933 at Sullivan's parties were less about Hayes's singing German lieder than about the frightening political developments in Germany. On April 1, some four months earlier, the Nazis had declared "Anti-Semitic Day," and the "official" boycotts of Jews began. Hughes, who had heard rumors of Nazi concentration camps before he left Russia, and was concerned about the worsening global scene in general, had written Noel Sullivan aboard the Trans-Siberian Express that "it sounds as if the whole world were falling to pieces."[3]

In the same letter he had also written, "I've taken the liberty of sending to myself at your address—things that would be difficult to get through the customs in Japan as they confiscate most written material coming out of the Soviet Union."[4] He was more than glad later that he had followed his intuition. The Japanese police, who did detain him, would probably have confiscated and destroyed all his photographs of Soviet Central Asia and the travelogues and short stories he wrote while in Russia.

Settling in at Sullivan's, Hughes caught up with the news at home and abroad. Except for the overthrow of Gerardo Machado, the Cuban dictator who had harassed him in Havana two years earlier, the news was nothing to cheer about. The young son of aviator Charles Lindbergh had been kidnapped and murdered months before; organized crime seemed to have increased coast to coast; unemployment was nationwide; shantytowns had sprung up everywhere; many banks and factories still had their doors closed; and many Americans doubted that the new President, Franklin Delano Roosevelt, inaugurated that March 4, could make his "New Deal" work.

In these circumstances, Hughes saw little for himself to do except what he knew how to do best: to write. Moreover, uncertain about his own finances, except for a July royalty check from Knopf and the sale of two pieces to the *American Mercury* and *Scribner's Magazine*, he welcomed the invitation from his always generous host to spend the next year, rent-free, at Ennesfree, Sullivan's beach home at Carmel-by-the-Sea. It meant a chance to write without financial worries and to complete the book of short stories he had started in Russia.

He was more gratified than he could express, and when he settled in as "writer-in-residence" that autumn, he was given the protection of Sullivan's German shepherd watchdog, the service of a houseboy who prepared his meals, and the professional assistance of a part-time secretary and researcher, Roy Blackburn, who would eventually serve as Hughes's "West Coast" secretary intermittently for the next three decades. Hughes and Blackburn shared a private joke: they had helped "integrate" Carmel. Except for the two of them, and three local black families, there were hardly enough Afro-Americans to count.

The picturesque beauty of its wide beach, the seaside cliffs, the quaint streets, had made Carmel-by-the-Sea a unique (and affluent) community, and an "artist's colony." Some well-known writers and artists had made it home since the 1920s, and they were followed by dilettantes. Curious tourists also wandered in and out as quickly as the tides, hoping to see such Hollywood stars as Greta Garbo, Jean Harlow, and other celebrities. When Prohibition ended that December, the village also attracted a few undesirable visitors known as "Vigilantes" who came from nearby Monterrey to drink in the local bars and make trouble for residents, including Hughes.

But throughout that autumn, he spent most of his time in peace and quiet at Ennesfree, working ten to twelve hours a day on his short stories, which he finished just before Christmas and gave to Noel Sullivan.

> DEAR NOEL:
> These stories are for you. You helped me with them, have listened to many of them before they were ever written, have read them all, have given me the music, and the shelter of your roof, and the truth of your friendship, and the time to work. You're a swell fellow and having cast your bread upon the waters, it comes back to you (this time) in manuscript. My first drafts.
> Happy Birthday! Merry Christmas! and a glorious New Year.[5]

The book of short stories, *The Ways of White Folks*, was published by Knopf some seven months later, in June 1934, and dedicated "To Noel Sullivan" with a quote from one of the book's characters:

> The ways of white folks,
> I mean some white folks...

It was certainly not a book about the ways of such white folks as Noel Sullivan. Every story in the book was biting, trenchant, and critical of the prevailing attitudes of whites toward Afro-Americans at the time. It represented Langston Hughes at the top of his literary talent for pathos and satire.

In several letters to Sullivan in 1933, he mentions "the Englishman" who may have helped him polish the final manuscript. Whoever that "Englishman" was, Hughes himself may never have known, except that he was an acquaintance of Sullivan's. In one letter Hughes told Sullivan, referring to the short story, "Red Headed Baby":

> Here is the poor little half-caste red-headed baby. Kindly turn him over to the Englishman and see if he can make him whiter than snow in the final draft.[6]

In another undated note from Carmel, he confided:

> I finished my story and here it is, if you will be so kind as to send it to the Englishman. Please tell him how much I appreciated the other being so beautifully done. If you wish to send me his address, I can post material directly to him and save you the trouble.[7]

Whatever the nameless Englishman did to make Hughes's fictional white characters "whiter than snow," Hughes himself gave them their essential character. He had begun to shape and write three of the stories while staying

at the New Moscow Hotel in the spring of 1933. He sent them via Blanche
Knopf to Maxim Lieber, a New York literary agent who had agreed to
represent him. In July 1933, Lieber wrote to Hughes:

> Several months ago, Mrs. Knopf sent me your story, "The Boy
> on the Block" with the information that you had asked me to
> represent you. I enjoyed the piece and promptly sold it to *Scribner*'s
> and now I hold a check for you. I wrote this to your Moscow
> address but apparently you had already left Moscow for your
> trip to Shanghai. . . . By all means send me all your material, I
> shall be very glad to represent you, and perhaps in the future we
> may make an arrangement to include your books as well as your
> magazine work.[8]

Upon his return to the States, while living temporarily in California,
Hughes wasted no time; he sent to Lieber two more stories in September
1933. "I cannot be too sanguine as to their sales possibilities," Lieber quickly
wrote him. "I enjoyed both of them, but I can imagine how shocked every
bourgeois editor in town would be with either of these pieces."[9]

One of the stories was "The Blues I'm Playing," which, despite Lieber's
skepticism about its marketability, was sold almost immediately to *Scribner's
Magazine*. Depicting a wealthy white New York dowager, Mrs. Dora Ellsworth, as patron to a young Harlem pianist, Oceola Jones, with whom she
disagrees about the meaning of art, love, and life, the story was the closest
Hughes ever came to giving his readers a glimpse of his own former patron,
Charlotte Mason. However, the fictional patron in his story encourages
none of the "exotic primitive" or blues and jazz syncopation in her protégée's work as Godmother Mason did with Hughes and others during the
Harlem Renaissance. Instead, the refined Mrs. Ellsworth is for classical
music, Old Master paintings, jade vases, French language and culture, wearing "black velvet and a collar of pearls," making uncomplimentary remarks
about Jews, and spending summers in Bar Harbor or Europe—all of which
fit the true Charlotte Mason's personal tastes, characteristics, and habits.
His opening description of Dora Ellsworth was actually Godmother:

> Poor dear lady, she had no children of her own. Her husband
> was dead. And she had no interest in life now, save art, and the
> young people who created art. She was very rich, and it gave her
> pleasure to share her richness with beauty. Except that she was
> sometimes confused as to where beauty lay—in the youngsters
> or in what they made, in the creators or the creation.

The other piece Lieber was doubtful about selling was "Home," a story
about a lynching. It was six months before he sold it to *Esquire*, where it

appeared in May 1934. A month earlier, the magazine had published another of Hughes's stories, "A Good Job Gone"—with even greater hesitation. "After making the purchase, the editor suddenly became alarmed and is wondering if he will ever have the courage to print the story," Lieber wrote Hughes.[10] But print it he did, and protest letters poured in to the editor for five months. Narrated by a black houseboy, "A Good Job Gone" was the story of a wealthy white *roué* with a paralyzed wife and a penchant for wine, women, and song. He succumbs to a Harlem chorus girl, who exploits him for all he has to give. The story infuriated some white readers, but "A Good Job Gone" was later reprinted in the *Bedside Esquire* anthology.[11]

Lieber was successful in placing in magazines ten of Hughes's fourteen stories before they were published in *The Ways of White Folks*. Some periodicals rejected the stories outright. *The Atlantic Monthly* refused "Home":

> Why is that authors think it is their function to lay the flesh bare and rub salt in the wound? The Langston Hughes story is both powerful and delicate, but we cannot forget that most people read for pleasure, and certainly there is no pleasure to be found here.[12]

Lieber was undaunted, though the work of his best-known white clients—Erskine Caldwell, John Cheever, Nathanael West, Thomas Wolfe—sold quickly and well. Nevertheless, he succeeded in putting Hughes's work into many major American magazines in 1934, including *American Mercury, Esquire, Harper's, The New Yorker, Scribner's*, and a few lesser-known periodicals such as *Abbott's Mercury*, the *Brooklyn Daily Eagle* and *Debate*. Finding the articles Hughes wrote in the Soviet Union unacceptable to most of the popular American publications, Lieber sent some of them to *New Masses*. The poet's controversial short story, "Mother and Child," and an excerpt from his booklet *A Negro Looks at Soviet Central Asia* appeared there that year. "My feeling about such things," Lieber wrote Hughes, "is that it's better to get them into the big bourgeois publications to give a glimmer of what it's all about to a large audience than to send them to already radical publics."[13]

Lieber, although he was more subtle about it, was no less a crusader for social justice and political reform than Hughes, and in time they became close confidants and friends. But even before their face-to-face personal meeting, Hughes, who was Lieber's junior by five years, had a sense of the man from his letters and their mutual friends. Lieber's preference for reading books instead of selling them had led him from being head of Brentano's publishing department to head of his own agency. With his Ivy-League tweeds and horn-rimmed glasses, he looked more like a young professor than a Fifth Avenue agent, but he knew the New York literary scene well, and would act as Hughes's protector in it for the next two decades.

Early in 1934, Lieber warned Hughes:

> Publishers have a way of beguiling authors with smiles, for they
> charge you plenty by attempting to get cuts of all sorts of rights
> on your books. I don't want to sound elementary except that
> authors are usually naïve when it comes to business matters so
> that a publisher sometimes gets from twenty-five to fifty percent
> of foreign rights, motion picture rights, and everything they can
> hog . . . of course the publishers would be outraged to hear this. . . . [14]

Lieber managed to negotiate a literary contract for *The Ways of White
Folks* better than any Hughes had previously received from Knopf. The
money came at a time of pressing financial need. Hughes's mother, Carolyn, was still quickly spending every dollar he sent her, and usually demanding more than he earned. The year before, she had satisfied her yearning to
be on the stage by appearing in a bit part in the Broadway production of
Hall Johnson's *Run Little Chillun*; now she was unemployed and too embarrassed to go on public relief. Besides, she wrote Langston that, having a son
who was a "great" writer, she wouldn't *dare* do such a thing.

Hughes was probably comforted by the fact that his mother was not
alone in her opinion of him as a writer. When *The Ways of White Folks* was
published that summer, a critic in *Books* wrote that "with the range of these
fourteen stories, . . . I suspect that Langston Hughes is revealing here that
mysterious quality in writing that we call genius."[15] The *New York Times
Book Review* praised him for writing "about the impact of one race upon
another with the confidence of the intelligent self-respecting man."[16] But the
critic in the daily *New York Times*, perhaps somewhat less enthusiastic,
though not unappreciative, and not without honest appraisal, even if with a
hint of nostalgia for the Jazz Age, wrote, "For short story purposes Mr.
Hughes has discarded the swinging vibrant rhythms of his poems in *The
Weary Blues* and *Fine Clothes to the Jew* . . . and is pretty well fed up with
members of his race who believe in the New Negro."[17]

It was that aspect of the book that angered Alain Locke. In a review in
The Survey Graphic, he wrote, "An important book for the present times,
but greater artistry, deeper sympathy and less resentment would have made
it a book for all times."[18]

Locke, still harboring deep resentment for Hughes and perennially expressing it in letters to Godmother, had even harsher words for *The Ways of
White Folks* in his correspondence to her. Assured that she would "instantly
see through it as self justification and willful egotism,"[19] he saw in it—probably
as well as she did—her resemblance to Dora Ellsworth. Forever eager to
turn up anything he could to give Langston a verbal flogging, that March he
had sent Godmother a clipping of Hughes's caustic essay, "Would You

Fight for the U.S. in the Next War?"—with a note attached: "The latest blast from Langston—in which his megolamania grows to ridiculous proportions—like Aesop's Frog."[20]

Locke's expressions of enmity for Hughes did not slacken even after Charlotte Mason had entered New York Hospital in the autumn of 1933. Confined for medical treatment of a broken hip, she would remain hospitalized as a cripple for the next thirteen years. Meanwhile, she clung to life for all it was worth, dictating letters, receiving mail and visitors, and living in the style to which she had become accustomed, with her hospital room decorated in a style reminiscent of a suite she had kept in New York's luxurious Barclay Hotel. Her income continued through the same sources from which it had flowed for thirty years since her husband's death: trusts from a few wealthy private donors who believed that Dr. Rufus Osgood Mason had "cured" them through therapeutic hypnotism. Whatever he had done through his work and his articles in such esoteric publications as the *Journal of the Society for Psychical Research*, he had convinced his wife and others like her of the "influence of the mind over various organs and functions of the body." For over a decade in the New York Hospital, she would defy death. Mind over matter kept her alive. It was no belief in God which sustained her, nor any faith in the Christian Science of Mary Baker Eddy, for like her long-deceased husband, Mrs. Mason was disposed to quote from his book, *Hypnotism and Suggestion*: "Eddyism has been evolved out of an exuberant, ill-regulated, emotional, subconscious mind without the supervision of disciplined intelligence, and the consequences have been simply disastrous."[21]

Although Locke continued to send Mrs. Mason clippings about Hughes's political posture in 1934, he appears not to have sent her the poet's most explosive verse of the year: "One More 'S' in the U.S.A." Being no reader of the Communist tabloid, the *Daily Worker*, where the poem was published as a "workers' song" to commemorate the eighth convention of the Communist Party held in Cleveland in April, Locke missed out on what he surely would have bombasted.

One More "S" in the U.S.A.

> Put one more S in the U.S.A.
> To make it Soviet.
> One more S in the U.S.A.
> Oh, we'll live to see it yet.
> When the land belongs to the farmers
> And the factories to the working men—
> The U.S.A. when we take control
> Will be the U.S.S.A. then.

Now across the water in Russia
They have a big U.S.S.R.
The fatherland of the Soviets—
But that is mighty far
From New York, or Texas, or California, too.
So listen, fellow workers,
This is what we have to do.

    Put one more S in the U.S.A. [Repeat chorus]

But we can't win out by just talking.
So let us take things in our hand.
Then down and way with the bosses' sway—
Hail Communistic land.
So stand up in battle and wave our flag on high,
And shout out fellow workers
Our new slogan to the sky:

    Put one more S in the U.S.A.

But we can't join hands strong together
So long as whites are lynching black,
So black and white in one union fight
And get on the right track.
By Texas, or Georgia, or Alabama led
Come together, fellow workers
Black and white can all be red:

    Put one more S in the U.S.A.

Oh, the bankers they all are planning
For another great big war.
To make them rich from the workers' dead,
That's all that war is for.
So if you don't want to see bullets holding sway
Then come on, all you workers,
And join our fight today:

    Put one more S in the U.S.A.
    To make it Soviet.
    One more S in the U.S.A.
    Oh, we'll live to see it yet.
    When the land belongs to the farmers
    And the factories to the working men—
    The U.S.A. when we take control
    Will be the U.S.S.A. then.[22]

ALMOST A YEAR after returning from the Soviet Union, Hughes was writing as if he were still there, innocently forgetting that there were too few Americans willing to join in his chorus for "One More 'S' in the U.S.A." Nevertheless, American Communists were not then considered *personae non gratae* and forced into isolation, as they later came to be. Even Republicans and Democrats sought their support in the 1930s; the Young Communist League was openly active on many college campuses, and the Communist and non-Communist left was already working toward the policy of the Popular Front adopted by 1935. But two decades later, during the McCarthy mania, Hughes would find those he once thought were in the chorus for "One More 'S' in the U.S.A." changing their tune to "God Bless America." Communist defectors such as Louis Budenz, a one-time managing editor of the *Daily Worker*, would become superpatriots, accusing Hughes and others of equal prominence of having been members of the Communist Party.

Writing a poem for the eighth convention of the Communist Party U.S.A. was no proof that he had joined it. But he made no secret of the fact that he supported it. In 1934, he also supported the celebration of the tenth anniversary of the *Daily Worker*. Along with his fellow writers in Carmel, Lincoln Steffens and Ella Winter, he wrote a personal message that "The *Daily Worker*, so far as I know, is the only daily voice in America that consistently and without deviation constantly calls for the complete liberation of the Negro masses, and works for their full and equal place in American life. Every Negro receiving a regular salary in this country should subscribe to the *Daily Worker*, and share it with his brothers who are unemployed."[23]

Living in comfort in Carmel-by-the-Sea that year never really saved Hughes from the tides of the economic depression. The signs of unemployment and class struggle were all around him in Northern California, where longshoremen in San Francisco and farm workers in the San Joaquin Valley were being arrested and often fired upon by police for striking and organizing unions. As soon as he finished *The Ways of White Folks*, he was more than ready to join Carmel's "resident radicals" such as Steffens and Winter and their friends in the local John Reed Club. Starting off the year in the Carmel branch of the National Committee for the Defense of Political Prisoners, he literally declared his sympathetic involvement in a poem "Ballad of Lenin," published in the proletarian review *The Anvil* and reprinted in the *Daily Worker*.

Ballad of Lenin

Comrade Lenin of Russia,
High in a marble tomb
Move over, Comrade Lenin,

And give me room.
    I am Ivan, the peasant,
    Boots all muddy with soil.
    I fought with you, Comrade Lenin,
    Now I have finished my toil.
Comrade Lenin of Russia,
Alive in a marble tomb,
Move over, Comrade Lenin,
And give me room.
    I am Chico, the Negro,
    Cutting cane in the sun.
    I lived for you, Comrade Lenin
    Now my work is done.
Comrade Lenin of Russia,
Honored in a marble tomb.
Move over, Comrade Lenin,
And give me room.
    I am Chang from the foundries
    On strike in the streets of Shanghai
    For the sake of the Revolution
    I fight, I starve, I die.
Comrade Lenin of Russia
Rises in the marble tomb:
On guard with the fighters forever!
The world is our room.

In cadences imitative of Carl Sandburg, Hughes's literary idol, his poetic tribute in 1934 to the tenth anniversary of Lenin's death was only one of the ways he involved his own spirit in the revolutionary struggle. International poet, voice of the underdog, weary of oppression and corruption, he was as ready to support the fight of California's striking workers as he had been to urge China's masses to break their chains. He made that fact clear in another poem published in the February 1934 issue of *New Masses*. The title was "Revolution."

Revolution

Great mob that knows no fear—
Come here!
And raise your hand
Against this man
Of iron and steel and gold

Who's bought and sold
You—
Each one—
For the last thousand years.
Come here,
Great mob that knows no fear,
And tear him limb from limb,
Split his golden throat
Ear to ear,
And end his time forever,
Now—
This year—
Great mob that knows no fear.

That same month, Hughes organized with the assistance of Carmel friends Ella Winter and Marie Short the Scottsboro Defense Fund Exhibit in San Francisco. The response was encouraging. Literary acquaintances and friends, "who based their inspiration (or a portion of it) on the life of the Negro peoples," contributed autographed works that brought in nearly $1,000. After three years of legal suits, the Scottsboro case was still a *cause célèbre* and would remain so throughout the decade and into the next. And Langston Hughes remained involved until the bitter end.

That April 1934, when Walt Carmon asked in *New Masses*, "What Are Revolutionary Writers and Artists in the U.S. Doing?" he praised Hughes as one of the vanguard who were using their pens in the battle against injustice. And Hughes was fighting that battle on all fronts. The very next month, responding to an announcement that President Roosevelt was about to end the nineteen-year American occupation of Haiti, Hughes declared in the *Daily Worker* that, "in regard to the American occupation which has lasted for nineteen years, the only thing which it has done which deserves any consideration has been the construction of a few half-way decent hospitals and a limited rural sanitary service. The roads are impassable and the schools are conspicuous by their absence."[24]

By that October, he was really concerned and angered by the imprisonment of his best Haitian friend, the poet-novelist Jacques Roumain. He had not seen Roumain in three years, but he had tried to keep in touch with him through correspondence and mutual acquaintances. Roumain had moved even further to the left than Hughes. No longer the *chef* in the Interior Ministry as he had been when the two poets met in 1931, Roumain had established the Communist Party in Haiti in 1934 and been active in the Communist underground. "Jacques believed," one of their friends later told Hughes, "that Communism was the only way to change the social and

economic conditions for the Haitian masses." But to the Haitian government, as to the government of the United States, orthodox Marxism was
completely unacceptable.

Grandson of a former Haitian President, Roumain had been arrested
numerous times during 1928–1930 for his nationalist activities; by 1933, he
was undermined and jailed for his Communist activities. His arrest again
the summer of 1934, followed by an unfair trial and a three-year prison
sentence in October, provoked Hughes to write letters of protest to editors
at home and abroad. His "Appeal for Jacques Roumain" appeared that year
in *International Literature, Dynamo: A Journal of Revolutionary Poetry, Com-
mune, New Masses,* and *The New Republic.*[25]

> Jacques Roumain, poet and novelist of color, and the finest liv-
> ing Haitian writer, has just been sentenced at Port-au-Prince,
> Haiti to two [sic] years in jail for circulating there a French
> magazine of Negro liberation called *Cri des Nègres.* Jacques
> Roumain is a young man of excellent European education, and
> formerly occupied a high post in the Haitian government and is
> greatly respected by intellectuals as an outstanding man of let-
> ters. He is one of the very few upper-class Haitians who under-
> stands and sympathizes with the plight of the oppressed peasants
> of his island home and who has attempted to write about and to
> remedy the pitiful conditions of 90 percent of the Haitian people
> exploited by the big coffee monopolies and by the manipulations
> of foreign finance in the hands of the National City Bank of
> New York.
>
> As a fellow writer of color, I call upon all writers and artists of
> whatever race who believe in the freedom of words and of the
> human spirit to protest immediately to the nearest Haitian Con-
> sulate the uncalled for and unmerited sentence to prison of Jacques
> Roumain, one of the few, and by far the most talented, of the
> literary men of Haiti.
>
> LANGSTON HUGHES
> *Carmel, California*

Believing like Eugene V. Debs "as long as one man is in prison, I am not
free," Hughes had also kept track of the case of Angelo Herndon, a young
black Communist organizer arrested in Georgia in 1932 on a charge of
"inciting insurrection" among black and white unemployed workers. Detained under a slave code established a century earlier, Herndon had been
sentenced to twenty years on a chain gang, but in August 1934, after several
appeals, he had been released on $15,000 bail. Hughes had begun to follow
the case even more closely as the inspiration for a play, *Angelo Herndon Jones.*

But what he spent much of his time and creative energy on in Carmel was a play he was writing with Ella Winter. *Blood on the Fields* had as its major theme the conflict between labor and capital; its dramatic core was the California farm workers' strike, which Hughes had actually seen end in bloody violence in the San Joaquin Valley the autumn of 1933. He and Ella based the play's fictional heroine, Jennie Martin, unmistakably on Caroline Decker, who in real life was one of the most militant union organizers on the Pacific Coast. *Blood on the Fields*, completed in mid-July 1934, but still in need of revision when Hughes sent it to Lieber that August 8, was as prophetic as it was historic. The play ends as unarmed strikers are attacked and wounded by local Vigilantes who raid a union office with guns and bricks. The scene was true to life: on July 20, 1934, in Caroline Decker's Sacramento headquarters, she and eighteen members of her Cannery and Agricultural Workers Union were arrested at gunpoint for "vagrancy" and "criminal syndicalism."

The "Vigilantes"—whom Ella and Langston cited and equated in their play as "Ku Klux"—were hardly fictional. The men who had begun drifting into Carmel in the autumn of 1933 became a threatening presence. Some local people referred to them as legionnaires, others as terrorist strikebreakers, who cooperated with police "Red Squads" and wealthy landowners bent on keeping agricultural workers' wages at twenty cents an hour. Parading under a banner of "Americanism," the Vigilantes used scare tactics against dissenters whenever and wherever they could. Although *Blood on the Fields* was neither published nor produced, word of it seems to have gotten around, and that, added to the general knowledge of Hughes's "radical" poems and some of the stories of *The Ways of White Folks*, and his membership in the local John Reed Club made him a target for the Vigilantes. They were determined to destroy the Club. They believed that John Reed, buried in the Kremlin as a hero, was an American "traitor" and that his eyewitness account of the Russian Revolution, *Ten Days that Shook the World*, was "propaganda." Langston Hughes, Ella Winter, and Lincoln Steffens had all been to Russia and praised John Reed's work, and that only increased the Vigilantes' fury. They accused Hughes of having an affair with Ella (who was four years his senior); they menaced her ten-year-old son and Steffens, his father. Years later, Ella Winter remembered that the Vigilantes went down to Hughes's "little cottage and danced their filthy devil's dances and shouted God knows what obscenities."[26] It was a summer night no one in Carmel's John Reed Club ever forgot.

For all those reasons, *Blood on the Fields* was abandoned that July when Ella, fearing threats against herself and her son, told Hughes to take her name off the script temporarily. Steffens, still bold and fearless, issued a statement to the Vigilantes from his sickbed: "Let them come and get me.

Let them send me to jail. I'd rather go there than to the White House. It's more honorable."[27]

That summer was the last Hughes would ever see of the legendary Steffens, who died two years later at the age of seventy. But he would never forget "Steffy" (as he called him) or Ella (called Peter by her friends) or their young son, Pete, whom he later said "were among my best friends in Carmel." They were among the last to see him before he escaped the Vigilantes, who came knocking at his door in the dead of night, in late July 1934. Fearing damage to Sullivan's Carmel property if he stayed, Hughes fled to Sullivan's house in San Francisco. There had been two lynchings in California that year, and Langston Hughes did not want to risk his own blood on the fields.

Over forty years later, Ella Winter recalled sadly, "Langston came out of the migratory workers strikes the only black there. We thought he would go on with this kind of 'revolutionary' activity, but he didn't; he went up the Valley and lived with Noel Sullivan, the non-active Catholic, gentle, gentleman. . . . I decided I had asked too much of a lonely black in our funny village."[28]

His time in Carmel in certain ways had been a lonely battle for Hughes, even though he showed no visible signs of it. A local friend and neighbor, Marie Short, once said that she never saw him without a smile. He did seem a peaceful rather than lonely fellow walking along the rugged California beach with Greta, his German shepherd companion, as Carmelites snapped his photo. Many of the local residents had taken to him, and visits from screen celebrities such as Jimmy Cagney (who had emceed Hughes's Scottsboro exhibit) made him a household name. That February, he had celebrated his thirty-second birthday with Una and Robinson Jeffers, Noel Sullivan, and a few of the neighboring literati at Tor House, the home with the tower that Jeffers had built by the sea. Jeffers, then famous for such books of verse as *Apology for Bad Dreams*, was as pessimistic about life as Langston was optimistic, but they seemed to balance each other, and they had in common a great admiration for Walt Whitman.

"The artists and writers at Carmel were mostly a serious hard-working lot and life was generally quiet," Hughes wrote later about his ten months in the seaside village.[29] For most of the time he was the only Afro-American writer or artist there. Nora Holt, the popular singer, who had left Shanghai shortly before he arrived there, stopped briefly in Carmel to see him, as did Roland Hayes during a West Coast concert tour. But the only black writer Hughes saw was Wallace Thurman. On furlough from Hollywood, where he was ghostwriting motion picture scripts, Thurman spent a May weekend drinking gin and tonic and talking about old times as Hughes's guest at Ennesfree.

The two had not seen each other in at least three years, and this was to be the last time. Maybe they both sensed it. They talked long and intimately about "things," "places," "people" they had never talked about—except casually, incidentally. One of the persons was Louise Thompson, who, having married Thurman in 1928, unaware of his homosexual proclivities, was still "Wallie's secret love." In 1934 Louise was working for the International Workers Order in New York, and although she had not seen Langston since they were together in Russia, she kept in closer touch with him than with Thurman, who still feared that any day she would go back to Reno and establish residence long enough to divorce him, as she had once tried to do before her mother fell ill with cancer and needed her constant care. During the Broadway run of his play, *Harlem*, the court had demanded that he pay Louise alimony, which he had long since ceased to pay, and which she didn't want anyway; she simply wanted out of the marriage, and Thurman didn't.

The old acquaintances talked of others, too: of their friends Countee Cullen and Yolande Du Bois, who had tied the nuptial knot the same year as Wallie and Louise and untied it just as quickly, and for the same reasons. They knew, however, that as a poet Cullen had come full circle from imitating the verse of John Keats to quoting the *Communist Manifesto* of Karl Marx and endorsing the Communist Party, and writing such poems as "Scottsboro, Too, Is Worth Its Song."

They knew, too, that Carmel circles were whispering that their long-lost Harlem Renaissance associate, Nathan Eugene Toomer, known to the literary world as Jean Toomer, was "passing for white." Toomer had long since left Carmel. In 1932 he had taken his white bride, Margery Latimer, there, and she had died soon after in childbirth. Toomer's search for racial identity had taken him many places, including rural Georgia, where he had spent four months among black folk in 1921 and surfaced in 1923 with publication of *Cane*, which Hughes had called a "beautiful book of prose and verse." Both Hughes and Thurman met him not long afterward, when he came to Harlem seeking disciples for the mystic movement of Georgi Gurdjieff, at whose Institute for the Harmonious Development of Man in Fontainebleau, France, Toomer had spent about as much time as he had in the cane fields of Sparta, Georgia. His stay in Harlem had been even briefer, for he found in Greenwich Village more converts to the "new race of Americans" of which he considered himself "one of the first conscious members."

Thurman, who had once followed Toomer into Gurdjieff and written in his second novel, *Infants of the Spring*, that Toomer was the only one of their generation "who has elements of greatness," had changed his mind. Hughes, who never had quite so lofty an opinion of Toomer, would say later in *The Big Sea* that "Negroes lost one of the most talented of all their writers." And

Toomer in his own autobiography would declare, "As I am not a Negro, I could not feature myself as one."[30] For most of his life he would "feature" himself as white, and he played the role like a Rudolf Valentino, whom many of his female admirers thought he resembled.

One of those admirers was Mable Dodge Luhan. She came to Carmel while Hughes was there and met him one afternoon at the Jefferses, where she and her fourth husband, Indian Tony Luhan, were guests. She told Hughes that she had heard about his poem, "A House in Taos," and she had no kind words for it. He had written the poem in 1926 when he heard rumors about Mabel and Toomer, in whose Gurdjieff project she had invested thousands of dollars, and whose affections Toomer had returned. "*My* house in Taos is nothing like that," she told Hughes. "You must come and see for yourself."

It was at least a year before he got to Taos, but in his meeting with Mabel in Carmel he found her as eccentric as he had always heard she was. Moreover, she brought to mind all the "free love" affairs he had heard Toomer reveled in, including one with the wife of one of Toomer's earliest and most enthusiastic literary sponsors, Waldo Frank. By September 1934, Toomer had married a second white wife, the wealthy and attractive Marjorie Content, daughter of a New York stockbroker. All that must have made Hughes remember the one Afro-American woman Toomer was once thought to care about: a sad-eyed, beautiful teacher of Spanish and aspiring actress named Dorothy Peterson, whose love for Jean Toomer was legend among their Harlem friends. To her, years later, Hughes would dedicate his own book of short stories, titled *Laughing to Keep from Crying*.

Laughing to keep from crying was what Hughes himself was doing that August 1934 when he packed his belongings for Reno, where he hoped to avoid any further threats from the Vigilantes. Although he had tried to keep his escape from Carmel to San Francisco a secret, Alain Locke had found out about it and was "reporting" as usual to Godmother: "Did you also hear that Langston was closed out of Carmel by the Vigilantes—the California Ku Klux Klan. He took refuge at the home of Noel Sullivan, to whom he dedicates *The Ways of White Folks*."[31]

Protecting Sullivan, not wanting any harm to come to him, or to impose any longer upon his hospitality, Hughes left San Francisco late that August to visit relatives and friends in Los Angeles and went thence to Reno via Lake Tahoe. In Los Angeles, he spent a few hours with his good friend, Arna Bontemps, who had recently moved there with his family. To him Langston confided little more about his Vigilante experience than he confided later to readers of *I Wonder as I Wander*, where he was silent about it. Langston Hughes, never one to express his innermost feelings, even to his best friends, was particularly reticent about "radicalism" with Arna, who never encouraged Langston to write about revolution, striking workers, or "political" matters. Knowing that Arna would have shaken his head, as he did in Alabama when Hughes took a personal risk to visit the Scottsboro inmates in prison, Langston told him little or nothing about his derring-do in Carmel.

But those who were sympathetic to him then and later knew that his having been pushed to the wall by right-wing mob violence broke his heart. His poetic vow—"For the sake of the revolution to fight, starve, and die" —had been easier to make than to keep, and the truth was no less difficult to accept. Having tried to be more than just an "artist" in Carmel, he had gone the limit, and ended up fighting for his life. Yet he could at least find some solace that September in the "Left and Leftward Writers" column of *New Masses*, which paid tribute to his revolutionary spirit:

> ... Salvation by art has been an even greater deterrent to revolu-
> tionary action among Negro intellectuals than among white in-
> tellectuals. Langston Hughes's work, in shattering its illusions,
> is of the first importance.[32]

With few illusions left about art or revolution, Hughes left California early that September to try to restore his spirit. In his suitcase was the draft of an article he had started more than once and been unable to finish. To complete it, he would need still more time and psychological distance than was then possible. Its title was "The Vigilantes Knock at My Door."

~ 16 ~

Mailbox for the Dead

"L ANGSTON HUGHES IS IN THE SIERRAS, buried in a far-away mountain resort writing his long deferred book on Soviet Central Asia"—
so said the first issue of *Controversy*,[1] an independent radical weekly which
Hughes helped launch in Carmel shortly before his departure. The news
blurb, which appeared in the weekly's "Sheer Gossip" column on October
24, 1934, was more gossip than truth—and probably a ruse to keep the Vigilantes off his trail. For one thing, "his long deferred book," *A Negro Looks at
Soviet Central Asia* had already been published that year in the Soviet Union;[2]
and he was no longer in the Sierras but in a Reno boarding house at 521
Elko Avenue, an address known only to his mother, Noel Sullivan, and
Maxim Lieber. If he went there to elude the Vigilantes, he had good reason
to keep his whereabouts confidential. Yet he could have stayed in the Sierras
if he had simply wanted a hideaway. Not even Arna Bontemps, whom he
had told he was "going to the mountains," knew where to find him. But a
desire for seclusion may not have been the only reason he kept the Reno
address secret. There is at least one clue to another consideration.

While Hughes was in Reno, Alain Locke, full of his usual gossip about
the poet's activities, and always on his trail, wrote to Godmother:

> ...ran into a former Washington friend, John Williams, now
> living in Los Angeles. It seems Langston had been staying with
> him—and in his answer to my question, did you leave him there
> when you came East, he said no, he is in Reno getting his
> divorce...he volunteered the information that his wife was a
> white woman, and that shortly after the marriage there was
> disagreement and an agreed plan to separate....[3]

Although Locke usually followed any leads about Hughes's activities
closely—he did not often err—he must have recognized the John Williams
story as a hoax. For if the professor could have proved any of it, he surely
would have spread the word. But he didn't. He never mentioned it again in

his correspondence with Charlotte Mason. The truth is that if Langston Hughes ever married and divorced a white woman, it was the best-kept secret of his life. And why he would tell John Williams[4] about it, when he never told Noel Sullivan, Eulah Pharr, Arna Bontemps, Maxim Lieber, Louise Patterson, Si-lan Chen, or Roy Blackburn—the people who knew Hughes best—is another mystery. None of them ever knew about any such marriage, and years later all of them would express complete disbelief that he had ever wed.[5]

Moreover, had he met and married a white woman in Carmel, it is doubtful that he could have kept it a secret for long—especially from the Vigilantes. Nor is there any record of a marriage license bearing his name in Monterrey County,[6] where such a record would have been preserved had he married in the Carmel vicinity. As Ella Winter later declared: "I never heard the slightest breath of Langston Hughes being married ANYWHERE AT ANY TIME. SOUNDS VERY UNLIKELY TO ME."[7]

Unlikely as Hughes's marriage may have seemed to his closest friends and associates, he was adept at keeping his private life private—even from those who thought they knew him best. He seems not to have told Ella, for instance, that he had added the name of a third collaborator to the script *Blood on the Fields* and changed the title to *Harvest*.[8] The other collaborator was Ann Hawkins. Ella said—much later—that she "never heard of [her] that I can remember."[9] It is curious that she did not. The Ann Hawkins by-line appeared occasionally on book reviews and articles in the *Pacific Weekly* —the successor to *Controversy*—at a time when Ella was writing regularly for it and Steffens was a columnist and an editor (until his death in 1936).

A few Carmelites remembered Ann as a rather outgoing young woman who tried especially to make herself known to people such as Hughes and Winter. During the autumn of 1933, when they were trodding through the fields of the San Joaquin Valley supporting the farmworkers' strikes, Ann had been there too. Perhaps Ella paid her no attention, but Hughes did. There is no real evidence as to how well the two knew each other—beyond their theatrical collaboration—or that she was the white woman he possibly married. All things considered, it seems doubtful that she could ever have been "Mrs. Langston Hughes." But two things are certain: she shared his political views and love for the theater. An aspiring theatrical director, she had spent a year visiting theatrical companies in Paris, London and Dublin, and in 1933-34 was a post-graduate student doing research at the University of California. Whatever her relationship to Hughes, it was of short duration, yet shrouded in as much secrecy as his brief, private stay in Reno.

Hughes spent eight weeks in the famous city of the "quickie divorce," but he would have needed to stay only six weeks, if he had indeed been there for that purpose. There is no record of a divorce decree in the name of Langston

Hughes (or his full name, James Mercer Langston Hughes) in Reno's Washoe County, or any county in Nevada.[10] If he ever entered into matrimony with a white woman, as reported by Alain Locke, he did it under an alias, and under circumstances which even the Federal Bureau of Investigation could not authenticate. The FBI preserved in its file on Langston Hughes false information, from a misinformed informant, that the poet had married a white Communist, Sonya Kroll, also known as June Croll. In fact, she was actually the wife of a black writer named Eugene Gordon.[11] The FBI, never infallible, followed Hughes's coming and goings for years, but it never leaked allegations of the marriage of the poet to a white Communist, as it surely would have done if the story were true, or even likely to be true.[12] Furthermore, there is no evidence in Hughes's passport records that he ever married anyone.[13]

Whatever the reasons for the almost total seclusion in Reno in late 1934, only Hughes really knew. His friend Arna Bontemps later thought the stay was motivated by a need for a complete retreat. Since Langston's preference for being with people rather than at a desk often got in the way of his work, Arna thought it was one of those periods when "he went into hiding" just to write.[14] In Reno, shut off from the world, Hughes did write prolifically for two months.

He was incognito to most local residents, in a town which he said "had no Negro section as such." But it did have a Negro weatherman, Oscar Hammonds, about whom Hughes later wrote a newspaper article, describing him as the only one of his race employed in that capacity in the United States. Some of the black settlers, like the Hammonds, had come to Reno in 1910, the year black heavyweight champion Jack Johnson came to town to fight the retired "Great White Hope," Jim Jeffries. But Hughes had come with the expectation of finding nothing too exciting in Depression-ridden Reno. He later claimed he "lived in a Negro boarding house, whose owner was on relief, as were most of her guests."[15]

The house he lived in on Elko Avenue was a two-family dwelling owned by the Durham Chevrolet Company and hardly large enough to accommodate more than one or two roomers.[16] Seeking complete privacy and an address known to only a few, he would not have harbored himself in a crowded boarding house anyway. Located near the railroad tracks, the house had none of the comforts of Ennesfree, but it was quiet enough for him to write in peace—away from the Vigilantes.

He spent most of his time in Reno at his typewriter, working on stories and poems which he hoped would bring him some income as quickly as possible. He had arrived nearly flat broke, faced with the need to meet his own expenses and support his mother in Cleveland. He no longer had time for the luxury of writing anything quite like the last piece he wrote in

Carmel. There, free of worries about food and shelter, he had written the foreword to *Hunger and Revolt*, a book of satirical cartoons by Jacob Burck, depicting "A Revolutionary History of the World Crisis." Now facing his own personal "crisis," he probably felt even more deeply what he wrote in the foreword: "Some of Jacob Burck's cartoons picture the harsh realities of today, the wall of struggle; others foreshadow the marching power of the proletarian future. Let the capitalists who pay for our oppression, laugh that future off, if they can."[17]

Proud that he was no "capitalist," even if he often joked with Noel Sullivan about the pleasures of creature comforts, Hughes gave no thought to making money for the sake of it. If he had been paid even a small sum for half of what he wrote during his lifetime, he would have had few financial worries. Despite the constant insecurity, he had long reconciled himself to poverty as the price he paid for publication of his radical works in small magazines that could not afford to compensate him. That meant not only the *Daily Worker*, but others, such as *New Masses*, to which he "donated" the poem "Cubes" in February 1934 and the article "White Gold in Soviet Asia" in August, and *The Crisis*, to which he gave two other pieces, "Going South in Russia" and "Cowards from the Colleges," in June and August. Only the more popular magazines, which bought some of his stories from *The Ways of White Folks* and noncontroversial articles about Soviet life, had provided him any income in Carmel.

Thanks to Lieber, who had sold "Boy Dancers in Uzbekistan" to *Travel Magazine*, and "Tamara Khanum: Soviet Asia's Greatest Dancer" to *Theatre Arts*, and "In an Emir's Harem" to the *Woman's Home Companion*, Hughes had been able to send his mother monthly checks. The *Woman's Home Companion* had paid him four hundred dollars, the largest sum he had ever received for an article, but most of it had been spent by the time he arrived in Reno.

Late that summer, he had applied for a Guggenheim Fellowship, with assurances and recommendations from the poet Robinson Jeffers and Noel Sullivan's good friend, Professor Benjamin Lehman, but he knew he wouldn't learn the result until the spring of 1935. Until then he had to live by his wits, hoping to survive the autumn and winter in Reno. Late that September, he finished "The Vigilantes Knock at My Door," and sent it to Lieber. The agent promptly submitted it to *The American Mercury*, which rejected it. The *Mercury*, then owned and published by Alfred A. Knopf, had a new editor, Charles Angoff, whom Knopf was soon to find too radical to keep for long. Hughes, knowing little about the *Mercury*, except that its controversial founder, H. L. Mencken, had stepped down months before, wired Lieber to send the piece to *New Masses*, where he was certain it would be accepted—with no revisions and no questions asked. What happened after that is a bizarre riddle, which may explain why Hughes apparently removed from Lieber's correspondence any evidence of whether the piece was accepted, rejected, or considered too risky to print.[18] The fact remains that the only piece appearing in *New Masses* that year under the title "The Vigilantes Knock at My Door" was signed by Ruth St. Ives, not Langston Hughes. It was published December 4, 1934, the sole piece in the issue not listed on the contents page. Datelined San Francisco, the text has no resemblance to Hughes's own experience with the Vigilantes, except in the opening paragraph:

> I had opened an official-looking letter lying on a pile of mail which had accumulated during a month in the Sierras. It was brief and read: Cease your Communist activities or suffer the consequences.

Otherwise, nothing about the tone, style, or content connected the events to Langston Hughes. Nor is the text the same as "The Vigilantes Knock at My Door" which he actually wrote and apparently never published.[19] In that thirteen-page article, he was fearless and uncompromising about events of the longshoremen's strike in San Francisco, the blood and terror of the cotton strikes in the San Joaquin Valley, the use of tear gas by the police and machine guns by the National Guard. He chastised the President, the Secretary of Labor, the governor of California, and the mayor of San Francisco for ignoring telegrams to protect the strikers. He blamed the ultra-patriotic American Legion for being behind the Vigilantes who stormed the John Reed Clubs in and around Carmel and organized local citizens against radicals. He explained how he, as the only Afro-American member of the John Reed Club, had been singled out as a target of attack, not only by the Vigilantes but by the *Carmel Sun*, which had appealed to race hatred by accusing him of having been seen in the company and cars of white women.

If he thought twice about publishing all that, he had reason: he feared for his life. He wanted no more open confrontation with the Vigilantes; he loathed them completely, but he would not risk a complete exposé of his personal experiences with them, even in a publication such as Carmel's crusading *Pacific Weekly*, which frequently attacked the Vigilantes in print and would have gladly published his true story. So personal and true was his story that it could never have been written under a pseudonym.

For quite a different reason than protection against the Vigilantes, he used a pseudonym for some of his writing in Reno. The name was "David Boatman," his pen name for nonracial, apolitical stories. Needing money badly, he told Lieber in early November that he had decided to write a story every week on "the eternal problem of love" under a pen name, considering that the market was too limited for his Russian and racial material, and that he saw no reason why he shouldn't turn to writing about romance for slick "American caucasian" magazines.

Having written ironically about love as a "problem" in every love poem he ever penned, it is no wonder that he expressed to Lieber his plan to write about this "eternal problem" with tongue in cheek. He did it in three stories entitled "Eyes Like a Gypsy's," "Hello Henry," and a "Posthumous Tale," which Lieber told him "certainly do you credit as a writer," and advised him that publishers should know that Langston Hughes and not David Boatman was the author. "I laughed myself sick reading three of Mr. David Boatman's stories," Lieber wrote him, "I am rushing this letter out to you by air mail before I begin selling the stories, so you may consider the advisability of using your own name and getting full credit for three humorous stories, perhaps as good as any humorous stories I have read recently."[20]

But despite Lieber's success in persuading Hughes to drop the pseudonym, he was not successful with editors. They had stereotyped Langston Hughes and refused to accept his nonracial fiction. Proving he could write slick humor as well as any white author did not make it acceptable to such editors as Wolcott Gibbs. The New Yorker editor rejected "Eyes Like a Gypsy's" with a note telling Lieber, "I'm afraid we're still not convinced that this kind of comedy is Mr. Hughes's forte; and wish frankly that he'd abandon it because he's so gifted the other way."[21]

Such responses were only another part of the sad dilemma that Hughes faced trying to make a living as a black author in the United States—then and throughout his career. It often seemed a losing battle. If he wrote honestly and forthrightly about his Afro-American experience, the market was limited. Yet white authors who adapted Negro material at will and sensationalized or distorted it found a ready market; at the same time publication seemed restricted to black authors who went beyond their own material, regardless of their literary skill. American literature, as Hughes knew so well, was segregated. Not even he could surmount its barriers with humor under a pen name. The name he chose, Boatman, perhaps had deep symbolic meaning for Hughes—the black bard of rivers and the merchant seaman—who tried everything he knew to stay afloat as a writer.

Although Lieber's enthusiasm for the nonracial stories had encouraged Hughes to write them, both knew the impetus was financial necessity rather than literary ambition. Determined not to give up, and expecting the response he received, Hughes continued writing racial stories and poems he hoped would sell. By late October he had sent at least three new ones to Lieber, who heaped praise on them. The story "On the Road," which Hughes had begun in Carmel as "Two on the Road"—about a black hobo's surreal encounter with Christ—Lieber told him was so "damned good" that he didn't know where to sell it. Another story, "Spanish Blood," was quickly

bought for the first issue of *Metropolis*, a New Jersey magazine, and a third
one, titled "Professor," went to *The Anvil*, which published it six months
later as "Dr. Brown's Decision." *Esquire* was considering his long new
poem, "Death in Harlem." But Hughes was less enthusiastic about all that
than about receiving a few checks. (Publishers, he lamented, didn't write
them as quickly as he wrote poems and stories.) Meanwhile, he had to
borrow from Sullivan to make ends meet.

At October's end, he complained to Noel, "Checks are conspicuous by
their absence, but there ought to be one in [Lieber's] next letter. It is certainly nice of you to send what you did for my mother, and certainly right
now is a *great* help. Nevertheless I hate to take it. There's no reason why
you should take care of 90% of the troubles of the world. No wonder you
never have any money for yourself anymore."[22]

That November, Hughes sent Sullivan his poem, "Ballad of Roosevelt,"
which appeared that month in *The New Republic*. It poked fun at the President for not living up to the promises of his "New Deal":

Ballad of Roosevelt

The pot was empty,
The cupboard was bare.
I said, Papa,
What's the matter here?
  I'm waitin' on Roosevelt, son,
  Roosevelt, Roosevelt,
  Waitin' on Roosevelt, son.

The rent was due,
And the lights was out.
I said, Tell me, Mama,
What's it all about?
  We're waitin' on Roosevelt, son,
  Roosevelt, Roosevelt,
  Just waitin' on Roosevelt.

Sister got sick
And the doctor wouldn't come
Cause we couldn't pay him
The proper sum—
  A-waitin' on Roosevelt,
  Roosevelt, Roosevelt,
  A-waitin' on Roosevelt.

Then one day
They put us out o' the house.
Ma and Pa was
Meek as a mouse
   Still waitin' on Roosevelt,
   Roosevelt, Roosevelt.

But, when they felt those
Cold winds blow
And didn't have no
Place to go
   Pa said, I'm tired
   O' waitin' on Roosevelt,
   Roosevelt, Roosevelt.
   Damn tired o' waitin' on Roosevelt.

I can't git a job
And I can't git no grub.
Backbone and navel's
Doin' the belly-rub—
   A-waitin' on Roosevelt,
   Roosevelt, Roosevelt.

And a lot o' other folks
What's hungry and cold
Done stopped believin'
What they been told
   By Roosevelt,
   Roosevelt, Roosevelt—

Cause the pot's still empty,
And the cupboard's still bare,
And you can't build a bungalow
Out o' air—
   Mr. Roosevelt, listen!
   What's the matter here?

"Ballad of Roosevelt" had a touch of humor and irony, as did much of what Hughes wrote in Reno. Nothing he published during those months showed the fury of the previous four years, and his fiction gave little hint that there was an economic Depression. Yet the Depression echoed, along with his social protest, in his short story "On the Road." Not until years later did he explain, in a speech "Concerning an Analysis of 'On the Road,' " some of what he had felt and seen in Reno during the Depression:

It was during the Depression, of course, and there were hobo jungles along the railroad tracks outside the town, and stacks of silver dollars on the gambling tables inside the town. Negroes weren't allowed in the hotels,...Negroes weren't allowed in the gambling places either, but neither were the American Indians who lived in Reno....Everybody in America was looking for work then; everybody moving from one place to another in search of a job. People who lived in the West were hoboing on trains to the east...sometimes they wouldn't get any further than Reno, whichever way they were going, and none of them had any money, they'd build these big fires near the railroad tracks...and they'd just live collected around those fires until they could make enough money at odd jobs to move farther on their way. I wrote in this story...about makeshift houses made out of boxes of tin and old pieces of wood and canvas. "You could not see them in the dark, but you knew they were there if you'd ever been on the road, if you had ever lived with the homeless and hungry in a depression," I wrote.

...."On the Road" was not carefully planned as to plot or character. As nearly as I can remember, it was written completely at one sitting, like a poem....All I had in mind was cold, hunger, a strange town at night whose permanent residents were not so cold and hungry, and a black vagabond named Sargent against white snow, cold people, hard doors, trying to get somewhere, but too tired and hungry to make it—hemmed in on the ground by the same people who hemmed Christ in by rigid rituals surrounding a man-made cross....His destination, Kansas City, being a half-way point across the country, half-way to somewhere.[23]

Perhaps he felt one story about all that was enough—and that people during the Depression didn't want to read about the Depression anyway. Sitting in his Reno room near the railroad track, watching the bonfires of vagabonds who had no rooms, he wrote fiction that had no connection with the reality of his life. One such story was "Mailbox for the Dead." He confided to Noel Sullivan that "it is about a man who writes a letter everyday to his dead wife who died in childbirth taking their baby with her. And after twenty years he gets an answer."[24] Nonracial, but more serious than his fiction of the Boatman variety, it met a dead end with editors. One sent the story back to Lieber with the message, "This has a nice quality, but it does seem a bit too sentimental."[25] In *I Wonder as I Wander*, his explanation for writing "Mailbox for the Dead" had nothing to do with the actual story he mentioned to Sullivan.

Every day in Reno, after a lengthy stint at the typewriter, in the afternoon I would take a long walk in the late autumn sunshine. One day I decided to follow a road that led outside the city and up the dusty slope of a barren hillside where there were no houses or trees. Far in the distance on the side of this parched hill, near its crest I saw a forlorn little mountain cemetery.... As I came closer, I was startled to see on the cemetery gate—with no house or living person about—what looked to be a mailbox.

How can that be? I asked myself. "A Mailbox for the Dead?"...As I came back down the hill in the sunset, I thought to myself, What a striking title for a story, "Mailbox for the Dead." So I began to think of a situation to suit the title. When I got back to my rooming house, after a Home Relief supper that night, I sat down and wrote the first draft of a story. Several times during the evening as I wrote, I kept thinking about my father. This was unusual, as I did not think of him often. But before I went to sleep, I thought perhaps I ought to drop him a line. Still I went to bed without writing him. The next afternoon word came that my father had died that night. He was dying during the time I was writing my story called "Mailbox for the Dead."

Hughes termed that a "psychic" experience. Possibly it was, but he had learned in early November that his father was gravely ill. Word had arrived—via mail forwarded from Carmel to San Francisco to Reno—suggesting that he come at once. The writer was one of the elderly Patiño sisters, whom he remembered from his youth as his father's most trusted friends in Mexico City. Why he didn't go immediately had perhaps as much to do with having no money to go as with the life-long distance between father and son. That distance had decreased only with the exchange of a few courteous letters in the thirteen years since they last saw each other. When news came at the end of November that James Hughes was dead, it was too late to heal old wounds or for Langston to attend the funeral. "When I got word that my father was dead," he wrote later, "the word came second-hand...a wire in Spanish had come for me to Carmel. The Filipino houseboy had relayed it to a friend of mine, who attempted to translate it, and who, in turn, advised me by wire in English that my father had died and the estate awaited my claim."

Hughes left Reno in early December on the first airplane flight of his life and flew over the mountains to San Francisco, then journeyed by train, via Los Angeles, with money borrowed from his Uncle John S. P. Hughes. It was his last desperate attempt to pay final respects to his father.

HUGHES arrived in Mexico City in mid-December, after being detained
for a weekend in Nogales, near the Arizona border. There, in a scenario fit
to make his father turn over in his grave, American immigration officials
insisted Langston could not enter Mexico without an entrance permit stat-
ing he was "colored." He was obliged to wait for hours for the permit to be
issued. Such unpleasant racial protocol had caused James Hughes to flee the
United States thirty-one years before and to visit very briefly only three
times again the rest of his life. At his death, his son could not cross the
American border without a racial permit.

Langston waited out the ordeal in Nogales by going horseback riding
with the train porters. In Mexico City, he was the guest of the elderly
Patiño sisters—Lola, Fela, and Cuca—who welcomed him like a long lost
son. They had cared for his ill father, seen to it that he received last rites of
the church, and chosen his gravesite. "I was grateful to them for what they
had done," Hughes wrote much later, "and for being with him at the end."

The aging Patiños, whom he had not seen in thirteen years, still lived in a
large, dark old apartment at San Ildefonso 73, where he had first met them
during his youth. Their apartment, filled as always with candles and statutes
of madonnas and saints, could not have looked more like a place of mourning that December when an aging Mexican lawyer came to read James
Nathaniel Hughes's last will and testament. Langston had prepared himself
for the result. "At the end of his testament in very black ink was my father's
signature," he said later. "Nowhere did it contain my name. . . ."

It is difficult to know how that really affected him. He said later that he
cried. Yet, considering what he wrote about his father, it is unlikely that he
shed tears of sorrow. He rarely let down the mask to show his innermost
feelings about anything—except his father, whom he seemed to loathe more
than love. But he had tried for a while to make a distant truce with him,
writing letters and postcards, telling him where he was, what he was doing.
Without such contact, the Patiño sisters might never have known where to
wire him of his father's death. Yet, at the stroke of a pen, the elder Hughes
had all but denied his only son's existence: he counted him out of his life and
his fortune. If he ever had loved or worshiped anything, it was money.
Money was his almighty god. James Hughes said as much to Louise Thompson, who visited him the summer of 1931 while she was in Mexico for the
Congregational Education Society's American Interracial Seminar. The
only question he seemed interested in asking about Langston was, "Is he
making any money?" When Louise answered that he had earned a world-
wide reputation as a poet, *pater* Hughes said he should not count on that.
"The *golden eagle*," he said, looking Louise straight in the eye, "is your only
friend."

Langston remained in Mexico City for nearly six months after his father's death. Having borrowed several hundred dollars from his Uncle John for the trip, he felt obliged to stay until he could repay it. The three Patiño sisters, to whom his father had bequeathed all property and assets, insisted that Langston stay as long as he wished, and that he share equally in the estate. It was difficult to refuse their hospitality during those soup-line days, but even in financial hardship he did not wish to accept part of an estate his father had denied him. "In the end," he wrote, "it was agreed that only the deposits of my father's bank account would be divided equally among the four of us."

But his quarter share did not come overnight. Berta Schultz, James Hughes's estranged widow, whom he left no more than he left Langston, had decided to sue for her share. As a result, it was May 1935 before Langston could repay his uncle. Although he later claimed in *I Wonder as I Wander* that he had to reimburse "Aunt Sallie," his father's sister in Indianapolis, it was actually his father's brother, John S. P. Hughes, who had made the generous loan—and who preferred to remain anonymous about it. John and James had not spoken for years, and as all their relatives discovered, James Hughes had left nothing to any of his blood kin.

That knowledge seemed as unsettling a way to begin the New Year as the news of the death of two friends in New York during Christmas week. Rudolph Fisher, a brilliant physician whose short stories and novels brought wit to the Harlem Renaissance, died the day after Christmas, 1934, a cancer victim at age thirty-seven. Wallace Thurman, tubercular and alcoholic at age thirty-two, had died a few days earlier, a charity patient on New York's Welfare Island.

Within a month's time, Hughes had had his share of "bad news" and "mailbox for the dead" messages. He was saddened by the loss of Thurman and Fisher, whose lives and talents seemed to promise so much, and whose deaths seemed to seal the coffin of the Harlem Renaissance. He later wrote of Fisher in *The Big Sea*:

> The wittiest of these New Negroes of Harlem, whose tongue was flavored with the sharpest and saltiest humor, was Rudolph Fisher, whose stories appeared in the *Atlantic Monthly*. His novel, *Walls of Jericho*, captures but slightly the raciness of his own conversation. He was a young medical doctor and X-ray specialist, who always frightened me a little, because he could think of the most incisively clever things to say—and I could never think of anything to answer....I used to wish I could talk like Rudolph Fisher. Beside being a good writer, he was an excellent singer, and had sung with Paul Robeson during their college days. But I guess Fisher was too brilliant and too talented to stay long on this earth.

Thurman was another story. Hughes had admitted and admired his literary talent but never quite understood the man, who seemed to turn on everyone he loved, including himself. Diabolical forces haunted him. Friends thought he might as well have killed himself, since he did nothing to prevent his death. From his hospital bed, he had sent for Louise to say a final farewell. He had wasted away to skin and bones. Laughing in tragic mockery, he drank a toast to death just before he died.

Unknown to Hughes, Louise, and perhaps anyone else at the time, Thurman left behind in his private papers several curious, undated typewritten letters addressed to "Dear Wallie" and signed "Langston" or "Lang."[26] One of the letters, typed in a rambling, unpunctuated style more reminiscent of Gertrude Stein than Langston Hughes, bears no signature—only the words "no I will not sign it." Three of the undated letters hint at some strange code figures and words suggesting homosexual encounters and an overriding concern that the correspondence "will benefit literary historians." In one such letter, uncharacteristic of Hughes, a portion reads: "I am undecided whether I should throw away my valuable correspondence during my collegiate years or not—leaving the autographs and slanders to posterity...would you, for example, care to see your noble letters in the HARLEM LITERARY MUSEUM fifty years after my death, all open to the public...or in the hands of some rich autograph collector?...it would take too long to sort them out and see which ones are not from people that I might later want to blackmail." Blackmail of Langston Hughes seemed the intent of some of these undated, typed letters, which are totally different in tone and style from anything he wrote in his own hand to Wallace Thurman—or anyone else. It is perhaps too late ever to know who really wrote them or why.

In any event, Hughes and Thurman had parted amicably enough a few months before Wallie's death. As friends they did not always agree, but they respected each other's work and usually offered mutual praise publicly and privately. When Hughes's *Not Without Laughter* appeared in 1930, Thurman had lauded it in *The New York Evening Post* as "an enviable first performance," noting that "with this volume he advances to the vanguard." Then two years later, when *Infants of the Spring* appeared, although Langston was satirized in it, he telegraphed Thurman from Kansas City: "You have written a swell book provoking brave and very true. Your potential soars like a kite breaking patterns for Negro writers...."[27]

In January 1935, another author-reviewer, Granville Hicks, in *New Masses*, still had *Not Without Laughter* in mind when he mistakenly referred to it, instead of *The Ways of White Folks*, in an assessment, "Revolutionary Literature of 1934."[28] However, there was no mistake about whether he considered the poet's first book of short stories a disappointment. "After the militant clarity of some of Hughes's poems," said Hicks, "the confusion of most of his stories—his emphasis on situations and events that the revolutionary must regard as of only secondary importance—was something of a shock." Much the same reaction had been voiced in the November 1934 issue of *Partisan Review*, where the critic wrote, "There is no doubt that the author of this volume is one of the more talented among the younger American writers. He is, however, more than that. He is also known as one of the outstanding revolutionary interpreters of Negro life in America. And yet, there is very little that is revolutionary about *The Ways of White Folks*."

Except when he was hiding out in Reno and receiving little mail or news, Hughes had kept up with all the reviews of *The Ways of White Folks* during late 1934. One of the most favorable reviews appeared in a November issue of *Controversy*, the newsweekly he had helped found in Carmel; and one of the book's stories, "Cora Unashamed," had been selected for inclusion in *The Best Short Stories of 1934*, and another, "Slave on the Block," for an *Editor's Choice* anthology.

But in Mexico, Hughes was too broke to think about resting on past laurels or worrying about book reviews. Except for a check received for a *New Yorker* short story, "Oyster's Son," which he had written in Reno, he had spent all he had left to send his mother a Christmas present. He had also pawned his wristwatch, while waiting for payment for a short story which Lieber sold to *Esquire* in January. Trying to earn enough to repay his Uncle John, while waiting for his father's estate to be settled, he stayed busy writing new stories which he sent Lieber as fast as the mail could carry them.

Hughes knew what it took to survive in the marketplace of "popular" fiction. But for leftist publications he wrote only the truth as he gauged and experienced it. Among radical writers he had a substantial following, and he was one of the first to sign a "Call for an American Writers Congress" to establish a League of American Writers to affiliate with the International Union of Revolutionary Writers that 1935. The call for a congress "devoted to exposition of all phases of a writer's participation in the struggle against war, the preservation of civil liberties and the destruction of fascist tendencies everywhere" was given a full page in the January 22 issue of *New Masses*, where the signers along with Hughes included Nelson Algren, Maxwell Bodenheim, Erskine Caldwell, Malcolm Cowley, Edward Dahlberg, Theodore Dreiser, Josephine Herbst, Granville Hicks, John Howard Lawson, Lincoln Steffens, Nathaniel West, Ella Winter, and Richard Wright.

A few weeks after signing, Hughes was invited to deliver a speech at the first session of the Congress, which was to be held in New York City on April 26 at the Mecca Temple. Not knowing that he would be too broke to make the trip from Mexico, he accepted, meanwhile preparing what some would judge one of his most revolutionary speeches of the decade, "To

Negro Writers," which he sent to be read by a substitute at the opening session of the First American Writers Congress.[29]

In February 1935, in collaboration with José Antonio Fernández de Castro, he began translating from the Spanish a selection of Mexican and Cuban short stories for an anthology. José Antonio, his old friend from Cuba, had come to Mexico City as secretary of the Cuban embassy. As Hughes put it, José Antonio the journalist and diplomat knew everybody "from generals on up or down," including their mutual acquaintance, the Mexican artist Miguel Covarrubias, who introduced Hughes to Diego Rivera. "I've met Diego Rivera and all his wives; about 600 other painters and almost as many writers," Hughes wrote jokingly to friends in Carmel.[30] Among those he knew best were the art and literary critic Luis Cardoza y Aragon, painters Maria Izquierdo and Rufino Tamayo, photographers Juan de la Cabada and Manuel Alvarez Bravo, and the poet "Francisca" (Nellie Campobello), some of whose poetry and prose he later translated.

But no one in Mexico seemed to fascinate Hughes so much as the tempestuous Lupe Marin, one of Rivera's ex-wives, to whom Langston devoted more space in I Wonder as I Wander than to Frida Kahlo, the Mexican surrealist painter to whom Rivera was then married. "I'd rather spend my time writing short stories and listening to Lupe talking about her love-life from Mexico to Paris and back," Hughes wrote in one letter. "Lupe is one of Diego's former wives—and is just about the most amusing person in the world. Diego painted her on half the walls in the country."[31]

Besides Diego Rivera, Hughes also met the other two most famous Mexican muralists then living: the brooding Orozco, and the powerful Alfaro Siqueiros, both of whom he liked and admired, even if he did not spell their names correctly in his autobiography.

Socializing with artists and writers, who invited him everywhere, Hughes found it difficult to meet the curfew hours of the elderly Patiño sisters, who bolted their door by nine P.M. and thought Hughes should be in bed at that hour. "The darling old-school Patiño sisters had not approved of the artists, writers, models and bullfighters who sometimes came by their house looking for me," he wrote later. Although he kept the Patiños' address for his mail, and often dined with them, he moved in March into a small flat near the Lagunilla Market with two roommates. One was Andrés Henestrosa, a Mexican folklorist and poet; the other was a French photographer, Henri Cartier-Bresson, who had his first major photo exhibit that spring at the Palacio de Bellas Artes. "Some of the pictures that hung in his show were taken in our Lagunilla courtyard, and in the streets surrounding the market," Hughes wrote later. "When the show came down, Cartier generously gave Andrés and me several of the prints."

With Cartier-Bresson, Hughes made a photo trip to Cuatla, a rustic

village beyond the mountains in Tierra Caliente, famous for its warm sulphur baths, palm trees, and sunshine. The scenery was worth the trip, but
they both agreed it was time to leave when they stopped for a beer in a local
cantina, where a Mexican military man pulled out a pistol and threatened the
orchestra leader's life if he didn't dedicate a song to him. "The Mexicans are
great *pistoleros*," Hughes joked, "but when they aren't shooting, they are
charming."[32] But no fears of the *pistoleros* kept him and his roommates from
"going on the town" in Mexico City nearly every night. If they weren't
listening to the *mariachis* playing their guitars in a bar, they were watching
folk dancing in a local dance hall. "I recall no period in my life when I've
had more fun with less cash," Hughes wrote in *I Wonder as I Wander*. His
camaraderie with Henestrosa and Cartier-Bresson was the beginning of a
friendship that was to last the rest of their lives. Later, Henestrosa would
come to study at Columbia University and see Hughes in New York, and
eventually write two articles about him. Cartier-Bresson, whose work would
bring him to New York as much as Hughes's would take him to Paris,
never lost touch with the poet.

That anthology, which they titled *Troubled Lands*, was never published in
book form, but some of Hughes's own translations appeared later that year
and the following in *Partisan Review*, *Pacific Weekly*, and *Esquire*. Among the
writers he translated were the Cubans Marcelo Salinas and Levi Marrero
and the Mexicans José Mancisidor, Francisco Rojas Gonzales, and Herman

Although Hughes might have preferred anonymity in Mexico, he didn't
have it. José Antonio saw to that. "When he found out I was in Mexico,"
Hughes wrote, he "immediately began broadcasting to the Mexican press
what an (in his view) 'important' writer I was, and he himself wrote a long
piece about my poetry which was published." That piece, "Langston Hughes,
poeta militante negro," appeared in Mexico City's large newspaper *El Nacional*
on March 3, 1935. Two weeks later, another piece, "Langston Hughes, el
poeta de los negros," by Luis Cardoza y Aragon, appeared in the same
newspaper, with a page of Hughes's poems accompanied by his photograph. Later, so lionized was he and pestered by requests for interviews that
(for eleven dollars a month) he took a "hide-away" apartment in the building where José Antonio and his wife lived. In May, he wrote to his Carmel
friends, "For the past month I've had a little apartment on the seventh floor
of the *Ermite*, Mexico's highest apartment house, which I took to escape my
friends and work on a Mexican-Cuban anthology of short stories José Antonio and I are translating. We have done 34 so far, and I think we will have
a swell collection. All stories of contemporary authors: the revolutions and
uprisings, sugar cane, Negroes, Indians, corrupt generals, American
imperialists—mostly all left stories, because practically all the writers down
here are left these days...."[33]

Litz Arzubide.[34] But his agent, Maxim Lieber, was not enthusiastic. "What hope can there be for you," he wrote Hughes, "if you persist in believing that the pieces you are translating are representative of the best that the Mexican authors are capable of. Without wanting to throw any bouquets at you, I would say that not a single one of these people, judging by the work you have sent me, can hold a candle to you...."[35]

It was typical of Hughes to try translations while living in Mexico, just as he had tried them while living in Russia. Poet of the people that he was, it was his way of being in touch with the people through their own language. In the case of translating Cuban short stories, it was also his—and José Antonio's—way of striking back at the corrupt regime of Carlos Mendieta, which had replaced the equally corrupt dictatorship of Gerardo Machado in 1935, and was being supported by a mendacious and dictatorial army sergeant, Fulgencia Batista. That spring, Langston and José Antonio heard and read about their friend, the Cuban poet, Pablo de la Torriente-Brau, who managed to escape from Cuba and write about it for *New Masses*.

Lieber encouraged Hughes in his sympathies for proletarian causes, but it concerned him that Hughes was writing and translating stories that were not selling. Hughes gave some of his translations to Ella Winter for publication in the radical *Pacific Weekly*, of which she was a contributing editor. But his stories? "I have written quite a few stories," Hughes wrote his friends in Carmel, "but have only sold one since January. That one went to *Esquire*. Most of the others seem too colored or too left to sell, so they are appearing in the little magazines devoted to ART AND LITERATURE AND THE MOVEMENT."[36] When his share of his father's estate finally came through, Hughes had barely enough to repay his uncle and redeem his pawned wristwatch. He wrote Noel Sullivan, "I have enough to maybe buy a serape."[37]

Meanwhile, he had also written Sullivan some good news: "I've just been notified that I am to receive a Guggenheim—$1500 for nine months—and I'm sure yours and Robin's [Robinson Jeffers] and Ben's [Benjamin Lehman] letters helped a lot, and I want to thank you for them. So I hope to begin work on the novel in the summer."[38]

News of the Guggenheim award had also reached Moscow. Si-lan (Sylvia) Chen wrote him from there: "Langston—congrats. I heard from Rose Carmon today about the fellowship and I'm so pleased about it. I thought I'd write and congratulate you too. I'm off to the Crimea tomorrow. The last time I saw you I was also going off to the Crimea....I won't write anymore because I know you won't answer."[39]

Hughes had been in and out of touch with Si-lan for two years. Evidently, his letters to her had been evasive, for in one of her letters, she wrote: "I see that it's almost as difficult to write to you as to try to talk to you—sketchy and superfluous—is it because you are really like that or is it habit or maybe protection from sentiment or—well it could be a hundred different things. . . . Excuse me for being serious . . . I'm always serious, when I'm serious I think of you, and then I sit and wish Langston dear, that sometimes you'd be serious too!"⁴⁰ The letter was signed, "All my love, Sylvia," touching serious questions of the heart that he had no inclination to answer.

Si-lan, the young and pretty ballerina, whose admirers were legion, and who was not without her share of personal vanity, did not know what to make of Langston Hughes, who sometimes seemed as distant as some remote planet. "I'm not going to write anymore, honest," she wrote him in June 1934. "I've written lots of times and received in return a Christmas card, a telegram and a book—now I ask you is that any way to treat a girl!"⁴¹ If he didn't pay her enough attention, she had her own way of paying him back. In December 1934, having received a copy of his article on "Tamara Khanum: Soviet Asia's Greatest Dancer," published a month before in *Theatre Arts*, she wrote him:

> . . . I read your article in the "Theatre Arts Monthly" and quite objectively speaking I found it somewhat flowery. Although I agree that Tamara is certainly one of the best dancers I've seen in the U.S.S.R. Did you notice an article in the same issue about Tishler, written by Jay Leyda? I mention this because he's a good friend of mine. What did you think of the article?⁴²

Si-lan cared less about what Langston thought of the article about Alexander Tishler, a Soviet theatre designer, than she did about the writer, Jay Leyda, who was by then, or was soon to be, her husband. A dashing young American filmmaker and writer, Leyda had come to work with Sergei Eisenstein in Moscow, where he met Si-lan in December 1933 and proposed soon thereafter. Langston Hughes never knew until it was too late.

He might have stayed in Mexico much longer than the end of May 1935 if circumstances had permitted. But Arna Bontemps, who was then living in Los Angeles and due to leave in August to accept a job in Chicago, had invited Langston to spend a few weeks in California working on another children's book. After that, Hughes wasn't sure where he was going to spend the period of his Guggenheim Fellowship. Carmel seemed out of the question because of the Vigilantes. Harlem had just exploded in racial violence that March 1935, and almost every other American city and town was still deep in the Depression. Meanwhile, Langston's mother beckoned from Cleveland, telling him how hard times were there, and that she and Gwyn had both been sick and needed money.

Langston spent his final days in Mexico City with the Patiños, trying to finish reading *Don Quixote* in Spanish, accompanying the three sisters to mass, and going to bullfights. He went to nearby Taxco, the quaint silver mining town high in the hills, where a few friends had moved from Carmel; and he made a brief journey to Guadalajara to see some Rivera frescoes. For old time's sake, he took a hike with the Dragones Club, which he had joined years before as a boy. Out of sentiment, he made one trip back to Toluca, his former homesite. If he really had ever considered it home, it was the last he would ever see of it. Indeed, he would not visit Mexico again until the decade he died.

❧ 17 ❧

Honor and Hunger

HUGHES PROVED HOW ADAPTABLE HE COULD BE when he moved from the home of the three elderly Patiño sisters in Mexico City into the household of three lively young children in Los Angeles. Except for a few quiet days in town as the guest of his Uncle John, Hughes stayed nearly eight weeks that summer of 1935 with the Bontemps family, while he and Arna finished their juvenile book in record time—and in cramped quarters. He was not accustomed to an early-to-bed, early-to-rise schedule, reading stories to children, and having no room of his own, but he adjusted to it all with good humor. Alberta Bontemps's home-cooked meals, the children's laughter, and talks with Arna made him sorry the summer ended so soon.

They spent over a month putting together *Bon Bon Buddy*, which included "Buddy at the Fair," "Buddy in the Big House," and "Buddy Grows Up," from Bontemps's childhood memories of his own Uncle Buddy, who was, in fact, his grandmother's younger brother. It was not the last Langston would hear of Arna's Uncle Buddy, especially after eleven publishers eventually notified them—through Lieber—that the book didn't seem worth publishing. Nevertheless, Langston seemed unable to say no to Arna on books which he would never have chosen to write himself.

He had been the Bontemps's houseguest briefly in 1931 when the two authors collaborated on *Popo and Fifina* in Huntsville, Alabama, where Arna had taught at Oakwood Junior College, before resigning after three years. Tired of the school's parochialism and enforced segregation, Arna had motored west with his family in 1934 and moved into his father's modest home in Los Angeles, where he completed his second novel, *Black Thunder*. By August 1935, he was preparing to go to the Midwest to teach at Shiloh Academy and study part time at the Graduate Library School of the University of Chicago. Meanwhile, believing that Hughes might soon be in some distant part of the globe again, Arna had tackled him to collaborate on children's literature.

That summer Hughes also let Bontemps coax him into drafting *The*

Pasteboard Bandit, a children's scenario about Mexico. Like *Bon Bon Buddy*, it was never printed. During the next eight years, while Bontemps lived in Chicago, Hughes spent intervals there collaborating on several projects—more Arna's than his own—that would bring them little more than the rewards of lasting friendship.

In Los Angeles that summer of 1935 they both talked of what had happened to some of their other Harlem Renaissance contemporaries. Bontemps, along with James Weldon Johnson, Countee Cullen, and Claude McKay, had begun contributing to *Challenge*, a new magazine started in March 1934 by Dorothy West, a writer who had traveled to Russia with Langston for the *Black and White* film. Hughes expressed an interest in sending her a new poem as soon as he could get around to it. McKay, a globetrotter like Langston, was a frequent subject of conversation. He had returned to the United States the year before, after more than a decade abroad in England, Russia, Germany, France, Spain, and North Africa. Meanwhile, Hughes had praised him in several articles, including one entitled "American Negro Writers—Claude McKay: The Best."[1] He still thought McKay the best Afro-American writer of their generation, even after seeing him inadequately represented in a massive new anthology entitled *Negro*, compiled, edited, and printed by Nancy Cunard in 1934. From North Africa, McKay had written Miss Cunard a scorching letter forbidding publication of an article he had written for the anthology, complaining that she had not paid him or any of the other contributors a cent. Nancy Cunard responded that McKay and the characters in his novels had "the wrong kind of race consciousness."[2]

The *Negro* anthology was more than a topic of literary conversation in Beverly Hills. There, at a party in Hughes's honor, guests buzzed about how Nancy Cunard, the wealthy English heiress, had dedicated the anthology to her black lover and had defended her relationship with him in an autobiographical and controversial pamphlet, *Black Man and White Ladyship*.[3] Hughes had no complaints about that, or her anthologizing five of his own poems, including four of the most outspoken: "Always the Same," "House in the World," "To Certain Negro Leaders," and "Goodbye, Christ." The angry poems left no doubt why Alain Locke, in his contribution to the anthology, declared Sterling Brown a greater "New Negro" folk poet than Langston Hughes.

Hughes certainly agreed that Sterling Brown had emerged as a preeminent folk poet with his 1932 book of poems, *Southern Road*. He considered him not only a poet but a scholar and critic whose articles and reviews—including one of the best ever written on *Not Without Laughter*—he had read in *Opportunity*. Hughes and Brown admired each other, but their paths had then rarely crossed. Brown, a Washingtonian, had not joined the Harlem

Renaissance; after receiving his B.A. from Williams College in 1922 and an M.A. from Harvard a year later, he had gone to teach in the South. The label for him as a "New Negro" was Locke's. Like Langston, Brown was not one to label himself.

On the other hand, Bontemps talked nostalgically about "New Negroes" and frequently referred to the Harlem Renaissance as "the golden days of paradise." But for Hughes "the golden days" had been dimmed by the Great Depression, and during the early 1930s, while Bontemps had been writing mostly lyrical verses, two noncontroversial novels, and children's happy stories, such as *You Can't Pet a Possum*, Hughes was publishing protest and proletarian poems and stories. Nevertheless, Bontemps was not without influence over Hughes. He encouraged his friend to embrace the "folk" tradition, as he himself had done in many passages of *Black Thunder*, his historical novel about Gabriel Prosser's slave insurrection. This was probably the reason that, by the following year, Hughes was bending over backward to be a folk dramatist as much as a militant spokesman.

Bontemps praised Hughes's long verse, "Death in Harlem"—with its mixture of folk blues and jazz rhythms—when it appeared that June 1935 in *Literary America*. Preferring that he continue writing in that spirit, Arna warned him against publishing pieces such as one in which their mutual friend Loren Miller attacked the Rosenwald Fund and its "philanthropic control" over twelve million Negroes.[4] Hughes was of no mind to attack the Fund, which had subsidized his tour of the South, even if Miller was a "comrade" from their days in the Soviet Union. If anything, the friendship with both Miller and Bontemps proved what a cross he was between them. Miller briefly left Los Angeles that 1935 to become a New York correspondent for the Associated Negro Press and contributing editor of *New Masses*. Bontemps would soon be on the payroll of the Chicago-based Rosenwald Fund, serving its director, Edwin R. Embree, who was certain that a "satisfactory and satisfying future for [the Negro] is already assured."[5]

Arna and his family left Los Angeles for Chicago the second week in August and Hughes moved into the all-Negro Clark Hotel before he headed east at the end of the month. But, as always, it seemed to be his luck to be in the right place at the right time, and to meet the right friends. Before he left California, he met Clarence Muse, a veteran black entertainer and composer in Hollywood, who was soon to appear in the 1936 blockbuster film, *Showboat*. Muse's ideas for other films and song lyrics made Hughes interested enough to spend a few days at the entertainer's mountain cabin trying tunes with him at the piano. It was the beginning of a collaboration which did not end then or there.

Through Muse and mutual friends, Hughes that summer also met the composer William Grant Still, who had made a national name for himself four years earlier with his *Afro-American Symphony*. Over cocktails, they chatted about how Still's *Symphony* had been performed the same year that Hughes wrote *Troubled Island*, his Haitian play which he hoped to turn into an opera. By the time the poet left Los Angeles, Still had agreed to compose the music for what they knew would be a first: the first opera in creative partnership by two Afro-American artists.

With such a possibility in the offing, Hughes was torn between keeping a promise to his mother that he would be in Ohio by early September and staying in Los Angeles as long as he could. For a dollar a day he could have continued to lodge at the Clark Hotel, or as a nonpaying, impecunious guest, he might have stayed at his Uncle John's or Cousin Flora's. But with checks arriving that month only from the *American Spectator* for the short story "Heaven to Hell" and *New Theatre* for "Trouble with the Angels," he considered it wiser to travel while he still had the train fare. He even skipped a planned trip to Carmel. After Noel Sullivan paid him a farewell visit in Los Angeles, Hughes departed in late August on his first journey to the East Coast in three years.

EN ROUTE, he stayed overnight in Santa Fe at the home of Witter Bynner. The poet was in New York, but his house was full of guests celebrating the annual summer fiesta. Hughes had hoped to see Jean Toomer, and to accept Mable Dodge Luhan's long-standing invitation to visit her "house in Taos." He had not forgotten her invitation when they met a year before in Carmel, and he had telegraphed her of his arrival before he left Los Angeles. However, he ended up seeing neither Mable nor Toomer, for reasons which he explained to Noel Sullivan in a long letter, written in a bus station—away from the bacchanalian fiesta atmosphere at Bynner's.

> This morning [they] came to tell me that Mabel had just passed through in an awfully bad humor, . . . and gone on saying that she would call me from Taos. So far she hasn't called (5 P.M.), and the town is full of stories of how badly she has been receiving guests lately (Edna Ferber, for one), and more recently Thomas Wolfe, who it seems, never did get in the house (after having been especially invited) so from the outside, he flung all sorts of bad words at her through the bed-room window, enlivening the night. . . . Jean Toomer, who lives outside Santa Fe, was most evasive on the phone as to when I might run out to see him, or just when he would be in town, or just where or when, anywhere! . . . so I've decided to take the evening train East, and am at the bus station now . . . because the floods are rising, trains are getting later and later, and all the Rain Gods know I don't

want to have to stay here much longer. It was raining last night when I arrived. The day was sunny, but it's raining again now that I'm leaving. Certainly, that Thunder of the Rain Gods part of my poem was right; concerning the rest of it about a house in Taos, I'm afraid I'll never know . . . the bus is off, the skies weep, and I am on my way.[6]

Probably no one had warned Hughes that, despite Mabel's eccentricity and aloofness, she would never have contacted him through Witter Bynner. Mabel and Bynner had been at each other like two rattlesnakes for years, even since she took *his* secretary and lover, Willard (Spud) Johnson, as *her* own secretary. Hughes probably expected the evasiveness of Jean Toomer, for racial and other reasons. For, by then, Jean had undoubtedly heard the rumors linking him to Mabel, as reflected in Langston's early poem, "A House in Taos," in which the lines "Through the red, white, yellow skins / Of our bodies" suggested some sensual *ménage à trois* (representing Mabel, her Indian husband, and possibly Toomer, her former lover). But whatever Hughes did or didn't know, he was as certain as Edmund Wilson—after his visit to Santa Fe and Taos during the thirties—that those two towns "had about the worst set of artists and writers to be found anywhere."[7]

In mid-September, Sullivan heard better news. Hughes had arrived in Oberlin, Ohio, just in time to help his mother move. "We now have a nice three-room and bath apartment which I think will be very comfortable for the winter, and which rents for only $9.00 a month."[8] The apartment, at 212 South Pleasant Street, was not far from the Oberlin campus where both his grandparents had attended college. Although he had lived for at least four years in nearby Cleveland, he had never visited the quiet, tree-shaded college town. There, where the local art museum stood on the property his maternal grandmother's parents once called home and where so much of his family history was lived, he still had cousins and other relatives, including descendants of Lewis Sheridan Leary, his grandmother's first husband, who had joined John Brown's raid on the arsenal at Harpers Ferry in 1859.

His mother, whom Langston had not seen since he went to Russia, was pleased with the new apartment, but she complained daily of not feeling well. Langston insisted that she see a physician, assuring her that he could afford to pay for whatever medical services were needed. Although he had arrived in Oberlin with only two dollars in his pocket, his financial situation had improved. Lieber had sent him a fifty-dollar check from the reprint sale of two short stories, along with the welcome news that a check was forthcoming from *Esquire* for "Tragedy at the Baths," which he had written in Mexico.[9] Moreover, the University of Minnesota was committed to pay him an honorarium of one hundred dollars for a lecture in October.

In late September, Hughes traveled to New York. After two years of correspondence by mail, he and Lieber met for the first time. The meeting established a strong personal bond between Hughes and his agent just at a time when he needed Lieber's professional competence most.

In 1931, before Lieber became Hughes's agent, Blanche Knopf had submitted Hughes's play *Mulatto* to the American Play Company, a quasi-brokerage firm for the theatre. But neither Mrs. Knopf nor the American Play Company had informed Langston Hughes of what had been done with his script. Four years later, Hughes learned quite by accident that *Mulatto* was scheduled for October 1935 production in New York. In *I Wonder as I Wander* he explained:

> In the fall, I thought it might be wise for me to go to New York and re-establish some of my old contacts there. . . so I left Oberlin for a while. I had hardly come up out of the subway in Harlem on a bright September morning, when I ran into an acquaintance on the street who said, "Oh, so you've come to New York for the rehearsals of your play!"
> "What play?" I asked.
> "What do you mean, what play?" the friend said, thinking I was joking. "According to the *Times*, your play is in rehearsal to open soon."

After a brief trip to Minneapolis, where he spoke to four thousand students—his largest audience to date—he returned to New York to attend rehearsals of his play. He found the script had been changed without his permission and, as he put it later, "a group of white and Negro actors reading lines I had never written. . . But eventually a scene came up that I recognized as my own."[10]

In the original two-act play, he had intended a "tragedy of the American South," dramatizing the fatal conflict between a white plantation owner and his Negro housekeeper-mistress and their mulatto, college-educated son, who kills his father and himself. The thematic focus of the play had been projected in a poem of the same title which Hughes had written in 1927, and a short story, "Father and Son," which he completed in Carmel. The drama marked the first time an Afro-American playwright had written about miscegenation for a predominantly white audience. In rehearsal, he found the focus had shifted from the social tragedy of miscegenation to a melodrama of violence and sex. Behind the changes was Martin Jones, the white producer, a "strange man of inherited wealth," Hughes remarked later, who "implied that if I as author would just leave him alone, we might have a box-office hit."[11]

There was much uncertainty and many changes before the curtain finally went up on *Mulatto* at the Vanderbilt Theatre on October 24—three nights later than scheduled. Even by October 16 Hughes was uncertain of the exact opening date himself. "Hold a thought for my mulatto chile on the 21st," he had written to Marie Short, a friend in Carmel. "Poor little illegitimate off-color proletarian opening in a theatre called ('shades of capitalism!!') the Vanderbilt!...only Shakespeare has more tragedy and death and destruction in a last act than *Mulatto* now promises."[12]

Angered that Jones had not permitted him one complimentary seat and had excluded him and the Negro members of the cast from a buffet supper backstage, Hughes did not attend the opening performance. He did, however, buy $73 worth of orchestra tickets so that his mother, his Aunt Toy, and relatives who came all the way from Ohio could attend; it cooled his anger and frustration a little. Later, he wrote: "At first at the Vanderbilt, the box office tried not to sell Negroes seats in the orchestra. When I learned of this, I not only protested, I bought as many orchestra seats myself as I could afford in the very center of the theatre. These I gave to the darkest Negroes I knew, including Claude McKay."[13]

His problems with *Mulatto* did not end with the box office. Most critics roasted the play and its author. Though some reviewers stated it less bluntly, they concurred with the opinion expressed in *Theatre Arts Monthly*: the "negroes in *Mulatto* are...someone to rape or to lynch, good for workin' and lovin'—good for nothing else...what destroys its effectiveness is Mr. Hughes' weak, amateurish writing, and the unvarnished fact that the negro is an ingrate and obnoxious as the villainous whites believe...."[14]

In the drama of his own life, in which moments of joy and satisfaction seemed inevitably followed by sadness and doubt, he received distressing news about his mother on the very day *Mulatto* opened on Broadway. A letter from his mother's physician in Cleveland informed him that she had cancer of the breast and recommended immediate surgery. Because his name was up in lights on Broadway, Langston's mother was in a state of euphoric pride, and he could not tell her the unhappy truth immediately, but when he did tell her, she took it with surprising calm. However, she insisted on having radiation treatments instead of the recommended operation. Such treatments were expensive, and since Gwyn, her foster son, was then in a Civilian Conservation Camp (CCC) somewhere in Ohio, and could not be counted on, and had never learned the value of a dollar, the total expense would fall on Langston, and very little of his Guggenheim stipend would be left.

There were other troubling matters and incidents, too, in the days immediately following the Broadway opening of *Mulatto*. As if Hughes did not have enough problems, who should create another but Alain Locke. Hughes found him backstage one evening in the dressing room of the leading

Afro-American in the cast, Rose McClendon. It was a scenario which Locke, of course, reported afterwards, in full, to Godmother Mason.

> I went around to the Vanderbilt Theatre to see Rose McClendon whom I didn't go backstage to see on Saturday since I knew a crowd would be there. On Monday I had a fine chat with her— told her frankly that I wished she would be more certain of the plays she does and if necessary wait. . .so that she would stop bolstering up dead horses. . . .Just as I was leaving who should come in but Langston—looking very well and slickly prosperous— toying at an unlit but filled bulldog English pipe. His greeting was almost disarmingly cordial and charming—for a moment I was thrown off-guard—but in a few more moments he gave me an opening—which must have been what had led me to go to the theatre. He said: "How did you like the play?" "Well, Langston, to tell the truth, I was sorry so grand and tragic a theme was prematurely exposed: the rarer the fruit the bitterer it is unripe." I guess this must have been Godmother talking through my lips—anyhow it was final. There was no answer of course. . . .[15]

Just before Thanksgiving, word came of the death of Hughes's Aunt Sallie, his father's sister in Indianapolis. He went to the funeral. Then he moved on to Chicago to visit the Bontemps—whose fourth child was born just before Christmas—and to collaborate with Arna on *When the Jack Hollers*, a comedy drama. But the pleasure of his working visit had not lessened his anxiety when he arrived in Oberlin on Christmas Eve. If *Mulatto* had brought in any revenue, there was no check from Martin Jones to prove it. Hughes had thirty-three cents in his bank account; his mother's medical bills and Gwyn's dental bills had piled up; the rent was due; his creditors, believing *Mulatto* was a big hit on Broadway, were hounding him for payment. Hughes wrote Lieber for an advance and wired Carl Van Vechten for a loan. That Christmas in the Hughes household in Oberlin, there was no Christmas tree, no Christmas dinner.

Hughes owed his financial woes to Martin Jones, who threatened to close the play rather than pay him a royalty of $88.50, which was due by contract. Moreover, Hughes was incensed that Jones had complained that Rose McClendon, formerly a star of *Green Pastures*, had been "paid too much for a Negro" before she dropped out of the *Mulatto* cast with pneumonia in December. Hughes wrote Lieber to tell Jones to pay up or ring down the curtain. By the first week in January, Hughes had his royalty, though future payments were to be waived until the play showed a profit.

It was not the end of the difficulties with Martin Jones, who continued for months to offer royalty alternatives which Hughes, Lieber, and the Dramatist's Guild refused. Although *Mulatto* stayed on Broadway a year—one of the longest runs of the 1935-36 season—and eventually went on tour, it took its toll on Hughes.

All the turmoil, however, did not stop him from writing other plays. Back in Ohio again, he learned that his old friends, Russell and Rowena Jelliffe in Cleveland, were anxious to have their drama company, the Gilpin Players, perform some of his dramatic works in their own theatre, Karamu House, which had opened in 1927, and was still the only theatre producing plays written and performed by Afro-Americans. Hughes was anxious to support such a venture. He put the Jelliffes in touch with Lieber, and arrangements were made for his three-act comedy, *Little Ham*, completed in Oberlin, to be produced in the spring in 1936. Their initial offer of ten dollars for each of five consecutive evenings of the play was all they could afford, and Hughes was glad to get it; *Little Ham* was eventually performed for two weeks that March.

Far from his best play, and a far cry from the melodramatic *Mulatto*, *Little Ham* was a slapstick comedy which must have made even his most ardent admirers wonder in which direction he was headed. During a decade when he was writing mostly proletarian works, and his leftist friends were raving about Clifford Odets's 1935 proletarian drama, *Waiting for Lefty*—and probably waiting for Langston Hughes to write a play with a similar theme— he came up with *Little Ham*, a so-called "folk comedy." It was neither folk nor comedy, and it had its limits for laughter. Depicting the adventures of Hamlet Hitchcock Jones, a shoeshine boy and sporty ladies' man in the Harlem of the twenties, it revealed that Hughes did not always practice what he had preached about some black writers falling into the trap of creating dramatic stereotypes. Rather than falling into traps, they sometimes set traps for themselves—as some critics thought he did with *Little Ham*.

Anyone listening to one of his serious lectures and then seeing one of his comic plays that 1936 must have considered him a schizophrenic at best. It was perhaps in his nature to write folk comedies when he was living tragedies, but it is difficult to understand and reconcile the heart and mind of the Langston Hughes who lectured on "The Negro Faces Fascism" in Cleveland's Public Hall for the Third United Congress Against War and Fascism on January 3, even as the Gilpin Players were rehearsing *Little Ham* across town at the Karamu Theatre.

Two weeks later, in Chicago, where he had gone primarily to collaborate with Arna Bontemps on *When the Jack Hollers*, he lectured on "Asiatic Peoples Under the Soviets" for the Friends of the Soviet Union. Near the end of the month, he received word that his one-act play, *Angelo Herndon Jones*, had won first prize of fifty dollars in a contest sponsored by the New

Negro Theatre League. Adapted from the life of Angelo Herndon, a militant black labor leader, the play's character, Angelo Herndon Jones, contrasted as sharply with Hamlet Hitchcock Jones of *Little Ham* as a lion's roar to a cat's meow. Hughes seemed unable to create in his plays the true-to-life characters and situations or the dramatic force of his poetry, short stories, and speeches.

His collaboration with Arna Bontemps on *When the Jack Hollers* did not help. Performed by the Gilpin Players in April 1936, this social comedy about black sharecroppers in the South carried dialogue as inane as any in *Little Ham*. Still, it was Hughes who brought to the play whatever elements of social realism there were in it; Bontemps had preferred to do an "out and out comedy which would develop the tale of the effect of a jackass mating call."[16] And from that incident came the title for a play that advanced neither Hughes's nor Bontemps's theatrical career.

Down and out in late 1935, with no checks coming in from *Mulatto*, Hughes had scheduled as many lectures as possible and written everything he knew how. That may explain the unevenness of the results. A one-act play that he completed during this period in Oberlin, *Soul Gone Home*, was not performed by Cleveland's Gilpin Players, possibly because Hughes's mother, ill with cancer, would have seen through it for what it was: an unresolved conflict between a mother and son with some implications that hit home. He told Noel Sullivan in January 1936 that he had completed a "one-act tragi-comedy of a wake in which the dead boy sits up to carry on the usual nightly family quarrel."[17] The play was not published until a year and a half later in *One-Act Play Magazine*.

When his mother moved from Oberlin into a Cleveland clinic for treatment in January 1936, Hughes stayed in Chicago and lectured to meet bills that were sharply increased by her medical expenses. Despite the Windy City's severe winter weather, his lectures were as well attended as those he had given in Cleveland. He was by turns entertaining and provocative. When he read from his poems or delivered a speech, he never failed to reach an audience—whether that audience was comprised predominantly of blacks or whites or was interracial. He had a message for all Americans, especially in his resounding and uncompromising poem, "Let America Be America Again," about "the poor white, fooled and pushed apart, the Negro bearing slavery's scars, the red man driven from the land, and the immigrant clutching the hope" that America would be the dream it was meant to be. Only half of this long poem was published that 1936 in *Esquire*, and not in full until two years later in his booklet, *A New Song*, but he recited it frequently in public, and it eventually became one of his most widely reprinted verses.

Hughes had sizable audiences for his lecture readings, but his income was hardly sufficient. "Honor and Hunger / Walk lean together," he wrote in a short poem entitled "Today"—and he meant every word of it.[18] From Chicago, he wrote Noel Sullivan: "I have come to the conclusion that Fate never intended for me to have a full pocket of anything but manuscripts, so the only thing I can do is to string along with the Left until maybe someday all of us poor folks will get enough to eat, including rent, gas, light and water—said bills being the bane of my life."[19]

He had hoped to do more than "to string along with the Left"; he wanted to be a part of it, but in Chicago, as elsewhere, he found the left fragmented. The Chicago-based *Workers Monthly*, a Marxist-Leninist organ of the Trade Union Educational League, to which he had submitted his first progressive poems in 1925, had changed its name to *The Communist*. Elsewhere, the city's once forceful John Reed Club had voted to disband the year before as a result of internal Stalinist-Trotskyite disputes. Some of the same political disagreements which had erupted in Moscow—in the Moscow trial of Kamenev and Zinoviev in January 1935—had spread to the John Reed Clubs, resulting in a directive from the high command of the Communist Party U.S.A. that the clubs should be dissolved instead of disintegrating from within.

In Chicago, Hughes made the acquaintance of Richard Wright, a young Mississippi-born black writer, who had been secretary of the local John Reed Club. Not yet the famous novelist he was to become, Wright was known in 1936 mostly for the poetry and prose he had published in small radical journals, including the *New Masses*. He had impressed Hughes with "Joe Louis Uncovers Dynamite," a piece on the psychological impact of Joe Louis's victory over a German former world heavyweight champion, Max Baer.[20] Wright had lectured on Hughes to the John Reed Club, but the two writers had missed meeting the year before in New York at the first American Writers Congress; Wright had attended, but Hughes had been unable to make the trip from Mexico. In Chicago, mutual friends, including Arna Bontemps, introduced them.

Unlike Bontemps and Wright, both of whom worked in the Federal Writers Project of the Works Progress Administration (WPA), Hughes was never involved in that New Deal project, which lasted from 1935 until 1943. As he later explained, "I was never able to enroll in the Federal Writers Project because I had two small volumes of poems published and a novel, so the government presumed I was well off—not realizing that a writer cannot eat poems, even when handsomely bound by Alfred A. Knopf."[21] In fact, he had published much more than that, but he was not as well off as some of the writers who were enrolled in the project. There were those who thought he was never accepted by the WPA because he was "too far to the left." Considering that the Federal Writers Project engaged some writers who were far to the left of Langston Hughes, that judgment made little sense. Years later, when Senator Joseph McCarthy, as chairman of the Senate

Committee on Government Operations, and Representative Martin Dies, as chairman of the House Committee on Un-American Activities, darkened the political climate with lies and false accusations, Langston Hughes was caught up in the storm, but so were some writers who had made the Federal Writers Project a commendable success.

But there were already some people trying to prove that Hughes was too "dangerous" for school children. In February 1936, the principal of the all-black Roosevelt High School in Gary, Indiana, forced the school to cancel a Hughes poetry reading. The same principal had been to Washington the year before to accuse President Roosevelt and New Dealers of communism. However, the organization of Negro ministers of Gary invited Hughes to lecture, and on February 10, the Afro-American citizens of the town, joined by others from nearby Chicago, filled a large auditorium to hear him.

A few days later, he again met some members of the Gary audience in Chicago, where the first convention of the National Negro Congress (NNC) was held on February 14, 15, and 16. The convention marked the beginning of a joint effort of Afro-American political, civic, fraternal, and religious organizations to overcome racial discrimination and Jim Crow laws and to attain and freely exercise the rights and privileges constitutionally guaranteed all American citizens no matter what their color, creed, sex, or national origin. The NNC became a rallying ground for exponents of equal rights for black Americans: voting rights, fair housing laws, integrated school, equal employment opportunities, and trade union representation. The delegates also forcefully called for an end to Hitlerism and fascism abroad and to lynching at home. During the three-day convention, the NNC elected as its first president A. Philip Randolph, founder and leader of the Brotherhood of Sleeping Car Porters and a progressive spokesman for the working class.

Langston Hughes, Arna Bontemps, and Richard Wright were invited to speak on Negro history and culture at the final session, which was attended not only by the official delegates, but by hundreds of visitors of both races, many of whom were outright Communists or Communist sympathizers. Because the Communist Party had officially endorsed the NNC convention, J. Edgar Hoover's FBI promptly labeled the National Negro Congress a "Communist front."

This was not peripheral to Langston Hughes, for the FBI tried to link the NNC to the League of Struggle for Negro Rights, of which Hughes had been listed as president in 1933-34, and which did indeed have Communists in its ranks. Hughes was not a Communist, but like John P. Davis, the principal organizer and first secretary of the NNC, he also "was willing to go down fighting for the rights of any Negro to exercise his rights as a free man to join the Communist Party or any other party he may choose to join."[22]

Hughes's sojourn in Chicago in 1936 was devoted principally to research for a historical novel he planned to write as a Guggenheim fellow. For his fellowship, scheduled to begin that February 24, he had considered a fictionalized account of the famous Haymarket Riot of 1886. For years he had heard talk of the mass protest in Haymarket Square where a bomb had been thrown into a crowd demonstrating for an eight-hour work day; the incident had sparked a massacre in which four workers and seven policemen were killed and hundreds of bystanders were wounded. In the ensuing trial of the alleged conspirators, the persons actually responsible for the bomb were never identified, but eight radical labor organizers were found guilty, and three were executed (one committed suicide). The events dealt a blow to organized labor and to the eight-hour day and to the career of John Peter Altgeld, the Illinois governor who later pardoned three of the accused. For Hughes, ever the champion of victims of injustice and inequality, the story of the Haymarket Riot was to be part of his great proletarian novel. He had discussed it in California with Noel Sullivan, who sent all Langston's notes and files to Arna's apartment in Chicago, where Hughes planned to gather oral history and information for the book.[23] But he found the city depressing, as he explained in a letter to Sullivan:

> I'm gathering my riot material for the novel and am finding that most interesting, since there were all sorts of tragic and humorous personal experience stories to be found from folks who were in it. This week I'm going to see a girl whose father was killed in front of the family by raiding ruffians. Today I was at the "Y" and saw the bullet marks on the front of the building, still there, and heard tales of how both whites and Negroes were killed in that vicinity. Chicago is still a savage and dangerous city. It's kind of an American Shanghai. And almost everybody seems to have been held up and robbed at least once. A few weeks ago Arna's two-room apartment was rifled while they were asleep, in both rooms. Luckily, he woke up as the robber was still in the closet, so most of the clothes were dropped on the way out. 85% of the Negroes are on relief. And there are whole apartment houses packed with people who haven't paid rent for months, and the landlords letting the houses [go] to rack and ruin, so that they look like nothing you ever saw inside and out. Kids rove the streets in bands at dusk snatching women's pocketbooks, so people are even afraid of children. And when you go to call on somebody, they never open the door until they have hollered

out to ask who it is, and are sure they recognize you. I really
never saw anything like Chicago!!!²⁴

News which Lieber wired prompted Hughes to leave Chicago for New
York a few days after the National Negro Congress convention ended. It
was good news, and it arrived just after his thirty-fourth birthday. Columbia
Pictures was interested in his *Cock o' the World* script—the musical play he
had begun in 1931 in collaboration with Kai Gynt, a Swedish woman, who
still projected Paul Robeson in the starring role. With news of Columbia
Pictures' interest, the historical novel on Chicago went by the board and
was, it seemed, completely forgotten.

But the sojourn in Chicago was productive in other ways. Some of the
people he met there became enduring friends and one, at least, a future
collaborator: the Afro-American pianist and composer Margaret Bonds.
She had appeared as a guest artist with the Chicago Symphony, and set to
music his poem "The Negro Speaks of Rivers" for Marian Anderson to sing
during a Chicago concert. It was the first but not the last Hughes would
hear of Margaret Bonds's interest in his poetry and librettos. In the future,
she would show in more ways than one that her interest in him was for
more than musical appreciation.

If there was any woman in whom Hughes was interested in 1936, it was
not Margaret Bonds, but a friend of hers: the beautiful Elsie Roxborough,
whom he had met in Cleveland that year. Following Hughes's stay in New
York in June to revise the *Cock o' the World* script, Elsie played a not-
unimportant role in his plans for another theatrical script. Like the few
women who had attracted him, she was actively involved in the theatre. By
that autumn, the two of them were discussing a stage production of his
Haitian drama, which she hoped to produce through her own theatre company, the Roxanne Players, in her native Detroit.

A senior at the University of Michigan when Hughes met her, Elsie had
already begun producing plays in Detroit, where her own play, *Wanting*,
had been performed by the Theatre Guild Players in the autumn in 1935.
That she was only twenty-two years old made no difference to the thirty-
four-year-old Langston Hughes: he found her charming, precocious, talented, and sophisticated beyond her years. They were introduced by a
mutual acquaintance, Evelyn Jackson, a Cleveland social worker, who thought
the two playwrights had much in common. Indeed they did. Besides their
interest in the theatre, they were both exemplars of what W. E. B. Du Bois
meant by the "Talented Tenth" of Afro-America. To a color-conscious,
class-conscious Negro élite, there could probably have been no more ideally
suited romantic match for Langston Hughes than the exquisitely attractive
and well-bred Elsie Roxborough. She did not share his consciousness of class

struggle, but she was his equal in family background, education, and intelligence. She was the daughter of Charles Roxborough—a prominent Detroit lawyer and the first of his race to serve in the Michigan state senate—and
she would graduate from the University of Michigan a year after meeting
Hughes, a major in journalism, ready to make a name for herself writing for
magazines, newspapers, and the theatre.

Langston could have told her the difficulties she would encounter with
racial discrimination in the publishing world and the theatre. Within a year,
she had discovered enough herself to surmount the obstacles her own way.
But in 1936 they both thought the best was yet to come—romantically and
otherwise.

Whether Hughes was really capable of any deeper emotional or more
lasting commitment to Elsie than he had felt for Si-lan is doubtful. But he
wanted to believe he was in love, and he wanted the world to think he was.
He displayed a portrait-size photograph of Elsie in his room until the day he
died. He had failed in his romance with Si-lan, who let him know it when
she wrote en route to Paris in 1936 and confessed her marriage. "I don't
remember whether I ever wrote telling you about my American husband,"
she announced. "Yes, I got tired of waiting for you to propose, so I got
myself a consort."[25]

A proposal to Elsie was surely not in Langston's mind at the time they
met. With the problems of his mother's illness and financial bills, then
would have been no time for matrimony, even if he had ever seriously
considered it—which he probably didn't. His mother had moved from
Oberlin to Cleveland to be near her physician for treatment, and it seemed
life had come full circle the spring of 1936 when Langston joined her and his
stepbrother at 2245 East 80th Street, the very building they had lived in
when Hughes was in high school. The small apartment was no place to
bring a bride, who probably would not have liked the small apartment, nor
was the five-room house he later moved into at 2256 East 86th Street.
Hughes resided at the latter address with his mother until the spring of 1937.
But whatever the drawbacks for both mother and son, it was a place they
could call a home. "It's just about the first time in years that we have not
lived in an attic or a basement," he wrote Noel Sullivan.[26]

The year in Cleveland was not his happiest year, but with income from
his Guggenheim fellowship, he could pay for food, rent, and his mother's
medical care. With the nation still in an economic depression and singing
the popular song "Pennies from Heaven," he was glad to have enough to
live on. Regular checks were finally coming in from *Mulatto*, even though
Martin Jones, out of resentment toward paying him, was still creating
problems when the play moved into an even larger Broadway theatre that
summer. Hughes wrote Sullivan that "Mr. Jones, the producer, is appar-

ently not very pleased that I won the arbitration, as he has been marking whatever letters come for me to the theatre: UNKNOWN, NOT HERE and sending them back to the senders. He has also sent out a publicity story that he himself completely rewrote the play for the stage—which I certainly don't mind. In fact, I'm delighted to have someone else want to take credit for the present version—which I think is pretty awful in lots of places. It's a melodrama, with a big M....[27]

Hughes's on-going battle with Jones was personal, but he saw it as another manifestation of white exploitation. His consciousness of that exploitation was heightened that summer when Italy bombed and annexed an African country, Ethiopia, causing him to vent his range in the denunciatory poem, "White Man": "You enjoy Rome / And *take* Ethiopia / White Man! White Man! / Let Louis Armstrong play it— / And you copyright it / And make the money...." But he ended it on a note that went beyond connotations of race:

> I hear your name ain't really White Man.
> I hear it's something
> Marx wrote down
> Fifty years ago—
> That rich people don't like to read.
> Is that true, White Man?
> Is your name in a book
> Called the Communist Manifesto?
> Is your name spelled
> C-A-P-I-T-A-L-I-S-T?
> Are you always a White Man?
> Huh?[28]

He still saw the class struggle as the catalyst of racial tension at home and abroad, and he ended his poem "Air Raid over Harlem" in the February 1936 issue of *New Theatre* with "Black and white workers united as one / There'll never be / AIR RAIDS over Harlem...."

In the September 1935 issue of *Opportunity*, he had already published another poem, "Call of Ethiopia," and by the summer of 1936 his poem "Broadcast on Ethiopia" in *The American Spectator* told how the Ethiopian capital of "Addis Ababa was across the headlines all year long...a tragisong for the newsreels." He also saw the headlines and newsreels showing other signs of the rise of fascism that 1936. In Germany, Adolf Hitler had been elected with 99 percent of the vote, and his Nazi Storm Troopers occupied the Rhineland. In Spain, the troops of the right-wing Generalissimo Francisco Franco had rebelled against the elected Republican government in July, causing an epical civil war.

When Lincoln Steffens died that August 9 in Carmel, Hughes read Ella's announcement in *New Masses* that "the last written message of my husband, Lincoln Steffens, to the world, . . . was one hailing the fight of the Spanish People's Front against the reactionary fascist uprising."[29] Only a year and a half before, Hughes had read in *Pacific Weekly* a description of Steffens which seemed to fit him best: "Lincoln Steffens is a prophet. What he writes today the world will not accept for another decade when it is probably too late. What he said a decade ago fell on deaf ears and we're paying for the deafness today."[30]

Hughes expressed his condolences to Ella and wrote Roy Blackburn—who had worked as secretary to both of them—that "all the newspapers out East carried front page stories of Steffy's death, which is certainly a great loss. And I'll miss him whenever I come to Carmel."[31]

For numerous reasons, a trip to Carmel was out of the question in 1936, for Hughes was traveling back and forth between Cleveland and New York City about *Mulatto, Cock o' the World*, and other literary matters. He was in New York in February to do a poetry reading sponsored by the Committee for the Release of Jacques Roumain, who was finally freed from a Haitian prison that June—after two years of incarceration. At the February meeting, Hughes bumped into Locke, whom Roumain had unwittingly visited and corresponded with in Washington in 1932 without knowing him well enough to trust him. Locke showed how much he could be trusted by telling Godmother that "I was only interested in going to the Roumain meeting to see L[angston] in action—because it is important, I think, to have him realize every once in a while that he has deserted the truth."[32]

Locke should have been the last person to speak of "deserting the truth," especially when it concerned Langston Hughes. The professor was the prototype for Hughes's satiric poem "Ph.D," published four years earlier in *Opportunity*:

> Always he kept his eyes
> Upon his books:
> And now he has
> Grown to be a man
> He is surprised that
> Everywhere he looks
> Life rolls in
> Waves he cannot
> Understand
> And all the world is vast and
> Strange—and
> Quite beyond his
> Ph.D's small range.

Locke's path crossed Langston's again in June 1936 while the poet was staying at the Harlem YMCA to work on *Cock o' the World*. "Langston has just reached New York," Locke wrote Godmother, "and (of all things) is staying at the Harlem Y!" He did not tell her of a related incident which Hughes considered significant enough to describe later in an article.

> ...Dr. Alain Locke, the Grandaddy of the New Negro, introduced me to the recently arrived Ralph Ellison in the lobby of the Young Men's Christian Association, and Ellison almost immediately expressed a desire to meet Richard Wright, who was coming briefly to New York for a week or so to attend a writer's conference. I introduced them. They became fast friends. Wright influenced Ellison in the nineteen forties, as I had influenced Wright in the thirties, as Claude McKay and James Weldon Johnson influenced me in the twenties.[33]

Hughes had not seen James Weldon Johnson for four years until that June 17, 1936, when he attended a party for him and Carl Van Vechten and Alfred A. Knopf, Jr., who all shared the same birthday. Hughes told friends how they gathered at Carl's and had three cakes—each red, white, and blue, and that, despite Carl's dislike for the "class struggle," it was an "anti-fascist party" for a Negro, a Gentile, and a Jew.

He had not forgotten his old literary acquaintances of the Harlem Renaissance era even when he was associated with what Carl Van Vechten called "reds" at the Convention of the Communist Party in New York that June. "When men as diverse as Westbrook Pegler, Langston Hughes and Heywood Broun join organized labor groups in greeting the Ninth National Convention of the Communist Party, it is a significant sign of the times," reported *New Masses*.[34] With 1936 being a Presidential election year, Hughes had his eyes and ears open to what the Communist Party candidate Earl Browder said about the Socialist Norman Thomas, the Republican Alf Landon, and the incumbent Democrat, Franklin Delano Roosevelt. Although he himself was inclined to support Roosevelt's New Deal policies, he had never quite forgiven the President and his Secretary of Labor, Frances Perkins, for not coming to the aid of striking workers in California a few years before.

At New York's leftist social gatherings, Hughes was still considered the leading black American radical writer of his day. Among the aspiring literati, Richard Wright and Ralph Ellison would soon join the same circles. Ellison, a twenty-two-year-old unpublished writer when he met Hughes in 1936, would soon follow him and Wright into the pages of *New Masses*. A native of Oklahoma and a former music student at Tuskeegee Institute, Ellison's first published piece was a book review in the autumn 1937 issue of

New Challenge, a short-lived magazine which Richard Wright helped to launch—with Dorothy West and Marian Minus—when he moved that year from Chicago to New York. Its first and only issue included Wright's piece, "Blueprint for Negro Writing," which defined his attitude on the relationship between political commitment and ethnic roots and made him a mentor to the younger Ellison. In Hughes, Ellison saw an older writer whose literary values he could admire, even if then and later he considered him somewhat too idealistic to take seriously at all times. He hinted at this early in their relationship when he inscribed a photograph he gave to the poet in April 1937: "To Langston, the 'dream keeper,' in sincerity and admiration, Ralph Ellison."

IN EARLY 1937, Hughes had accepted the position of travel director for an eight-week foreign trip organized by a progressive New York group known as Edutravel, Inc. A special travel brochure and ads in *New Masses* announced that "under the personal guidance of Langston Hughes, well-known author and playwright, an interracial group of travellers will spend July and August 1937 in Europe and the Soviet Union studying different racial minorities." Hughes was still popular in the Soviet Union, where *The Ways of White Folks* had been translated and published the previous year, and many of his other works were still circulating. He still had as much faith in the Soviet regime as did *New Masses*, whose correspondent, Joshua Kunitz, reported on the Moscow treason trials and Leon Trotsky's exile to Mexico. The Soviet political trials and the 1936 executions of Kamenev and Zinoviev, who had been blamed for the assassination in 1934 of Sergei Kirov, did not then appear to disturb Hughes, who was eager to go to Russia again.

The group was to set sail on July 3 aboard the S.S. *Berengaria*. Hughes stayed busy in the months between lecturing in Boston, New York, Brooklyn, Dayton, and Toledo and attending to theatrical projects in Cleveland, where his three-act comedy, *Joy to My Soul*, opened in March.

With the expiration of his Guggenheim fellowship in December 1936, he had concentrated on the theatre and on lectures to make ends meet. Having given up hope of hitting the jackpot with Columbia Pictures on *Cock o' the World*, after hearing nothing definite about his script or its musical score by Duke Ellington, he had greater hopes for his opera libretto *Troubled Island*. William Grant Still had invited him to continue work on it in California. The Gilpin Players had already performed a mini-version of the dramatic script just before Christmas, and a Detroit production under the title *Drums of Haiti* was in rehearsal with Elsie Roxborough's Roxanne Players.

Meanwhile, the romance with Elsie was continuing as well as a romance could by mail and telephone. In Chicago, Margaret Bonds was playing cupid and writing Langston: "After this you can save our letters—Elsie's and mine. We're making history. Just turned out a song hit in the past half hour. 'That Sweet Silent Love.'...If Elsie comes down the 12th of Feb., are you coming? Does your heart go pitty-pat about her or anything? Not that it's any of my business, but it's what Mother Margaret had hoped for."[35] Their matchmaker, "Mother Margaret," was only one year older than Elsie, and had romantic designs on Langston herself, but she knew better than to reveal them. Hughes saw Elsie again in April in Detroit, where he went for the opening of her stage production. By then they were talking about the possibility of seeing each other in Hollywood. She was planning to go there after graduation from the University of Michigan in June, and Langston thought he might be working on his libretto with William Grant Still.

By early May, some of his plans had changed. When he arrived in California to work with Still at the composer's country home in the San Dimas Canyon, his Edutravel tour had already been cancelled, because of developments in the Spanish Civil War, and he had accepted an invitation to speak in Paris in July at the Second International Writers Congress. He had also planned to attend the Second American Writers Congress in New York City on June 4, 5, and 6, but he had to forgo the Congress when he accepted speaking engagements in Denver and Salt Lake City on the way east.

When he arrived in Cleveland, he found a letter from the *Baltimore Afro-American* newspaper asking him to consider traveling to Spain as a correspondent to cover black Americans in the International Brigades on the front lines of the Civil War. Having heard and read about the inhumane church bombings and the daily bombardments by the Germans and Italians, he was wondering what he could do about it all beyond writing a long, militant poem, "Song of Spain." That poem, which was read at a mass rally of the National Negro Congress and the American Committee to Aid Spanish Democracy that summer, exhorted workers to "make no bombs again...lift no hand again / To build up profits for the rape of Spain!"[36] He was ready to go to the Spanish front for ideological reasons, even if it did mean risking his life. "Since the *Afro-American* offered me four to six months abroad at what seemed to me a good rate of pay, I made up my mind to accept," he said later. "The *Cleveland Call and Post* and *Globe* magazine also said they would pay for articles. So on very short notice I made ready for the trip."[37]

He should have known he might encounter official difficulties, and he did. The League of American Writers had been complaining that summer about the U.S. State Department and major American newspapers showing no great interest in siding with the Spanish Loyalists over Franco's fascists in reporting the war. Roosevelt's Secretary of State, Cordell Hull, future winner of a Nobel Peace Prize, seemed bent on appearing impartial even during Franco's siege of Spain.

Hughes prepared for the trip, uncertain whether he would have a press pass until the last minute.[38] Meanwhile, he opened a bank account in his mother's name in Cleveland, arranged with a doctor and a housekeeper for her care, paid the rent for three months in advance and had his will written by Arthur Spingarn. "The papers were full of news of bombing raids on Spanish cities where the Germans and the Italians were trying out their new planes, so I thought I might not come back," he wrote later.[39]

On June 30, eleven days after celebrating Joe Louis's victory as the new world heavyweight champion, Hughes sailed for Europe on the S.S. *Aquitania*. Among the many friends waving goodbye at the New York pier were Aaron Douglas, Ralph Ellison, and Louise Thompson, all of whom had heard him joking that the war in Spain might mean, "I might not come back." Philosophical as usual about death, he had laughed it all off, as if he meant every word of a short poem he had published two months before:

Note in Music

Life is for the living
Death is for the dead
Let life be like music
And death a note unsaid.[40]

⚜ 18 ⚜

Nightmare Dream

HUGHES HAD NOT BEEN TO PARIS IN FOURTEEN YEARS when he arrived there in July 1937 for the Second International Writers Congress. As one of four American delegates invited by the Writer's International Association for the Defense of Culture, he was not the unknown poet he had been on his first visit to Paris. Among the widely acclaimed writers from twenty-eight different nations were friends he had made around the world. One was his comrade Jacques Roumain, then living in political exile after a two-year imprisonment in Haiti. Nicolás Guillén was there from Cuba, and he, too, had recently been released from prison for his political activities. Louis Aragon, the French poet-novelist, whom Hughes had not seen since 1933 in Russia, extended a warm welcome as host-delegate and editor of the influential Paris newspaper, *Ce Soir*. They were all there to talk about more than literature. The Spanish Civil War was at the top of the agenda.

Over seventy representatives to the Congress had arrived via Valencia, Madrid, or Barcelona, where the first sessions had been held in support of Spanish writers fighting the Fascist revolt. The three other American delegates—Malcolm Cowley, Anna Louise Strong, and Louis Fischer—had all traveled to Paris via Spain. Because of problems with visas and press credentials from the U.S. State Department, Hughes had no choice but to come straight from New York to Paris. In his speech at the concluding session of the Congress on July 17, he left no doubts among the politically *engagé* writers there that he was angry with the State Department. He ended his talk on a note that brought cheers and roaring applause from the international representatives who filled the hall.

> Why is it that the British police seized [the Indian writer] Raj Anand's passport? Why is it that the State Department in Washington has not yet granted me permission to go to Spain as a representative of the Negro Press? Why is it that the young Negro leader, Angelo Herndon, was finding it most difficult to

secure a passport when I last saw him recently in New York? Why? We know why!

It is because the reactionary and Fascist forces of the world know that writers like Anand and myself, leaders like Herndon, and poets like Guillén and Roumain represent the great longing that is in the hearts of the darker peoples of the world to reach out their hands in friendship and brotherhood to all the white races of the earth. The Fascists know that we long to be rid of hatred and terror and oppression, to be rid of conquering and being conquered, to be rid of all the ugliness of poverty and imperialism that eat away the heart of life today. We represent the end of race. And the Fascists know that when there is no more race, there will be no more capitalism, and no more war, and no more money for the munition makers, because the workers of the world will have triumphed.[1]

Neither his speech nor much about the Congress was mentioned in *I Wonder as I Wander* two decades later. Then he said only, "At the International Writers Congress in Paris that summer I met Stephen Spender and W. H. Auden from London, also John Strachey and the beautiful Rosamund Lehman, Pablo Neruda from Chile, José Bergamin from Spain, Michael Koltsov and Ilya Ehrenburg from Russia, and a great many French writers, including Tristan Tzara and André Malraux. At one of the sessions, the young actor, Jean-Louis Barrault, recited some of my poems in French."

I Wonder as I Wander, published three years after his Senate testimony during the McCarthy era, was a cautious book. Hughes never mentioned that he ultimately ignored the State Department's efforts to deny him press credentials to go to Spain, and that he obtained them by other means and got there anyway via the French border, which was the route taken by many Americans serving in the International Brigades. He had all the help he needed from friends such as Louis Aragon, who had arranged with the French *préfecture de police* the visas and papers needed by international writers traveling back and forth between France and Spain.

Also unmentioned was any hint of what it meant to Hughes to talk again to Jacques Roumain, whom he had not seen in six years and whose plight he had taken up in appeals at home and abroad. In Paris that summer, the two poets had long discussions about how Roumain's quest to bring communism to the Haitian masses had led to his imprisonment, and how the Haitian élite had also labeled Hughes a Communist for criticizing them in such articles as "People without Shoes"; and why Roumain's underground activities had kept him from speaking out publicly for Langston as Haitian intellectuals such as René Piquion had done.[2]

Rather than referring to such political matters, the autobiographical reminiscences of the visit to Paris showed only the more entertaining side of Langston Hughes—the one who enjoyed the Folies Bergères, where he saw and met Josephine Baker; the tourist who had a happy reunion with his old friend Bricktop at her nightclub on the rue Pigalle, where Mabel Mercer was singing; and the poet who danced in the streets on Bastille Day and watched boat fêtes on the Seine with Cartier-Bresson and his wife.

It was a brief stay, with nostalgic moments spent walking through the Montmartre streets Hughes had known in 1924 and seeing people he had not seen since then, such as René Maran, the Martinican author, who hosted a party for him that 1937. He also paid a visit to Mercer Cook whose mother, Abbie Mitchell, was then touring in the lead role in *Mulatto*. Cook, a scholar of French language and literature, was studying in Paris. He had not yet met Jacques Roumain, whose novel *Gouverneurs de la Rosée (Masters of the Dew)* he translated with Hughes some years later. But he had become acquainted with two *Négritude* poets, Leopold Senghor of Senegal and Léon Damas of French Guiana, who had discovered Hughes's poems in the *Revue du Monde Noir* during the early 1930s.[3] Cook would later write and lecture on Hughes's influence on those and other poets of the West Indies and Africa. Meanwhile, that summer they both saw much of Léon Damas, whom Hughes met at the Writers Congress.

"I found a great many old friends in France and made a number of new ones," Hughes said later. Louis Aragon introduced him to one of those new friends, Nancy Cunard. Hughes had corresponded with her briefly a few years before, for her *Negro* anthology, and now was instantly fascinated by this tall, thin, attractive woman, who had been Aragon's great passion before he met and married Elsa Triolet. Heiress to the Cunard steamship fortune, and an aspiring poet, Nancy had spent most of her money on social causes that alienated her from her family and the English aristocracy into which she was born. In *I Wonder as I Wander*, Hughes discreetly wrote little about her: "Nancy Cunard had a fondness for Negro music, so together we visited Bricktop's." Their friendship, as platonic as any could be, did not end in Paris.

Hughes saw her again a few weeks later in Spain, where she was traveling with an Irish painter, John Banting, who later remembered Hughes as "a magnificent and a magnetising man—with his sense of humanity and wide understanding of life."[4] Nancy had been living in Spain on and off since the outbreak of the war in 1936, devoting herself to the Loyalist cause with the same energy she had poured into her *Negro* anthology. She had begun writing articles on the war for the Associated Negro Press and, after meeting Hughes, Guillén, and Roumain at the Writers Congress in Paris, had written about them for the London-based *Left Review*. In "Three Negro

Poets," she praised Hughes as "the travelling star of coloured America, the leader of the younger intellectuals."[5] She and Pablo Neruda anthologized Hughes's "Song of Spain" in *Deux Poèmes*, one of a series of leaflets called *Les Poètes du Monde Défendent le Peuple Espagnol* (The Poets of the World Defend the Spanish People), published in 1937.

For these and other reasons, Hughes years later had his own words of praise for Nancy Cunard. Six years his senior, she seemed to him one of the unforgettable women of her generation.

> Nancy Cunard was kind and good and catholic and cosmopolitan and sophisticated and simple all at the same time and a poet of no mean abilities and an appreciator of the rare and the offbeat from jazz to ivory bracelets and witch doctors to Cocteau but she did not like truffles at Maxim's or chitterlings in Harlem. She did not like bigots or brilliant bores or academicians who wore their honors, or scholars who wore their doctorates, like dog tags. But she had an infinite capacity to love peasants and children and great but simple causes across the board and a grace in giving that was itself gratitude and she had a body like sculpture in the thinnest of wire and a face made of a million mosaics in a gauze-web of cubes lighter than air and a piñata of a heart in the center of a mobile at fiesta time with bits of her soul swirling in the breeze in honor of life and love and Good Morning to you, *Bon jour*, Muy Buenos, Muy Buenos! Muy Buenos![6]

Like Nancy Cunard and many progressive-minded foreigners who flocked to Spain that 1937, Hughes was there hoping fascism would be defeated. It had triumphed in Germany and Italy, but in Spain at least there was still hope that the Republic might be saved. Toward that end, thousands came from Europe, the United States, Canada, and Latin America to join relief committees and the International Brigades and demonstrate support for Republican Spain.

Writers such as André Malraux had already risked their lives in the war. Shortly after the Civil War broke out, he had gone to the Spanish front and formed an international air squadron, "Escadre España," later known as "Escadre Malraux." Two poets Hughes admired and translated had already been killed early in the war. One was Pablo de la Torriente-Brau of Cuba, killed in a Peasant Battalion on the Ponzuela de Alarcon front in the defense of Madrid in December 1936. The most famous Spanish poet of the day, Federico García Lorca, was murdered mysteriously by Fascist Falangists in Grenada in August 1936. Hughes later learned that many Republican Loyalists believed García Lorca was shot by the Spanish Civil Guard, whose souls the poet had likened to the substance of patent leather. In

"Ballad of the Spanish Civil Guard," which Hughes later translated for *New Masses*, García Lorca had written, "With their patent leather souls / They came marching down the road," and "They never weep," for "They have skulls of lead."[7]

Organizations with medical aid and relief committees to aid the Republic had sprung up in nearly every country. "Save Republican Spain," "Save democracy," were the cries of the day. Europeans embroiled in the Spanish Civil War saw their destiny and freedom linked to the conflict. Historically, Spain's crises had proved to be Europe's crises—and some, like the Cuban war for independence from Spain, had also proved to be America's crises. For over three centuries some of the major political ideas of Europe had been resisted by conflicting forces in Spain. Those internal Spanish conflicts erupted in civil war in July 1936 when Spain's liberal and Socialist Popular Front majority in Parliament threatened the interests of the Monarchists, the military, and the Catholic Church—the pillars of economic and political power in Spain for centuries. The old order, joined by the new Fascist *Falange*, rallied to the side of military forces led by Generalissimo Franco. Their revolt against the elected President of the Spanish Republic, and his electoral alliance of liberal Republicans, Socialists, and Communists, split Spain wide open into insurrection and revolution—a battle between Franco's right-wing Nationalists and the left-wing Republicans, known as Loyalists. In July 1936, there were virtually two Spains, with thousands of Spaniards supporting one side or the other, depending in part upon whether they happened to be in Nationalist or Loyalist territory when the war broke out. The Loyalists, supported by powerful trade unions, working-class groups, and Anarchists, resisted Franco's generals wherever possible. Church burnings, press censorship, political murders, and general strikes turned into a civil war which would last two and a half years and conclude with nearly a half million dead.[8]

When Hughes arrived in Spain in early August 1937, Franco's Nationalist forces had captured key cities in the south and the Basque provinces in the north. Supplied with munitions, pilots, and planes by Hitler and Mussolini, the Nationalists had bombed but not taken the Mediterranean cities of Barcelona and Valencia, which were Hughes's first two stops. Valencia, the temporary seat of the Spanish Republican government in 1937, did not look like the town he had known thirteen years before as a merchant seaman. But the war had not ravaged beautiful Valencia so much as Madrid, the capital, which was the major battlefront. It was Madrid where Hughes chose to stay during most of his five-month stint as a newspaper correspondent in Spain, and where he wrote some of his strongest poems denouncing Franco's war.

Three of his poems, "Air Raid: Barcelona," "Moonlight in Valencia:

Civil War," and "Madrid—1937" were written at white heat soon after he arrived. The words of "Air Raid: Barcelona," with its "echoes out of hell in a nightmare dream," came after an aerial attack which he and his traveling companion, Nicolás Guillén, barely missed. He wrote about it in his first article from Spain to *The Afro-American Newspapers*.

> I came down from Paris by train. We reached Barcelona at night. The day before there had been a terrific air raid in the city, killing almost a hundred persons in their houses and wounding a great many more. We read about it in the papers at the border: AIR RAID OVER BARCELONA.[9]

The *Afro-American* ran the piece with the headline "HUGHES BOMBED IN SPAIN," although by then he had left Barcelona and was in Madrid trying to escape the bombardments there. His long and passionate war poem, "Madrid—1937" was not published until thirty-six years later.[10] Inscribed and sent that September to his friend and lawyer, Arthur Spingarn, it revealed a city under siege. "Madrid / Beneath the bullets! / Madrid / Beneath the bombing planes! / Madrid! / In the fearful dark!" Madrid's civilian population, the Madrileños, still remained fiercely Loyalist, and Hughes found them holding out bravely against Franco's continual aerial attacks. For months the besieged Spanish capital had been hit from the air by Nationalist artillery, while Franco's Moorish cavalry advanced below in mobile units with machine guns. Against this onslaught, Madrid's men, women, and children fought back with the help of the International Brigades and Russian tanks and aircraft.

Franco's Moorish troops, recruited from Morocco, had become known as his "Army of Africa." It was that Army, fighting against black volunteers of the International Brigades, that Hughes wrote about in his early dispatches from Spain. Shortly before he arrived, the International Brigades had suffered severe losses in the bloody battle of Brunete, near Madrid. There, for twenty-four hours, in the blistering heat of July, the heaviest aerial bombardment in modern warfare, up to that time, took place. A black American commander of the Washington Battalion, Oliver Law, was among the first to fall. Bearing the brunt of the Loyalist offensive at Brunete were some one thousand Moroccans. "Divided Spain," Hughes wrote later, "with men of color fighting on both sides."[11] His first piece on that subject, "Negroes in Spain," appeared that September in *El Voluntario de la Libertad* (*The Volunteer for Liberty*), organ of the English-speaking battalions of the XVth International Brigade.

> In Spain, there is no color prejudice. Here in Madrid, heroic and bravest of cities, Madrid where the shells of Franco plow through

the roof-tops at night, Madrid where you can take a streetcar to
the trenches, this Madrid to whose defense lovers of freedom
and democracy all over the world have sent food and money and
men—here to this Madrid have come Negroes from all over the
world to offer help.

On the opposite side of the trenches with Franco, in the company of the professional soldiers of Germany, and the illiterate
troops of Italy, are the deluded and driven Moors of North
Africa. An oppressed colonial people of color being used by
Fascism to make a colony of Spain. And they are being used
ruthlessly, without pity. Young boys, men from the desert, old
men and even women, compose the Moorish hordes brought by
the reactionaries from Africa to Europe in their attempt to crush
the Spanish people. . . .

He expressed something of the same sentiment in a poem, "Letter from
Spain Addressed to Alabama," which The Volunteer for Liberty published
two months later, and again in "A Postcard from Spain Addressed to Alabama," in April 1938. In an article for The Afro-American, with the caption
"HUGHES FINDS MOORS USED AS PAWNS BY FASCISTS IN SPAIN," he wrote of
the ironies of the colonial Moors fighting against a republic that sought a
liberalized policy toward them, the paradox of a Catholic general Franco
bringing Moslems to fight Spanish Christians, and the tragedy of men of
color from different countries fighting each other. "But I could not find that
the enemy's use of these colored troops had brought about any increased
feeling of color consciousness on the part of the people of Spain," he wrote
later. "I was well received everywhere I went, and the Negroes in the
International Brigades reported a similar reception."[12]

Hughes took up the banner of the International Brigades, especially the
XVth Brigade, with its American, British, Irish, Canadian, Cuban, and
Puerto Rican volunteers in units known as the Lincoln, Washington,
Mackenzie-Papineau, and 24th Battalions. He praised them for their valor
and for being integrated long before the American military services, and for
having Negro commanders over white troops, a policy then unheard of in
the U.S. Army. The fact that most of the European volunteers in the
International Brigades were recruited by the Comintern went unmentioned
in his articles. He certainly knew it, but he also knew that the Spanish
Loyalists, like the Nationalists, had a censorship board. His articles for The
Afro-American Newspapers focused on the high morale of the black volunteers in the Brigades, their background, and their belief in the Loyalist
cause.

He wrote twenty-two such articles, which he hoped to publish in a booklet. Most of the pieces appeared, with photographs, exclusively in *The Afro-American*, word for word from the text he sent from the Spanish front. The *Afro* took the liberty only of changing some of his titles, as did *The Cleveland Call and Post*, which also published a few of his articles. He dispatched five from Madrid, beginning in early October 1937, five more from Valencia, one from Barcelona, and several from unnamed places in-between. His stories of black volunteers who joined the war effort as combat soldiers, ambulance drivers, truck drivers, clerks, nurses and cooks brought the Spanish Civil War home to thousands of black Americans. He documented a side of their history which few other correspondents in Spain touched. Years later, in *I Wonder as I Wander*, he said of those who went to the Spanish front:

> Who were they? There were a hundred or so that I talked with in the various hospitals, or on the Ebro front, at Albacete, Valencia, Tarragona and Madrid. I put their names in my notebook. Yet their names cannot tell us who they really were, nor could any additional pages I might write about them. But they were there in Spain in 1937-38, American Negroes. History has recorded it. Before that time, the leading ambassadors of the Negro in Europe were jazz-band musicians, concert artists, dancers or other performers. But these Negroes in Spain were fighters— *voluntary fighters*—which is where history turned another page.

One "voluntary fighter" he wrote about but never met was Angelo Herndon's brother, Milton, who died in combat at Fuentes del Ebro on October 13, 1937—while Hughes was on his way there. He devoted an entire article to him in *The Afro-American* and later included parts of it in *I Wonder as I Wonder*. He never forgot a comrade's reminiscence about remarks Herndon made shortly before he died: "Yesterday, Ethiopia. Today, Spain. Tomorrow, maybe America. Fascism won't stop anywhere—until we stop it."[13]

Other black American volunteers also confessed they had decided to fight in Spain after Mussolini's 1936 invasion of Ethiopia. "By fighting against Franco they felt they were opposing Mussolini," he wrote.[14] In a way they were. The most devastating bombing raids over Barcelona were from Mussolini's planes, and Il Duce frequently boasted how Franco owed some of his victories to him. To Hughes, Franco and Mussolini were one and the same. "Give Franco a hood and he would be a member of the Ku Klux Klan," Langston wrote in the *Afro*.[15] Then and later, he never wavered in his contempt for the Spanish generalissimo who eventually was recognized as an ally by the United States. Even in *I Wonder as I Wander*, where his leftist sympathies were muted, he condemned Franco. " '*War and fascism*'—a great

many people at home in America seemed to think those words were just a
left-wing slogan" he said. He had seen first-hand in Spain that war and
fascism were more than words.

He wrote of the foreigners of all races and nationalities who, despite the
barriers of language, volunteered to serve side by side with the Loyalists in
the trenches, hospitals, and kitchens. He expressed their spirit of unity in
the opening lines of a Spanish folk-song that he translated for *The Volunteer
for Liberty*:

> *Frontiers that divide the people,*
> *Soon we'll tear apart.*
> *The masses speak a thousand tongues*
> *But have one heart....*[16]

When he wasn't writing and translating, he tried boosting the morale of
the wounded in hospitals. Another writer who did the same was Ernest
Hemingway. Hughes read one of Hemingway's dispatches for the North
American Newspaper Alliance, in which he jocularly told of the hospitalized American soldier and would-be author who said, "They tell me Dos
Passos and Sinclair Lewis are coming over too." Not to disappoint the
soldier, Hemingway answered, "Yes, and when they come I'll bring them
up to see you."[17]

Dos Passos had been in Madrid that spring to work with Hemingway and
film director Joris Ivens on a documentary, *This Spanish Earth*, but he was
gone by the time Hughes arrived. However, other literary figures were
there, enough for him to say later, "During the months that I was in Spain I
became acquainted with more white American writers than at any other
period in my life."[18] He exaggerated slightly, for he had known as many in
Carmel and New York. But in Spain he encountered some he had seen at
the International Writers Congress in Paris and others he had never met,
including Lillian Hellman, who made an impassioned broadcast to Americans via Madrid radio. Also in Madrid was Dorothy Parker, who he said
"came quietly and went away quietly," and Alvah Bessie, who later anthologized Hughes's poetry in *The Heart of Spain*, published by the Veterans of
the Abraham Lincoln Brigade. Poets such as Stephen Spender and W. H.
Auden, and novelists such as Hemingway and Malraux, embraced the cause
of Loyalist Spain and immortalized it through literature and film.

"Certainly the most celebrated American in Spain was Ernest Hemingway," Hughes wrote later. "I found him a big likable fellow whom the men
in the Brigades adored. He spent a great deal of time with them in their
encampments."[19] At one of the Brigade encampments, someone took a
group photograph of Hemingway, Hughes, Guillén and Michael Koltsov,

the leading foreign correspondent of *Pravda*. Hughes put the photo in a suitcase with his memorabilia of Spain, unaware then that Koltsov would later be portrayed as the fictional character Karkov in Hemingway's 1940 novel, *For Whom the Bell Tolls*, or that the bell would toll soon for the Russian journalist, who was shot in 1938 in one of Stalin's purges. Whatever Hughes knew about any of that, he kept it to himself. He also kept out of *I Wonder as I Wander* whatever he and Ernest Hemingway may have discussed in Spain. He later wrote in his autobiography that he "spent a whole day with Hemingway . . . but I don't remember now what we talked about, nothing very profound, I'm sure." His restraint, not lack of memory, was the reason he could not "remember." Like an elephant, he could remember everything he wanted to; he could also conveniently "forget" anything he preferred not to divulge.

Most writers around Hemingway in Spain, especially Martha Gellhorn, his future wife, knew he planned to write his next novel on the Spanish Civil War. Hughes knew it, too. He was aware but discreet about Hemingway's visits to Gaylord's Hotel, the center of the Russian information operations in Madrid—a location that was a setting of *For Whom the Bell Tolls*. Hemingway had no illusions about communism. He drew favorably the character of Koltsov (alias Karkov), but he had a less pleasant sketch of the doctrinaire André Marty, who was in reality the French commander of the International Brigades training base at Albacete, and whom Hemingway did not disguise with a fictitious name. Like Malraux in *L'Espoir (Man's Hope)*, Hemingway admired the Communists for their discipline, but not for their political purges. Privately, Hughes probably agreed with both authors, even if he never said so publicly.

He had begun reading Malraux in June 1936, after he heard him lecture in New York and told Ralph Ellison to read *Man's Fate* and *Days of Wrath*, two of the Frenchman's novels published in English translation. In Carmel, he had heard much of Malraux, as well as his translator, Haakon Chevalier, a progressive professor of French literature at the University of California, who had also translated Aragon. Reading Malraux's novels—or suggesting that Ellison read them—went unmentioned in Hughes's autobiographies, where he mentioned few of the books he read during his adult life. Being considered an intellectual was an image he shied away from, but he kept abreast of the work of his contemporaries at home and abroad.

His admirers on the left had elected him one of seven vice presidents of the League of American Writers when they gathered in June 1937 at Carnegie Hall in New York for the Second American Writers Congress. Hughes had missed the Congress, but he had heard all about it, especially the speech by Hemingway, who told a packed audience that the war in Spain proved "fascism is a lie told by bullies."[20]

In Madrid, Hemingway stayed at the Hotel Florida, which had been hit by artillery shells so many times that some of the walls were missing. Langston lived in a not much safer location on the top floor of the Alianza de Intelectuales Antifascistas, a Spanish writers' and artists' club, which he described in The Volunteer for Liberty as "no ivory tower." The former palace of a Spanish marquis, the Alianza escaped bombardment while Hughes was there, but one of its residents, Gerda Taro, a French photo-journalist, was killed while taking pictures on the battlefront.

Traveling from place to place, Hughes was lucky not to have been killed himself. Except for a dum-dum bullet which nicked him in the elbow at Madrid's University City, he was spared any wounds. But he said later, "Several times in Spain I thought I might not live long."[21] En route from the International Brigades' training camp at Albacete, he just missed being blasted out of a Brigade battalion's new field headquarters. At Alcala de Henares, the camp headquarters of El Campesino, "the daredevil general of the war," Hughes and Guillén barely escaped a hand grenade that fell a few feet from them. At the village of Quinto, Langston dodged the line of sniper fire as he trudged through the ruins after a Loyalist victory. But only once did he go to the front line under battle conditions: at Fuentes del Ebro. There, in pouring rain, in a tent near the trenches, he waited for the men who had served in the machine gun unit with the slain Milton Herndon.

"With no trains running in or out of the city, and with no car, I had to depend on the kindness of others to travel," he wrote later.[22] He hitchhiked or rode in military convoys nearly everywhere he went. He made a friend of a driver in the XVth International Brigade truck unit, Bernard ("Bunny") Rucker, of Columbus, Ohio. Hughes devoted an article and several paragraphs in I Wonder as I Wander to this black corporal who drove supplies and troops through enemy fire in the Brunete offensive. When the two men met on a chilly day at Rucker's encampment outside Madrid, Langston was shivering in a lightweight jacket, lamenting that he had not brought any winter clothes to Spain. Before driving him back to Madrid in the Brigades' convoy truck, Rucker gave his overcoat to the poet and told him to keep it. Langston was reluctant, but Rucker insisted. The coat was better than any Hughes had ever had, and he was still wearing it three years later when Rucker saw him in Columbus during a lecture tour.[23]

Without a coat, Hughes might have left for the warmer shores of Valencia before December. There he would also have been less hungry. In the "garden of Spain" on the Mediterranean, people still ate fresh fruit and fish, and were not starving, as were many in Madrid, where horsemeat and potato peelings were often considered luxury items. Onions, grapes, and bread were the only foods in abundance in the beleaguered city that Franco was trying to starve into submission. But the weary Madrileños held on, remembering the words of their militant saint of the war, Dolores Ibarurri, "La Pasionaria" (The Passion Flower), who reminded them, "It is better to die on your feet than to live on your knees." For unknown reasons, Hughes's articles from Spain never mentioned "La Pasionaria," the fiery Communist member of the Parliament whose radio broadcasts made the slogan *No pasaron* (They shall not pass) the rallying cry of the Loyalist resistance. But he did say in *I Wonder as I Wander*, "Due to the miracle of 'No pasaron!'. . . the city did not fall—not that week, nor that month, nor that year. Madrid held out."

Hughes held out in Madrid as long as he could, despite chilly weather and food shortages that increased as fall turned to winter. He also held out on chain smoking, since cigarettes were as hard to come by as food. The rationed menu at the Alianza consisted of two meals a day: breakfast of a roll and coffee at nine, and whatever the cook could find for dinner at eight. "At the house where I am staying, sometimes a meal consists largely of bread and soup made with bread. Everybody tightens his belt and grins," he wrote in "Laughter in Madrid," an article published a few months later in *The Nation*.[24] His belt-tightening was more than a joke, for he had lost fourteen pounds by the time he left Spain. "But the longer I stayed in Madrid, the more I liked it," he wrote. "I might get hungry there, but I never got bored."[25]

There was no time for boredom at the Alianza, where a spirit of hope seemed to pervade the entire place, as artists and writers stayed busy making posters, writing songs, poems, and plays to boost the Loyalists. Hughes added his spirit to the memory of "Spain's Martyred Poet, García Lorca," the title of a piece the wrote for a Madrid radio broadcast on November 8. With the assistance of the Spanish poets Rafael Alberti and Manuel Altolaguirre, he also began translating García Lorca's *Romancero Gitano* and his play *Bodas de Sangre*.[26] Alberti, a prolific poet whose verses of the war frequently appeared in *The Volunteer for Liberty*, directed the Alianza's activities along with his wife, María Teresa Léon, an actress and theatrical director. The Alianza, which Hughes described in *The Volunteer for Liberty* as "Madrid's House of Culture" where "creative miracles continually happen," had grown out of the First International Writers Congress in Paris in 1935. By 1937, it had brought to Spain the Second International Congress, which held sessions in Madrid, Barcelona, and Valencia. The Alianza's president, José Bergamin, another famous poet of the war, welcomed foreign guests such as Hughes and Guillén. Many others came and went. Some of them Hughes had met during his travels; others he knew only by name, such as Egon Ervin Kisch—the German writer whose book on Soviet Central Asia the Knopfs had decided to publish instead of his own. He also met Miguel Hernández, whom he described as "a young poet in peasant's shoes," who

came to the Alianza for one week. Hernández told him about the death of
Pablo de la Torriente-Brau, who had fought with him in the same regi-
ment, and Langston shared with him Pablo's short story, "The Hero,"
which he had translated for *The Champion* magazine.[27]

Langston wrote little about Hernández, whom he did not know well,
but he greatly admired this Spanish poet. Hernández had once been a
shepherd in the hills of Orihuela, and had taught himself to read with the
help of a priest. By 1937 he was as widely known for his well-crafted poems
as for his service as a Communist soldier in the Republican army. That July
he was hailed when he attended the International Writers' Congress in
Madrid. Five years later, he was dead, at the age of thirty-two, having
starved to death in Franco's jail at Alicante.

Yet every day offered the promise of a better tomorrow in the minds and
hearts of Loyalists in 1937. Whenever the Republican side scored victory on
the battlefront, the Madrileños celebrated in the streets, in the bars, and in
the theatres, where gypsy guitarists and flamenco dancers clapped and sang
and tapped their heels. Nothing in the Spanish cultural tradition, except
perhaps a bullfight, excited Hughes more than gypsy flamenco music. The
bullfights had ceased in war-ravaged Madrid, but Spain's greatest flamenco
singer was still there, Pastora Pavón, La Niña de los Peines, whom Hughes
went to see perform many times. He was awed by this "plain old woman"
who "could make the hair rise on your head, could do to your insides what
the moan of an air-raid siren did, could rip your soul-case with her voice."[28]
She had refused to leave Madrid, and the strength of her wailing flamenco
voice echoed the strength of the city's resistance against defeat.

The songs and courage of the people of Madrid inspired Hughes to write
to Arthur Spingarn in September that "it's a thrilling and poetic place to be
at the moment. There's surely nothing else like it in the world."[29] Still, he
knew by December that he had no choice but to leave. Franco was threatening to cut the Madrid-Valencia road, the lifeline to the coast. Americans
were urged to evacuate before the city was surrounded. "Like the Madrileños,
even under doom, I did not want to leave," Hughes wrote later. "But there
was no real reason for me, an American, to stay there any longer, eating up
their meager food, taking up their fighting time. I had gotten the stories for
my paper, overstayed the time for which the editor had agreed to pay me,
and seen almost all there was to see."[30] All the cities he had hoped to
see—Malaga, Seville, Cordova, Santander, San Sebastian—were in rebel
hands; the only site he visited which was not a battle front was the sixteenth-
century monastery and palace of Escorial, in the Guadarrama Mountains,
twenty-four miles from Madrid. This ancient national treasure of Spanish
kings was one of the few places that the Monarchist-minded Franco generals did not bomb. It was one of Hughes's few memories of what had once
been the glory and history of Spain.

He joined many Americans leaving Madrid in early December, as rumors increased that Franco planned an attack either on Teruel or Guadalajara and then the capital. Hemingway was preparing to leave—only to return a few months later. Hughes's friend, Louise Thompson, who had been there briefly to work on a relief committee, had already left, taking with her one of the mascot souvenirs seen on Loyalist postcards and posters during the war: the figure of a small child waving a flag in one hand and a determined fist in the other—*La Mascota de la Revolución.*

When Hughes finally began packing his suitcases at the Alianza, he had accumulated more souvenirs, inscribed books, and photographs than he could carry—but could never leave behind. Along with his manuscripts, he had notebooks and photos of nearly all the people and places he had written about in Spain, mementos of what he called "a world without end."

For a time, he thought his own world might end the night before he left Madrid. That evening, one of the heaviest shelling attacks on the city occurred as he groped his way through the dark streets to the Victoria Hotel, where a farewell party was being hosted for him by Hemingway, Herbert Matthews of the *New York Times* and several other newspaper correspondents. The venerable hotel, located away from the firing line, was not hit, but the party started late and ended late, with wine and scotch flowing until the wee hours of the morning. A very drunk Langston Hughes stumbled back to the Alianza to finish packing. He barely made the bus leaving for Valencia.

ALONG with his Cuban friend, Guillén, Hughes spent nearly a week in crowded Valencia trying to find transportation to Barcelona. Trains to the north were booked for weeks and crowded with refugees from destroyed villages. Langston's appeals to Constancia de la Mora y Maura, the head of the government press bureau, brought no promise of a train seat before Christmas. In desperation, Hughes finally walked into Cook's Travel Service and bought deluxe *wagon-lit* tickets for himself and Guillén. Such expensive accommodations had usually been reserved by the government, and it was not by choice that "we traveled the following night to Barcelona in style in a private room with plenty of space, while in other coaches people were packed in like sardines," he said later.[31]

In Barcelona, Guillén remained to write articles for his Cuban newspaper, *Mediodia,* and Hughes stayed only a few days before leaving for Paris via the Pyrenees. Rumors that the Republican government planned to move from Valencia to Barcelona were a reality before he left the Catalonian port. Rebel planes were still zooming in nightly to the sound of air-raid sirens, but he found the city still trying to go on with life as usual, with the Orquesta Simfonica Catalana performing the music of Rimsky-Korsakov, Gershwin, Wagner, and Revueltas at a concert he attended the night he arrived. As in Madrid, he found the Loyalists trying to raise the cultural and musical appreciation of the workers and peasants. At one music hall where he went to see a troupe of Basque dancers, the programs were printed with a notice from Spain's largest labor unions, urging the workers "to have the greatest respect for all the comrades you are going to see on the stage." The notice—signed by the Confederación Nacional de Trabajo (CNT), an Anarchist union, and the Socialist-controlled Unión General de Trabajadores (UGT)—showed a rare effort at unity between the two powerful unions which, in Hughes's words, were not always unified. "They had formerly been bitter rivals, and even now in the midst of war, they did not always see eye to eye," he wrote later.[32]

His newspaper dispatches, stamped by the Republican government's censorship bureau, revealed nothing of the bitter internal rivalry of some of the leftist factions fighting Franco. He did not mention how, early in the war, the militant Anarchists were distrustful of the International Brigades and tried to refuse them entry into the fighting forces. He knew all that and more, but not until much later did he confess it. "In fact," he wrote in *I Wonder as I Wander*, "it seemed to me a major weakness of Loyalist Spain that, even in regard to the conduct of the war, action and opinion varied so greatly between the Socialist, Communist, Anarchist, and Republican parties as to cause not infrequent confusion in military plans." But he defended the Communists against outside charges that they controlled the Loyalists. "The Communists, although an important party," he said, "by no means controlled the government, the military forces, the press, the arts, or anything else so far as I could see."[33]

Staying in Spain as long as he did, he surely knew that the Loyalists paid for military aid from Stalin. The Russian leader had sold them munitions after announcing that other nations should either observe nonintervention or let the Spanish Republic buy arms. In October 1936, Stalin had already declared that the liberation of Spain was not the concern of the Spaniards alone, but the common cause of progressive people throughout the world.

Russia's aid, although no favor, seemed more noble to Hughes than the nonintervention policy of the United States. Like Britain and France, the United States sent relief committees, medical aid, and cigarettes to the Loyalists but no arms for defense against the weapons of Franco, Hitler, and Mussolini. "The democratic nations have let Spain down," Hughes said in a magazine interview after he left there. "The French frontier must be opened and the American neutrality law changed to allow arms to be sold to the Loyalists. Spain does not need cigarettes as much as it needs guns with which to obliterate the fascists."[34]

With France having pursued a nonintervention policy and closed its borders to Spain on August 9, 1937, and with the Nationalists threatening vital railroad points, Hughes was unable to travel by train from Barcelona northeast through Port Bou to the French border, the route he had followed five months before. That December he went from Spain through the Pyrenees-Orientales to the French village of Tour de Carol, where he boarded the night express train to Paris.

He arrived in the French capital just in time for a home-cooked Christmas dinner with American friends. At the Ethiopian hotel in Montmartre where he stayed during the holidays, the talk there was as much about the Italian occupation of Ethiopia as the war in Spain. News reports from the Spanish front were not good. By Christmas, Barcelona Radio had announced the fall of Teruel and a crucial turning point for the Republican Army. In the ferocious battle in subzero temperatures, the casualties had been as heavy as the continual snowfall. On political orders, Spanish troops had tried to defend the walled town of Teruel without the International Brigades— and lost. The brutal counteroffensive begun by Franco on December 29 was still raging as Hughes tried to observe the New Year, hoping for a turn for the better.

In Paris, his friends who had worked and hoped for a Loyalist victory had begun to despair. Jacques Roumain, who had published a deeply felt poem, "Madrid," early in the war, now saw ominous signs looming elsewhere in Europe. "The charming but sad Jacques Roumain said, 'I expect the world will end,' " Hughes wrote later.[35] Equally concerned about the mounting casualties in Spain was Cartier-Bresson, who had directed a Spanish documentary film, *Return to Life*, about medical aid to Loyalist hospitals in Barcelona, Madrid, and Valencia. Nancy Cunard, worried but determined the Loyalists could still win, was in tears about Teruel when Hughes saw her the day after Christmas. "Paris did not seem as happy that winter as it had been in the summer," Hughes wrote. "There was much talk of war in the air—not just war in Spain."[36]

Trying to forget rumors of impending disaster, Hughes spent his last days in Paris going to the opera, the theatre, nightclubs, and parties. His French publisher, Pierre Seghers, tried to encourage him to stay in Paris longer, and so did Louis Aragon, who introduced him to George Adam, a young Frenchman who had translated some of Langston's short stories. For a while, he seriously considered spending the winter in France, but his mother's letters beckoned him home. Concerned about her illness and news that she had given up their rented house in Cleveland and moved in with cousins, he made plans to leave immediately. Having sent her most of his earnings from his *Afro* articles, he had barely enough to book his transatlantic passage.

He sailed for New York the second week in January on the Cunard Star Line's S.S. *Berengaria*, the same ship on which he had been scheduled to travel as a tour guide for Edutravel six months before. "Nothing I ever plan happens quite the way I plan it," he once told Arna Bontemps. "Fate has a way of making its own plans."[37]

He must surely have felt that way at the beginning of 1938, as he sailed across the icy Atlantic, leaving behind a world whose fate seemed more uncertain than at any time in his life.

❧ 19 ❧

A World Apart

WHATEVER HUGHES'S WORRIES WERE ABOUT GLOBAL CONDITIONS, he had immediate personal concerns when he docked in New York. That cold morning of January 17, 1938, he was too broke to pay his travel expenses to Cleveland and uncertain where he would live once he arrived there. Accepting a longstanding invitation from his old friends Toy and Emerson Harper, he moved into their Harlem apartment and began making plans for a lecture tour.

Meanwhile, he was none too heartened by the news from his mother in Cleveland. She had moved in with relatives after squandering most of the money Langston had deposited in her bank account during his absence. Much of it had been spent on his stepbrother, Gwyn, who had persuaded her to let him return to college in Wilberforce, where he had flunked out a second time. His bragging that "he had lots of fun during the process" did not help matters. Langston had spent the royalties from *Mulatto* on "Kit's" unsuccessful first semester, and he had been in no mood to indulge him a second time. Nor did he quite understand why his mother had indulged Gwyn either, since she had been less interested in his own college education than in his finding a job to support her. With her capricious and unambitious stepson, she had been just the opposite, giving in to his every whim, often at Langston's expense. While he was in Spain, she had also taken in a long-lost cousin, who arrived pregnant out of wedlock.

Langston, always willing to forgive his mother for her impulses and excesses, wrote in *I Wonder as I Wander*, "That year my brother, plus this distant cousin, used up all the money I left at home and most that I airmailed or cabled from Europe. My mother had even sold some of our belongings—including an ancient Aztec statuette Miguel Covarrubias had given me in Mexico. . . ." It was Aunt Toy who convinced him that his mother might be better off in New York where they could both keep an eye on her. Indeed, they had no choice. She was a terminal cancer patient when she arrived in

March, and in mid-spring, when Langston could pay the cost, she entered Edgecombe Sanatarium as a private patient.

A few weeks before her arrival, Hughes had rented a Harlem studio apartment at 66 St. Nicholas Avenue. It was a hideaway from the telephone calls, mail, and visitors at the Harpers', where everyone thought he lived. There was never a dull moment at Toy and Emerson's residence nearby at 634 St. Nicholas Avenue, where his friends and theirs seemed always to be ringing the doorbell, but it was no place for him to write. For that he retreated to his studio. While he lectured out-of-town at the end of March, his mother stayed there, at an address known only to a few. She could not have had more privacy. During her brief stay, she guarded his private address as closely as he did. In her diary, which Langston found sometime later, she had written, "moved to 66—apt. 53—3/31st 1938. In Langston's apartment. Very swell," as if she were keeping a secret of the name of the street.[1]

But meeting the cost of his mother's bills and his own was not easy, although Lieber, his agent, had thought Langston "in the luck and in the money" at the first of the year from his writings. Those checks—for articles and poems written in Spain—along with earnings from a February lecture engagement in Montreal, were barely enough to make ends meet. For additional income, he booked himself solid for lecture engagements through the spring—Chicago, Milwaukee, Cincinnati, Cleveland, Buffalo, Durham, Richmond, and Washington, D.C. Otherwise, he was in Harlem as much as possible to check on his mother and to carry out a theatre project he had begun in February. The project was the Harlem Suitcase Theatre, a community-based theatrical group which he had organized on a shoestring. Using techniques he had observed in Russia and Loyalist Spain, where members of the working class were encouraged to pursue the arts as participants and observers, he put the same methods to work in Harlem. Aboard the S.S. *Berengaria* he had written Noel Sullivan, "I'm afraid there's nothing left for me to do except to start a theatre and produce plays. That will be equal to anybody's battlefront!"[2]

Soon after arriving in New York in January, he had discussed the idea with Louise Thompson, who was then on the staff of the International Workers Order (IWO). Her suggestion that they use the IWO Community Center resulted in the Suitcase Theatre's first production, *Don't You Want to Be Free?*, which was sponsored by the Harlem branch of the IWO. Rehearsals for the play, with fifteen performers and a chorus, began in early April while Langston was busy lecturing in the Midwest. In his absence, Aunt Toy took over, making costumes and rehearsing the music with the chorus, while Louise helped with other arrangements. Hughes had purposely wanted a theatre in the round, without set designs or decorative props, and there were none when *Don't You Want to Be Free?* opened on April 21, 1938, in a loft at 317 West 125th Street.

Billed as a poetry-play "From Slavery Through the Blues to Now—and Then Some—with Singing, Music and Dance," it featured dramatic excerpts set to music from *The Weary Blues, Fine Clothes to the Jew, The Negro Mother, The Dream Keeper, Scottsboro Limited,* and *A New Song.* As Langston had hoped, the production educated and entertained. There were no curtains for a curtain call, but after the opening performance he took a bow as "executive director" and told the enthusiastic crowd that his dream of creating a "people's theatre" had come true. He had named his troupe the Suitcase Theatre because their limited paraphernalia could have fit into a suitcase. He hoped, he said, to carry *Don't You Want to Be Free?* just like a traveling suitcase into other black communities.

Performed three times each weekend, at an admission price of thirty-five cents, his musical play was a big enough hit among Harlemites to move eventually into a larger space in the basement of the Harlem Branch of the New York Public Library on West 135th Street. Featuring unpaid community actors such as James Earl Jones, Sr. (whose career was launched at the Suitcase Theatre), *Don't You Want to Be Free?* was performed 135 times in two years; it was the longest running play in Harlem during Hughes's lifetime.

Soon after the play opened, the IWO's Chicago branch center and the New Theatre League there requested Hughes to direct performances for them. By then, he was over-committed, and the Chicago group handled its own production. The national IWO—which published his booklet *A New Song* that 1938—had invited him to lecture on "A Negro Poet Looks at a Troubled World" in several cities during the spring. He also had been asked to direct a special performance of his "Chant for May Day," a verse from *A New Song* that was to be read by a workman with a chorus of over fifty voices. Although unable to accept, Hughes thought the reading a good idea, and he did it himself during a few appearances that May. The deeply felt verse, which called upon workers of all races to join together, was Hughes's great theme in the 1930s.

Chant for May Day

The first of May:
When the flowers break through the earth,
When the sap rises in the trees,
When the birds come back from the South,
Workers:
Be like flowers,

Bloom in the strength of your unknown power,
Grow out of the passive earth,
Grow strong with the Union
All hands together—
To beautify the hour, this spring
And all the springs to come
Forever for the workers!
Workers!
Be like the sap rising in the trees
Strengthening each branch,
No part neglected—
Reaching all the world.
All the workers:
White workers,
Black workers,
Yellow workers,
Workers in the islands of the sea—
Life is everywhere for you,
When the sap of your own strength rises
Life is everywhere.
May Day!
May Day!
When the earth is new.
Proletarians of all the world
Arise,
Grow strong,
Take power,
Till the forces of the earth are yours
From this hour.

That May he had more requests for lectures than he could accept. A young woman he had hired as a part-time secretary became, in effect, his lecture agent. Seeking secretarial help soon after he arrived in New York, he had walked into the Harlem YWCA office and inquired of a pretty receptionist named Frances Wills. She knew of no one to recommend, but she offered to help him herself, and Langston hired her on the spot. Fresh out of college, she was planning to enter graduate school the following year, but she was Hughes's right hand through most of 1938 and 1939, booking his lectures through notices she placed in *Opportunity*. Not one to mix business with pleasure or social cordiality, Langston addressed her only as "Miss Wills" for months. Several years passed before he asked her for a social date.

Aunt Toy, possessive of him as ever, liked Frances Wills better than she liked most of Langston's female acquaintances. Frances liked her, too, and she was receptive to being taught how to sew and how to play poker, two of Toy's favorite activities. Occasionally, Frances was invited to meals when Langston was there, but he tried to ignore Toy's subtle remarks about "this pretty young thing who had helped him so much." He knew better than anyone that if he had shown any romantic interest in Frances, Toy would have seen through it and tried to discourage it.

Only reluctantly had he brought Si-lan Chen Leyda to visit Mrs. Harper for tea the year before, during one of his brief trips from Cleveland. Even though Si-lan by then was a married woman, who spoke of her American husband, his studies in Russia, and his work in the film department of the Museum of Modern Art, Aunt Toy sensed the rest of the story in Langston's eyes. But whatever she sensed mattered less to Langston than what he himself expressed to Si-lan when he walked her to the subway that afternoon. The tears broke through his voice when, in an uncharacteristic scenario, he blurted out, "Why did you do it!? How could you give up what we had and marry someone else when I met you first?" Probably no answer Si-Lan could have given would have consoled him. They waved goodbye as the subway train sped away. It would be a decade before they saw each other again. But Si-lan had an address where she sent occasional letters to Langston. He kept them all, though he rarely answered.

But Toy Harper knew even less about Elsie Roxborough, although Langston's large photograph of Elsie was proudly displayed on the Harpers' grand piano. What Toy did know was what any reader of *I Wonder as I Wander* would learn later.

From Valencia I wrote a long letter to the girl I was in love with then, Elsie Roxborough, in Detroit. Elsie...was ambitious to become a director in the professional theater, radio, or motion pictures. She was a lovely-looking girl, ivory-white of skin with dark eyes and raven hair like a Levantine. Each time that we met in Detroit or Cleveland or Chicago, Elsie would tell me about her dreams, and wonder whether or not it would be better for her to pass for white to achieve them. From what I knew of the American entertainment field and how Negroes were then almost entirely excluded from the directorial or technical aspects of it, I agreed with her that it was difficult for any colored person to gain entrance except as a performer....Elsie was often mistaken for white in public places, so it would be no trouble at all for her to pass as white. While I was in Spain she wrote me that she had made up her mind to do so. She intended to cease being

colored.... When I got back to the United States, Elsie had
disappeared into the white world.

Elsie had not quite disappeared into the white world in 1938, but she was
on her way. Except for occasional rumors later linking her romantically
with heavyweight champion Joe Louis—whose trainer-manager was Elsie's
uncle—she was all but invisible to her friends. She would appear and then
disappear—no one exactly knew where. Some claimed to see her in the
company of black comedian-actor Stepin Fechit, about whom she supposedly once said, "If he's the best the Negro race has to offer, then I don't
want any part of it." She was still in New York City in 1938, and she knew
Langston was there, too, but if they ever met together, it was in such
secrecy that none of their friends were aware of it. Her decision to pass for
white seemed to make it futile to continue their short-lived romance except
through letters. For a time she continued to write Langston, but she gave
no return address.

When Carolyn Clark died that June 3, Elsie was not among the close
friends who gathered at the small funeral home chapel on West 131st Street
to pay their last respects. The Sunday afternoon funeral service was stark
and simple and humble; Langston could not afford an elaborate one. Sapped
financially by his mother's medical expenses, he had to borrow the money
for her funeral from Mrs. Amy Spingarn. Whatever sadness he felt at the
last rites, he was stoic throughout, knowing as surely as his mother must
have known in life that he had given as much as he could give.

Less than a month after his mother died, Langston's friend and mentor,
James Weldon Johnson, was killed in an automobile accident in Maine. On
June 30, Hughes joined over two thousand mourners at Johnson's funeral
service at the Salem Methodist Church in Harlem. Ten years earlier, some
of the same people there had packed the church for the wedding of Countee
Cullen and Yolande Du Bois. Strange coincidences seemed to touch his
friends and loved ones and himself that summer of 1938. His mother's
funeral had been held next door to the same house at 234 West 131st Street
where he had once lived with Countee Cullen during the 1920s. James
Weldon Johnson had met his tragic end on the way to Great Barrington,
Massachusetts, the birthplace of W. E. B. Du Bois. The untimely death of
Johnson, eminent lawyer, professor, librettist, diplomat, and NAACP
official, made headlines in the black press, and eulogies were still being
written and talked about as Hughes prepared to sail for Europe that July.
Along with Theodore Dreiser, he had been invited to represent the United
States in Paris at a Peace Congress sponsored by the International Association of Writers for the Defense of Culture. With so much to concern
him before he left, he nearly forgot to renew his passport; a new one was

issued only four days before he sailed on July 13, 1938, on the S.S. *Normandie*.

At the pier, the ship was moving away from its berth when a distraught Elsie Roxborough arrived—too late to bid Hughes goodbye. However anonymous she may have thought she was in the crowd, most of Langston's friends knew who she was. They had all seen the dark-eyed, dark-haired beauty in the photograph on the piano at the Harpers. But this was the last time any of them would ever claim to recognize her in person—and the last chance that Hughes would ever have to see her of the "raven hair like a Levantine."

Elsie Roxborough was soon to become a blonde, and to adopt her middle name, Patricia, alias Pat Rico, one of the pseudonyms she used in the white world. As Pat Rico she would become a fashion model and an occasional writer of fictional romance stories, after trying unsuccessfully to become a screen actress in Hollywood. For nearly eight years on the East Coast she would be Mona Monet, owner of a cosmetic firm. An ambitious and beautiful woman who was ahead of her time, cut off from her past, she lived out an uncertain identity in her own glamorous fantasy world. Her destiny would end with an overdose of barbiturates in October 1949, at the age of thirty-five.

HUGHES AND ELSIE were worlds apart in more ways than one when he arrived in Paris that July. Some of the same writers who had been in the French capital one year before for the Second International Writers Congress were there again for the Peace Congress. Their attitude toward "creeping fascism" was even more somber than in 1937. They wondered what they could do in the face of the increasing persecution of Jews in Germany and Austria and the defeat of Loyalist strongholds in Spain. Authors from China brooded over the fall of key Chinese provinces to Japan and Hitler's recognition of the puppet Manchukuo state. All the delegates seemed worried about the military maneuvers of the Nazis, who were goosestepping steadily toward Czechoslovakia after seizing Austria in March and declaring it a part of the Third Reich. French writers who wondered what Hitler and Mussolini had been up to during a May meeting in Rome feared the worst for France. Their fears were not unfounded, for the worst was yet to come.

The Congress ended two months before the Western powers, in the hope of averting a world war, established an "appeasement policy" with Nazi Germany. On September 28 and 29, France's premier and war minister, Edouard Daladier, joined Great Britain's Neville Chamberlain in signing the Munich Pact with Germany and Italy, permitting Hitler immediate occupation of the Sudeten region of Czechoslovakia. Hughes commented later to friends at home that the atmosphere in Paris that summer created only the illusion of peace. Signs of the Anglo-French solidarity were everywhere. Flags were waving along the grand boulevards and the Champs-Elysées in celebration of the state visit of the British monarch, George VI. Evening *son et lumière* festivals were held with greater pomp and ceremony than ever. Pageantry was everywhere, obscuring the economic and political troubles which had recently led to the devaluation of the French franc. Uncertain of exactly what was going on, Hughes wrote Arthur Spingarn that the city was the same as ever, beautiful, inexpensive, and full of tourists.

Sensing that it might be a long time before he saw Paris again, he made the most of it. He stayed two months, working on two plays and seeing all his old friends. Some, including Jacques Roumain, he would never see again. Others he would not see for almost a decade, such as Henri Cartier-Bresson and his wife, to whom he later dedicated *Simple's Uncle Sam*. It would be even longer before he saw Nancy Cunard, who that summer posed with him for a photograph and dedicated it "with love and admiration and appreciation of our days in Spain."

By the time Hughes sailed from Le Havre on September 10, talk had increased about the fateful month of August 1914 and the hope that Europe was not on the brink of another world war. To his sorrow, he knew that the Peace Congress he had attended had not really lessened the chances. He and the delegates had hailed the courage of Thomas Mann in leaving Germany and denouncing Hitler, but all had wondered whether the pen was really mightier than the sword.

BACK IN THE UNITED STATES, where Americans were less concerned than Europeans about the threats to peace, Hughes turned his attention to his work. While he was in Europe Frances Wills had scheduled appearances for him (and Arna Bontemps) on the West Coast, beginning in late November. Meanwhile, the modest earnings from his lectures in Stamford, Bridgeport, New Haven, and Hartford, Connecticut, and Poughkeepsie, New York, allowed him to continue his unpaid labor of love: writing and directing for the Suitcase Theatre. With an eye toward future Suitcase productions in Harlem, he finished a libretto with composer James P. Johnson for a folk opera, *The Organizer*, and started rehearsals of his two one-act satirical sketches, *Limitations of Life* and *Em-Fuehrer Jones*, which he had written in Paris.

The routine of lectures and theatrical work suited his habit of writing until dawn and sleeping until noon. "Come early to work," he would tell Frances Wills. She soon learned that "early" meant afternoon and "late" usually meant Cinderella midnight and beyond. That autumn, adapting herself to his schedule, she typed his play *Front Porch*. The Gilpin Players began rehearsing it before the last act was written, and had to improvise. Hughes, unruffled, went to Cleveland for the November production.

Constantly on the go before his trip to California, he nearly missed seeing his old friend Marie Seton, who was in New York on a brief visit from London. They had kept in touch after their meeting in Moscow. Though she had lent him the volume of stories by D. H. Lawrence, he had never told her they had influenced his own career.[3] Not long before her New York trip, Hughes had sent her a letter of introduction to a white literary acquaintance, John Trounstine, "who had passed himself off as a great friend of Langston's in Europe."[4] In New York Trounstine threw a party in Marie's honor and, for racial reasons, did not invite Hughes. Trounstine's confession that he had feared being "thrown out of his fancy flat" had so infuriated Marie that she left the party and went straight to Harlem in a taxi to apologize to Langston. He comforted her by laughing it off. He had experienced so many similar racial incidents that one more seemed not to matter; it seemed to Marie that "beneath his deep sensitivity, he was in fact wiry and tough."[5]

At the time, Trounstine was the literary agent of Arna Bontemps, but Bontemps eventually grew dissatisfied enough with his behavior and his services to become a client of Maxim Lieber. But that decision was still months off when Bontemps and Hughes teamed up to lecture late that autumn in Chicago and California for their series on "Making Words Sing, Talk and Dance." The lectures were paid for by the Fillipa Pollia Foundation, and Langston and Arna went into nearly every high school in Los Angeles before Christmas. Lecturing together in the California schools had been Bontemps's idea, and he had another project idea that also involved Langston. Bontemps's play, *St. Louis Woman*—fashioned from his novel *God Sends Sunday* with the collaboration of Countee Cullen—needed to be revised for a production by the Federal Theatre in Los Angeles. Langston agreed to help out. Since the Federal Theatre salary was not much for the script revision, Clarence Muse, the theatre director and an old acquaintance of Langston, had another idea. Believing that, if music and lyrics were added, the play had Broadway and screen possibilities, Muse persuaded Hughes to write the libretto. Bontemps and Countee Cullen would share in profits from performances outside the Federal Theatre. Arna was all for it, and so was Langston.

The decision to collaborate on the musical meant a longer stay in California than Hughes had expected. Originally, he had planned only to spend Christmas with his Uncle John and cousin Flora Coates and to make a short visit to see Noel Sullivan. He had kept his New York studio (at 66 St. Nicholas Avenue) and the rent was past due. Needing money immediately, he asked Lieber to collect what was owed for the use of "Let America Be America Again" in Harold Rome's popular musical revue, *Pins and Needles*, which had been playing off Broadway and on tour for over a year.[6] Hughes

paid his New York debts out of the $100 royalty payment he received and
had enough left to visit Noel Sullivan at his new Hollow Hills farm in
Carmel Valley. Hughes found the peaceful farm in a scenic canyon ideal for
writing, and he stayed there that January 1939 long enough to write "Inside
Us," the first short story he had written in four years.[7] Then, summoned by
Clarence Muse, he returned at the end of the month to Los Angeles to
collaborate on *St. Louis Woman* and a filmscript, *Way Down South*.

HAD ANYONE TOLD HUGHES even five years before that he would be working in Hollywood before the thirties ended, he probably would have laughed
it off as a joke. He had heard Sergei Eisenstein's horror stories about the
way he had been treated there. But the New Year of 1939 ushered in a new
period in Hughes's career, in more ways than one. The world of show
business added a new dimension to the pattern of his life. It was that
experience, as much as the gathering storm in Europe, that modified what
he wrote and marked the beginning of the end of his steady, activist political
involvement on the left. Although privately he held to most of his political
beliefs of the 1930s until the day he died, he could never again be described
as unbending in his leftist political posture after 1939. Perhaps battle fatigue,
hinted at in "Poem," published in *Challenge* in June 1936, overtook him:

> Beating your fists against the wall,
> Sometimes you break your bones
> Against the wall—
> But sometimes not.

Some of the leftist magazines he wrote for also reflected the tired fists and
broken bones. One after another he had seen them go down to defeat. *The
Champion*, organ of the Young Communist League, which for two years
had championed the "popular Front" of liberal democrats, union leaders
and reformers, had ceased publication in 1938 for lack of support. Elsewhere, Jack Conroy, editor of *The Anvil*, complained that his magazine had
been "swallowed up and completely effaced in an ill-advised merger with
the *Partisan Review*."[8] After the merger ended, *Partisan Review* had reorgan-
ized, in 1937, and changed its dedication from a 1934 editorial defending the
Soviet Union, combating fascism, and promoting a working class literature
to a "tradition of aestheticism."
    If Hughes saw few ways to go in early 1939, except to write entertaining
scripts or to lecture to school children on "Making Words Sing, Talk and
Dance," it was because he had experienced enough disillusionment on almost every other front. It was no April Fool's joke when he heard Franco
announce to the world via radio broadcast, on April 1, 1939, his victory

over Republican Spain. That was three days after Hughes had finished an eight-week Hollywood contract as co-author of the film script for *Way Down South*. He was completely exhausted, and the Loyalist defeat depressed him beyond words.

The movie script was the first that Hughes ever wrote, and he meant and hoped that it would be the last. Though originally offered only three hundred dollars, Hughes, urged on by Lieber, demanded more, and in the end he and Muse received five hundred dollars apiece for the script and song lyrics. It was low-scale for Hollywood, and the conditions under which the production was completed—long hours on the location, dining on sandwiches in the boiling sun while making the film—were just as unrewarding. When Hughes saw the film edited and finished, it gave him little comfort to write Noel Sullivan, "Now that I know how movies are made, it might have been worse. I assure you it is not as bad as *Mulatto!*"[9]

Hughes could not have done much more to make the script better in a Hollywood where black screenwriters and lyricists were even rarer than black performers. The RKO movie moguls seemed content with the portrayal of contented slaves in the Old South melodrama. Hughes was not. Muse, who knew Hollywood well—he eventually performed in 217 films—tried to calm Hughes when he demanded that they make their views known. Muse had written himself into the script as one of the slaves, the beloved Old Uncle Caton who never made trouble, and Muse didn't want to make any for himself. The film, set in antebellum Louisiana, was high on offerings of Negro spirituals sung by the Hall Johnson Choir as a supporting cast for the white star, Bobby Breen, owner of Bobby Breen Productions, which made *Way Down South*. In it, young Bobby played the role of a white Southern orphan boy trying to save the plantation and the devoted slaves left behind when his father was killed by runaway horses. Hughes took pride only in writing the lyrics of two of the songs, "Good Ground," and "Louisiana," both with music by Muse. When the film opened nationally to not-so-rave reviews, Langston told interested friends to go see it just to hear "Louisiana."

He took greater pride in having formed the New Negro Theatre in Los Angeles. That March, he had organized the theatrical group in much the same way he had the Harlem Suitcase Theatre. It opened with a production of *Don't You Want to Be Free?* In April, when he left Los Angeles on a lecture tour with Arna Bontemps, Clarence Muse took over the supervision of the company.

Sponsored again by the Fillipa Pollia Foundation, Hughes and Bontemps lectured—mainly in schools—in Kansas City, Missouri; Lexington, Kentucky; Cincinnati, Dayton, Columbus, Cleveland, and Toledo, Ohio; Chicago; Indianapolis; Buffalo; and Pittsburgh over a two-month period. Hughes interrupted the tour on June 2 to address the opening session of the Third American Writers Congress at New York City's Carnegie Hall. As one of the regional vice-presidents of the League of American Writers, he scarcely needed an introduction, but Donald Ogden Stewart, the president, introduced Hughes in the same formal and laudatory tone with which he introduced Thomas Mann, the keynote speaker. The applause was thunderous when Hughes rose to speak his mind on "Democracy and Me":

> Twice now I have had the honor and the pleasure of representing the League of American Writers at Congresses held abroad in Paris and Spain. In Europe I spoke first as an American and as a writer, and secondarily as a Negro. Tonight, here in New York at the Third American Writers' Congress, I feel it wise in the interest of democracy to reverse the order, and to speak first as a Negro and a writer, and secondarily as an American—because Negroes are secondary Americans. All the problems known to the Jews today in Hitler's Germany, we who are Negroes know here in America—with one difference. Here we may speak openly about our problems, write about them, protest and seek to better our conditions. In Germany the Jews may do none of these things. Democracy permits us the freedom of a hope, and some action towards the realization of that hope. Because we live in a democracy, tonight I may stand here and talk to you about our common problem, the problem of Democracy and me....[10]

The rest of his speech focused on the bread-and-butter issues of survival for black American writers; he hit hard at their limited access to the publishing world, the lecture circuit, and the movie industry. And though he did not say so, he undoubtedly had his own work on *Way Down South* in mind when he said that "no motion picture studio in America, in all the history of motion pictures has yet dared make one single picture using any of the fundamental dramatic values of Negro life—not one."

The following day, at the New School for Social Research, where the Writers Congress held a seminar on American film, he heard Donald Ogden Stewart talk about the "Hollywood Progressive Movement." He did not then understand the full implications of what Stewart meant when he said that "writers, actors and directors have come to the realization that the social responsibility is theirs to protect the vast motion picture audience... against any possible use of the pictures by anti-democratic forces."[11] During the McCarthy years, Hughes would discover the deeper meaning when he learned that Stewart, an Academy Award-winning screenwriter, was blacklisted along with the Hollywood Ten.[12] With Ella Winter, whom Stewart

married in 1939, he would be forced to flee to England. At the Writers
Congress in 1939, Stewart told Hughes that "Democracy and Me" was so
good that it should be published. He meant it: the following year he excerpted it himself in the anthology *Fighting Words*.

Hughes stayed in New York after the Writers Congress only long enough
to sublet his Harlem studio apartment and to visit briefly with the Harpers,
with Carl Van Vechten, with Lieber, and with Paul Robeson, who was
soon to leave for London. He had a short reunion with Richard Wright,
who was celebrating the completion of his novel *Native Son*. Together, they
dashed off a poem, "Red Clay Blues," which appeared under both their
names that August 1 in *New Masses*. By then, Hughes had returned to
California via Chicago, and decided to accept Noel Sullivan's invitation to
spend a year at Hollow Hills Farm. A special Mexican-style guest house
had been built for Hughes on the edge of the farm. There he could finish his
autobiography, the first draft of which he had begun at the Grand Hotel in
Chicago. The book was to be called *The Big Sea*. Arna had been urging
Hughes for months to complete it, a fact that Hughes later recorded in an
inscribed copy: "For Arna, who prodded me into starting this BIG SEA on
a train between Toledo and Chicago when we were on a lecture tour...."[13]

Not until late August did he get back to writing the book in California.
Stopping in Los Angeles for the premiere of *Way Down South* on July 18, he
stayed around a month working with William Grant Still on their opera
Troubled Island. Convinced there was a "revival of interest in things Negro
on Broadway," he had hopes that *Troubled Island* or another of his theatrical
ventures would bring a stroke of luck. He was still betting on *Cock o' the
World*, which Duke Ellington was revising the music for again that summer. Except for *Way Down South*, and his brief stint with the Los Angeles
Federal Theatre, none of Hughes's theatrical efforts had brought any income that year. He had received little more than applause for performances
of *The Organizer* at the Suitcase Theatre in March and at the International
Ladies Garment Workers Union convention in May; performances of *Don't
You Want to Be Free?* in Atlanta, New Orleans, and Nashville were earning
no royalties, even though he was glad the show was getting national exposure; the Karamu Theatre had paid fifty dollars to perform *Mulatto* on seven
nights in April; and he and Muse had ended up with a few dollars for
"Refugee Road," a song lyric that had been played on the radio.

When he finally got to Hollow Hills Farm in August, he felt like a
refugee himself, a beggar. His money had been so low in New York that he
had pawned a suit to pay his train fare to California. Admitting that he was
without funds, he told Noel Sullivan that he was broke after "flirting with
the theatre." He wanted no more of it for a while, even when a young black
scenarist, Carlton Moss, wrote from Los Angeles asking him to send some

song lyrics "with light social meaning" for a Cafe Society show. Instead, he was ready to get back to "literature." For a year and a half, he had published next to nothing in the way of poetry, except for *A New Song*, and most of that was not really new. He had written not an article since he left Spain.

But in spite of not having published much since 1937, he was still being anthologized and praised for the reputation he had already made for himself. That 1939, the urbane and sensitive critic Saunders Redding in *To Make a Poet Black*, the first serious evaluation of Afro-American literature ever published, called Hughes the "most prolific and the most representative of the New Negroes." His critical appraisal, however, covered only Hughes's published books up to that time, and so omitted mention of the theatrical works and the less conventional writings of social protest published in rather obscure "little magazines."

Significantly, *The Big Sea* gave no hint of Hughes's radical works or activities. There was no mention of the proletarian magazines he had published in or the proletarian organizations he was associated with. Except for quotes from "Advertisements for the Waldorf Astoria"—from which he carefully deleted the revolutionary ending—the decade that Edmund Wilson called "The American Earthquake," the thirties, never surfaced in *The Big Sea*. Hughes ended his story in 1931. Reviewing it with some dismay in *New Masses*, Ralph Ellison wrote that Hughes had not been explicit enough about his activism, "for after 1930 Hughes was the more conscious artist." Noting that *The Big Sea* was written in a narrative style that was "charming in its simplicity," Ellison said "many *New Masses* readers will question whether this is a style suitable for the autobiography of a Negro writer of Hughes's importance."[14]

No one was more conscious of his "importance" than Langston Hughes, who kept an archive on every aspect of his career, and whose simple, almost childlike language in *The Big Sea* only masked his complexity. So conscious was he of his place in literary history that he drew a line, as it were, through a part of that history in his first autobiography. The picaresque book, devoid of anger and protest, was an entertaining, innocuous memoir which Blanche and Alfred Knopf were pleased to publish. Throughout much of his career, Hughes wrote differently for different audiences—one for his commercial books, another for noncommercial magazines. The duality at times made him look like a chameleon, a cop-out. That must have been his own feeling when he worked on *The Big Sea*.

During that time, on at least two occasions, he felt deluded and betrayed. He surely felt betrayed the summer of 1939 after hearing the news that, on August 18, Stalin had signed a nonaggression pact with Hitler. It hit Langston like a thunderbolt. Four days before, his own name, along with others, had been mentioned in the *Daily Worker* decrying accusations that the Soviet

Union and the totalitarian states were alike. Then suddenly to see Josef Stalin and the Communist regime ally with the Nazis was the last straw. "Write about your life," Bontemps had told him. "Don't write about the Communists, they change their line too much."[15]

Purposely, *The Big Sea* chronology ended in 1931 and revealed almost nothing about the Soviet Union, which was then held suspect by many important public figures in the United States. Nothing about Hughes's experiences in Russia or his work published in *Krasnaya Nov, Zemlya Kolumbia,* and *Izvestia* was mentioned. Least of all did he say that he, along with a hundred other prominent authors, had put his career on the line in 1938 by signing the "Statement of American Progressives on the Moscow Trials":

> The measures taken by the Soviet Union to preserve and extend its gains and its strength therefore find their echoes here, where we are staking the future of the American people on the preservation of progressive democracy and the unification of our efforts to prevent the fascists from strangling the rights of the people. American liberals must not permit their outlook on these questions to be confused, nor allow their recognition of the place of the Soviet Union in the international fight of democracy against facism to be destroyed. We call upon them to support the efforts of the Soviet Union to free itself from insidious internal dangers, principal menace to peace and democracy.[16]

Readers who saw his name also signed with four hundred others in an open letter in the September 1939 issue of *Soviet Russia Today*—calling for closer cooperation with the Soviet Union—saw only what he had signed *before* the Nazi-Soviet Pact. Not until after June 1941, when Russia was invaded by the Germans, did he take up the banner of the U.S.S.R. again— but never quite so proudly as before.

He completed *The Big Sea* in record time, dispatching the manuscript to Lieber before Thanksgiving. He had also found time to write some poetry. Two poems were quickly picked up by *The New Yorker*. "Hey-Hey Blues," appeared in the November 25 issue, three weeks before the magazine accepted another of his poems. Though he had little money for Christmas, his spirits lifted when Lieber wrote that the *The New Yorker* had just dropped thirty-six dollars in his sock for "Sunday Morning Prophecy."[17]

He celebrated the Christmas holidays with Noel Sullivan, whose Yuletide birthday party brought old friends from Carmel for a joyous reunion. If it all seemed like old times, the feeling was only temporary. When the bells rang in the New Year (1940), Hughes's life had already changed for the new decade. For him and most of the people he had known in Carmel during the turbulent thirties, it was the end of an era.

❧ 20 ❧

The Need for Heroes

THE FIRST MONTH OF THE NEW YEAR brought ups and downs which were an omen of what was to follow for Hughes in 1940. Both troubles and blessings seemed to touch him and his close friends. Eulah Pharr, Noel Sullivan's long-time housekeeper, had skidded and turned over three times in her automobile on New Year's Eve but luckily escaped without a scratch. The Jelliffes wrote from Cleveland that they had lost their theatre in a fire but hoped to raise funds to build a phoenix from the ashes. Hughes himself was numb from revisions Knopf requested on *The Big Sea*. Preparing for lectures scheduled to begin in Pennsylvania on February 19 didn't make his life any easier. Trying to adjust his lecture topics to fit the political climate was a chore. In a New Year's letter, he told Louise Thompson: "I'm laying off political poetry for awhile, though, since the world situation, methinks, is too complicated for so simple an art. So I am going back (indeed have gone) to nature, Negroes and love."[1]

If there was any compensation for his literary compromise on "political poetry," it was a $101.75 check that January for his poem "Seven Moments of Love: An Unsonnet Sequence in Blues." The highest amount he had ever received for a poem, it arrived with news from Lieber that *Esquire* planned to publish the work in May, with drawings by a well-known black cartoonist, E. Simms Campbell. It all seemed agreeable enough to Hughes, who received the money in time to celebrate his thirty-eighth birthday in San Francisco, where he saw *Gone with the Wind* before departing on a three-month lecture tour.

The tour, which he had coordinated through the mail with Frances Wills for weeks, was a whirlwind trip through thirty-five cities in eight states. At the modest honorarium of twenty-five dollars a lecture, he had accepted a full schedule. However, the actual nonstop itinerary by rail through parts of the Northeast, Midwest, Tennessee, and coal-mining towns of West Virginia wore him out. Without a day's rest between some of his lectures at colleges and high schools, he had laryngitis from speaking and a backache from sitting up all night on trains. The Jim Crow rail coaches, when he could not get a sleeping berth, added to his weariness. His only pleasure at being in the South again was the "southern cuisine deluxe" served him by some cousins he found in Kentucky. "Had not my tour caused me to have to move on," he wrote Noel Sullivan, "I'm sure I'd come back to California looking like Fats Waller."[2] By mid-May, he was in Chicago, at the black-owned and operated Grand Hotel, working on two projects he had promised to do with Arna Bontemps. One of their efforts was another children's book, *Boy of the Border*, which Arna had written him about in January, suggesting he pack up and come immediately to work on it. Trying to oblige, Langston had stopped in Chicago in February, en route from the West Coast, and picked up the manuscript to read during his lecture tour. It would eventually end up as another of their unpublished collaborations, although only a mild disappointment compared to a theatrical fiasco they were involved in that summer: *Jubilee: A Cavalcade of the Negro Theatre*, a musical production commissioned by the American Negro Exposition.

Before and during Hughes's spring tour, Bontemps had written him several letters raving about the American Negro Exposition to be held in Chicago from July 4 through Labor Day. Scheduled as part of the "Diamond Jubilee" of the Illinois State Fair, the Exposition was intended to celebrate seventy-five years of Negro freedom with a series of historical exhibits, lectures and musical entertainment programs. Money was to come from a federal appropriation, plus the Julius Rosenwald Fund, the state of Illinois, and various local business enterprises. Bontemps, engaged by the Exposition as a research advisor on historical murals, suggested Hughes might be interested in collaborating on the musical shows. Enthusiastic about the idea, Langston sent Arna an outline for a suggested theatrical program, and it was soon authorized by Truman K. Gibson, a Chicago attorney and executive director of the Exposition. In early May, Hughes rushed to New York to discuss it with Lieber, who drew up a written agreement for a collaboration contract on *Jubilee: A Cavalcade of the Negro Theatre*.

For two months Hughes and Bontemps researched and wrote their material into a book-length script, while Expo promoted it in the media as the major musical event of the fair. For their production using slave songs, spirituals, blues and jazz, they hoped to have Duke Ellington compose the finale, Abbie Mitchell appear as the nineteenth-century troubadour, "Black Patti," and a one-hundred-voice chorus to reenact the Fisk Jubilee Singers' performance before Queen Victoria. Programs were printed and rehearsals were scheduled. But during the opening week of the show, when the total Exposition expenses exceeded the budget by $30,000, *Cavalcade* was cancelled. Hughes, assured from the beginning that he would be compensated for his time and labor, was flabbergasted when Gibson replied vaguely about payment and showed him and Bontemps $63,000 worth of indebtedness to union hands, musicians, and nearly everyone else. Rumors that Chicago underworld figures and politicians were trying to get a cut of Expo's federal grant only added to the confusion. Langston told Arna that he expected to get no more out of the venture than a good chapter for his next autobiography. Meanwhile, Lieber sent Gibson a memorandum agreement of the collaboration contract setting forth the terms of copyright and remuneration for Hughes and Bontemps.[3]

After Expo opened, further disappointment followed for Langston and Arna, who had also written a short musical show called *Tropics after Dark* for the fair. They found it being performed as cabaret entertainment in a beer hall concession, instead of in a theatre as originally planned. Scaled down for financial reasons, most of their libretto—set to music by Margaret Bonds and Zilner Randolph—had been cut out, leaving only four of their original songs. Lieber intervened to get Hughes ninety dollars for his lyrics and told him, "My only regret is that you and Bontemps spent so many weeks of valuable time on a project one could have foreseen would flop, because, after all, neither Gibson nor any of his associates are equipped with the necessary experience to handle a fair, but I daresay hindsight is always better than foresight."[4]

Both Hughes and Lieber tried to use their hindsight to good advantage when offers came in August for Langston to return to Hollywood as a script director for a stage production billed as a "Negro Revue." Ambivalent about another theatrical effort after the *Cavalcade* failure, Hughes was not enthusiastic about returning to Hollywood either. Flat on his back with a cold, which he was certain resulted from worry about his "art," he told Lieber he wanted more time to think about the whole matter and to discuss it with him in New York the following month.

He was only sorry that, because of a few lecture commitments, he couldn't leave Chicago immediately. "This Chicago is really the most fantastic town (outside of Shanghai that I have ever been in)," he wrote Noel Sullivan. "It is certainly one of the chief abodes of the Devil in the Western Hemisphere."[5] His sojourn in Chicago that summer prompted his poem, "Big City Prayer" which was printed that October in *Opportunity*:

> Gather up in the arms of your pity,
> The sick, the depraved, the desperate, the tired,
> All the scum of the weary city,
> Gather up in the arms of your pity.
> Gather them up in the arms of your love—
> Those who expect no love from above.

His preoccupation with *Cavalcade*, and irritation with Chicago, had kept him from feeling the immediate impact of the tragedy in Paris that summer. In June, the German Army had marched in and occupied the city, with the cooperation of octogenarian Marshal Henri Philippe Pétain, the acting French "chief of state." In correspondence to Sullivan, Hughes reacted with deep sorrow:

> Only that I have been so busy has kept me from feeling unbearably the fate of Paris and the French people. I judge that you know the Negro papers (as well as all American papers I have seen) have lamented the great loss to liberty and...the world that the fall of Paris symbolized. And a fund has been started by Prof. Mercer Cook (Abbie Mitchell's son) at Atlanta University, for the aid of French Negro writers and intellectuals, such as René Maran, who are trying to escape with a few of their manuscripts and books to the West Indies and French possessions or other friendly shores on this side of the water. My heart bleeds for them, and for hundreds of other anti-Hitler writers and artists, German, Spanish, Czechoslovakian, who had sought asylum in France. (And many of them, dear Noel, were NOT communist). What has become, what will become of them? Have you had any personal news from your godchild or any of your friends there? I hope they are all safe, at least, and unharmed physically by air raids or otherwise. The barbarism of the whole thing is more than I can ascribe to human intelligence.[6]

The events in Paris made him slightly less enthusiastic than he would have been about the publication that summer of the biography, *Langston Hughes: Un Chant Nouveau* by the Haitian author, René Piquion. Although it was the first biographical study of him (in any language), with French translations of some of his best-known poems, it was also a political statement by Piquion condoning the Hitler-Nazi Pact and calling Britain and France "bourgeois, imperialistic" nations. Appearing the same summer that the British and French were attacked in a declaration of war by Germany and Italy made the book seem badly timed to Hughes and French-speaking Afro-American intellectuals such as Mercer Cook, who did not like Piquion's translations or his politics. Reviewing *Un Chant Nouveau*, Cook wrote that "René Piquion was interested in combining two books: one an enthusiastic appreciation of Langston Hughes; the other an equally ardent plea for communism. The result is something of a hodge-podge which does justice neither to poetry nor to propaganda. American readers will note numerous errors in translation which indicate that M. Piquion's English is somewhat inadequate or that his book was hastily written."[7]

Hughes was mute in public about the book, although privately pleased with Arna's introduction calling him the "Robert Burns of America."

Of more far-reaching concern than the biography was the August 26 publication of *The Big Sea*, which had already caught on with both black and white readers. Excerpts had been published earlier that summer in *The Saturday Review of Literature* and *Town and Country* and in a twenty-two part serialization in *The Afro-American Newspapers*. Early reviews of the book were favorable, and *Newsweek* and *The New York Times* took the lead in recommending it. However, *The Saturday Review*, having excerpted it, did not altogether praise it, calling it "vulgar in spots, trivial elsewhere, . . . but a well-worthwhile book which should have been written; a most valuable contribution to the struggle of the Negro for life and justice and freedom and intellectual liberty in America."[8] *The New York Herald Tribune Books* critic went so far as to call it a "ramblingly anecdotal chronicle characterized by a tolerance, simplicity and unpretentiousness that borders on the naive."[9] Reviews in newspapers and magazines continued through the late summer and early autumn, with one of the most laudatory appearing in *Opportunity*, where Hughes's old acquaintance from the *Black and White* film, Henry Lee Moon, wrote that "*The Big Sea* reveals the personality of the man—a charitable spirit, unembittered by experience, gifted with a leavening sense of humor, and sensitive alike to beauty and human suffering."[10] In *The New Republic*, Richard Wright praised both the book and the author, saying "Hughes is tough; he bends but he never breaks, and he has carried on a manly tradition in literary expression when many of his fellow writers have gone to sleep at their posts."[11]

Wright, who himself had achieved a national reputation that 1940 with the Chicago-based novel *Native Son*, was back in town in July to research a book on black migration. Hughes had a chance to chat with him again for the first time in a year. They were both enthusiastic that *Native Son* had been made a Book-of-the-Month Club selection and was being considered for the stage. Wright was already glad to have earned sufficient royalties to move his mother into a comfortable home. He also confided at least enough about his private life to confirm what Langston had heard through the grapevine: that in August 1939 Ralph Ellison had been best man at Wright's marriage to Dhimah Meadman, a white woman; the couple had lived briefly in Mexico but had recently separated. As far as Hughes was concerned, it was confidential, and he refused to spread gossip some eight months later when Wright took as his second wife an attractive Jewish brunette named Ellen Poplar.

Hughes said his farewell to Wright in Chicago at a lively party given by Jack Conroy and Nelson Algren, editors of *The New Anvil*. Both hosts told the crowd they would all be invited back to toast Hughes on publication of

The Big Sea. Conroy held the gathering to celebrate the book in September. Hughes stood around signing autographs for literary lions such as Maxwell Bodenheim and joking that the party was held in a penthouse "because the proletariat had moved up in the world." Conroy had moved to Chicago in 1938, joined the Federal Writers Project, and met there a future collaborator, Arna Bontemps. Reminiscing about that, he said: "I was pleased when Arna, upon being introduced to me, at once identified me as editor of *The Anvil* and author of the novel *The Disinherited.* I learned though, that Langston had spoken of them to him."[12]

It was partly through Arna's influence that Hughes finally decided to try the *Negro Revue* project in Hollywood that autumn. Bontemps's rationale that the war atmosphere had created more show business opportunities for black Americans—because the United States wanted to project itself as a democracy abroad—seemed to Hughes to make sense, at least at the time. After speaking for Northwestern University's radio program, "Of Men and Books," he left Chicago in early October for California—first for Carmel, then Los Angeles.

Over a month later, not a word had been heard from him by Lieber, who awaited a response to Hughes's contract sent for the *Negro Revue.* "Are you in Hollywood now?" he wrote in mid-November. It was almost Christmas before Langston replied. His contract, which Lieber had drawn up under terms of the Dramatists Guild, was the least of his worries. He had other tales of woe. He was demoralized and tired. No place in Hollywood would accept Negro guests; he had commuted daily by bus to and from the Clark Hotel in Los Angeles. Leaving for the studio at dawn and returning to the hotel after midnight had left him little time for writing letters. Besides all that, the atmosphere at the Hollywood studio had gotten him down. The New Negro Theatre, in order to produce the *Negro Revue,* had affiliated itself with the predominantly white Hollywood Theatre Alliance, causing internal squabbles about writing and editing material. Some of the skits, written by eight to ten people of varying temperaments, had produced chaos. Except for Donald Ogden Stewart, who was editing a few of the comedy scripts, and Charles Leonard, the producer, who had staged the Wallace Thurman play, *Harlem,* on Broadway, Hughes couldn't see eye to eye with several of the white writers. They seemed familiar with writing sophisticated Chaplinesque humor but unfamiliar with creating black characters beyond Amos 'n' Andy. He was unable to convince them that presenting material in Negro dialect did not always make it humorous. They could not make up their minds whether the production should be "half-Negro," "half-white," "very Negro," have a social message, or none at all. Hughes thought the material had no feeling for black characters, even if it was to be performed by black actors.

He told Lieber he was ready to call it quits and return to Hollow Hills Farm for Christmas, since his twenty-five dollar weekly advance against royalties was barely enough to cover his transportation and hotel expenses. His most rewarding experience with the revue had been writing the lyrics for a song called "America's Young Black Joe" for a skit about the Joe Louis-Max Schmeling fight. Set to music by Elliott Carpenter, a Los Angeles composer, the song had been requested by the NAACP and several predominantly black high schools. Beyond that, Hughes left Hollywood with no desire to return for rehearsals of the *Negro Revue*. His experience reminded him all over again of the theme of a poem he had composed after his Hollywood stint the year before. Written at Hollow Hills Farm in September 1939, it was published in *The Crisis* in March 1940. The title, "Note on Commercial Art," was subsequently changed to "Note on Commercial Theatre":

You've taken my blues and gone—
You sing 'em on Broadway
And you sing 'em in Hollywood Bowl,
And you mixed 'em up with symphonies
And you fixed 'em
So they don't sound like me.
Yep, you done taken my blues and gone.

You also took my spirituals and gone.
You put me in *Macbeth* and *Carmen Jones*
And all kinds of *Swing Mikados*
And in everything but what's about me—
But someday somebody'll
Stand up and talk about me,
And write about me—
Black and beautiful—
And sing about me,
And put on plays about me!
I reckon it'll be
Me myself!

Yes, it'll be me.

It bothered him deeply that black Americans had little power over their image in the American theatre. They might be "script directors," as he had been for the *Negro Revue*, or "Hollywood screenwriters," as he had been for

Way Down South, or "Broadway playwrights," as he had been for *Mulatto* —and still be powerless to change the ways of the white establishment even as it exploited black talents. For the duration of his career, his prose and poetry would touch on that theme. The number of his song lyrics and librettos would increase, as if he were determined that songs and plays about his own people would be written and performed by them. Earlier in 1940, he had welcomed the news that his poem "Songs for a Dark Virgin" had been set to music for Marian Anderson to sing in a concert, and that the arranger, Florence Price, was eager to set more of his verses to music.

A popular poet, playwright, song lyricist, lecturer and author was how he hoped and thought most people saw him at the end of 1940. He had begun contributing regularly again that year to *The Crisis* and *Opportunity*, both of which had favorable pieces about him in their December issues. *The Crisis* book critic, while not overwhelmed by *The Big Sea*, nevertheless called it "a valuable addition to Hughes's growing volume of prose." *Opportunity* published a glowing short profile by Verna Arvey, William Grant Still's wife, who wrote, "Indeed Langston Hughes may well be termed a crusader, for the Negro race as a whole, and for his fellow artists." Appearing with her article were three of his "Ballads." These were new to *Opportunity* readers, although his "Ballad of the Landlord" had been published seven years before in Russia.

"Ballad of the Landlord" was one of the poems of the early 1930s that Hughes still felt comfortable with. The same was not true of a poem which *The Saturday Evening Post* reprinted on December 21, 1940 without his permission: "Goodbye Christ." If he had said goodbye to it, some other people were just discovering it. Already that November 15, during a Book and Author Luncheon at the Vista Del Arroyo Hotel in Pasadena, he had been met by a picketing delegation. Sent from the temple of evangelist Aimee Semple McPherson, the picketers distributed copies of the poem while a sound truck played "God Bless America." They then marched into the luncheon, waving a poster of "Goodbye Christ," to denounce Hughes and the presiding host, George Palmer Putnam, in front of over five hundred guests. The stunt was arranged by Aimee's publicity man, who was quickly arrested. Meanwhile, to avoid further embarrassment to the hotel management and luncheon officials, Hughes politely withdrew from the program. Outside the hotel, where a few well-wishers tried to shake his hand as he entered a waiting car, one of Aimee's Four Square Gospel supporters shouted, "Down where I come from, we don't shake hands with niggers." Blaring in the background, the sound truck continued with "God Bless America."

It was not the first time he had been hounded for "Goodbye Christ."

Seven years before, a black clergyman had attacked him in *The Pittsburgh Courier* while he was in Russia. A vigorous response had followed from Hughes's fellow poet and Lincoln alumnus, Melvin B. Tolson, who defended Hughes and the poem as a challenge to the contradictions of Christianity. After the poem was reprinted in 1938 in Benjamin Mays's anthology, *The Negro's God*, various detractors had surfaced here and there, but Hughes had tried to ignore them. Then *The Saturday Evening Post* got into the act. That 1940, he spent part of his Christmas holiday at Hollow Hills Farm writing a "press statement" to the editors.[13] Signed and dated New Year's Day 1941, copies went to Alfred A. Knopf's lawyers, as well as to his own lawyer, Arthur Spingarn, and to his agent, Maxim Lieber. His statement explained, as truthfully and tersely as it could, his entry into American radicalism during the 1930s, his long trip through the South, his journey to Russia, where he wrote the poem which "contrasted...those, who, on the religious side in America...had said to Christ and the Christian principles, Goodbye...." Having attacked *The Saturday Evening Post* in the poem, he did not retreat in his statement from attacking it as a "magazine whose columns, like the doors of many of our churches, has been until recently entirely closed to Negroes."

Although the text mentioned that his foes "failed to see the poem in connection with [his]...many verses most sympathetic to the true Christian spirit," he did not try to defend himself with a poem he had published in 1933, one year after "Goodbye Christ":

Personal

In an envelope marked:
Personal
God addressed me a letter.
In an envelope marked:
Personal
I have given my answer.[14]

Whatever that "answer" was, some people surely wondered why the final lines of his press release on "Goodbye, Christ" seemed an *apologia* for a poem intended to attack hypocrisy.

> Now in the year 1941, having left the terrain of "the radical at twenty" to approach "the conservative of forty," I would not and could not write "Goodbye Christ," desiring no longer to *épater le bourgeois*...Goodbye Christ does not represent my personal viewpoint. It was long ago withdrawn from circulation and has been reprinted without my knowledge and consent....

Hughes's belief that he could wave a magic wand and the poem would suddenly be "withdrawn from circulation" seemed wishful thinking to Lieber. He wrote Hughes: "I am shocked to learn about the disaster that has befallen you in connection with the *Post's* reprint of a poem that you have taken out of circulation—although God knows how one can take out of circulation something one has published."[15] His long silence in letters to Lieber between November and December had been partly due to a reluctance to confess to him the Pasadena incident. The tough-minded Lieber would have expected him to confront his hecklers, instead of caving in to them. But Hughes's reaction to "Goodbye, Christ" revealed the lengths he would go to avoid public ostracism. If there was one thing he feared most, that was it. Like a turtle, he withdrew into a protective shell whenever he felt threatened. In his craving for public approbation and affection, he sometimes let himself be guided by what was expedient.

Arna Bontemps, knowing Hughes felt wounded by the "Goodbye Christ" episode, tried consoling him. "As nifty a piece of writing as you ever did is that statement of 'Goodbye Christ,' " he said in a January letter. "It seems to me to put the stopper in the bottle most neatly."[16] Hughes might have wished it were so neat and simple, and that the New Year had not signaled other problems. There were new arbitration costs on *Mulatto*, after Martin Jones refused to pay a royalty on the Boston production, claiming a theatre manager had absconded with the money. That news followed a notice of eviction on his Harlem studio apartment; he had sublet it to Zell Ingram and a few struggling artists, and they had fallen behind in the rent. Before Hughes could send the amount himself, he landed in Carmel's Peninsula Community Hospital. Louise Thompson Patterson, who had recently married and moved to Chicago, was among the first to hear from him about his condition. "For the past two weeks now," he wrote, "I've been flat on my back here in the hospital—a kind of arthritis-like infection of one leg—very painful, and unable to set foot to floor, so I just lie here mostly in a fog from pain pills. You can hear me moaning and groaning for miles. Too much trouble all at once, I guess...."[17]

Released in late January, he returned to Hollow Hills Farm with orders from the doctors to stop traveling and lecturing and "stay close to home." He could have had no better place to recuperate than his "little house" on the hillside above a pear orchard. With its enormous windows and sun patio overlooking the valley, it was his private retreat from the many houseguests Noel Sullivan frequently entertained. To Sullivan, he referred to the cottage as "mi casa y la suya"—"my house and your house," and he liked it as much as the seaside house, Ennesfree, which his host had given up for the tranquil farm in Carmel Valley. Nothing seemed to threaten the serenity of the scenic canyon which they both called "God's Country." But unknown to either man, the Federal Bureau of Investigation would soon have its eyes on them both, paying informants to watchdog their activities and their friends. Already in 1938, Martin Dies had become chairman of the newly formed Committee on Un-American Activities (HUAC) of the U.S. House of Representatives, and for the next decade J. Edgar Hoover was busy behind the scenes with "internal security reports" on suspected political dissenters. Bent on finding "Communists," the FBI did not spare such gentle Catholics as Noel Sullivan, who was targeted for harboring Langston Hughes. "Investigations" turned up the following:

> Hollow Hills Farm is owned by Noel Sullivan, a well-known musician, who spends most of his time at the farm "entertaining all kinds of persons." Further, Sullivan is reported to be a "Negro lover" with very liberal views, but it was not known if he was interested in Communism. . . . No further information regarding the subject. . . . Sullivan receives his mail through P.O. Box Q, and through the Jamesburg Route out of Monterey, California.[18]

Under Hoover, the FBI would become the closest thing to the Gestapo the United States ever had, but its surveillance reports on Sullivan were mild compared to the ones on Hughes. Hoover eventually launched his own personal attack against "Goodbye, Christ" vilifying it in a speech titled "Secularism—A Breeder of Crime."[19] His negrophobia, more than "Goodbye, Christ," caused him to begin extensive files on Hughes, whose poem was no more anti-Christian or "un-American" than the venerated Carl Sandburg's "To a Contemporary Bunkshooter."[20]

On Hughes, the FBI reports revealed only "limited information obtainable regarding subject's activities while in Carmel Valley, California, 1941." They were looking for evidence to link him with communism, and there was none at Hollow Hills Farm. The Bureau could hardly have been interested in visits by such Afro-American artists as the concert singer Dorothy Maynor, the sculptor Richmond Barthe, the actress Ethel Waters, and the dancer Katherine Dunham, all of whom were guests at the farm that year. His prose and poetry during those months likewise showed no leftist sentiments. Poems such as "Dust Bowl," "Southern Mammy Sings," "Crossing Jordan," and "Black Maria" which appeared in the April issue of *Poetry* had no resemblance to "Goodbye, Christ." He had begun the New Year writing about his old Carmel friends, Una and Robinson Jeffers, with a touching unpublished verse, "To Una Jeffers," and a poetic prose piece, "Jeffers: Man, Sea and Poetry," which appeared in the January 10 issue of the *Carmel Pine Cone*. His other literary efforts went toward a new book he had begun in November 1940 and hoped soon to publish. Already he had written his friend, Louise, "Would you like to have a book of poems dedicated to you?

Such is *Shakespeare in Harlem*, the present collection I'm assembling for Knopf. Folk, blues, and lyric verse in the lighter manner—but not too light."[21]

If anyone was conscious of the "lighter manner" he had turned to in his creative writing, it was Louise. Her strong leftist convictions never changed with the times. Like a sister, she had been with him through thick and thin, in Harlem, in Russia, and in Spain, although then and later she thought that "no one really knew Lang." To her and the few close friends who knew him best, he was the deeply private man who seemed both simple and complex. "I have just written an article for *The Crisis* on the need for heroes in Negro literature," he wrote Louise in March 1941. "To read it, you would almost think I was a hero myself. Such is the power of literature to deceive."[22]

The piece was "The Need for Heroes," and he wrote it especially for *The Crisis*, in observance of his twentieth year as contributor to the NAACP magazine. His words embodied the spirit and the tone of the writer who, during the next two decades, would become known increasingly as "the poet laureate of his race."

> The written word is the only record we will have of this our present, or our past, to leave behind for future generations. . . . We have a need for heroes. We have a need for books and plays that will encourage and inspire our youth, set for them patterns of conduct, move and stir them to be forthright, strong, clear-thinking and unafraid. . . . It is the social duty of Negro writers to reveal to the people the deep reservoirs of heroism within the race. . . . We need in literature the kind of black men and women all of us know exist in life; who are not afraid to claim our rights as human beings and as Americans. . . .

The piece was published that June 1941 together with a reprint of his 1921 poem "The Negro Speaks of Rivers" and a new verse entitled "NAACP." A month later, he followed with publication of his short story, "One Friday Morning."[23] Of Hughes's works appearing in *The Crisis* during a twenty-year period, most had appeared between 1921 and 1928. During the thirties, he had been conspicuous by his absence, except for four racially oriented articles between 1932 and 1937, two poems about love and death in 1930, and "Personal" and "A New Song" in 1933. For ideological reasons, he knew better than to submit any "workers-of-the-world-unite" prose and poetry to *The Crisis*, especially about Scottsboro. He had quietly sided with the Communist-oriented International Labor Defense (ILD), instead of the NAACP, in the Scottsboro case, and he also had been a contributing editor to *Labor Defense*, an ILD publication. Moreover, during the early thirties, he had preferred to remain neutral in the internal disputes at the NAACP, where his friends, W. E. B. Du Bois and executive secretary Walter White were feuding, and where Du Bois, opposed by White and the NAACP Board, resigned as editor of *The Crisis* in mid-1934.[24] By 1940, when Hughes was becoming a less vocal political poet, he welcomed the opportunity to return to the magazine which had given him his first literary encouragement.

Telling friends in early 1941 that "he wanted to do something special for *The Crisis*," he sent out to people from coast to coast 250 cards printed with "The Negro Speaks of Rivers." In addition, he wrote the his poem "NAACP" especially for the thirty-second annual NAACP Convention, held in Houston that year. After having tried so to be dutiful, he perhaps felt like a stepchild when the organization, at its August convention, awarded the coveted Spingarn Medal to Richard Wright, who had never published a word in *The Crisis*. Furthermore, while Hughes had been trying his best for a year to be "conservative," Wright was then an avowed member of the Communist Party. Not until nineteen years later, in 1960, would Hughes receive the gold medal which Joel Spingarn had established in 1914 for the "highest or noblest achievement by an American Negro during the preceding year." Meanwhile, he would be denied the prize by persons on the nine-member Award Committee who insisted that his epithet "bastard" in the poem "Christ in Alabama" was inexcusable.[25] Damned for "Goodbye, Christ," he was punished as well for "Christ in Alabama" and his apologies seemed to mean little to people in high places.

Nevertheless, he sounded more than ever like a respectable civil rights spokesman in 1941. In California, he wrote racial essays such as "What the Negro Wants" with the same force he had shown a decade before in his proletarian prose. So direct was "What the Negro Wants" that Lieber told him "I'm afraid you are doomed to disappointment, because with the possible exception of *New Masses*, no other publication will venture it."[26] Louis Adamic, editor of *Common Ground*, ventured it, and the piece appeared that autumn in the quarterly published by the Common Council on American Unity. For the next four years, Hughes would be a regular contributor to *Common Ground*, serving on its editorial board with Pearl Buck, Van Wyck Brooks, Thomas Mann, and Lin Yutang.

Recuperating in Carmel Valley and not returning to the lecture circuit that 1941 resulted in more articles, stories, and poems than Hughes had written in four years. He also began drafting the second volume of his autobiography, resuming where *The Big Sea* left off. The longer he stayed at Hollow Hills, the more he wrote, and the less interested he was—at least temporarily—in any more forays into show business. If there was "no business like show business," he had begun to believe he had no business in it. That spring, disappointments about some of his theatrical ventures had come tumbling down all at once. *Mulatto* was still in arbitration, with

Hughes paying the cost of an arbitrator while Martin Jones skipped and postponed meetings and gave excuses for not sending overdue royalties.[27] The *Negro Revue* in Hollywood was at an impasse, with no production date set. Meanwhile, the executive director, irked because Hughes would not return to Hollywood for rehearsals, had cut his song "America's Young Black Joe" from the production. He also denied him permission to sell elsewhere any of his "collaborated material" not used in the *Revue*.[28] Except for $175 in back wages sent him by the Hollywood Theatre Alliance, no royalties according to his contract could be expected. Lieber was angry about it, and Hughes was hurt. But he felt worse that the Los Angeles Federal Music Project appropriation had been cut, making it impossible to produce *Troubled Island*, which he and William Grant Still had worked toward for six years. *Cock o' the World*, to which he had devoted as much time, now offered no hope of being produced on stage or screen. Meanwhile, payment from the American Negro Exposition for *Cavalcade* still seemed only a remote possibility.

All Hughes's catastrophic theatrical ventures had finally gotten the best of Lieber, who told him in March, "A peculiar misfortune certainly dogs your footsteps, Langston, for almost everything you get tied up with, turns sour. It's a miracle that you have been able to preserve your charming and carefree manner."[29] The news in May that he had been awarded a Rosenwald Fund fellowship was a boost—financially and spiritually. He received the fellowship to research and write a series of dramatic sketches on Frederick Douglass, but it also meant a steady income for a few months. He had been depressed about hospital bills and debts and had barely enough money to buy a new suit that spring. Trying to joke about it, he told Louise that "my main interest is centered in trying to get a new brown suit...never having had one...I'd just as well go back to waiting table and get a suit on credit. You know, being a 'great' author doesn't give one the credit rating of a guy with a $12.00 a week job...."[30]

A few weeks later, he bought a new brown suit, matching shoes, and a tie. For Noel Sullivan's luncheons and dinners—to which came European royalty, educators and celebrities—he thought he should look presentable, instead of like a hobo. After years of not being clothes-conscious, he was becoming so. In July, he sported the new brown suit when he met with dancer Katherine Dunham in San Francisco to discuss a new movie libretto. The lure of show business came and went from month to month, even though he swore he was through with it. He tried to fight it by concentrating on short stories and poetry. In late July, he sent over one hundred of his retyped, unpublished poems to Lieber to select for the *New Directions* Poet of the Month series. Some were lyrical, some ballads, and some blues; others were about Jim Crow discrimination, which he was writing about

increasingly. He could not forget about segregation, even if he was removed from it in Carmel Valley, where he wrote "Daybreak in Alabama,"
"Sunset in Dixie," "Merry Go Round," and "Southern Negro Speaks." The
latter, published that October in *Opportunity*, expressed his ambivalence
about America's willingness to fight a war to defend European democracy
when racial equality had not been achieved at home. It was the first half of a
dozen of his poems on that theme during the war years. Some would appear
two years later in *Jim Crow's Last Stand*.

Already in the June 1940 issue of *The Crisis* he had expressed an opposing
view:

Comment on War

Let us kill off youth.
For the sake of *truth*.

We who are old know what truth is—
Truth is a bundle of vicious lies
Tied together and sterilized—
A war-makers' bait for unwise youth
To kill off each other
For the sake of
Truth.

The same month that poem appeared, *New Masses* published a statement
sponsored by the League of American Writers opposing American entry
into the European war. In the partial list of names with the statement,
Hughes was not included, although he was among three hundred who
signed it.[31] His name, however, did appear in the Call of the Fourth American Writers Congress, which was held in New York City June 6-8, 1941.
He was still a member of the League and in 1940 had been listed as a director
of the California chapter along with Donald Ogden Stewart, John Stein-
beck, and Upton Sinclair, even though he was absent too often to really be
active. He did not go to New York for the Fourth Congress, the "Congress
in Defense of Culture," as some preferred to call it. It was, in reality, the last
Congress. The next year would mark the dissolution of the League, which
had lost some of its prominent members after the Third Congress; some
had resigned from the Communist Party and the League after the Nazi-
Soviet Pact; some non-Communists had dropped out, believing the League
was becoming more political than cultural. Hughes had been in neither
camp, but he was no longer a regional vice-president after the Fourth
Congress elected new officers.[32]

The war was a major issue at the Writer's Congress. Richard Wright

delivered an impassioned address entitled "Not My People's War." Hughes
heard about it and concurred. Like Wright, he resented segregated armed
forces, and he had seen them in increasing numbers at nearby Fort Ord,
outside Monterey. He had also heard the war debated from all sides by
foreign and American guests at Noel Sullivan's. Those who argued that war
would finally bring America out of the economic depression; those who
quoted Theodore Dreiser's *America Is Worth Saving*, on why the nation
should avoid militarism and imperialism; and those who echoed Archibald
MacLeish, Lewis Mumford, and Malcolm Cowley that Americans should
fight to defend democracy as a matter of conscience.

Meanwhile, the headlines seemed full of signs that President Franklin
Roosevelt and his Secretary of War were preparing the American people to
plunge into battle. The situation looked grim, with no peace in sight.
Hughes, regretting that he had never seen London, wondered if he ever
would, as reports of Nazi blitz attacks over the city continued. In May, the
British House of Commons was destroyed in an air raid. A month later
came news of the German invasion of the Soviet Union, where 300,000
Russians were taken prisoner. One by one, countries were falling to the Nazi
storm troopers, who that year had also captured Bulgaria, and occupied
Yugoslavia, Albania, Macedonia, and Greece. In Asia, the Japanese were
waging war as if they intended to conquer the world. In Africa, the British
were on the offensive to save their territories. The only positive news that
Hughes could see was that British troops had liberated Ethiopia from the
Italians. That August, in *Opportunity*, he published "Death in Africa," a
poem which spoke of helpless witch doctors and missionaries "in the path
of a speeding plane."

When the poem appeared, he was in the Arizona desert recuperating from
what he called "another-itis." The doctors were uncertain whether it was
arthritis or bursitis, which this time affected his arm instead of his leg. He
blamed the damp, cool Carmel weather for his aches and pains, and he
welcomed the chance to be in the desert sun—for more reasons than one.
What he could not tell his kind host, Noel Sullivan, but confessed in a letter
to Arna, was that he needed to get away from it all. "I'm trying to work on
a schedule these days, which is why I have an arm ache," he told him. "Also
Edna Ferber was right when she says it looks like there ain't no place where
a writer can write in peace uninterrupted and unbothered. To tell the truth,
Carmel might as well be 42nd Street and Fifth Avenue—so many white
folks and Negroes are always passing through."[33] For two weeks he soaked
up the Phoenix sun and stayed anonymously as "James Hughes" in the
home of the local president of Colored Women's Clubs. His friend Arna
understood the gregarious Hughes who loved people but loved his privacy
too, and who wrote him from Arizona that "I'm delighted not to have to

dress for dinner."[34] On their lecture tours together, Arna had seen Langston leave banquets and receptions to go off and hide, after shaking hands and signing autographs to the point of exhaustion. To school children's questions about "the secret of success," he had heard him answer that it was knowing what you want to do, setting a course for yourself, having discipline, good health and getting enough sleep.[35] He did not confess that one of his own "secrets" was also having hideaways where he could "write in peace uninterrupted and unbothered."

Nevertheless, Hughes could never stay secluded very long. After stopping in Tucson, he was in Los Angeles, where he was eager to see friends and relatives again. He was back and forth between his Uncle John's house and his cousin Flora's; Loren Miller and his wife entertained him in their new home, and Clarence Muse invited him for a weekend at his ranch. Hearing that Zora Neale Hurston was then living in Los Angeles and trying to sell a novel to Hollywood, he considered looking her up, but decided against it, after learning that she'had bad-mouthed him all over Pasadena. He, too, was in Hollywood to talk to Hollywood producers, after having told Noel Sullivan and Arna that he would "NEVER" bother with show business again. To be or not to be in show business, that was the question, and he was like Hamlet trying to decide. Word that his song, "America's Young Black Joe," was being performed on college campuses, and that a rendition of "Let America Be America Again" had been sung by a one-hundred-fifty-voice chorus in Chicago, had put him in the mood for show business again. He swung back and forth like a pendulum. However, he was far more interested in being recognized for his literary accomplishments and being represented in such important anthologies as *The Negro Caravan*, which Sterling Brown, Arthur P. Davis, and Ulysses Lee compiled and edited that year. In February, he had told Arna, "Me, I have retired from the show business and shall devote the rest of my creative life exclusively to words on paper not on the stage."[36] By the end of September, after nearly a month in Los Angeles, he had a different story.

> It looks like I can't get away from this town, but I am positively leaving tomorrow! Have been having some conferences with movie producers, but no results. I think only a subsidized Negro Film Institute, or the revolution, will cause any really good Negro pictures to be made in America. And right now, we need them badly to underscore our democratic aims and help change the American mass mind away from its Hitlerian attitude toward us. In a single day more people see a picture at the Paramount than read any one of our Negro writers' books in a year....[37]

To a few Hollywood producers he proposed a film based on "The Negro Speaks of Rivers." He had in mind "using a visual theme of the rivers of the world along whose banks the Negro had lived in his transition from Africa to America." He should have known Hollywood would turn a deaf ear, even if he was celebrating the twentieth anniversary of publication of his poem. Three years later, he gave a synopsis and suggested treatment for the film as a gift to two friends: he inscribed one copy to "Charles S. Johnson, Who has started so many good things for the Negro People and America." Another was inscribed to the playwright Owen Dodson, who was then executive secretary of the American Film Committee for Mass Education in Race Relations.

Like many other ideas Hughes had for stage and screen, the film of "The Negro Speaks of Rivers" never materialized. The same was true of the screen adaptation of *St. Louis Woman*, which he had collaborated on with Clarence Muse. A new libretto, *Carmelita and the Cuckatoo*, which he submitted to Katherine Dunham as a dance idea interested her, but not enough to cause her to pay a fifty-dollar advance on it.

Returning to Hollow Hills Farm, he concentrated on writing short stories again. By late October, he had sent Lieber six new ones: "The Bottle of Wine," "Mysterious Madame Shanghai," "Two at the Bar," "The Star Decides," "Banquet in Honor," and "Sailor Ashore." Lieber liked only four of the stories; "Sailor Ashore" and "Banquet in Honor," he told Hughes, were taboo subjects. In the crystal ball of Hughes's literary future, Lieber was not wrong about "Sailor Ashore." It would be eleven years before this story about a Negro sailor and prostitute could be published. Even then it appeared in two of Hughes's own collections, not in a magazine. The other "taboo" story appeared in 1942 in *Negro Story*, though it was never reprinted elsewhere.[38] Mirrored in the fictional character who spoke his mind at a banquet was a little of Hughes himself speaking about Hollywood and his own career:

> Ladies and Gentlemen of the Athenia Arts Club, you think you are honoring me when you invite me here tonight. You're not honoring me a damn bit! The way you could have honored me all these years would have been to buy a piece of my music and play it, or a book of mine and read it, or boo off the screen a few of the *Uncle Toms* thereon and tell the manager you'd never come back to see another picture in his theatre until he put me in it, or some other decent hard-working Negro. But you didn't do no such thing. You let me starve until I was mighty nigh blue-black in the face. . . .

Of the five other stories he sent Lieber, only one was never published.[39] None was as well-crafted as the stories in *The Ways of White Folks*, which

Sherwood Anderson had called a "good book," and none was published in a magazine that paid much, if anything to the author. He had written the stories in great haste, following Lieber's suggestion that it was time to begin working toward a new volume of short stories. Hughes himself was more interested in continuing the second volume of his autobiography. He had no title for the draft, but already he had written the section about his experiences in Russia and told Arna and Louise about it. Arna, who had thought it was not the time to write about Russia in *The Big Sea*, had reconsidered. In a letter dated "Sunday, June 22, 1941—The Day the Nazis Marched Against the U.S.S.R.," he told Hughes, "This, incidentally, should set the stage beautifully for volume II of your autobiography, since Russia is sure to come into better favor in this country."[40] The stage was not set exactly as Bontemps envisioned, and Hughes was wise not to put too much hope in early publication of the book.

He was relieved that *Shakespeare in Harlem* finally went to press at the end of October, after page proofs were delayed. The book was scheduled for publication in February 1942, and Hughes had plans to be on the East Coast to promote it. Meanwhile, he prepared to leave Hollow Hills in mid-November for Chicago. There the officers of the Rosenwald Fund were expecting him to begin work on his fellowship, and he was committed to lecture at the Chicago Book Club on November 21 with Arna Bontemps. He had also agreed to joint public readings with him for his new anthology, *Golden Slippers*. At one of their programs the concert artist Etta Moten was to sing "The Negro Speaks of Rivers." For Arna's sake, he had agreed to make his first public appearance wearing black tie. It was not his style and he was not prepared for it. "I haven't any tuxedo," he wrote Arna. "But if *absolute* necessity dictates one, I'll either have to buy it or rent it—according to how my funds are—And they ain't much."[41]

His funds were low when he packed to leave Carmel Valley, and so were his spirits. After nearly a year there, he was reluctant to go. Despite the frequent houseguests, his stay had been one of the most productive and peaceful periods of his life, with no worries about food or shelter; and he was sad to leave Noel, Eulah, the farm, and seven barking dogs. He departed on a thirty-day, one-way ticket to New York via Chicago, uncertain when he would return again. From Chicago, he wrote Sullivan:

> I have found you always the most thoughtful person in all the world to those whom you love. To say what your friendship has meant to me would take more pages than I have ever written in any of my books. The way you stood by me last winter in my various and varied vicissitudes makes me believe in you like the early Christians must have believed in that rock on which the church was founded...

How I hated to leave Hollow Hills! And I hope it will not be
too long before I may return. And remember, if you ever need
me, let me know, and I'll be there![42]

The two friends would not see each other again for two and a half years.
Three weeks after Hughes left California, Japan attacked Pearl Harbor, and
the United States immediately found itself at war.

America's entry into the Second World War coincided with Hughes's
decision to return to Harlem. In all his travels it had been the place which
remained with him wherever he went. In his early poem, "Aesthete in
Harlem," he had written:

> Strange,
> That in this nigger place
> I should meet life face to face,
> When for years, I had been seeking
> Life in places gentler speaking
> Until I came to this near street
> And found Life—stepping on my feet.[43]

He had adopted Harlem in his youth, and he returned to it in his prime. For
the next twenty-five years, it would be his residence no matter the frequent
trips he made elsewhere. When he returned to Harlem for Christmas in
1941, he already had plans to be in Chicago two months later. To those who
asked *why* he chose Harlem, he answered, *why not?* For a decade his home
had been nowhere except on the way to somewhere. Like Odysseus after ten
years of wandering, Langston Hughes had finally come home.

EPILOGUE

Full Circle

THE 1940S ADDED NEW DIMENSIONS TO HUGHES'S CAREER. Although he had opposed everything about the Second World War, he made every effort to help America win it. Battling with his pen to defend the nation and boost morale, he was just as determined to fight Jim Crow. His song lyrics, radio scripts, and verses expressed the hope that America would be victorious abroad and end racial discrimination at home. "Look like by now / Folks ought to know / It's hard to beat Hitler / Protecting Jim Crow," he wrote in "How About It, Dixie." Such opinions occasionally met with opposition: in February 1942 officials in Washington refused to broadcast a radio script in which he linked Franklin Roosevelt's "Four Freedoms" to black Americans. Having heard Roosevelt declare, in his famous January 6, 1941, "Four Freedoms" speech, that freedom of speech and worship, and freedom from want and fear, applied to all the world, Hughes was puzzled when his script was rejected. "The President's Four Freedoms / Appeal to me / I would like to see those Freedoms / Come to be," he wrote.

Following the production of his musical play, *The Sun Do Move*,[1] in Chicago in the spring of 1942, he returned to New York to devote himself to patriotic duty as a member of the Writers War Committee. His radio script, "Brothers"—about a black soldier's heroism during a convoy—was broadcast nationally by the Writers War Board, as was his musical script, "In the Service of My Country." He contributed jingles to the Treasury Department's Defense Bond campaign. His marching song, "Freedom Road," set to music by Emerson Harper, was heard coast to coast on the *March of Time* and *Treasury Star Parade*. Another Hughes-Harper song, "That Eagle of the U.S.A.," was entertainment for troops at New York's interracial Stage Door Canteen, where Hughes was a volunteer waiter.

Never before had his name been on the radio so often as during the war years. In 1943, his lyrics to Earl Robinson's tune, "We'll Hammer It Out Together" were sung by Paul Robeson on NBC's *Labor for Victory*. Paul Muni read Hughes's long dramatic poem "Freedom's Plow" to musical

308

accompaniment on the Blue Network. A year later, on the same network, Hughes joined a panel on *Town Meeting of the Air* to discuss "Let's Face the Race Question." The BBC in London broadcast his script, "Ballad of the Man Who Went to War."

Some of his lyrics were set to music by popular composers and often heard at Negro freedom rallies and Armed Forces programs. Among them were "Go and Get the Enemy Blues," written with W. C. Handy and Clarence Muse; "The Day of Victory" with Irving Landau; "New Wind a-Blowin' " and "When a Soldier Writes a Letter Home" with Elie Siegmeister. His lyrics were the title songs for two Madison Square Garden pageants: "For This We Fight," with a musical score by Herbert Haufrecht in 1943, and "Carry On, America, Victory Is What You Make It," written with Norman Corwin and Howard Fast in 1945.

He made the most of the defense effort, but his real thoughts about all the singing and marching were in the irony of his poem "World War II," which was not published until later: "What a grand time was the war! / Oh, my, my / ...Did somebody die?" Along with some of his other more critical verses such as "Green Memory" and "Wisdom and War," the poem was later anthologized; others, including "Total War," "Will V-Day Be Me Day Too," "Uncle Sam and Old Jim Crow," were destined to disappear. "Underground" (alternately titled "Our Spring") appeared in 1943 in *New Masses* and several poetry collections, including *Lament for Dark Peoples*. (The Dutch underground privately printed 250 copies of the latter in 1944.)

During the war years, his literary canon expanded to include a newspaper column. It began on November 21, 1942, in *The Chicago Defender*, the nation's largest circulation black weekly. Two months earlier, in the newspaper's magazine section, he had published "Klan or Gestapo? Why Take Either," in which he declared, "It is the duty of Negro writers to reveal the international aspects of our problems at home, to show how these problems are merely a part of the great problem of world freedom everywhere." His first regular column, with the folksy title "Here to Yonder," continued that theme. "Things that happen way off yonder affect us here," he wrote. In succeeding weeks the topics ranged from a sixtieth birthday tribute to W. C. Handy to a premature eulogy to Josephine Baker, whom most of the world then believed was dead at the hands of the Nazis. Then, on February 13, 1943, in "Conversations after Midnight," he introduced what some considered his most enduring contribution to literature: the folk character Jesse B. Semple—nicknamed "Simple."

The "conversations" with "Simple" were to last for twenty-three years. "The character of My Simple-Minded Friend is really very simple," he wrote soon after he created him. "It is just myself talking to me....I have developed this inner discussion into two characters: the *this* being me, and the *that* being Simple, or vice versa. We are both colored, American and Harlemized."² The legendary Jesse B. Semple was the result of an incident in a Harlem bar where Langston "once met a fellow who worked in a war plant."

While Hughes's readers were becoming acquainted with Simple in *The Chicago Defender*, he introduced another urban folk character that year in *Common Ground, Negro Today, Negro Story, Poetry* and *Contemporary Poetry*: the spunky "Madame" Alberta K. Johnson. During the summer of 1942 and 1943 at Yaddo, a writers' colony in Saratoga Springs, New York, he wrote a series of eighteen verses about her, a dozen of which were collected in his poetry volumes *One-Way Ticket* and *Selected Poems*.

"Simple" and "Madame" both reflected the new humor and irony in his prose and poetry of the 1940s. With them came a new identity for Hughes, whose popularity grew with theirs. Through his new characters and his varied contributions to new black periodicals such as *Negro Digest, Negro Quarterly, Harlem Quarterly, Ebony*, and *Our World*, plus his columns in *The Chicago Defender*, his reputation soared. Communicating with and about his own people made him a household word to readers of the black press. Through such articles as "The Case Against Segregation," "Solving the Race Problem: A State or Federal Issue," "Is Hollywood Fair to Negroes?" and "The Future of Black America," they began to recognize him not only as a poet but as a spokesman for race relations. He varied his *Defender* columns with humorous stories, satire, historical incidents, and vignettes of famous Afro-Americans, foreshadowing the material of some of his books of the next decade. The Associated Negro Press service eagerly requested verses, and sometimes he sent doggerel, such as "Uncle Tom when he was alive / Filled the white folks / Full of Jive," but the message was clear and increasingly effective.

At the same time, his voice continued to be heard in interracial publications such as *Direction, The New Republic*, and *Common Ground*, where his views on racial matters, including the 1943 urban riots, were not soon forgotten. "Looky here America / Look what you done done / Let things drift / Until the riots come," he wrote in the poem "From Beaumont to Detroit: 1943." Ever the voice of the underdog, he took up the plight of his people wherever and whenever the occasion called for it. He often wrote with tongue in cheek, but he rarely held his tongue or turned his cheek against racial injustice. He lashed out at Dixiecrat politicians, the Ku Klux Klan and Jim Crow laws. "Certainly it is not the Negro who is going to wreck our democracy," he commented in the essay, "My America," published in 1943. "But democracy is going to wreck itself if it continues to approach closer and closer to fascist methods in its dealings with Negro citizens."³ That tone, however, varied with the publications he was writing

for. By then he had become "respectable" enough to appear in the pages of
The Saturday Evening Post, which no longer recognized him as the poet of
"Goodbye, Christ" but of "Wisdom" and "Refugee in America." Slowly,
but surely, his name was catching on to a wider, more diverse audience.
Some people who had remembered his speech on "A Poet's Campaign
Against Racial Prejudice and Intolerance" at Boston's famous Ford Hall
Forum in 1937 heard another Langston Hughes lecture there in 1946. By
then, with the war over, "Are We Solving Our Race Problem" showed
more of the hope and optimism of his long poem, "Freedom's Plow." Its
message, "America / Land created in common / Dream nourished in common / Keep your hand on the plow! / Hold on!" was the message Hughes
tried to hold on to for the next two decades—with great difficulty.

Already in 1944, he had seen some of the charges he would have to
contend with later. In the October 23, 1944, issue of *The New York Sun*, the
conservative columnist George Sokolsky declared him to be on a Justice
Department list of twelve "subversive organizations." Knowing the *Sun* to
be an anti-Roosevelt newspaper during the 1944 campaign, Hughes ignored
the allegations about "subversive organizations," since most of the organizations he had belonged to in the 1930s were by then defunct. Moreover, his
opponents could not really complain then about such poems as "Good
Morning, Stalingrad" and "To the Red Army," both published when Russia was an ally of the United States. In 1946, before the Cold War set in, he
had published a series of articles in *The Chicago Defender* praising the Soviet
Union, and a memorial poem to Lenin in *New Masses*. If he had sublimated
his leftist sentiments a few years before, his deeper feeling emerged in his
eulogistic, unpublished tribute to his late friend, Jacques Roumain, who
died in Haiti in August 1944, at age thirty-seven.

A Poem for Jacques Roumain

When did you
Find out about the world,
Jacques?

You certainly found out about it
Before you went away.

When did you learn to say,
Without fear or shame,
Je suis communiste?

You had no job to lose
But you had
What lots of people think
Is more.

None amounted to much,
Though, did it?
When did you realize that?
I can't answer for you,
And you are gone.

You are gone—
Have gone—
Are gone.
You've gone.
Where?
If I knew
I'd be a celestial
Houdini.

You've gone—
But you are still here—
From the point of my pen in New York
To the toes of the blackest peasant in the *morne*.
Because you found out
What it is all about.

Never will you become
Anonymous.
Never will your dust
Become air—
Then nothingness—
Invisible—
Never will you become
Less than a name—
Or less than you.

Always
You will be
Man
Finding out about
The ever bigger world
Before him.
Always you will be
Frontiersman,
Pathfinder,
Breaker down of
Barriers,
Hand that links

Azelie to the Pope,
Damballa to Lenin,
Haiti to the Universe,
Bread and fish
To fisherman
To man
To me.

Strange
About eternity
Eternal
To the free.[4]

With Mercer Cook, Hughes translated Roumain's posthumously published novel, *Gouverneurs de la rosée*, which appeared in the United States in 1947 as *Masters of the Dew*. A year later, he translated with Ben Carruthers the book of poems, *Cuba Libre*, by Nicolás Guillén.

By 1949, when he anthologized *The Poetry of the Negro 1746–1949* with Arna Bontemps, he had published in every literary genre. His vow to devote himself to literature had become a reality, but the intention he had expressed at the beginning of the decade to abandon show business was an illusion. After 1941, he wrote one song lyric after another. Not just for the war effort, but for every imaginable occasion. His lyrics to "Let My People Go" became the campaign song for Adam Clayton Powell's first Congressional race in 1944. For Harlem Week in 1945, Hughes collaborated with Duke Ellington to write "Heart of Harlem," and it was later performed at Carnegie Hall. His song lyric "African Dance," with music by Clarence Muse and Connie Bemis, was tapped out by Bojangles Bill Robinson in the popular 1940s movie *Stormy Weather*. With bandleader Noble Sissle he did the script for *Swing Time at the Savoy*, a five-part musical series that NBC radio aired the summer of 1948. Many more of his lyrics and scripts were not produced or published, but he took pride in the fact that some of his poems were set to music. None of his songs ever made the hit parade, although his "Night Time" was the radio theme song on the Blue Network for over a year. He fretted in his "Here to Yonder" column about the hazards of "The Song Writing Game," but he kept at it for the rest of his career.

Occasionally, it paid off, as in *Street Scene*. This Broadway musical, based on a book by Elmer Rice, opened at the Adelphi Theatre on January 9, 1947, with Hughes's lyrics and Kurt Weill's music. However, so many problems did he encounter with the arrogant Weill and the unpredictable Rice—over who got credit for what and who split what percentage of

what—that Hughes said later he was "sure the Lord had nothing to do with
the theatre, it had to be the devil's work." He later wrote a long article
about Kurt Weill, "My Collaborator," in which he told only part of the
story, but decided against publishing it. *Street Scene* lasted only four and a
half months on Broadway, after two years of work, although it became a
musical recording and eventually played abroad.

Hughes gained more personal satisfaction a year later when his opera
libretto, *Troubled Island*, finally reached the New York stage. Eighteen years
after he wrote it in Haiti, and fourteen years after he brought it to the attention of composer William Grant Still, the production premiered at the New
York City Opera Company, March 31, 1949. They owed much of the credit
to Leopold Stokowski. In 1944, while musical director of the City Center of
Music and Drama, he had put the opera into rehearsal, announcing it as a
work which "should be made known to the world, because it is one of the
most inspired expressions of Negro art in the United States."[5]

When the opera opened, Hughes was in Chicago, on a three-month
assignment as a resident poet and teacher at the University of Chicago
Laboratory School. Two years earlier, he had lectured one semester at
Atlanta University. These two teaching experiences were the first and last
of his mid-career, for he thought he was better on the lecture circuit than in
the classroom. He did more lecturing between 1942 and 1949 than at any
time in his life—making more than a hundred appearances in the United
States and Canada. Many of his readings were delivered before high school
assemblies; a new generation of young people had discovered him on Asch
Recordings, in book introductions, in an edited volume of Walt Whitman
for young readers, and through his own poetry. He also wrote more poems
in the 1940s than in any other decade, most of them appearing in *Shakespeare
in Harlem* (1942), *Fields of Wonder* (1947), *One-Way Ticket* (1949), and a
thirty-page booklet, *Jim Crow's Last Stand* (1943).

The decade brought its honors and rewards, immortalizing Hughes for
his contributions to American culture. In May 1943, along with the revered
poet of his youth, Carl Sandburg, he received an honorary doctorate from
his alma mater, Lincoln University, where he heard Sandburg deliver that
year's commencement address. Three years later, at a special ceremonial
dinner, he was honored by American Academy of Arts and Letters, together with Gwendolyn Brooks, Kenneth Burke, Malcolm Cowley, Peter
De Vries, Marianne Moore, Arthur Schesinger, Jr., and Irwin Shaw. At the
Academy's blue-ribbon ceremony, he was awarded a one-thousand-dollar
cash grant, the largest single sum he had ever received during his career.

He saved the grant for a down payment on the Harlem townhouse he
bought two years later with Toy and Emerson Harper. Until then their
address had been a three-room apartment at 634 St. Nicholas Avenue.

Hughes had joked that "Toy did her sewing in the bedrom, Emerson practiced his music in the living room, and he himself did his writing in the hall." In July 1948, they settled into 20 East 127th Street, a three-story, ivy-covered dwelling. Hughes's home-office suite on the top floor was the closest thing he ever had to an ivory tower.

As he was establishing his roots ever more firmly in Harlem, death claimed two of his friends from the Harlem Renaissance. Countee Cullen died in 1946, the year that his and Arna Bontemps's play, *St. Louis Woman*, finally reached Broadway. Their friend Claude McKay died in 1948, five years after suffering a stroke from which he never recovered. No obituary announced the passing of another figure who had once touched McKay's life and Hughes's own: their former patron, Charlotte Mason, whose end came at age ninety-one, on April 15, 1946, at New York Hospital.

THE 1950S FOUND Hughes surrounded by an ever-expanding group of new associates and collaborators in the literary, theatrical, and musical worlds. One was Jan Meyerowitz, a gifted German-born composer and postwar emigré. He contacted Hughes in 1947 about making an opera of *Mulatto*. The result of their collaboration was *The Barrier*, which the Columbia University Opera Workshop presented for ten evenings at Brander Matthews Hall in January 1950. Most reviewers echoed *The New Yorker* critic, who wrote that "few musical events have stirred me quite so deeply as the first performance...of a new opera, *The Barrier*, with a libretto by Langston Hughes and music by Jan Meyerowitz." The production reached Broadway in November, and then went on tour in the United States and abroad. Despite Hughes's problems with the producer, Joel Spector, who tried to cut him out of an advance on the Broadway production (and failed), the opera was the first of a number of successful Hughes-Meyerowitz collaborations.

Hughes showed his theatrical versatility the following year when he teamed up with Joe Sherman, Abby Mann, and Bernard Drew to create a musical comedy, *Just Around the Corner*, for a summer stock production at the Ogunquit Playhouse in Maine. With his ability to shift easily from a libretto to a song lyric, he found no hardship working on more than one production at once. In 1954, his libretto for a cantata with Jan Meyerowitz, *Five Foolish Virgins*, premiered in February; and another one, *Ballad of the Brown King*, written with Margaret Bonds, was presented in December (exactly six years before a longer version of the cantata was televised by CBS on "Christmas U.S.A."). In 1957, *Esther*, a Biblical opera he wrote with Meyerowitz, was produced at the University of Illinois Festival of Arts in March, five months before Hughes's musical folk comedy, *Simply Heavenly*, opened on Broadway (where it soon closed and moved to a Greenwich Village theatre).

Based on his 1955 book, *Simple Takes a Wife*, the popular musical, with tunes by David Martin, reached Hollywood the same year, London a year later, and American television in December 1959. During that time, he was collaborating with Margaret Bonds on a musical adaptation of *Shakespeare in Harlem*, which played at the White Barn Theatre in Westport, Connecticut, in August 1959. Meanwhile, after a brief run of *Esther* at the New England Conservatory in Boston in 1958, Hughes was again collaborating with Meyerowitz—on a choral composition, *How Godly Is the House of God*, and on a one-act opera, *Port Town*, for an August 1960 performance at the Tanglewood Music Festival.

His stamina and productivity often astonished his colleagues and friends. They wondered how he could lecture, travel, and write all at the same time. Only a few knew that he was then also working on a long list of proposals, outlines, and scripts for shows that, for one reason or another, never happened. Among them were *Wide, Wide River*, a folk opera with Granville English; a musical about Pennsylvania with Elie Siegmeister; *The Train That Took Wings and Flew*, a children's musical program with a narrator and orchestra; *I Wish You'd Let Me Love You*, an outline for a movie; *Dear Old American Southland*, a ballet drama of the American South; and an untitled one-act opera about Adam and Eve. Between 1949 and 1952, he drafted a biography and screenplay, called *Battle of Harlem*, based on the dramatic life and times of Samuel J. Battle, with whom he collaborated at length. Clarence Muse also thought the story had great possibilities for a movie, but they finally gave up on the battle to do it.

The early fifties found Hughes fighting many battles of his own. The Cold War of the late forties had shown its chilling effects all too soon. The flag-waving America First group of Gerald L. K. Smith and similar organizations had begun harassing him at his lectures, picketing with "Red" signs at auditoriums, and booing from the audience. In Arizona, opponents petitioned the governor to forbid Hughes to speak on the campus of Arizona State College in April 1948. Several weeks earlier, Senator Albert Hawkes of New Jersey had stood up in the United States Senate and called him a Communist, and read "Goodbye, Christ" and "One More 'S' in the U.S.A." into the *Congressional Record*.[6] By autumn a conservative coalition in California had accused him of having once been a member of the Central Committee of the Communist Party. These were isolated incidents, but alarming enough to cause Hughes to revise his militant poem "Let America Be America Again" when a publisher asked permission to reissue it that year. The revision brought a response from Maxim Lieber that Hughes surely never forgot. "I am a little amused," Lieber wrote him, "to see that you have revised the poem, bringing it up to date. While I suppose there is no law against such a procedure, it does seem somewhat strange. What would have happened to the original of Shelley's poem to the men of England—and to some of the work of our own American poets written within a certain period? For instance, what would have happened to Francis Scott Key's Star Spangled Banner, if he had a chance to revise it some twenty years later?"[7]

The House Un-American Activities Committee (HUAC) was reaching out like an octopus and, by 1950, was referring to Hughes in its documents. He occasionally tried to escape the onslaught with humor, as he did in "When a Man Sees Red," published that year in *Simple Speaks His Mind*:

> "I am black," said Simple, "also I will be red if things get worse. But one thing sure, I will not be yellow. I will stand up for my rights till kingdom come."
>
> "You'd better be careful or they will have you up before the Un-American Committee."
>
> "I wish that old Southern chairman would send for me," said Simple. "I'd tell him more than he wants to know.... I would say your Honery, I wish to inform you that I was born in America, I live in America, and long as I have been black, I been an American. Also I was a Democrat—but I didn't know Roosevelt was going to die. Then I would ask them, How come you don't have any Negroes on your Un-American Committee?"

Hughes soon got his chance to appear before an "Un-American Committee," but by then it was no laughing matter. His subpoena came not from the HUAC but from the Permanent Subcommitee on Investigations of the Committee on Government Operations—better known as the McCarthy Committee. The reign of terror of Joseph Raymond McCarthy had begun on February 9, 1950, with a speech in which he announced he had a list of subversives working in the State Department. By the time he became chairman of the Subcommittee on Investigations in 1953, the double-edged sword of his accusations and those of the HUAC had dealt piercing blows to Hughes and to almost everyone he knew. The publishing industry was shuddering from blacklists. Franklin Watts, the publisher of Hughes's *First Book of Negroes*, felt compelled in 1951 to distribute an advance notice that the selection of the author was "carefully deliberated" and that Langston Hughes was not a Communist. Meanwhile, purges were rampant from Hollywood to Broadway. And in August of that year, Hughes was directly affected: his loyal literary agent and friend Maxim Lieber was forced to abandon his agency and flee to exile in Mexico.[8]

Hughes did not know what the repercussions would be when he appeared before the McCarthy Committee on March 26, 1953. He did know that some witnesses, in order to save themselves, had destroyed others by "naming names," which he was determined not to do. He knew, too, that others who had taken the Fifth Amendment had ended up in jail or, worse, as suicides. Having seen enough careers broken, he could not be sure that the same would not happen to him. Two months before the subpoena came, McCarthy had hired as the Subcommittee's chief counsel, Roy Cohn, a twenty-five-year-old lawyer who had helped prosecute Ethel and Julius Rosenberg at their trial for espionage in 1951. So relentless and bumptious was the young Cohn in his interrogation of witnesses before the Subcommittee that McCarthy once remarked that he was "as indispensable as I am." Hughes was summoned only a month before Cohn and a consultant, G. David Schine, went on a seventeen-day, seven-country tour in search of alleged pro-Communist books in State Department Information Service centers abroad. McCarthy opponents called it a "book-burning" trip, but already Cohn and Schine had probed into Hughes's books, which were the major reason for the subpoena. The whole scenario of their behind-the-scene interrogation of Hughes never became part of the public record. And it was not a story Hughes liked to tell.

When McCarthy sounded the gavel at the public hearing and came face to face with Hughes and his lawyer for this encounter, Frank D. Reeves, it appeared they were meeting for the first time. In fact, they had already met privately in executive session—first with Cohn and Schine, and then in the Senator's office. Cohn, a harsher interrogator than Schine, had grilled Hughes about some of his writings. McCarthy, however, was anxious that a renowned American author should not become a "hostile witness." He had worked out an arrangement whereby Hughes would not be asked to "name names" of known Communists, but only in order to admit tacitly his own pro-Communist sympathies and writings. Having been indecisive about whether he would testify at all, after much private discussion with Reeves, he finally agreed to cooperate in the McCarthy scenario. He feared the worst if he didn't. Raising his right hand, he said, "I do," when the Senator asked him, "Do you swear to tell the whole truth and nothing but the truth, so help you God?"[9]

On the witness stand, Hughes confessed that "that there was such a period" when Cohn asked whether he had been a believer in the Soviet form of government; and "I certainly did," when questioned whether he wrote poetry which reflected his feelings during that time; and "That is correct, sir," when Cohn added, "I understand your testimony to be that you never actually joined the Communist Party." But so hard did he try to tell the truth about his past Soviet sympathies and at the same time sound like a patriotic American that he was only a shadow of himself. "A complete reorientation of my thinking and feelings occurred roughly four or five years ago," he offered, but Cohn quickly interjected "I notice that in 1949 you made a statement in defense of the Communist leaders who were on trial, which was in the *Daily Worker.*" Hughes said he believed "one can and does" get a fair trial in America. Pressed to defend "When a Man Sees Red" and other works, he got away with, "They do not represent my current thinking," and "I have more recent books I would prefer." Asked to explain his "complete change in ideology," he affirmed, "I have always been a believer in the American form of government." There were momemts when, pulverized into submission, he did disparage the Soviet Union. Praised by Southern Senator John McClellan for his "refreshing and comforting testimony," Hughes finally asked McCarthy, after about an hour of the inquisition, "Am I excused now, sir?" McCarthy finally let him go, after announcing he had "included in the record, on request," Hughes's earlier poem "Goodbye, Christ" "to show the type of thinking of Mr. Hughes at that time." To show he also had a "friendly witness," he sought assurance from the poet that he had not been "in any way mistreated by the staff or by the Committee." The capitulation was complete, from beginning to end.

After his testimony, Hughes wrote about it for the NAACP. Its officials, Walter White, Roy Wilkins, and Henry Lee Moon, had stuck with him through the ordeal and contacted Washington attorney Frank Reeves to represent him. His article, "Langston Hughes Speaks,"[10] published in *The Crisis* in May 1953, resembled his remarks on the witness stand. All that didn't stop one black man named Manning Johnson from testifying two months later to the HUAC that Langston Hughes was a Communist. More disappointments soon followed. His lecture bureau, Colston Leigh, dropped him like a hot potato—after representing him since 1946.[11] From other sources he was later criticized for not acting like Paul Robeson, who told the HUAC in 1956 that "I am here because I am opposing the neo-fascist cause which I see arising in these committees." Others wondered why Hughes's *First Book of Negroes*—which he had quoted proudly at the McCarthy hearing—carried no references to Robeson or Du Bois.[12] In 1921 he had thought enough of Du Bois to dedicate his poem "The Negro Speaks of Rivers" to him; in 1951 Du Bois had been indicted and threatened with jail under the Foreign Agents Registration Act; Hughes had defended his hero in *The Chicago Defender*, but omitted mentioning him in the *First Book of Negroes* (1952) and in a subsequent book of sketches on renowned Afro-Americans. Lieber chastized him in a letter. More than anything, Langston had not wanted to abandon his friends on the left, and he was at least relieved when Lieber in another letter said: "It made me feel damned good to see you quoted as one of the many well-wishers of Mike Gold on his 60th birthday....for this brings home the fact that despite your session before the McCarthy fascists you had not abandoned your former friends and acquaintances. In these days when so many weaken and turn tail, one wants to embrace one who stands up in human dignity."[13]

McCarthy died in 1957, three years after being condemned by his own Senate colleagues in a censure vote of 67–22. Hughes ultimately emerged from the witch-hunting era with his literary career intact. To play it safe, he had even begun drafting such things as *Dog and Cat Tale: A Story for Small Children.* If he was laughing to keep from crying—the title of his 1952 book of short stories—he put on his best smile. His lectures had fallen off, but he was more prolific than ever, turning out an average of two books a year, plus his librettos. The content of these works could not have been more acceptable to USIS libraries. He told friends his books were getting "simpler and simpler and younger and younger." It was more truth than jest. Having started the decade with *Simple Speaks His Mind*—and a dramatic sketch, *Just a Little Simple,* which played in Harlem briefly in September 1950—he produced two more "Simple" books, *Simple Takes a Wife* (1953) and *Simple Stakes a Claim* (1957) in addition to *Simply Heavenly* (1959). Following the *First Book of Negroes,* he produced three more historical and biographical works in the Franklin Watts First Book Series for young readers: *First Book of Jazz* (1955) and *First Book of Rhythmns* and *First Book of the West Indies* (both in 1956). Simultaneously, he expanded his scope with *Famous American Negroes* and *Famous Negro Music Makers,* both published in 1954 and later widely translated abroad. They were followed by the equally popular *Famous Negro Heroes of America* in 1958.

That same year he used his research to write the text for *A Pictorial History of the Negro in America,* in collaboration with Milton Meltzer, and edited *The Book of Negro Folklore* with Arna Bontemps. He wrote an essay to accompany the photographs of Roy De Carava in *Sweet Flypaper of Life* (1955). His major medium during the decade was prose, the best of which was the second volume of his autobiography, *I Wonder as I Wander,* published in 1956.

His poetry dropped off during the fifties, but his comments on poetry, as well as his editing of poetry, increased. He edited the "Negro Poets Issue" of *Voices* in 1950, and with two former Lincoln University classmates, Waring Cuney and Bruce McWright, he co-edited *Lincoln University Poets* in 1954. He and Cuney had also hoped to prepare an anthology called *Opportunity Poets,* with poems from the literary magazine, *Opportunity* (by then defunct). Having edited with an introduction *I Hear the People Singing: Selected Poems of Walt Whitman* in 1946, Hughes expanded his life-long interest in the poet to include several columns about him in 1953 in *The Chicago Defender.* "Whitman: Negroes' First Great Poetic Friend" evoked a heated response from an English professor who disagreed with him about Whitman's racial attitudes and caused Hughes to respond with "Like Whitman, Great Artists Are Not Always Good People." Hughes held on to to his belief later in an article, "Walt Whitman and the Negro," published in 1955 in the Brooklyn College magazine, *Nocturne*.

He also contributed articles on writing to *Phylon, Mainstream,* and *CLA Bulletin* and did some of his best translations from the Spanish during the 1950s. The 1957 publication of his *Selected Poems of Gabriela Mistral* was the first significant English-language translation of the Chilean Nobel-prize winning poet. After numerous revisions, his translation of fifteen of Federico García Lorca's *Gypsy Ballads* appeared the autumn of 1951 in the *Beloit Poetry Chapbook*. Even if Hughes had never translated a Hispanic poet, his reputation in the Spanish-speaking world would have been assured. Widely known for his writings on the Spanish Civil War, he had been acclaimed as a poet in Mexico and Cuba from the early thirties, and his critical reputation in Latin America had grown by leaps and bounds. Some of his major prose and drama had been translated into Spanish by the fifties, especially in Argentina, where Julio Galer translated Hughes's autobiographies and some of his fiction and also anthologized him. His *Poemas por Langston Hughes* in 1952 included more than sixty Hughes poems. Poets of African descent in Latin America hailed Hughes in verse and song. One of the most influential was the Afro-Uruguayan poet, Pilar Barrios, who paid him tribute as his "brother" in the long poem "Voces" in his first book of poems, *Piel Negra,* published in 1947.[14]

Hughes's *Selected Poems*, published in 1959, was his last book of the decade, and it represented nearly forty years of his productivity as a poet. Included in it were verses from his only other poetry volume of the 1950s—*Montage of a Dream Deferred*. Arranged in thirteen subject groups, *Selected Poems* showed his versatility and craftsmanship; the poet who could display as much comic relief as pathos, who could translate rural folk expression and urban folk expression, who could write ballads and blues, poems of social protest and verses about dreams, love, and death. Looming large in the collection were poems about Harlem from almost all his previous collections: the jazz-inspired Harlem of *The Weary Blues*, the disillusioned metropolis of *Shakespeare in Harlem*, the melancholy urban ghetto of *Fields of Wonder*, and the restless Harlem of *One-Way Ticket* and *Montage of a Dream Deferred*. There was nothing about the wide selection of poems to indicate a chronology, but obviously missing were any of his more radical ones from the 1930s; not even his revised version of "Let America Be America Again" was included. Nobody knew better than Langston Hughes why they were not there. He had selected not his best poems, but those he thought would go over best with the public. He aimed to please. *Selected Poems* reflected that desire as much as *The Langston Hughes Reader*, a 1958 sampler of his short stories, novels, plays, poetry, song lyrics, essays, speeches, translations, and verses for children. It was perhaps a paradox that, several months after it appeared, an obscure writer with an axe to grind and a pen dipped in far-right vitriol attacked Hughes and the *Reader* in an article entitled "Langston Hughes: Malevolent Force."[15] Such attacks did not end when the McCarthy era ended, but enemies mattered less to Hughes than his friends, for he had many more of the latter than the former. His deepest regret of the decade was not political persecution but the loss of his close friend of twenty-five years—Noel Sullivan, who died of a heart attack on September 15, 1956. Through all Langston's "red-baiting" agony, Sullivan had told him, "Don't worry, God will see you through."

HUGHES ENTERED THE 1960s with a reputation as the "Dean of Negro Writers." To younger literary protégés, such as the poet Gwendolyn Brooks and the novelist Julian Mayfield, whose works he encouraged and reviewed, he was a revered example and friend.[16] Playwright Lorraine Hansberry had adapted a line from his poem "Harlem" as the title of her play *Raisin in the Sun*, the Broadway hit of the 1958–59 season. But Hughes and the Harlem-born writer James Baldwin never quite hit it off. Reviewing *Selected Poems* in the *New York Times Book Review*, March 29, 1959, Baldwin declared "this book contains a great deal which a more disciplined poet would have thrown into the wastebasket." Three years earlier, Hughes had offered his own critical observations on Baldwin's first book of essays, *Notes of a Native Son*. Although he rarely reviewed the books of black authors unfavorably, believing they had a hard enough time getting published, he did not bite his tongue about Baldwin in a *New York Times* review of February 26, 1956, "From Harlem to Paris." He thought the young writer had not only a racial and cultural identity crisis but a personal identity crisis for attacking his father figure and literary mentor, Richard Wright.

Hughes saw Wright for the last time in Paris in November 1960. Three days later, in London, he learned the author was dead. For *Ebony* magazine, he wrote about their last meeting in a short reminiscence called "Richard Wright's Last Guest at Home," which was published three months later.

A trip to Paris in 1960 was Hughes's first in twenty-two years, but it was not the last. He found himself going to Europe and Africa on several trips on cultural grants from the State Department. If he thought anything about the irony of all that, he never said so. He never knew that until 1959 he was on the "security index" of the FBI's New York office, which kept files on his lecture engagements, publications, and activities. By 1961, he was considered a good enough American to be invited to a White House reception for an African diplomat, after Attorney General Robert F. Kennedy requested a memorandum security clearance on him from the FBI. By 1962, he was a short-term cultural emissary, criss-crossing Africa and attending literary conferences in Kampala, Accra, and Lagos. In 1960, enthusiastic about newly emerging independent African nations, he published *The First Book of Africa* and *An African Treasury*, an anthology of articles, folk tales, essays, short stories. He quickly followed in 1963 with *Poems from Black Africa, Ethiopia and Other Countries*, a collection representing thirty-eight poets from eleven nations. At home and abroad, he made contact with African writers, notably the South African, Bloke Modisane, who for a time was a guest in Hughes's Harlem home. In Nigeria, Hughes adopted an African godson, Sunday Osuya, a young merchant who had befriended him. He collaborated with the American jazz composer-musician Randy Weston to write the lyrics for "Uhuru Kwanza," which was recorded on a popular album of Afro-percussion music under the title "Uhuru Afrika" (Freedom Africa) in 1966.

His keen interest in Africa was only one indication that he had come full circle to embrace some of the same causes and themes which occupied him during the 1920s. His love for jazz and blues was also more evident, especially in *Ask Your Mama*, his 1961 book of poems subtitled "12 Moods for Jazz." He was proud that his *First Book of Jazz* had been translated into a half dozen languages, and that it was popular in Canada, where he read his poetry to jazz at the Stratford, Ontario, Festival in 1958. The American jazz poetry movement, made popular in the late fifties by white poets such as Lawrence Ferlinghetti, was nothing new to Hughes: he had started it in the twenties. During the late fifties, he made a jazz and poetry album with musician Charlie Mingus. He was a board member of the Newport Jazz Festival and narrator for one of its concerts in 1960. He frequently read his poetry to jazz—until an incident on June 21, 1961, at the Boston Arts Festival. There pickets calling themselves "American Patriots" paraded about with signs saying, "Hughes Affiliated with Communist Fronts." Only one week before, he had written a friend that, "after my Blues and Jazz night at the Boston Arts Festival next week, I am retiring from the public platform FOREVER to devote myself to writing."[17] The picketing incident occurred some eight months after *Time* magazine, in its October 3, 1960 issue, wrote that "the left-wing poet Langston Hughes dropped into the Theresa to pay respects" to visiting Cuban Premier Fidel Castro, who was staying in Harlem during a New York visit to the United Nations. Hughes shot back a letter to *Time* saying, "I have not been in the Hotel Theresa for several weeks, and was certainly not there during Mr. Castro's stay." *Time*'s erroneous report had followed a similar one by Leonard Lyons in the September 2 *New York Post*. (Lyons, however, a day later, had retracted his statement that Hughes had been a guest at a Castro dinner.)

Hughes was then less inclined to political dinners in Harlem than to eating in small "soul food" restaurants and listening to gospel music in storefront churches. Always a lover of gospel music, he turned his fervor into the creation of the "gospel song play." An innovative dramatic form, it achieved an international reputation after his *Black Nativity* opened at New York's 41st Street Theatre in December 1961. After its New York run, it became a hit at the Festival of Two Worlds in Spoleto the summer of 1962, and successfully toured in Europe and Sydney, Australia, before returning for the Christmas holidays to New York's Lincoln Center. It got bravos when it played a few American cities, and it was the one show which made Hughes some money; it also cost him some when he filed a lawsuit after the Chicago production closed abruptly, owing him $7,000 in royalties.

Believing the gospel song play translated the Bible into a folk milieu, he tried the narrative technique with several different composers, including the talented Jobe Huntley, but none of the subsequent efforts was as successful as the first. His *Gospel Glory*, conceived as *Gospel Glow*, had only a few performances at the Washington Temple in Brooklyn in 1962. *Tambourines to Glory*, adapted from the novel of the same title, had a try-out in Westport, Connecticut, before opening in November 1963 at New York's Little Theatre; it closed after twenty-five performances. On December 28, his rousing *Jerico-Jim Crow* was presented in coordination with the NAACP, CORE, SNCC, and Stella Holt Productions; its gospels, hymns, and freedom songs packed audiences into the Sanctuary of the Village Presbyterian Church and Brotherhood Synagogue, where it played on weekends through April 1964. A month after it closed, the one-act musical play *Prodigal Son* opened to much foot-stomping and hand-clapping at the Greenwich Mews Theatre; it played until autumn before going on a tour abroad. In 1965, as companion piece to *Prodigal Son*, he wrote *Tell It to Telstar*, which never made it to the stage.

The gospel song plays were only one manifestation of the religious themes of Hughes's earlier career. In his final decade, the poet of "Goodbye, Christ" had made his truce with Christ, and his musical and literary works showed it. His poems and texts on Bibilical themes proliferated. Some, like his penitent, unpublished verse "Prayer for the Mantel Piece"—an arietta from his libretto, *Five Wise, Five Foolish*—were largely unknown. He wrote one libretto for an Easter cantata with Margaret Bonds (*Simon Bore the Cross*) and another with Jan Meyerowitz (*The Glory Around His Head*). In 1959, he narrated *Lamp Unto My Feet: Out of Faith* for a televised production with the vocalist Odetta. Many more such readings followed, including several appearances in a "Spiritual Spectacular" musical narrative program written by his editorial secretary, George Bass. He took Bass with him on a 1963 trip to the Holy Land, where he baptized him in the Jordan River "in the name of art and higher things." Between 1960 and 1966, Hughes offered publishers five different proposals for religious anthologies: *These Prayers*, a collection of short texts from major religions; *Prayers Around the World*, the first book of ecumenical prayers; *Poems of the Spirit*, verses on Biblical themes by well-known poets; *Spread Your Wings and Fly: Poems of Faith*; and a *Christmas Sampler*, a collection of short stories, sketches, and translations on the theme of Christmas. *The Crisis* in 1958 printed some of the Christmas poems, one of which was "On a Pallet of Straw," later set to music by Jan Meyerowitz, but none of the religious anthologies was ever published.

During his twilight years, as during his early career, publishers still had trouble identifying him with any book which was not racial in content. All of his other books released during the sixties carried the mark of race: *The Best of Simple* (1961), *Fight for Freedom: A History of the NAACP* (1962), *Something in Common and Other Stories* (1962), *Simple's Uncle Sam* (1965), *The Panther and the Lash* (1967), plus his edited collections—*New Negro Poets, U.S.A.* (1964), *The Book of Negro Humor* (1965), and the bilingual *La Poésie Négro-Américaine* (1966). With Arna Bontemps he was already preparing a revised, updated version of their *Poetry of the Negro* and considering an anthology of Harlem Renaissance authors. With Lindsay Patterson—one of the many young, aspiring black writers he encouraged—he had made notes for two proposed anthologies they hoped to edit: *Distinguished Stories by White Americans about Black Americans*, and *Advice to My People*, biographical sketches of twenty-five prominent persons of African descent.

At the heart of the "poet laureate of the Negro people" was the great humanitarian whose words often transcended race. His nonracial poems, such as the lyrical verses in *Fields of Wonder* were often overlooked by the public, and others were never printed widely enough to be noticed. Some were also written for special occasions, such as the testimonial dinner honoring his life-long friends Russell and Rowena Jelliffe upon their retirement from Karamu House in March 1963. He also wrote such prose as "A Reader's Writer," a special tribute for the Ernest Hemingway memorial issue of *The Mark Twain Journal* in 1962. He never believed that black writers should be confined to writing about the racial issue, any more than he believed in Jim Crow accommodations. "The most heartening thing for me," he wrote in *Phylon* in 1950, " is to see Negroes writing works in the general American field, rather than dwelling on Negro themes solely." He rarely got that chance himself until he became a columnist for the *New York Post*; there, until 1965, he wrote about everything from the "Woes of a Writer" to the woes of his folk hero, Simple.

Those same years were the turbulent ones in which he also chronicled sit-ins, the Birmingham church bombing of four little girls in Sunday school, protest demonstrations, assassinations, the Selma-Montgomery march, and "riots" in Harlem and Watts. By the end of 1965, he had abandoned his twenty-three-year effort to use humor as a weapon in the civil rights strug-

gle. "No more Simple stories,...the racial climate has gotten so complicated and bitter that cheerful and ironic humor is less understandable to
many people," he told colleagues at *The Post*. The newspaper's first black
staff writer, Ted Poston—with whom Hughes had long since settled old
grievances from their days in Russia—encouraged him to continue the Simple column. Hughes had abandoned it briefly in August 1963—because, in
Poston's words, "Black nationalists lost their sense of humor."[18] In his
August 16, 1963, column, titled "A Dissent," Hughes printed a letter he
received from a Harlemite: "Why do you continue to perpetuate the stupid,
ignorant offensive character you call Jess Semple?" the reader asked. "I say
he is dead and died with all the other Uncle Toms like him.... You have
had a measure of success and it is now time to lay Jess Semple to rest...."

He did lay Simple to rest for a while, and did not publish another piece in
the *Post* until December 13, 1963, when a front-page banner announced
"Langston Hughes Is Back." He was back, not with Simple, but with a
mournful tribute to the slain President John F. Kennedy, assassinated in
Dallas, November 22, 1963. Not until two years later, on December 31,
1965, did he say "Hail and Farewell" to Simple and the *Post*. Simple was not
dead, he was simply moving to suburbia, never to be heard from again.
That month, *The Chicago Defender* and the Associated Negro Press received
a personal message: "This is to advise you that my column, including
Simple, will no longer be distributed."

Six weeks before his last newspaper column, Hughes's last concert work
had its world premiere at the San Francisco War Memorial Opera House on
November 15. It was the cantata, *Let Us Remember: A Requiem for Martyrs*,
composed and conducted by David Amram and presented by the Union of
American Hebrew Congregations. Hughes's text linked the civil rights struggle with the persecution of all oppressed people of all times. "Remember
Auschwitz, Dachau, Buchenwald / Let not the oppressed become the op-
pressors / Remember—Montgomery, Selma and Savannah.... / Where man
must live and man must forgive."

Three months later, his last script for a musical production was used on
national television in Harry Belafonte's *Strollin' Twenties*; it aired on February 21, 1966. By April, free of commitments of newspaper columns and
musical collaborations, he was on an honorary committee representing the
United States at the First World Festival of Negro Arts in Dakar, Senegal.
At one colloquium, he presented a paper, "Black Writers in a Troubled
World." The festival was a major event, and he appeared in distinguished
company with many friends he had not seen in years and would never see
again: Mercer Cook, then American ambassador to Senegal; Leopold Sedar
Senghor, the Senegalese President; Jean François Brierre, Haitian poet in
exile; Katherine Dunham, Josephine Baker, and so many others that he

wrote Arna that almost everyone he knew was there from all over the world. Before he left on a journey to Khartoum, Addis Ababa, Nairobi, and Dar es Salaam, he spent several hours walking the beach near the Senegalese port he had visited forty-three years before as a merchant seaman.

On the way home from Africa, he spent several days in Paris. He had told Arna Bontemps in March 1965 that he hoped he could "get back to Paris one more time once."[19] He got there two months later on a lecture tour for the United States Information Agency (USIA).[20] Four times since 1960 he had been to the French capital, and it had grown on him. He had read Hemingway's posthumously published *A Moveable Feast*, about Paris in the twenties, and it had reminded him of his own days there in 1924. In his column of November 13, 1964 in the *New York Post*, he wrote his own nostalgic reminiscence of Paris. "There are other cities, of course, other countries, no doubt other worlds—but there is none like Paris. I think solely because Paris becomes you, whoever you are...."

By April 1967 he was talking seriously of going there in July for the promotion of the French publication of one of his *Simple* collections and looking for an apartment. He did not plan to stay indefinitely until later, because of the illness of Toy Harper, who had been hospitalized and was slowly wasting away, Meanwhile, Emerson Harper was languishing over Toy and afraid to go out into the Harlem night after having been mugged several times. During Toy's absence the house was being painted, and there was such upheaval that Langston took a room at the Wellington Hotel in midtown Manhattan. From there, he penned his last letter to Arna Bontemps, expressing the hope that he could stay in Paris for "toujours."

Now, at age sixty-five, and not in the best of health, Hughes had something to look forward to in the trip to Paris. He would have liked nothing better than to sit at an outdoor café and watch the world go by. He had written himself out about America's escalating war in Vietnam and the racial unrest at home. Knopf was soon to publish some of his poems about those events in his anthology *The Panther and the Lash*. With its forty-four new poems and twenty-six selected from previous volumes, it was to be his final testament, the most militant book of verse he had published since the thirties. He had considered calling it *Words Like Freedom*, until the words didn't fit the times anymore. He also thought he had exhausted the word *freedom*, using it in many songs and poems—"Freedom," "Freedom Seekers," "Freedom Train," "Freedom's Plow," "Freedom Road," and "Freedom Land," a song in *Jerico-Jim Crow* for which he wrote both the music and the words.

He was disappointed that, in mid-1967, racial freedom was still a "dream deferred." He had written all he could on the subject, both as America's defender and its critic. At home and abroad he seemed to be recognized for his efforts. During his final years, there were more tributes, testimonials, and special programs in his honor than he could attend. The *Lincoln-University Bulletin* devoted a special issue to him in 1964; the BBC, the Berlin Arts Festival, the Library of Congress, and civic, labor, fraternal, and cultural organizations besieged him with requests for poetry readings and personal appearances. The University of Grenoble, the University of Colorado, and the University of Nigeria wanted him to be writer-in residence. Howard University presented him with a Litt.D in 1963, and Western Reserve University followed with another a year later; Columbia University intended to bestow the same honor in June 1967.

During his forty-six-year career, he had represented many things to many people: poet, playwright, novelist, song lyricist, librettist, journalist, essayist, editor, translator, lecturer, humorist, social activist, agnostic, freedom fighter, dream-keeper, integrationist, Pan-Africanist, world traveler, and international voice of the oppressed everywhere. Few knew him better than he knew himself. In the end, he was uncertain what he had accomplished by his work, despite all he had tried to do. His last poem in *The Crisis* seemed to say so.

Flotsam

On the shoals of Nowhere,
Cast up—my boat,
Bow all broken
No longer afloat.

On the shoals of Nowhere,
Wasted my song—
Yet taken by the sea wind
And blown along.[21]

No one ever seemed to know when he was feeling downcast, because he didn't talk about it. Like so much about his personal life, he kept his physical ailments to himself. He had no personal physician, having tried consistently to avoid doctors, physical check-ups and hospitals, unless his life depended on it. The night of May 6, 1967, was one of the times he voluntarily sought emergency care. He took a cab to the Polyclinic Hospital, after suffering an attack—of he knew not what—in his room at the nearby Wellington Hotel. What actually happened after that, the hospital preferred later not to reveal.[22] He registered anonymously as "James Hughes," and for several days was treated much like an indigent and given no special medical attention. Not until he was recognized by a black orderly, who told hospital authorities, did emergency care begin. By then it was too late. He was diagnosed as having an infection of the prostate gland, and it was later reported that he entered the hospital with a heart condition. He had both. He had hoped to keep his illness and his hospitalization a secret, except from his literary asistant Raoul Abdul and from Emerson Harper and a few other close friends. He wrote Amy Spingarn a postcard saying he expected to be up and about in a few days. Indeed, he thought so, and he looked like himself when George Bass and Raoul Abdul visited him before an operation scheduled for May 19. After that, they hardly recognized him as the same person. Uremia had set in, and he deteriorated rapidly.

If the end was near, he had prepared for it. His will had been written four years earlier; in his papers he had left full instructions about his funeral service; he did not want it held in a church with liturgical music but in a Harlem funeral home, with musical accompaniment by a jazz combo. He specified that the musicians were to be paid union wages; the service was not to be an occasion for mourning. He was to be cremated.

On May 22, Hughes took a turn for the worse. Toy Harper, herself in intensive care at another hospital, had not been told of his illness. But Langston and Emerson often said she had "supernatural" powers, and perhaps she did. Weak from hardening of the arteries, she was thought to be delirious when she told her nurse of a frightful dream: Langston Hughes had climbed atop a pole to reach toward a tower and had fallen. "Death is a tower / To which the soul ascends / To spend a meditative hour / That never ends," he had written in 1930.[23] His end came quietly the same night as Toy Harper's dream. Alone in a room in the Polyclinic Hospital, he died in his sleep.

The memorial service three days later was carried out as he wished. It was held in the Benta Funeral Home at 630 St. Nicholas Avenue, only a few doors from the Harlem residence where he had lived many years with the Harpers. Music was played by the Randy Weston Trio. Solos and readings were exactly as he wanted them. There were remarks by Arna Bontemps. The memorial program carried the words of "I Dream a World," from the libretto of the opera *Troubled Island*:

> I dream a world where man
> No other man will scorn,
> Where love will bless the earth
> And peace its paths adorn.
> I dream a world where all
> Will know sweet freedom's way,
> Where greed no longer saps the soul
> Nor avarice blights our day.
> A world I dream where black or white,

Whatever race you be,
Will *share* the bounties of the earth
And every man is free,
Where wretchedness will hang its head,
And joy, like a pearl,
Attend the needs of all mankind.
Of such I dream—
Our world!

Notes

The following abbreviations and key words are used in the notes to refer to persons, archives, and collections:

ABSP   Arthur B. Spingarn Papers, Moorland-Spingarn Research Center, Howard University Library

ALP   Alain Locke Papers, Moorland-Spingarn Research Center, Howard University Library

Bancroft The Bancroft Library, University of California, Berkeley

Beinecke Beinecke Rare Book and Manuscript Library, Yale University

Fisk   Special Collections, Fisk University Library

JWJ   James Weldon Johnson Memorial Collection, American Literature Collection, Beinecke Rare Book and Manuscript Library, Yale University

LH   Langston Hughes

MDLC   Manuscript Division, Library of Congress

NSP   Noel Sullivan Papers, The Bancroft Library, University of California, Berkeley

Schomburg Schomburg Center for Research in Black Culture, New York Public Library

Chapter 1: From These Roots

1. It is not known whether *Mercer* was included in Hughes's full name at birth or whether he adopted it later out of family pride. It was his mother's legal middle name, given her in honor of her uncle John Mercer Langston. In 1971, the author requested a search for a birth certificate for Langston Hughes in the Division of Health of Missouri, Jefferson City, where records are maintained for persons born in Joplin. Because records of the period have not survived, no birth certificate is on file to reveal Hughes's full legal name. The author credits Arnold Rampersad for bringing to her attention that the name Mercer does not appear as part of Hughes's full name in official documents, such as passports or the last will and testament. The name James Mercer Langston Hughes appears in this biography as the name Hughes preferred—and the one given by his executors on the printed program of the memorial service for last rites in May 1967.

2. Langston Hughes allegedly first learned in 1958 of his deceased brother from a New York friend and former Joplin resident, Max Baird (1912–77), a writer-editor and professor. Baird's research into Joplin's history provided information about the Hughes family records, which the poet corroborated. Hughes visited Joplin's Fairview Cemetery accompanied by Attorney Ralph Baird, Max's brother. The location of the unmarked burial site is Terrace 3, West 136, Grave 4, on record for an unnamed son of J. N. Hughes, interred February 8, 1900.

For this biography every effort was made to document the birth and date record of the Hughes infant in Jasper County, where such records for the city of Joplin are registered. However, as the state of Missouri did not require the registration of births and deaths prior to

1910 in certain counties, no record of his birth or death is registered in the Bureau of Vital Records, or in the Records Management and Archives Service in the state capital at Jefferson City, Missouri. Nevertheless, U.S. Census records for the year 1900 in Jasper County do reveal a deceased child of James Nathaniel and Carrie Mercer Langston Hughes, though such records do not provide the name, age, or sex of the deceased.

For information about Hughes's visit to Joplin and the location of the grave site, the author is grateful to Ms. Linda Tarpley, a Joplin resident, and to Mr. Ralph Baird, who confirmed Hughes's trip to the cemetery and Max Baird's research. Ralph Baird, whom the author corresponded with and interviewed in 1977–78, died May 25, 1980.

3. Cited in Herbert Aptheker, ed., *A Documentary History of the Negro People in the United States*, 2 vols. (New York, 1963), 1:62.

4. See Jacob R. Shipherd, *History of the Oberlin-Wellington Rescue* (Boston, 1959). See also Aptheker, *op. cit.*, 1: 423–33; Benjamin Quarles, *Black Abolitionists* (New York, 1969), pp. 213–14.

5. Mary Sampson Patterson Leary was of African, French, and Indian ancestry. She and Charles Langston were married by the Reverend F. L. Kenyon in January 1869 at Elyria, Ohio (*Lorain County News*, January 20, 1869). Source provided by Dr. and Mrs. William Cheek.

6. *The Colored Citizen* (Topeka, Kansas), August 9, 1879.

7. "The Death of Charley Langston," *Lawrence Weekly Record*, November 25, 1892. Information furnished by the Kansas State Historical Society to author, July 10, 1971.

8. Information on dates of enrollment and attendance of Carrie Mercer Langston furnished by Certifications Supervisor, Office of the Registrar, University of Kansas, to author, August 12, 1971.

9. John Mercer Langston (1829–97) was the youngest of the three Langston brothers. Gideon Langston (1809–55), the eldest, died at age forty-six of tuberculosis in Ohio. He had attended Oberlin College and later entered business in Chillicothe and Cincinnati as an owner of livery stables.

10. James Hughes arrived in Mexico on October 29, 1903, and established residence there. He did not visit the United States until 1907, when Langston was five years old.

11. LH, *The Big Sea* (New York, Alfred A. Knopf, 1940; reprinted New York: Hill & Wang, 1963). Here and later I have drawn upon this autobiographical volume for direct quotations about Hughes's early life. To avoid repetitive footnotes, I shall usually cite only once—at the beginning of each chapter, the pages where incidental relevant quotations may be found. In this chapter, on Hughes's early life in Lawrence, Kansas, I have quoted from *The Big Sea*, page 13, 14, 15, and 26. All quotations are used by permission of the Langston Hughes Estate, George Houston Bass, Executor; the agent Harold Ober; and the publisher, Hill & Wang, a subsidiary of Farrar, Straus & Giroux, Inc..

12. The date of the earthquake, which Hughes does not give in *The Big Sea*, was March 26, 1908.

Chapter 2: Significant Moves

1. LH, *The Big Sea*, p. 16. Subsequent quotations in this chapter not otherwise attributed are taken from *The Big Sea*, pages 16–17, 21, 23–24.

2. See LH, "Things I Don't Like Much," *The Chicago Defender*, July 17, 1961. See also LH, "Family Tree," *Simple Speaks His Mind* (New York, 1950), pp. 26–30; "Simple on Indian Blood," *The Best of Simple* (New York, 1961), pp. 17–20.

3. *The Crisis*, July 1921, p. 121.

4. LH to Arthur Spingarn, December 6, 1930 (ABSP).

5. LH, "Empty Houses," *Simple's Uncle Sam* (New York, 1965), p. 15.

6. LH, *The Big Sea*, p. 18.

7. LH, "God to Hungry Child," *The Workers Monthly*, March 1925, p. 234. Reprinted in Faith Berry, ed., *Good Morning, Revolution: Uncollected Social Protest Writings by Langston Hughes* (New York, 1973), p. 36 (hereafter cited as *Good Morning, Revolution*).

8. LH, "Prayer," *The Buccaneer*, May 1925, p. 20. Reprinted in LH, *Selected Poems* (New York, 1959), p. 18.

9. Hughes's mother, for personal reasons, often spelled her second married name as *Clarke*. However, Hughes, in *The Big Sea* and in personal papers, spells it *Clark* when he refers to her marriage to Homer Clark. Milton Meltzer, in *Langston Hughes*, spells the name *Clarke*. Both spellings have appeared elsewhere. In this biography I use the spelling *Clark*, which Hughes himself believed to be correct.

10. LH, *The Big Sea*, p. 24.

11. LH, "My School Days in Lincoln, Illinois." Excerpt from a tape-recorded talk for the Illinois Education Association, Central Division Centennial, 1954 (Schomburg).

12. LH, *The Big Sea*, p. 24. Hughes used the variant spellings Welch and Welsh; in *The Big Sea* he used the latter.

13. Dunbar's famous poem "We Wear the Mask" is a rare exception.

Chapter 3: The Making of a Poet

1. LH, *The Big Sea*, p. 29.

2. Ibid.

3. LH, *I Wonder as I Wander* (New York, 1956), p. 308.

4. LH, *The Big Sea*, p. 52.

5. Ibid., p. 34.

6. Ibid., p. 35.

7. Porfirio Diaz ruled Mexico from 1877 to 1880 and from 1884 to 1911.

8. LH, *The Big Sea*, p. 47.

9. Ibid., p. 49.

10. Ibid.

11. Ibid., p. 51.

12. Saunders Redding, *They Came in Chains* (New York, 1950), p. 247.

13. May 1919.

14. LH, *The Big Sea*, p. 39.

15. LH, "Soul Gone Home," *One-Act Play Magazine*, 1937. Reprinted in LH, *The Langston Hughes Reader* (New York, 1958), pp. 241–42; Webster Smalley, ed., *Five Plays of Langston Hughes* (Bloomington, Ind., 1968), p. 41.

16. LH, *The Big Sea*, p. 54.

17. Hughes's poems, with few known exceptions, appeared exclusively in *The Crisis* until 1924. In the same month "The Negro Speaks of Rivers" appeared there, it was also published in *The Literary Digest*; the poem "Negro," first published in *The Crisis* of January 1922, appeared two months later in *Current Opinion*. "The Weary Blues" was among the first of his poems to be originally published elsewhere, in *The New York Amsterdam News*, April 8, 1923; it never appeared in *The Crisis*.

18. *The Brownies' Book* was published monthly from January 1920 to December 1921.

19. LH to Locke, February 9, 1923 (ALP).

20. LH, *The Big Sea*, p. 80.

Chapter 4: Hail and Farewell

1. LH, *The Big Sea*, p. 81.

2. LH, "The Twenties: Harlem and Its Negritude," *African Forum*, Spring 1966, p. 12.

3. LH, "My Early Days in Harlem," in John Henrik Clarke, ed., *Harlem: A Community in Transition* (New York, 1964), p. 63.

4. For information about the dates, titles, and pen names of poems in *The Spectator* attributed to Langston Hughes, the author is grateful to Arnold Rampersad. A scrapbook of poems, having a table of contents in Hughes's own hand, shows four printed poems from *The Spectator*: "Passionate Love" and "Utopia" for April 1922, and "Reasons Why" and "Times Prohibition Bar" for May 1922. All were signed "LANG-HU," except for "Utopia," which was signed "LANGHU."

5. In a later version of this poem, this line was changed to "They lynch me still in Mississippi."

6. LH, "Danse Africaine," *The Crisis*, August 1922, p. 167; "Song for a Banjo Dance," *The Crisis*, October 1922, p. 267.

7. LH, *The Big Sea*, p. 93.

8. Ibid., p. 84.

9. Ibid., p. 86.

10. Ibid., p. 87.

11. Ibid.

12. William White, ed., *Daybooks and Notebooks: The Collected Writings of Walt Whitman*, 3 vols. (New York, 1978).

13. *The Crisis*, December 1922, p. 87.

14. LH, *The Big Sea*, p. 89.

15. Pio Baroja y Nessi (1872–1958), Spanish author who conceived most of his books as trilogies and strongly identified with the oppressed and the disinherited. His titles in English translation include *Zalacain the Adventurer* (1909), *The Tree of Science* (1911), *Caesar or Nothing* (1919), and *King Paradox* (1937).

16. In the case of D'Annunzio, by coincidence rather than influence, the title of a Hughes book of verse, *A New Song* (1938), resembles one D'Annunzio titled *New Song* (1881).

17. Of eleven Hughes poems published in *The Crisis* in 1923, only one, "When Sue Wears Red," written some four years previously, was not new.

18. *The Crisis*, May 1923, p. 35.

19. LH to Locke, February 6, 1923 (ALP).

20. LH to Locke, February 19, 1923 (ALP).

21. LH, *The Big Sea*, p. 97.

22. LH to Locke, n.d. [1923] (ALP).

Chapter 5: Africa and Europe

1. LH, *The Big Sea*, pp. 97–98. Subsequent quotations in this chapter not otherwise attributed are taken from *The Big Sea*, pages 114, 115, 143, 144, 145, 146, 154, 155, 189, and 197.

2. LH, "Ships, Sea and Africa," *The Crisis*, December 1923.

3. LH, "The Little Virgin," *The Messenger*, November 1927, pp. 327–28.

4. LH, *The Big Sea*, p. 10.

5. Excerpt of "The Same," published in full in *The Negro Worker*, September-October 1932, p. 31. See also LH, "Always the Same," *The Liberator*, November 4, 1932; ibid., in Nancy Cunard, ed., *Negro* (1934; reprinted New York, 1970), p. 263; and ibid., in Faith Berry, ed., *Good Morning, Revolution* (New York, 1973), p. 9.

6. LH, "Fog," *Palms*, October 1926, p. 24.

7. LH, "Liars," *Opportunity*, March 1925, p. 90.

8. LH, *The Big Sea*, p. 102.

9. Ibid., p. 103.

10. "Burutu Moon," written some eight months before it was published in *The Crisis* (June 1925), later appeared in slightly altered form in *The Big Sea*.

11. LH to Carrie Mercer Langston Hughes Clark, July 3, 1923 (Property of the Estate of Langston Hughes). Quoted by permission of the Executor, George Houston Bass. The letter was found in a trunk of Hughes's belongings after his death.

12. "African Morning" was first published as "The Outcast" in *Pacific Weekly*, August 31, 1936. Reprinted in LH, *Something in Common* (New York, 1963), pp. 45–49.

13. LH, *The Big Sea*, p. 234.

14. "The Sailor and the Steward," whose theme is the exploited worker, was published in the July-August 1935 issue of *The Anvil*, a magazine of proletarian literature. The story's resolve that a young seaman must organize and unionize for better wages and working conditions reflects the proletarian thrust of the nineteen thirties that Hughes adopted in much of his writing of that decade.

15. LH, *The Big Sea*, p. 139.

16. The old city of Rotterdam, which Hughes describes in *The Big Sea* as "quaint, picturesque and beautiful," was destroyed completely by German bombardment, May 14, 1940, the year *The Big Sea* was published.

17. The Witter Bynner undergraduate poetry contest, sponsored by the Poetry Society of America, awarded second prize to Cullen for "Ballad of a Brown Girl."

18. LH to Locke, February 4, 1924 (ALP).

19. The incident was the basis of Hughes's poem "Death of an Old Seaman." See LH, *The Weary Blues* (New York, 1926), p. 81, and *The Dream Keeper* (New York, 1932), p. 26.

20. From the typescript of "Just Traveling," an unpublished draft of *The Big Sea* (Marie Short Collection, Bancroft). The piece was published as a vignette in the *Carmel Pine Cone*, May 2, 1941, pp. 6–7. (It is probable that Hughes drew upon this incident for "The Sailor and the Steward.")

21. LH, *The Big Sea*, p. 151.

22. Ibid., pp. 156–57.

23. LH to Locke, May 27, 1924 (ALP).

24. LH, *The Big Sea*, p. 163.

25. LH, "Song for a Suicide," *The Crisis*, May 1924, p. 23. The poem, with slightly different wording, appears under the title "Exits" in Hughes's poetry volume *Fields of Wonder* (New York, 1947), p. 65.

Having learned that Cullen was contemplating suicide, Hughes included the poem on the back of a letter to him with the dedication "For Countee Cullen—November 18, 1925—Washington" (Countee Cullen Papers, Amistad Collection, Dillard University).

26. "Poem," *The Crisis*, August 1924, p. 173. The poem, with slightly different wording, appears under the title "Mammy" in *Fine Clothes to the Jew* (New York, 1937), p. 76.

27. LH to Locke, April 23, 1924 (ALP).

28. LH to Locke, May 27, 1924 (ALP).

29. René Maran, the Martinique-born writer, had won the Prix Goncourt in 1921 for his novel *Batouala*.

30. Seventeen years later, in a letter dated February 14, 1941, to Professor Rayford Logan, Hughes noted that "Anne Cousey [sic], who was Mary in *The Big Sea*," was known to be living in Trinidad with "lots of children and married to a leading young colored barrister of the island." (Correspondence of Dr. Rayford Logan; quoted by permission.)

31. Raymond Duncan was the brother of the American dancer Isadora Duncan (1878–1927).

32. LH, *The Big Sea*, p. 170. See also Edwin Embree, ed., *Thirteen Against the Odds* (New York, 1944), p. 118. "The Breath of a Rose" was set to music by William Grant Still.

33. "Youth," first published in *The Crisis* in August 1924, later appeared in *The Weary Blues* as "Poem." For publication of *The Langston Hughes Reader* in 1958, Hughes added these new lines to the end of the poem: "We march! / Americans together, / We march!" See *The Langston Hughes Reader*, pp. 147–48.

34. Hughes ultimately contributed twelve poems to the special issue of *The Survey Graphic* that appeared in March 1925. Nine of these were included among the eleven poems he contributed to *The New Negro*.

35. LH, *The Big Sea*, p. 185.

36. Hughes contributed the poem "Our Land." Articles by Locke, Barnes, and Guillaume were "A Note on African Art," "The Temple," and "African Art at the Barnes Foundation," respectively. See *Opportunity*, May 1925.

37. LH to Locke, April 23, 1924 (ALP).

38. LH to Locke, April 6, 1923 (ALP).

39. LH to Locke, August 12 [1924] (ALP).

40. LH to Locke, August 24 [1924] (ALP).

41. LH, *The Big Sea*, p. 189.

42. Ibid., p. 190.

43. LH to Locke, n.d. [1924] (ALP).

44. Ibid.

45. "I, Too" was enclosed in a letter LH to Locke, September 25 [1924] (ALP). The poem was first published in *The Survey Graphic*, March 1925, and was reprinted in *The Weary Blues* as "Epilogue."

46. LH, *The Big Sea*, p. 196.

Chapter 6: Spring Cannot Be Far Behind

1. In *The Big Sea* Hughes gives as the date of his return from Europe November 24, 1924, saying he attended a benefit dance held by the NAACP the same evening. The actual date of his arrival was November 10, which did coincide with an NAACP affair held under the auspices of the Committee of One Hundred Women, at the Happy Rhone Orchestra Club, 143rd Street and Lenox Avenue.

2. James Weldon Johnson included two of Hughes's poems in his social history of Harlem, *Black Manhattan* (1930), and ten poems in his anthology, *Book of American Negro Poetry* (1931).

3. Carl Van Vechten, "Introducing Langston Hughes to the Reader," *The Weary Blues* (New York, 1926), p. 11.

4. LH, *The Big Sea*, p. 203. Quotations not otherwise attributed in this chapter dealing with aspects of Hughes's life in Washington, D.C., are taken from pages 205 and 213 of *The Big Sea*.

5. LH, *The Big Sea*, p. 204.

6. Hughes also lived at 1917 Third Street, N.W., and 1749 S Street, N.W., during his months in Washington, D.C.

7. LH, *The Big Sea*, p. 208.

8. LH to Locke, August 20, 1924 (ALP).

9. "Drama for a Winter Night" and "God to Hungry Child" appeared in a March issue, and "Poem to a Dead Soldier," "Rising Waters," and "Park Benching" in an April issue. The publication of Hughes's poetry in *The Workers Monthly* came soon after the periodical's November 1924 merger with *The Liberator*, a radical magazine which lasted from March 1918 until October 1924, and to which Hughes had tried submitting poems in high school. *The Workers Monthly*, in its new format, was a consolidation of *The Liberator*, *The Labor Herald* (March 1922–October 1924), and *Soviet Russia Pictorial*. It was dedicated to the theory and practice of Marxism-Leninism and was the official organ of the Chicago-based Workers Party of America Trade Union Educational League. It is not known whether Hughes at the time believed he was submitting his poems to a newly named *Liberator* magazine, or that he had indeed begun to identify with Marxist-Leninist ideology. He contributed to the magazine only during the spring and summer of 1925, although *The Workers Monthly* survived until February 1927. A month later, the title changed to *The Communist*, which it remained until December 1944, before becoming *Political Affairs* in 1945.

10. LH, "Park Benching," *The Workers Monthly*, April 1925, p. 261. (A different poem, with the title "Park Bench," later appeared in Hughes's volume of political poetry, *A New Song*.)

11. Carter G. Woodson (1875–1950), author and educator, received his bachelor's and master's degrees from the University of Chicago and his doctorate from Harvard University. He founded the Association for the Study of Negro Life and History in 1915. The name was changed to the Association for the Study of Afro-American Life and History in 1972.

12. *Negro History Bulletin*, May 1950, p. 13.

13. *Opportunity*, August 1927, p. 226.

14. LH, "These Bad New Negroes: A Critique on Critics, Part I," *The Pittsburgh Courier*, April 9, 1927. (Part II appeared in *The Courier* a week later, on April 16, 1927.)

15. LH, "The Weary Blues," *Opportunity*, May 1925; reprinted in LH, *The Weary Blues*, pp. 23–24; *The Dream Keeper*, pp. 34–35; *The Langston Hughes Reader*, pp. 87–88; and *Selected Poems*, pp. 33–34.

16. "A Negro Renaissance," *The New York Herald Tribune*, May 7, 1925, p. 16; *Opportunity*, June 1925, p. 176.

17. "The Weary Blues" was reprinted in *The Forum*, August 1925. The wife of Henry Goddard Leach made possible the first *Opportunity* contest by contributing $500. For two successive years the contests were funded largely by Caspar Holstein, a West Indian merchant. The *Opportunity* prize contest was suspended in 1927.

18. Hughes and Charles S. Johnson corresponded while Hughes was in Paris, but evidence is inconclusive as to whether they actually met before the first *Opportunity* banquet in May 1925.

Charles Spurgeon Johnson (1893–1956), sociologist, author, and educator, was editor of

Opportunity from 1923 until 1928, when he joined the faculty at Fisk University. He became president of the university in 1947 and remained in that post until his death.

19. Blanche Knopf to LH, May 18, 1925 (JWJ).

20. The first of Hughes's poems to appear in *Vanity Fair*—the first he ever *sold* to a magazine—appeared in the September 1925 issue: "Fantasy in Purple," "Suicide's Note," and "To Midnight Nan at Leroy's."

21. "Cross" was first published in *The Crisis*, December 1925, p. 66; reprinted in LH, *Selected Poems*, p. 158.

22. "Minstrel Man" was first published in *The Crisis*, December 1925, pp. 66–67; reprinted in LH, *The Dream Keeper*, p. 38. In various reprintings, punctuation was slightly changed from the original.

23. Winold Reiss's pastel drawing of Hughes appeared on the March 1927 cover of *Opportunity*.

24. LH, *The Big Sea*, pp. 216–17. Though Hughes said he spent two years in Washington, he actually spent only fourteen months there—from November 1924 to February 1926.

25. Lincoln was established in 1854 by John Miller Dickey, a Presbyterian minister.

26. The Wardman Park Hotel later became the Sheraton Park Hotel and then the Sheraton-Washington.

27. LH to Walter White, October 29, 1925 (Walter White Papers, MDLC). The Mr. Johnson referred to in the letter is believed to be James Weldon Johnson, who was a trustee of the Garland Fund, also known as the American Fund for Public Service, which provided generous aid to civil rights organizations during the twenties and thirties through a bequest from Charles Garland, a wealthy white benefactor.

28. Walter White to LH, December 15, 1925 (Walter White Papers, MDLC).

29. LH to White, December 17, 1925 (Walter White Papers, MDLC).

It is not known whether LH ever actually wrote any part of the autobiography that he mentioned to White in 1925; but he appears to have fully abandoned the title *Scarlet Flowers: The Autobiography of a Young Negro Poet*. A year later, however, he had begun drafting his autobiographical first novel, which eventually was titled *Not Without Laughter*.

30. LH, *The Big Sea*, p. 212.

31. In a conversation with the author, February 27, 1971, Mrs. Spingarn, then eighty-eight years old, remarked, "[Langston] was very careful in his book never to say that I had helped him, because he thought I would be bothered by other people. He told me that." Hughes acknowledges his gratitude for Mrs. Spingarn's help, without mentioning her by name, in *The Big Sea*, p. 219.

32. Amy Spingarn, "Amy Spingarn Prizes," *The Crisis*, September 1924, p. 199.

33. LH to Mrs. Joel E. Spingarn, December 18, 1925 (Private correspondence of Mrs. Joel E. Spingarn). Reprinted by permission of Mrs. Joel E. Spingarn and the Langston Hughes Estate.

34. The line is quoted from a poem by Mrs. Spingarn.

35. Private correspondence of Mrs. Joel E. Spingarn. Reprinted by permission of Mrs. Joel E. Spingarn and the Langston Hughes Estate.

Chapter 7: A Temple for Tomorrow

1. LH to Locke, March 8, 1926 (ALP).

2. The reference is to Walter Wright, a mathematics professor who later became president of Lincoln.

3. Review of *The Weary Blues*, by Langston Hughes, *Times Literary Supplement*, July 29, 1926, p. 515.

4. DuBose Heyward, Review of *The Weary Blues*, by Langston Hughes, *New York Herald Tribune Books*, August 1, 1926, p. 4.

5. LH, "The Negro Artist and the Racial Mountain," *The Nation*, June 23, 1926, p. 692.

6. Ibid., p. 693.

7. In 1926 Hughes's poems appeared in *The Crisis, Fire!!, Lincoln News, Literary Digest, The Messenger, New York Herald Tribune, New Masses, The New Republic, Opportunity, Palms, Poetry, Vanity Fair,* and *Anthology of Magazine Verse*. The poem "Youth" appeared

on the May cover of *The Orange Jewel*, and "Feet o' Jesus" on the October cover of *Opportunity*.

8. *Lincoln News*, February 1927, p. 4.

9. LH to Locke, March 8, 1926 (ALP).

10. All of Hughes's poetic contributions to the *Lincoln News* were previously unpublished works, only a few of which were later reprinted elsewhere. In order of publication, they were: "Salome," March 1926, p. 5; "Lincoln Monument" and "Stars," November 26, p. 5; "Montmartre Beggar Woman," "A Letter to Anne," and "In the Mist of the Moon," February 1927, p. 4; "Mazie Dies Alone in the City Hospital" and "Barrel House: Chicago," October 1928, p. 7. Of these, he later anthologized only two in his own poetry collections: "Montmartre Beggar Woman" (as "Parisian Beggar Woman" in *The Dream Keeper*) and "Stars" (in *Fields of Wonder* and *Selected Poems*).

11. LH to Locke, March 29, 1926 (ALP).

12. LH, *The Big Sea*, p. 225. Quotations not otherwise attributed in this chapter dealing with Hughes's life at Lincoln University and in New York City during the Harlem Renaissance are taken from *The Big Sea*, pages 235, 236, 239, 244, 272, 296, 301, 303, 309, 310, 311, and 317.

13. LH to Locke, May 4, 1926 (ALP).

14. LH to Locke, June 4 [1926] (ALP).

15. George Schuyler, "The Negro Art-Hokum," *The Nation*, June 16, 1926, pp. 662–63. Hughes's piece appeared a week later.

16. LH to Locke, June 4 [1926] (ALP). In *The Big Sea* Hughes recalled—mistakenly—beginning the first draft of his novel only in 1928. The evidence of the letter to Professor Locke confutes this. He began writing the novel, first referred to as an "autobiography" when he mentioned it to Locke, no later than June 1926. There is also evidence that, before 1928, he had shown parts of a manuscript using his early life as background, to the wife of one of his Lincoln University professors.

17. Wallace Thurman's two novels—*The Blacker the Berry* (1929) and *Infants of the Spring* (1932)—were later published by Macauley.

18. Bruce Nugent interview with author, 1977.

19. These settings, unlike many of Hughes's poems that were later set to music by various composers, are not known to have been published. Rosamond Johnson is best known for the music to "Lift Every Voice and Sing," popularly called the Negro National Anthem. (James Weldon Johnson wrote the lyrics.)

20. LH, *Opportunity*, August 1926, p. 258.

21. "House-rent parties," also referred to as "social whist parties," were gatherings held in small apartments where refreshments and musical entertainment were provided, usually for an admission fee that helped raise money for the rent.

22. LH, *The Big Sea*, p. 233.

23. Ibid., pp. 262–63. The playmate to whom Hughes refers was to become the character Buster in *Not Without Laughter*.

24. Ibid., p. 262. "Mulatto" first appeared in *The Saturday Review of Literature*, January 29, 1927, shortly before publication in *Fine Clothes to the Jew*, pp. 71–72. Reprinted in *Selected Poems*, pp. 160–61.

25. LH to Locke, August 12, 1926 (ALP).

26. The name "The Dark Tower" was taken from Countee Cullen's poem "From the Dark Tower." (Cullen also wrote a column called "The Dark Tower" in *Opportunity*.) A few of his Harlem contemporaries suggested it was a fitting name for the room where A'Lelia frequently entertained on West 136th Street.

27. LH, *The Big Sea*, p. 251.

28. Van Vechten, who loved parties and sprinkled them through his fiction, eventually titled one of his books *Parties* (1930).

29. LH to Locke, August 12, 1926 (ALP).

30. LH, "These Bad New Negroes...Part II," *The Pittsburgh Courier*, April 16, 1927, p. 8.

31. Manuscript notes to the Carl Van Vechten Papers in the JWJ, Beinecke. Hughes's "Blues" appear on pages 34–35, 52, 137, and 139 of *Nigger Heaven*.

32. LH, *The Big Sea*, p. 262.

33. Mabel Dodge Luhan (née Ganson), who was married four times during her life—her married names were sequentially Evans, Dodge, Sterne, and Luhan—first met Carl Van Vechten in 1912. She briefly recounts their early relationship in *Movers and Shakers*, the third volume of *Intimate Memories* (New York, 1936). Van Vechten, who described her in his memoirs as someone he thought "had more effect on my life than anybody I ever met," modeled the character Edith Dale after her in his first novel, *Peter Whiffle* (1922). Despite one breach lasting sixteen years, they remained friends until her death in 1962. (Van Vechten is not known to have visited her home in Taos until 1927, a year after Hughes's poem was published.)

34. Lawrence first went to Taos in 1922 at the invitation of Mabel (then Sterne). She believed she had willed his visit by telepathy (but had not foreseen his wife Frieda). Lawrence stayed in and near Taos intermittently during three separate periods until September 1925. During part of that time he lived on a ranch that Mabel (now Luhan) gave him. Hughes is believed to have acquired some of this information from his acquaintance with the writer and critic Witter Bynner. Bynner, who frequented New York artistic circles, maintained a home in Sante Fe, and the Lawrences and the Luhans were occasional guests there. Bynner later recounted Lawrence's New Mexico sojourn in *Journey with Genius* (New York, 1951).

35. The cash prize was provided by Witter Bynner, who made the undergraduate contest available for over a decade. It was awarded by the Poetry Society of America through the magazine *Palms*, where "A House in Taos" was first published, in November 1926. (Hughes, in *The Big Sea*, erroneously gives the publication date as 1927.)

36. Quoted in *The Big Sea*, p. 237.

37. Alain Locke, *The Survey*, August 15–September 15, 1927, p. 563.

38. For reasons discussed in Chapter 16, the author doubts the attribution to Hughes of this and several other undated letters allegedly written by him to Wallace Thurman. The letters are preserved in the Wallace Thurman Papers, Beinecke Rare Book and Manuscript Library, Yale University.

39. Ibid.

40. DuBose Heyward, Review of *Fine Clothes to the Jew*, by Langston Hughes, *New York Herald Tribune*, February 20, 1927, p. 5.

41. Herbert S. Gorman, Review of *Fine Clothes to the Jew*, by Langston Hughes, *New York Times Book Review*, March 27, 1927, p. 2.

42. Review of *Fine Clothes to the Jew*, by Langston Hughes, *Boston Transcript*, March 2, 1927, p. 4.

43. Babette Deutsch, Review of *Fine Clothes to the Jew*, by Langston Hughes, *The Bookman*, April 1927, p. 221.

44. Julia Peterkin, Review of *Fine Clothes to the Jew*, by Langston Hughes, *Poetry*, October 1927, p. 45.

45. Margaret Larkin, Review of *Fine Clothes to the Jew*, by Langston Hughes, *Opportunity*, March 1927, pp. 84–85.

46. Dewey Jones, Review of *Fine Clothes to the Jew*, by Langston Hughes, *The Chicago Defender*, February 5, 1927, including a letter quoted from Langston Hughes.

47. Quoted in *The Big Sea*, pp. 265–66.

48. Charles S. Johnson, "The Negro Renaissance and Its Significance," in *The Negro Thirty Years Afterward*, ed. Rayford Logan, Eugene Holmes, and G. Franklin Edwards (Washington, D.C., 1955), p. 83.

49. Alain Locke, Review of *Fine Clothes to the Jew*, by Langston Hughes, *The Saturday Review of Literature*, April 9, 1927, p. 112.

50. Walter White, Review of *Fine Clothes to the Jew*, by Langston Hughes, *New York World*, February 6, 1927, p. 9m.

51. *The Pittsburgh Courier*, April 16, 1927, p. 8.

52. LH to Locke, n.d. [1927] (ALP).

53. Allison Davis, "Our Negro Intellectuals," *The Crisis*, August 1928, p. 269. *Fine Clothes to the Jew* is dedicated to Carl Van Vechten.

54. LH, Letter to the Editor, *The Crisis*, September 1928, p. 302.

55. LH, *The Big Sea*, pp. 263–64.

56. LH, "Day," *Opportunity*, March 1927, p. 85. "For an Indian Screen," "Lincoln Monument," and "Passing Love" all appeared in this same issue. The last two poems were later published in *The Dream Keeper*.

57. Two more of these stories were published in *The Messenger* that year, "The Young Glory of Him" and "The Little Virgin," in the June and November issues, respectively.

58. LH to White, February [n.d.], 1927 (Walter White Papers, MDLC).

59. LH (postcard) to Locke, April [n.d.], 1927 (ALP).

60. Hughes, though pleased with *Four Negro Poets* and his inclusion in it, wrote a long letter to Locke after its publication outlining printer's errors in his own poems and requesting they be corrected in a subsequent printing.

61. LH, *The Big Sea*, p. 316.

62. Ibid., p. 312.

63. Charlotte Mason died April 15, 1946, just before reaching the age of 92; Hughes died May 22, 1967, at age 65.

64. Hughes never made public in his published works the name of Mrs. Rufus Osgood Mason or any information about her private life; Zora Neale Hurston did so on several occasions, including her autobiography, *Dust Tracks on a Road* (Philadelphia, 1942; reprinted New York, 1969, 1971), pp. 183–85.

65. During World War II, Hughes wrote a critical poem titled "Red Cross," which appeared in a pamphlet of his poetry, *Jim Crow's Last Stand* (Atlanta, 1943), p. 8. The poem reads: "The angel of Mercy's / Got her wings in the mud / And all because of / Negro blood."

66. LH to Mr. and Mrs. Arthur B. Spingarn, June 28, 1927 (ABSP).

67. LH to Mr. and Mrs. Arthur B. Spingarn, July 14, 1927 (ABSP).

68. Zora Hurston later combined some of her materials for a program of black folklore titled "Sun to Sun," produced at the New School for Social Research in New York City, March 29, 1932. Notes on the program of that production say that Miss Hurston spent four years collecting material in the South (1927–31); and that "throughout these years this work of salvaging some of the surviving portions of the original primitive life of the Negro has been actively supported by Mrs. R. Osgood Mason of New York." (Miss Hurston's autograph to Mrs. Mason on the program of "Sun to Sun" reads: "To my Godmother, the mother of the Primitives, in faith and devotion, Zora Hurston" [ALP].)

Robert Hemenway, author of *Zora Neale Hurston: A Literary Biography*, writes that Zora did not meet Mrs. Mason until mid-September 1927. This author, through information from interviews in 1971 with Mrs. Katherine Garrison Chapin Biddle, a close family friend of Mrs. Mason, believes the date to have been earlier. According to Mrs. Biddle, whose younger sister, Cornelia Van A. Chapin, and brother, L. H. Paul Chapin, were also privy to Mrs. Mason's personal and business affairs, both Hughes and Hurston were receiving the personal support of Godmother during the summer of 1927.

69. See Zora Neale Hurston, *Dust Tracks on a Road*; Robert Hemenway, *Zora Neale Hurston: A Literary Biography*; and Arthur P. Davis, *From the Dark Tower: Afro-American Writers 1900 to 1960* (Washington, D.C., 1974).

70. Contract between Charlotte L. Mason and Zora Neale Hurston (ALP).

71. The exact date of Hurston's birth is not known. Some accounts give 1903, others 1901. Her biographer, Robert Hemenway, notes on page 13 of *Zora Neale Hurston* that "Hurston had been born in Eatonville on January 7, probably 1901; birth records of the period do not survive, and she was purposely inconsistent in the birth dates she dispensed during her lifetime, most of which were fictitious."

72. LH, *The Big Sea*, p. 296.

73. LH to Locke, October 8, 1927 (ALP).

74. LH, "Being Old," *The Crisis*, October 1927, p. 265; W. S. Braithwaite, ed., *Anthology of Magazine Verse* (New York, 1928), p. 181.

75. *Porgy*, adapted in 1927 by Dorothy and DuBose Heyward from the latter's 1925 novel of the same title, later became the George and Ira Gershwin musical *Porgy and Bess* (1935).

76. Mrs. R. O. Mason, one of whose primary interests was music, funded several white choral groups in New York City and carried on her late husband's interest in the New York Philharmonic Society. She did not encourage Hughes's interest in this music.

77. LH to Locke, February 27, 1928 (ALP).
78. LH, *The Big Sea*, p. 315.
79. LH to Locke, January 3, 1928 (ALP). In fact, Gwyn was fifteen years old.
80. LH, *The Big Sea*, p. 318.
81. LH to Locke, February 27, 1928 (ALP).
82. "Sunset Coney Island," *New Masses*, February 1928, p. 13; "Johannesburg Mines," *The Crisis*, February 1928, p. 52; and "Lover's Return," *The Carolina Magazine*, May 1928, p. 21. Hughes reviewed *Rainbow Round My Shoulder*, by Howard W. Odum, in *Opportunity*, May 1928, p. 49.
83. Hughes later published a poem about her: "Anne Spencer's Table," *The Crisis*, July 1930, p. 235.
84. Harold Jackman (1901–62), a New York school teacher interested in literature and the theatre arts, and a friend of Cullen's from early boyhood days in Baltimore, later established the Countee Cullen Memorial Collection in the Trevor Arnett Library, Atlanta University.
85. Francis Carco (1886–1958), French poet and novelist; Pio Baroja y Nessi (1872–1958), Spanish novelist; Maxim Gorki (1868–1936), Russian novelist and playwright. Hughes's reference is to the picaresque novels of these authors.
86. LH to Locke, March 1 [1928] (ALP).
87. Three of Hughes's poems—"Hurt," "Lady in Cabaret," and "Mazie Dies Alone in the City Hospital"—appeared that November in *Harlem*, p. 38, as did his short story, "Luani of the Jungles," pp. 7–11.
88. The result was *Four Lincoln University Poets*, ed. Langston Hughes (Lincoln University, 1930), which included the work of Waring Cuney, William Allyn Hill, Langston Hughes, and Edward Silvera.
89. LH, *The Big Sea*, pp. 306–7.
90. LH, "Cowards from the Colleges, *The Crisis*, August 1934, p. 228. (Hughes was careful to point out in his autobiography, published in 1940, that "Lincoln today is not the Lincoln of my survey . . . many changes have been made. There are Negro members of both the faculty and the Board of Trustees. . . ." [*The Big Sea*, p. 310].)
91. Natalie Curtis [Burlin] (1875–1921), an American musician whom Charlotte Mason encouraged to record the music, rites, and legends of American Indians, produced *The Indians' Book* in 1907. Its preface notes: "Grateful acknowledgment is made to . . . Mrs. Osgood Mason, whose help made possible the original undertaking, and without whose continued devotion the present edition could never have been accomplished." At Charlotte Mason's suggestion, Natalie Curtis also compiled collections titled *Negro Folk Songs* (New York, 1918) and *Songs and Tales from the Dark Continent* (New York, 1920).
92. LH, *The Big Sea*, p. 311. Copies of Hughes's survey, parts of which are quoted in *The Big Sea*, are available in the library collections of Lincoln University, Atlanta University, and Yale University.
93. "Dr. Brown's Decision" first appeared in *The Anvil*, May–June 1935, pp. 5–8; the title was later changed to "Professor" when published in *Laughing to Keep from Crying* (New York, 1952), pp. 97–105, and in *Something in Common* (New York, 1963), pp. 136–43.
94. Some of Hughes's works that refer to Booker T. Washington are *Not Without Laughter, The Big Sea, I Wonder as I Wander*, and several poems, as well as a radio script, "Booker T. Washington in Atlanta," which Hughes wrote at the invitation of the Columbia Broadcasting System and Tuskeegee Institute on the occasion of the issuance of a commemorative Booker T. Washington stamp by the Post Office Department. Hughes later referred to this script as a "special occasion script" "since we are not normally a part of radio drama, except as comedy relief." "Booker T. Washington in Atlanta," was published in Erik Barnouw, ed., *Radio Drama in Action: Twenty-five Plays of a Changing World* (New York, 1945), pp. 283–94.
95. Mason to LH, July 29, 1929. Dictated on that date to Katherine Garrison Chapin Biddle. Made available to the author through the private papers of Mrs. Biddle. Property of the Estate of Katherine Garrison Chapin Biddle (Mrs. Francis Biddle). Quoted by permission.
96. Mason to Hurston, August 18, 1929 (Private Papers of Mrs. Francis Biddle). Quoted by permission.
97. Mason to LH, August 3, 1929. Dictated to Katherine Garrison Chapin Biddle. Property

of the Estate of Katherine Garrison Chapin Biddle (Mrs. Francis Biddle). Quoted by permission.

98. LH, "The Negro Artist and the Racial Mountain," *The Nation*, June 23, 1926, p. 693.

99. *Appearances* (1925) by Garland Anderson; *Meek Mose* (1928) by Frank Wilson; and *Harlem* (1929) by Wallace Thurman (in collaboration with William Jordan Rapp, a white author).

100. LH, *The Big Sea*, p. 305.

101. Theresa Helburn figures in a subchapter to Hughes's second autobiographical volume, *I Wonder as I Wander*, as someone he meets at a dinner party given in his honor in Beverly Hills. They had actually met before.

102. Hughes, though he never admitted it publicly, was deeply dismayed by the Theatre Guild's attitude toward serious plays by black playwrights and by the Guild's role in what eventually happened to the comedy Miss Helburn suggested he write. It was occasionally his device, in autobiography as well as in fiction, to camouflage his feelings and convey his own thoughts through the words of someone else; we may assume he was doing this in *I Wonder as I Wander*, where an acquaintance angrily tells Theresa Helburn that the Theatre Guild is "nothing but a great louse on the tree of the American theater...a Broadway bloodsucker! a commercial leech'"—while Hughes sits on the sidelines trying to make peace (*I Wonder as I Wander*, pp. 303–6).

103. Review of *Not Without Laughter*, by Langston Hughes, *New York Times*, August 3, 1930, p. 6; *New York Herald Tribune*, July 27, 1930, p. 5; *The Nation*, August 6, 1930, p. 157; *The Saturday Review of Literature*, August 23, 1920, p. 69.

104. Sterling Brown, Review of *Not Without Laughter*, by Langston Hughes, *Opportunity*, September 1930, pp. 279–80; Walt Carmon, Review of *Not Without Laughter*, by Langston Hughes, *New Masses*, October 1930, pp. 17–18. (Excerpts of Hughes's novel appeared in *New Masses* prior to book publication.) Review of *Not Without Laughter*, by Langston Hughes, *Times Literary Supplement*, October 2, 1930, p. 778.

105. LH, *The Big Sea*, pp. 319–20.

106. One tangible result of the Cuban trip was the article about Ramos Blanco, "A Cuban Sculptor," *Opportunity*, November 1930, p. 334.

107. LH, *The Big Sea*, p. 324.

108. Zora Neale Hurston, *Dust Tracks on a Road*, p. 183.

109. Hurston to Mason, October 10, 1931 (ALP).

110. LH, *The Big Sea*, p. 325.

111. LH, "Afro-American Fragment," *The Crisis*, July 1930, p. 235. The physical form of the poem was later slightly changed from the original by Hughes. The form here corresponds to its printing in *Selected Poems*, p. 3, rather than to its original appearance in *The Crisis*.

112. Hughes's five poems in *The Crisis*, appeared in the July issue, p. 235; two poems in *Opportunity* in the June issue, p. 182; the June cover of the *Tuskeegee Messenger* carried a poem which appeared four months later in the *Epworth Era*, p. 93.

113. LH, *The Big Sea*, pp. 320–21. (The Waldorf-Astoria formally opened in 1931.)

114. See Faith Berry, ed., *Good Morning, Revolution: Uncollected Social Protest Writings by Langston Hughes* (New York, 1973), pp. 19–22.

115. LH, "Pride," *Opportunity*, December 1930, p. 371. The poem, which also appeared in Hughes's volume of poetry *A New Song* (New York, 1938), p. 16, was published some thirty years later under the title "Militant" in the posthumously printed poetry collection, *The Panther and the Lash* (New York 1926), p. 39. In the 1930 version of the poem, the final lines differ slightly from the later version (which is reproduced in the text). They read: "And so my fist is clenched— / Too weak I know— / But longing to be strong / To strike your face!"

116. LH, "Poet to Patron," *American Mercury*, June 1939, p. 147.

117. LH, *The Big Sea*, pp. 325–26.

118. Ibid., p. 328.

119. Ibid., pp. 327–28.

120. Ibid., p. 328.

Chapter 8: A Bone of Contention

1. Hughes's name appeared on the masthead of *New Masses* as a contributing editor from September 1930 until 1933, although he remained a regular contributor throughout the 1930s and for a time during the 1940s. The magazine was published until January 12, 1948, and was later superseded by *Masses and Mainstream*.

2. Michael Gold, "Carnevali and Other Essays," *New Masses*, December 1926, p. 18. Michael Gold (1893–1970), author of *Jews Without Money* and other works, was one of the founding editors and members of the executive board of *New Masses*. A well-known Communist, he lived on both the East Coast and the West Coast during his literary career and was a columnist for the *Daily Worker* and the *People's World*.

3. The manuscript of *De Turkey and de Law* was received by the Register of Copyrights October 28, 1930, and registered the following day as entry Number 52659 under the name Zora Neale Hurston.

4. Hurston to LH, January 18, 1931 (ABSP).

5. The Gilpin Players, named in 1922 after the actor Charles Gilpin, grew out of the Dumas Dramatic Club organized by Russell and Rowena Jelliffe in 1920. The Players' first theatre, the Karamu Theatre, remodeled from a pool room, opened in 1927.

6. Hurston to LH, January 20, 1931 (ABSP). A duplicate of this letter, sent by Zora Hurston to Mrs. Rufus Osgood Mason, appears in the Alain Locke Papers.

7. LH to Hurston, January 22, 1931 (ABSP).

8. Arthur Spingarn to LH, January 24, 1931 (ABSP).

9. Arthur Spingarn to LH, January 27, 1931 (ABSP).

10. Rowena Woodham Jelliffe to Arthur Spingarn, January 30, 1931 (ABSP).

11. Louise Thompson's patronage relationship with Charlotte Mason lasted less than a year and ended abruptly several months before Hughes's own break with the patron.

12. In a letter to Arthur Spingarn (March 15, 1931), LH confirms this date: "Have just had my tonsils out this week...." (ABSP).

13. The play was never produced. After Miss Hurston's death, part of Act 3 appeared, with Hughes's permission, in *Drama Critique*, Spring 1964, pp. 103–7.

14. Hurston (telegram) to Mason, February 3, 1931 (ALP).

15. Locke (telegram) to LH, January 29, 1931 (ALP). The original telegram reads slightly differently from Hughes's version of it in *The Big Sea*: "YOU HAVE HARMON AWARD SO WHAT MORE DO YOU WANT?" (*The Big Sea*, p. 334).

16. LH (telegram) to Locke, January 28, 1931 (ABSP).

17. Locke to Mason, January 29, 1931 (ALP).

18. Locke to Harmon Foundation, August 3, 1930 (Harmon Foundation Papers, MDLC). The Harmon Foundation (1928–1967), which made awards for Afro-American achievement in the arts and letters, was endowed by William Elmer Harmon, a wealthy white philanthropist. Alain Locke was one of the foundation's cultural advisors during the early years. When the foundation ceased its activities in 1967, its records went to the National Archives and Record Service and to the Library of Congress.

19. LH to Arthur Spingarn, January 30, 1931 (ABSP).

20. Locke to LH, February 5 [n.d.] (ALP).

21. Arthur Spingarn to LH, March 5, 1931 (ABSP).

22. LH to Arthur Spingarn, March 6, 1931 (ABSP).

23. Hurston to Mason, May 17, 1932 (ALP).

24. The volume was privately printed and distributed by Mrs. Amy Spingarn, who also did a frontispiece drawing of Hughes for the collection. "Drum," one of the poems iterating the death theme, was published in the spring 1931 issue of *Poetry Quarterly*, p. 12, along with two other poems, "Request to Genius" and "Snake," not included in *Dear Lovely Death*.

Chapter 9: South of the Border

1. LH, "Flight," *Opportunity*, July 1930, p. 182.

2. LH, *I Wonder as I Wander* (New York, 1956), p. 4. In this chapter I have drawn upon *I*

Wonder as I Wander for details of Hughes's life in the Caribbean and in New York in 1931. Quotations in the text not otherwise attributed are taken from pages 11, 15, 16, 19, 25, 26, 28, 29, 31, and 47.

3. Mary McLeod Bethune (1875–1955), Afro-American educator, was founder in 1904 of Daytona Normal & Industrial Institute for Negro Girls (later Bethune-Cookman College), of which she was president until 1942. Appointed an official of the National Youth Administration by Franklin Delano Roosevelt, she was a friend and confidante of Eleanor Roosevelt, and founder and organizer in 1935 of the National Council of Negro Women.

4. April 8, 1931.

5. "Conversación con Langston Hughes," *Diario de la Marina*, March 9, 1930.

6. For the Cuban journal *Social*, José Antonio Fernández de Castro translated Hughes's poem "I, Too." His essay appeared in March 1930. His first meeting with Hughes came through a letter of introduction from their mutual friend, Miguel Covarrubias.

7. LH, "White Shadows in a Black Land," *The Crisis*, May 1932, p. 157.

8. The Langston Hughes Papers, Fisk.

9. The poem "Langston Hughes" was reprinted and translated by Edna Worthley Underwood in *The Poets of Haiti, 1782–1934* (Portland, Maine, 1934), p. 66. It appeared in French in the *Haiti Journal*, October 20, 1931. See also Langston Hughes and Arna Bontemps, eds., *The Poetry of the Negro: 1746–1949* (Garden City, N.Y., 1949).

10. Gerardo Machado (1871–1939) was president of Cuba from 1925 to 1933.

11. LH, "My Adventures as a Social Poet," *Phylon*, Fall 1947.

12. Documents on Hughes received through the Freedom of Information Act indicate that an FBI file was begun on the poet in 1940 and continued until shortly before his death in 1967, although he had been removed from an "active" file to an "inactive" file by the late 1950s.

13. Ethel Dudley Harper (August 15, 1887?–January 6, 1968) had a show-business career during her youth and occasionally was confused with Ethel Ernestine Harper (1904–79). The latter had appeared in the theatrical productions *Hot Mikado* and *Negro Follies*, and later became better known as "Aunt Jemima" in a Quaker Oats campaign of the 1950s. The two women were not related, and neither was a relative of Hughes's.

14. Full details of the *Mule Bone* dispute are given in Chapter 8.

15. Hurston to Mason, August 14, 1931 (ALP).

16. Hurston to Mason, January 20, 1931 (ALP).

17. Mason to Hurston, January 20, 1932 (ALP).

18. Robert Hemenway, *Zora Neale Hurston: A Literary Biography* (Urbana, Ill., 1977), p. 127.

19. Hurston to Mason, July 23, 1931, October 15, 1931, and February 29, 1932 (ALP).

20. Locke to Mason, May 7, 1932 (ALP).

21. Locke to Mason, May 19, 1932, "Special Memorandum Re: Louise Thompson" (ALP).

22. Locke to Mason, March 5, 1931 (ALP).

23. LH to Locke, November 20, 1933 (ALP). Affixed to Hughes's letter is a note in Locke's handwriting—"sent *Negro Poetry*." However, it is not known whether he ever actually replied to LH's request.

24. April 10, 1931.

25. Excerpt of LH, "Scottsboro," *Opportunity*, December 1931.

26. Seven years later, in 1938, "Union" was reprinted in Hughes's anthology *A New Song*. There he added two lines at the end: "And the rule of greed's upheld / That must be ended."

27. LH to Arthur Spingarn, n.d. [1931] (ABSP).

28. LH, "The Twenties: Harlem and Its Negritude," *African Forum*, Spring 1966, p. 11.

Chapter 10: On the Cross of the South

1. LH, *I Wonder as I Wander*, p. 43. For this chapter I have drawn upon *I Wonder as I Wander* for Hughes's poetry tour of the South and West. Quotations in the text not otherwise attributed are taken from pages 46, 47, 48, 52, 53, 55, 61, 62, 63, 64, 65, and 66.

2. In *I Wonder as I Wander* Hughes inaccurately refers to his essay as "Southern Gentlemen,

White Women and Black Boys." As published in *Contempo* on December 1, 1931, it was "Southern Gentlemen, White Prostitutes, Mill Owners and Negroes."

3. Dr. E. C. L. Adams's *Congaree Sketches*, based on folk tales by South Carolina blacks, was a book Hughes knew well, for Charlotte Mason had once given it to him and praised two of his poems quoted in the foreword by Paul Green. In 1928, Adams had published a similar volume, *Nigger to Nigger*, whose dialect he described as "pure nigger." If Hughes ever knew that, he never mentioned it in *I Wonder as I Wander*, where he presents an anecdote of his South Carolina meeting with Adams and refers to him erroneously as "A. C. L. Adams."

4. Hughes appreciated the cordial welcome he received from Will Alexander Percy in February 1932, but he later had mixed feelings about Percy's 1941 nonfiction book *Lanterns on the Levee*, which portrayed the attitudes of Southern aristocratic plantation owners toward Afro-Americans after Emancipation.

5. LH, "My Most Humiliating Jim Crow Experience," *Negro Digest*, May 1945, pp. 33–34; reprinted in *The Langston Hughes Reader* (New York, 1958), pp. 500–501.

6. Sterling Brown, "Arna Bontemps: Co-Worker, Comrade," *Black World*, September 1973, p. 95.

7. LH, "Alabama Earth," *Tuskeegee Messenger*, June 28, 1930, cover; ibid., *Epworth Era*, October 1930, p. 93.

8. LH, "Red Flag on Tuskeegee," *The Afro-American*, June 25, 1932. The same poem, with slight emendation, was published under the title "Open Letter to the South" in *A New Song*, pp. 27–28.

9. Loren Miller, "South O.K. for $5000 a Year Negroes, Says Langston Hughes," *The Afro-American*, June 25, 1932.

10. "August 19th" [1938] was originally printed in editions of the *Daily Worker* and distributed by the Communist Party in Birmingham in support of the Scottsboro Defense (Langston Hughes Papers, JWJ, Beinecke). Norris's death sentence was commuted on July 5, 1928 by Governor Bibbs Graves to life imprisonment. Eleven years younger than Hughes, Norris was destined to outlive him, and to be the last survivor of the nine Scottsboro Boys. He was formally pardoned by Governor George C. Wallace, October 25, 1976.

11. LH, "Childhood of Jimmy," *The Crisis*, May 1927, p. 84.

12. LH, "Trek to Texas" (Langston Hughes Papers, Fisk).

13. LH to Sullivan, January 31, 1933 (NSP, Bancroft).

14. Fisk.

15. LH (telegram) to Thompson, March 11, 1932 (Private papers of Louise Thompson Patterson). Quoted by permission.

16. LH (telegram) to Thompson, June 6, 1932 (Private papers of Louise Thompson Patterson). Quoted by permission.

17. Fisk.

18. Ibid.

Chapter 11: Black and White

1. Locke to Mason, [June 1932?] (ALP).

2. Locke to Mason, June 9, 1932 (ALP).

3. Ibid.

4. Hughes, in *I Wonder as I Wander*, writes, erroneously, of "crossing the Atlantic on the *Bremen*," perhaps because the group members did originally plan to sail on that ship until they were booked on the *Europa*.

5. Locke to Mason, June 16, 1932 (ALP).

6. Ibid.

7. In addition to the chairman, W. A. Domingo, the membership of the interracial American planning committee seeking volunteers for the film included Bessye Bearden, Malcolm Cowley, Waldo Frank, Rose McClendon, and John Henry Hammond, none of whom made the trip to Russia with the group of twenty-two. Hughes, Miller, Moon, and Thompson were originating sponsors who did go to make the film.

8. W. A. Domingo, May 31, 1932, letter written as chairman of the Co-Operating Committee for Production of a Soviet Film on Negro Life. Courtesy of Louise Thompson Patterson.

9. LH, *I Wonder as I Wander*, p. 70. The twenty-two members of the *Black and White* film group were: Lawrence O. Alberga, agricultural worker; Matthew Crawford, insurance clerk; Sylvia Garner, singer-actress; Leonard Hill, social service worker; Langston Hughes, poet-author; Katherine Jenkins, social worker; Mildred Jones, art student; Juanita Lewis, singer; Mollie Lewis, graduate student; Thurston McNary Lewis, actor; Allen McKenzie, salesman; Loren Miller, editor; Frank C. Montero, student; Henry Lee Moon, reporter; Lloyd Patterson, paperhanger; Theodore R. Poston, reporter; Wayland Rudd, actor; George Sample, law student; Neil Homer Smith, journalist-postal clerk; Louise Thompson, labor research assistant; Dorothy West, writer-actress; Constance White, social worker.

10. Ibid., p. 70. In this chapter I have drawn upon *I Wonder as I Wander* for information on Hughes's trip to Russia. Quotations in the text not otherwise attributed are taken from pages 71, 76, 79, 80, 87, 89, 90, 92, 94, 95, 98, 99.

11. Ibid.

12. Locke to Mason, August 17, 1932 (ALP).

13. LH, "Moscow and Me," *International Literature*, July 1933, p. 61.

14. Lydia Filatova, "Langston Hughes, American Writer," *International Literature*, Spring, 1933, pp. 99–111.

15. Louise Thompson, "The Soviet Film," *The Crisis*, February 1933, pp. 37, 46.

16. Locke to Mason, September 14, 1932 (ALP).

17. "Langston Hughes Spikes Lies on Negro Film," *Daily Worker*, September 8, 1932, p. 3.

18. "Promise to Print Negro Film Facts," *Daily Worker*, October 24, 1932, p. 2. See also "Soviet Abandons Negro Photoplay," *New York Amsterdam News*, August 17, 1932, p. 1; "Claims Russians Will Make Film," *New York Amsterdam News*, August 31, 1932, p. 16.

19. *Daily Worker*, September 8, 1932, p. 3.

20. "Seek to Produce Boss Negro Film," *Daily Worker*, October 14, 1932, p. 3. See also "Newspaper Men Expose Tactics of Soviet in Making Film," *The Afro-American*, October 15, 1932, p. 2.

21. "Soviet Film Policy Refutes Slanders about Negro Movie," *Daily Worker*, October 15, 1932, p. 4.

23. *The New York Amsterdam News*, November 23, 1932, p. 5.

24. *Daily Worker*, September 24, 1932, p. 3.

25. W. R. Benet, *The Saturday Review of Literature*, November 12, 1932, p. 241.

Chapter 12: Dust and Rainbows

1. LH, "Going South in Russia," *The Crisis*, June 1934, pp. 162–63. See also *Good Morning, Revolution*, p. 77.

2. LH, "The Soviet Union and Color," *The Chicago Defender*, June 15, 1946, p. 14. See also *Good Morning, Revolution*, pp. 84–86.

3. No poem with the English title "Shoeshine Boy" exists in Hughes's literary canon. Koestler's reference was undoubtedly to Hughes's poem "Porter," which was translated into German and included with some thirty of his verses in the anthology *Africa Singt*, edited by A. Nussbaum and published in Vienna in 1929.

4. Arthur Koestler, *The Invisible Writing* (New York, 1954), p. 137.

5. Ibid., p. 136.

6. Ibid., p. 134.

7. *I Wonder as I Wander*, p. 120. For this chapter I have drawn upon *I Wonder as I Wander* for details about Hughes's life in the Soviet Union. Quotations in the text not otherwise attributed are taken from pages 110, 111, 113, 114, 115, 116, 120, 122, 126–27, 132, 143, 176–77.

8. *The Selected Works of V. I. Lenin*, English edition (Moscow, 1952), Vol. 1, Part 1.

9. The Special Collections Division of Fisk University Library and the James Weldon Johnson Memorial Collection of the Beinecke Rare Book and Manuscript Library at Yale University both contain early drafts of *I Wonder as I Wander*.

10. LH, "The Soviet Union and Color," *loc. cit.*

11. Arthur Koestler, *The Invisible Writing*, p. 140.

12. Ibid.

13. Ibid., p. 149.

14. LH, "Farewell to Mahomet," *Travel*, February 1935, pp. 28–31.

15. *Selected Works of V. I. Lenin, loc. cit.*

16. LH, "The Soviet Union and Health," *The Chicago Defender*, July 20, 1946, p. 14. Reprinted in *Good Morning, Revolution*, pp. 88–90.

17. LH, "Two Somewhat Different Epigrams, #1," in Rolfe Humphries, ed., *New Poems by American Poets* (New York 1957), p. 80; ibid., in Robert Hayden, ed., *Kaleidoscope* (New York, 1967), p. 89.

18. Gafur Gulam, "On the Turksib Roads," trans. Langston Hughes and Nina Zorokovina, with the author's assistance, appeared in *International Literature* 5 (1933–34), p. 67.

19. LH, "The Soviet Union and Women," *The Chicago Defender*, June 29, 1946, p. 14. Reprinted in *Good Morning, Revolution*, pp. 86–88.

20. LH to Sullivan, January 31, 1933 (NSP, Bancroft).

21. LH, "Light and the Soviet Union," *The Chicago Defender*, August 10, 1946, p. 14. Reprinted in *Good Morning, Revolution*, pp. 92–94.

Chapter 13: Zero Hour

1. *I Wonder as I Wander*, p. 194. For this chapter I have drawn upon *I Wonder as I Wander* for details of Hughes's life in Moscow. Quotations not otherwise attributed in the text are taken from pages 147, 194, 196, 213, 230, 232, and 256.

2. LH to Sullivan, January 31, 1933 (NSP, Bancroft).

3. LH, "Negroes in Moscow," *International Literature* 4 (1933), p. 79.

4. *Krasnaya Nov*, a literary and scientific journal founded in 1921, had the early backing of Lenin and his wife, N. K. Krupskaya. It ceased publication around 1935. "Ballad of the Landlord" appeared in the November 1933 issue.

5. *Opportunity*, January 1933, p. 23.

6. Alain Locke, "Outstanding Books of 1932," *Opportunity*, January 3, 1933, pp. 14–18.

7. Locke to Mason, September 14, 1932 (ALP).

8. Si-lan Chen Leyda interview with author, November 28, 1977.

9. Si-lan Chen [Leyda] to LH, December 3, 1934 (Beinecke). Quoted by permission of Si-lan Chen Leyda.

10. "Poem" first appeared in *The Crisis* in May 1925, and was reprinted in *The Weary Blues* and *The Dream Keeper*. Hughes never publicly identified F.S., but it is conjectured he was Ferdinand Smith, a merchant seaman whom the poet first met in New York in the early 1920s. Nine years older than Hughes, Smith first influenced the poet to go to sea. Born in Jamaica in 1893, Smith spent most of his life as a ship steward and political activist at sea—and later in New York as a resident of Harlem. In 1936 he led a strike as a steward on the S.S. *Horace Lukenbach*, and later he helped organize the National Maritime Union, of which he became vice president and then national executive secretary. Hughes attended and was a sponsor of a dinner in Smith's honor at the Hotel Commodore in New York City, September 21, 1944—the year Smith resigned his post with the National Maritime Union following publicity over his alleged Communist activities. He was expelled from the union six months after he was arrested in 1948 as an illegal alien and detained on Ellis Island. In 1951, under pressure from the Immigration and Naturalization Service, he was deported with his wife to Jamaica. He died there in 1961. Hughes maintained a lasting, if distant, friendship with Smith until his death.

11. LH, "Spring for Lovers," *The Crisis*, July 1930, p. 235.

12. Si-lan Chen Leyda to author.

13. From a sheaf of poems and a letter dated February 3, 1933, Si-lan Chen [Leyda] to LH (Langston Hughes Papers, Beinecke). Quoted by permission.

14. John Sutton to author.

15. Marie Seton to author.

16. The closest Hughes came to publication of *Dark People of the Soviet Union* was his booklet *A Negro Looks at Soviet Central Asia*, issued by Iskra Revolutii, the Moscow Cooperative Publishing Society, in 1934.

17. Egon Erwin Kisch, *Changing Asia* (New York, 1935).

18. Hughes's translations of three poems by Mayakovsky exist in typescript in the Fisk University Library, Special Collections. Translated with the assistance of Lydia Filatova, they are "Black and White," "Syphilis," and "Hygiene." The latter was published in *I Wonder as I Wander*, page 198.

19. LH, trans., "Magnitogorsk," by Louis Aragon, *International Literature* 4 (1933–34), pp. 82–83.

Chapter 14: Chains of the East

1. *I Wonder as I Wander*, p. 240. In this chapter I have drawn upon *I Wonder as I Wander* for details of Hughes's life in China. Quotations not otherwise attributed in the text are taken from pages 242, 246, 248, 249, 250, 268, 277, 278, 281.

2. National Archives, File 800.00B—Hughes, Langston, listed as "The Communistic Activities of Langston Hughes." This file remained confidential and unopen to the public until after Hughes's death.

3. *New York Times*, July 25, 1933, p. D7. Although Hughes says in *I Wonder as I Wander* Stanley Wood was the *Times* reporter in Japan at the time, no such by-line appears on *Times* reports on Japanese affairs during that period. The AP dispatch carried no by-line.

4. National Archives, File 800.00B.

Chapter 15: Blood on the Fields

1. LH, *I Wonder as I Wander*, p. 282.

2. LH, *Famous American Negroes* (New York, 1954), p. 127.

3. LH to Sullivan, June 12, 1933 (NSP, Bancroft).

4. Ibid.

5. LH to Sullivan, December 25, 1933 (NSP, Bancroft).

6. LH to Sullivan, n.d. [1933] (NSP, Bancroft). Sullivan appears to have kept this information and the identity of the Englishman confidential even from his own best friend (and later literary executor), Benjamin Harrison Lehman, a professor who, in correspondence with the author in 1975, said he did not know who the Englishman was.

7. LH to Sullivan, n.d. [1933] (NSP, Bancroft).

8. Maxim Lieber to LH, July 13, 1933 (Beinecke). Quoted by permission of Maxim Lieber.

9. Maxim Lieber to LH, October 4, 1933 (Beinecke). Quoted by permission of Maxim Lieber.

10. Maxim Lieber to LH, November 15, 1933 (Beinecke). Quoted by permission of Maxim Lieber.

11. Arnold Gingrich, ed., *Bedside Esquire* (New York, 1940), pp. 97–103.

12. Editors, *The Atlantic Monthly*, to Lieber, January 8, 1934 (Beinecke).

13. Lieber to LH, April 5, 1934 (Beinecke). Quoted by permission of Maxim Lieber.

14. Lieber to LH, January 3, 1934 (Beinecke). Quoted by permission of Maxim Lieber.

15. Horace Gregory, *Books*, July 1, 1934, p. 4.

16. *New York Times Book Review*, July 1, 1934, p. 6.

17. John Chamberlain, *New York Times*, June 28, 1934, p. L21.

18. Alain Locke, *Survey Graphic*, November 1934, p. 565.

19. Locke to Mason, June 28, 1934 (ALP).

20. Locke to Mason, March 1, 1934 (ALP).

21. Rufus Osgood Mason, "Psychic Element in Therapeutics," *Hypnotism and Suggestion* (New York, 1901), p. 37.

22. LH, *Daily Worker*, April 2, 1934, p. 7.

23. LH, *Daily Worker*, October 9, 1934, p. 5.

24. LH, "People Have No Shoes," *Daily Worker*, May 7, 1934, p. 5.

25. The title of Hughes's letter to the editors of these publications varied—"Free Jacques Roumain," "Jacques Roumain Imprisoned," or "An Appeal for Jacques Roumain"—though the text in all was the same.

26. Ella Winter to author, June 7, 1978.

27. Statement given to the press by Lincoln Steffens and quoted by Hughes to Lieber, August 8, 1934 (Beinecke).

28. Ella Winter to author, June 7, 1978.

29. LH, *I Wonder as I Wander*, p. 284.

30. Darwin Turner, ed., *The Wayward and the Seeking: A Collection of Writings by Jean Toomer* (Washington, D.C., 1980), p. 127.

31. Locke to Mason, September 30, 1934 (ALP).

32. Isidor Schneider, "Left and Leftward Writers Series," Review of *The Ways of White Folks, New Masses*, September 25, 1934, pp. 25–26.

Chapter 16: Mailbox for the Dead

1. *Controversy*, October 25, 1934, p. 4. (*Controversy* was a forerunner of *Pacific Weekly*, taking the latter name in January 1935.)

2. LH, *A Negro Looks at Soviet Central Asia* (Moscow: Cooperative Publishing Society of Foreign Workers in the U.S.S.R., 1934).

3. Locke to Mason, December 10, 1934 (ALP).

4. The only John Williams known to any of Hughes's relatives or friends at the time was a *Pittsburgh Courier* correspondent who went east to live briefly and then returned to Los Angeles, where he later suffered a nervous breakdown. He died in the early 1960s.

5. Except for Noel Sullivan, who had died before the author conducted research and interviews for this biography, all the named persons were questioned about Hughes's putative marriage and divorce. All disclaimed any knowledge of such events, as did Professor Benjamin Lehman, executor of the Noel Sullivan Estate.

6. Office of the County Recorder, Monterrey, California, to author, 1975.

7. Winter to author, June 7, 1978.

8. The copyright of *Blood on the Fields* is registered under the names Langston Hughes and Ella Winter, dated August 8, 1934, and recorded August 13, 1934. The copy which Hughes retained in his personal papers bears the title *Harvest*, by Langston Hughes, Ella Winter, and Ann Hawkins, but it was never copyrighted under that title. As Ella Winter acknowledged in 1978: "Langston was disturbed a bit by the implications of the title that it might be thought to be the object we women wear once a month. . . . We may well have changed the name of our play to *Harvest* since Langston felt we could not call it *Blood on the Fields* for obvious reasons" (Winter to author, June 7, 1978).

9. Winter to author, *op. cit.*

10. The author's father, Attorney Theodore M. Berry, traveled to Reno in 1977 and personally conducted a legal search of the files of divorce records of the Second Judicial District Court of Washoe County Courthouse, in an effort to obtain evidence of a divorce granted to Langston Hughes (or James Langston Hughes) in 1934 or any succeeding year. None was found. Additionally, the author in 1976 wrote to the county clerk of each county in Nevada to determine whether local records reflected any divorce action ever filed under the name Langston Hughes. All replies were negative.

11. Documented by the author's research from material obtained under the Freedom of Information Act.

12. Evidence from declassified reports under the Freedom of Information Act.

13. Information from the Deputy Assistant Secretary of State, Office of the Assistant Secretary for Consular Affairs, Department of State, to author, February 2, 1978.

14. Arna Bontemps interview with author, 1970.

15. LH, *I Wonder as I Wander*, p. 286. Hughes's life in Reno is covered only sparsely in *I Wonder as I Wander*; I have drawn only upon pages 286 and 287 in quoting from this text. All other information about the Reno period is drawn from personal research and primary sources. For the portion of this chapter dealing with Hughes's life in Mexico in 1934 and 1935, quotations in the text not otherwise attributed are taken from pages 289, 290, 292, 293, and 295 of *I Wonder as I Wander*.

16. Information obtained by Attorney Theodore M. Berry in Reno, Nevada, through a legal

title search and on-site observation of the property of 521 Elko Avenue. A frame house when Hughes lived in it, the dwelling was later renovated as a brick house on the same site.

17. Langston Hughes, "The Negro," a foreword to Jacob Burck, *Hunger and Revolt* (Daily Worker, 1935), pp. 141–42. Hughes's contribution appeared along with pieces by ten other authors in this book of satirical cartoons.

18. Maxim Lieber, who was eighty years old when the author spoke with him in 1977, had suffered two strokes and did not trust his memory for exact details as to why Hughes may possibly have removed a page from a December 24, 1934, letter which Lieber wrote him about the contents and publication of "The Vigilantes Knock at My Door." A page of that letter—with a reference to the article—appears to have been expunged, while all other details concerning other matters therein remain intact.

19. The author is grateful to George Houston Bass, literary Executor-Trustee of the Langston Hughes Estate, and to Arnold Rampersad, the official biographer, for permission to examine the unpublished manuscript of "The Vigilantes Knock at My Door" in the Langston Hughes Papers at the Yale University Library, in order to compare the typescript with the article of the same title published in *New Masses*.

20. Lieber to LH, December 5, 1934 (Beinecke). Quoted by permission of Maxim Lieber.

21. Gibbs to Lieber, January 28, 1935.

22. LH to Sullivan, October 24, 1934 (NSP, Bancroft).

23. Langston Hughes, excerpt of "Revised Version of Remarks Concerning an Analysis of 'On the Road,' " June 1957 (Schomburg).

24. LH to Sullivan, October 4, 1934 (NSP, Bancroft). (Hughes's story "Mailbox for the Dead" is not known to have been published under that or any other title.)

25. Oscar Graeve, editorial staff of *The Delineator*, to Lieber, January 29, 1935 (Beinecke).

26. The letters are in the Wallace Thurman Papers, JWJ, Beinecke. In the judgment and firm belief of this biographer, who examined the original correspondence, several letters attributed to Hughes and allegedly signed by him in the Wallace Thurman Papers bear no resemblance to Hughes's tone, style, or penmanship (in the signature). Of five letters supposedly from Hughes, this biographer would vouchsafe that only two were actually composed and signed by Langston Hughes. The remaining three, all undated and typed on the same kind of paper, as if they were composed during the same sitting, are suspect. While they contain allusions to Hughes's personal life and career, the signatures appear to be forgeries.

The Wallace Thurman Papers were made available to the Yale University Library through Carl Van Vechten, who initiated plans for the James Weldon Johnson Memorial Collection and began locating Afro-American manuscript materials for it in 1941. On February 28, 1942, Harold Jackman wrote Van Vechten: "You are indebted to the Misses Helene Grant and Georgia Washington for the Wallace Thurman material. . . ." Helene Grant and Georgia Washington, both friends of Thurman during the Harlem Renaissance, located his literary papers and saved them after his death. Thurman died intestate, leaving no will, no estate, and no literary executor.

It is not known whether Hughes ever saw, or verified as his own, all the letters attributed to him in the Thurman Papers at Yale—to which he began donating his own material in 1942 (also for the JWJ Collection). But he saw enough there to cause him to write to Arna Bontemps on May 17, 1942: "I would just as leave you did *not* give my letters away. How about yours? Do you want them to go to Yale? The ones of mine to Wallie look very juvenile now. I do not like the idea of writing to one's friends—for posterity and the world" (In Charles Nichols, ed., *Arna Bontemps—Langston Hughes Letters* [New York, 1980], pp. 98–99).

27. LH (telegram) to Thurman, March 12, 1932 (Wallace Thurman Papers, JWJ).

28. Granville Hicks, "Revolutionary Literature of 1934," *New Masses*, January 1, 1935, p. 36. Hicks, one of the foremost literary critics of the thirties, was editor of the anthology *Proletarian Literature in the United States* (1935), which included three of Hughes's poems: "Ballad of Lenin," "Sharecroppers," and "Park Bench."

29. Hughes's speech and others evolving out of the first Congress (April 26, 27, 28, 1935) were published in Henry Hart, ed., *American Writers Congress* (New York, 1935). See also "To Negro Writers," in *Good Morning, Revolution*, 125–26.

30. LH to Marie and Doug Short, May 20, 1935 (Marie Short Papers, Bancroft).

31. Ibid.

32. Ibid.

33. Ibid.

34. See LH, trans., "Three Mexican Stories," *Partisan Review*, July 1935, pp. 20–27; idem., "The Protector," *Pacific Weekly*, October 28, 1935, pp. 200–201; idem., "Juice of the Cane," *Pacific Weekly*, June 22, 1936; and idem., "The Survivor," *Pacific Weekly*, September 7, 1936, pp. 150–51.

35. Lieber to LH, June 11, 1935 (Beinecke). Quoted by permission of Maxim Lieber.

36. LH to Short, *op. cit.*

37. LH to Sullivan, May 22, 1935 (NSP, Bancroft).

38. LH to Sullivan, March 28, 1935 (NSP, Bancroft).

39. Si-lan Chen [Leyda] to LH, June 4, 1935 (Beinecke). Quoted by permission.

40. Si-lan Chen [Leyda] to LH, n.d. (Beinecke). Quoted by permission.

41. Si-lan Chen [Leyda] to LH, June 26, 1934 (Beinecke). Quoted by permission.

42. Si-lan Chen [Leyda] to LH, December 3, 1934 (Beinecke). Quoted by permission.

Chapter 17: Honor and Hunger

1. The undated, unpublished draft is in Hughes's papers in the JWJ Collection, Beinecke Rare Book and Manuscript Library, Yale University. Another piece, "Negro Art and Claude McKay," was published in *The New Sign*, October 24, 1931.

2. Claude McKay himself confessed to his disagreements with Nancy Cunard in "On Belonging to a Minority Group," the final chapter of his autobiography, *A Long Way from Home*, published in 1937.

3. The pamphlet, divided into two sections, was privately printed by Nancy Cunard in 1931 and concerned her unnamed friend, Henry Crowder, an Afro-American musician whom she met in Venice in 1928 and to whom she dedicated her *Negro* anthology in 1934.

4. Loren Miller, "Mail-Order Dictatorship," *New Masses*, April 16, 1935, pp. 10–12.

5. Ibid. Miller is quoting from Embree's *Brown America: The Story of a New Race* (New York, 1931), p. 285.

6. LH to Sullivan, August 31, 1935 (NSP, Bancroft).

7. Leon Edel, ed., *Edmund Wilson: The Thirties* (New York, 1980), p. 92.

8. LH to Sullivan, September 13, 1935 (NSP, Bancroft).

9. "Big Meeting" was reprinted in *Fiction Parade* (September 1935) and "Spanish Blood" in *Modern Story* (October 1935).

10. LH, *I Wonder as I Wander*, p. 310.

11. Ibid., p. 312.

12. LH to Marie Short, October 16, 1935 (Marie Short Papers, Bancroft).

13. LH, *I Wonder as I Wander*, p. 313.

14. Review of *Mulatto*, *Theatre Arts Monthly* 19, no. 12 (December 1935), p. 902.

15. Locke to Mason, October 30, 1935 (ALP).

16. Arthur Spaeth, "When the Jack Hollers Is Comic 'Tobacco Road,' " *Cleveland News*, April 29, 1936, p. 18.

17. LH to Sullivan, January 29, 1936 (NSP, Bancroft).

18. *Opportunity*, October 1937, p. 340.

19. Ibid.

20. Richard Wright, "Joe Louis Uncovers Dynamite," *New Masses*, October 8, 1935, p. 18.

21. LH, "The Twenties: Harlem and Its Negritude," *African Forum*, Spring 1966, p. 12.

22. John P. Davis, secretary and organizer of the National Negro Congress, quoted from page 5 of the booklet "Resolutions of the National Negro Congress"; statements also appear in documents obtained under the Freedom of Information Act.

23. Arna Bontemps indicated in an interview with the author in 1970 that during the mid-1930s Hughes considered writing a proletarian novel set in Chicago, because the Midwestern metropolis symbolized to him "an American Shanghai" and the center of historic events such as the Haymarket Riot of 1886 and the "Red Summer" race riots of 1919. Not having been privy to the notes which Hughes wrote for the novel—and because no such novel

survives—I have relied on Bontemps's personal recollections of Hughes's intentions. Hughes's authorized biographer, Arnold Rampersad, has literary evidence that Hughes hoped to write a trilogy, the first novel of which was *Not Without Laughter* (a portion of which is set in Chicago in 1918). In a sequel, Hughes planned to have his protagonist, Sandy, return to Chicago after World War I. Rampersad's biography, based on Hughes's complete personal papers, should be considered the definitive source on the subject.

24. LH to Sullivan, January 29, 1936 (NSP, Bancroft).

25. Si-lan Chen [Leyda] to LH, August 16, 1936.

26. LH to Sullivan, May 27, 1936 (NSP, Bancroft).

27. Ibid.

28. *New Masses*, December 15, 1936, p. 34. Reprinted in *Good Morning, Revolution*, p. 5.

29. Ella Winter, *New Masses*, August 18, 1936, p. 11.

30. *Pacific Weekly*, March 15, 1935, p. 2.

31. LH to Roy Blackburn, August 26, 1936 (Bancroft). The complete papers of Ella Winter, including all correspondence from Langston Hughes, were sealed at the Yale University Library at the time this biography was written. Only letters from Ella Winter to the author are quoted in this book.

32. Locke to Mason, February 29, 1936 (ALP).

33. LH, "The Twenties: Harlem and Its Negritude," *African Forum*, Spring 1966, p. 11. There is literary disagreement about whether Hughes introduced Ellison and Wright in 1936 or 1937. It is a fact that Ellison arrived in New York City in June 1936 and stayed at the Harlem YMCA, where, within a few days, he met Hughes, who also stayed there for most of the month. From Hughes's account, it appears that he introduced the two authors in 1936, before Richard Wright moved to New York (in 1937). This dating is disputed by Michael Fabre, Wright's biographer, who gives June 1937 as the date of the meeting in *The Unfinished Quest of Richard Wright*. Ellison's recollection of the exact year appears uncertain, and none appears in Robert G. O'Meally's *Craft of Ralph Ellison*, the first biographical-critical work on Ellison. In an interview with Hollie West, published in the *Washington Post*, August 21, 1973, Ellison acknowledges, "I had read some things of Wright's in the *New Masses* and I asked Hughes about him and Hughes wrote Wright saying that [there was] this young writer who was interested and it turned out that Wright was coming to New York. . . ." While he mentioned no year, Ellison did say he met Wright before going to Dayton in February 1937 and staying there for seven months following the death of his mother. This might be taken as determinative, if it were not established that Ellison had returned to New York City by June 30, 1937, when Hughes sailed for Europe on the S.S. *Aquitania*: a photograph of Hughes's friends at the pier shows Ralph Ellison among the well-wishers—and a note in Hughes's own hand identifies him. Considering that Hughes was in New York City infrequently and was living in Cleveland during most of 1936 and 1937, until his departure for Europe in June 1937 (where he remained until January 1938), the exact month when he introduced Ellison and Wright must remain conjecture. See also "The Alain Locke Symposium," *Harvard Advocate*, Spring 1974, pp. 9–28.

34. "The Communist Convention," *New Masses*, June 30, 1936, p. 3.

35. Bonds to LH, January 26, 1937 (Langston Hughes Papers, Fisk). The Register of Copyrights records show that Langston Hughes wrote the lyrics to "That Sweet Silent Love" and Margaret Bonds composed the music. The song was copyrighted in both their names, March 18, 1937.

36. "The Song of Spain" was published that same year in *International Literature* 6 (1937), p. 67, and in *Deux Poèmes*, ed. Nancy Cunard and Pablo Neruda, before being reprinted in Hughes's collection *A New Song*, in 1938.

37. LH, *I Wonder as I Wander*, p. 315.

38. In a letter dated July 8, 1937, *The Baltimore Afro-American* requested the assistance of the U.S. State Department in arranging for Hughes to go to Spain from France as a correspondent. There is no evidence that such official permission was ever granted. Hughes was not denied a passport; his passport had been reissued February 20, 1936.

39. LH, *I Wonder as I Wander*, p. 315.

40. LH, "Note in Music," *Opportunity*, April 1937, p. 104.

Chapter 18: Nightmare Dream

1. LH, "Too Much of Race," speech for the Second International Writers Congress, Paris, July 17, 1937. *The Volunteer for Liberty*, August, 1937; *The Crisis*, September 1937; reprinted in Nancy Cunard, "Three Negro Poets," *Left Review*, October 1937. See Faith Berry, ed., *Good Morning, Revolution*, (New York, 1973), pp. 97–99.

2. Léon Damas interview with author, Washington, D.C., April 1973.

3. See Mercer Cook, "Some Literary Contacts: African, West Indian, Afro-American," Conference on Comparative Literature, University of Southern California, 1970, vol. 6; reprinted in Lloyd Brown, ed., *The Black Writer in Africa and the Americas* (Los Angeles, 1973).

4. John Banting, "Nancy Cunard," in Hugh Ford, ed., *Nancy Cunard: Brave Poet, Indomitable Rebel* (Philadelphia, 1968), pp. 179–85.

5. Nancy Cunard, "Three Negro Poets," *Left Review*, October 1937, pp. 529–36.

6. LH, "Nancy: A Piñata in Memoriam, If One Could Break It in Her Honor," Prologue to *Nancy Cunard: Brave Poet, Indomitable Rebel*, ed. Hugh Ford (Philadelphia, 1968). © 1968 by the author. Reprinted with the permission of the publisher, Chilton Book Company, Radnor, Pa.

7. LH, trans., "Ballad of the Spanish Civil Guard," by Federico García Lorca, *New Masses*, March 1938, p. 6.

8. Various figures have been given for the number of casualties on both sides during the Civil War. Hugh Thomas, in *The Spanish Civil War*, suggests 410,000 violent deaths, and also cites a 1940 Nationalist press release that put the total casualties at 1,000,000. The figure in the text is taken from combined figures from newspaper reports of the period.

9. LH, "Air Raid: Barcelona," was the original title of the first of a series of weekly articles. It was written October 3, 1937, from Spain, for the *Baltimore Afro-American*, which published it under the title "Hughes Bombed in Spain: Tells of Terror of Fascist Raid," October 23, 1937.

10. "Madrid—1937" was first published in *Good Morning, Revolution*, pp. 105–6.

11. LH, *I Wonder as I Wander*, p. 327.

12. Ibid., p. 351.

13. LH, "How Milton Herndon Died," was written in Valencia, December 1, 1937, and published in the *Afro-American Newspapers*, January 1, 1938, under the title "Milton Herndon Died Trying to Rescue Pal...." Except for the difference of a few words and slightly different punctuation, Hughes included the Herndon quote in *I Wonder as I Wander*—from an identical paragraph in the 1937 article. In the later version, he added the word "Czechoslovakia" to Herndon's quote. Several other passages from the *Afro-American* series were included in the 1956 autobiography.

14. LH, *I Wonder as I Wander*, p. 354.

15. *The Afro-American*, December 18, 1937, p. 1.

16. Langston Hughes, trans., "Spanish Folk Songs of the War," *El Voluntario de la Libertad* 2, No. 21, Barcelona (June 15, 1938), p. 15.

17. Ernest Hemingway, "A New Kind of War," NANA Dispatch, April 14, 1937. Reprinted in *By-Line, Ernest Hemingway*, ed. William White (New York, 1967), p. 233.

18. LH, *I Wonder as I Wander*, p. 362.

19. Ibid., p. 363.

20. Ernest Hemingway, "Fascism Is a Lie," speech to the Second American Writers' Congress, June 4, 1937; excerpted in *New Masses*, June 22, 1937, p. 4.

21. LH, *I Wonder as I Wander*, p. 357.

22. Ibid., p. 370.

23. Bernard Rucker interview with author, November 1977.

24. LH, "Laughter in Madrid," *The Nation*, January 29, 1938, pp. 123–24.

25. LH, *I Wonder as I Wander*, p. 385.

26. The Hughes translation of García Lorca's Gypsy Ballads was published in *The Beloit Poetry Chapbook*, No. 1, Autumn 1951, at Beloit College. The translations made in Spain were later revised in 1945 in New York with the assistance of Miguel Covarrubias. Hughes's translation of García Lorca's *Bodas de Sangre* (*Blood Wedding*) was not published, though other English-language versions of the play are in print.

27. LH, trans., "The Hero," by Pablo de la Torriente-Brau, *The Champion*, November 1937, p. 39.

28. LH, *I Wonder as I Wander*, p. 333.

29. LH to Arthur Spingarn, September 18, 1937 (ABSP).

30. LH, *I Wonder as I Wander*, p. 384.

31. Ibid., p. 397.

32. Ibid., p. 398.

33. Ibid.

34. George Harris, "The Worker's Poet: An Interview with Langston Hughes," *The Champion*, May 1938, pp. 14–15.

35. LH, *I Wonder as I Wander*, p. 401.

36. Ibid.

37. Arna Bontemps interview with author, 1970.

Chapter 19: A World Apart

1. Diary of Carolyn Langston Clark(e). Courtesy of George Houston Bass, surviving Literary Executor-Trustee, the Langston Hughes Estate.

2. LH to Sullivan, January 15, 1938 (NSP, Bancroft).

3. Marie Seton to author, October 20, 1977: "I'd no idea that the D. H. Lawrence short stories which I lent him set him off to writing short stories."

4. Ibid.

5. Ibid.

6. Harold Rome confirmed that Hughes's poem suggested the prelude of "Men Awake" in his musical about the International Ladies Garment Workers Union (ILGWU), *Pins and Needles* (Rome to author, November 6, 1978). A portion of the poem was included with a dance number in the first act of the revue, which opened off-Broadway on November 27, 1937. The show lasted 1,108 performances and for a decade was the longest-running musical in New York theatrical history. With some changes in format, it toured the nation twice, and was revived for a short run in November 1978 at New York's Off-Broadway Roundabout Theater.

7. The title "Inside Us" was later changed to "One Friday Morning." First published in *The Crisis* in July 1941, the story was later widely reprinted in anthologies, including Hughes's short story collection, *Laughing to Keep from Crying*, and *The Langston Hughes Reader*.

8. Jack Conroy, "Memories of Arna Bontemps, Friend and Collaborator," *American Libraries*, December 1974, p. 602.

9. LH to Sullivan, July 26, 1939 (NSP, Bancroft).

10. See Faith Berry, ed., *Good Morning, Revolution: Uncollected Social Protest Writings by Langston Hughes* (New York, 1973), pp. 127–30.

11. Archives of the League of American Writers, Bancroft Library, University of California, Berkeley.

12. The Hollywood Ten were among the screenwriters, directors, and actors subpoenaed by the House Committee on Un-American Activities and accused of Communist activities or sympathies and subsequently blacklisted after the "Hollywood Hearings," which began in 1947. The ten who adamantly claimed the protection of the First Amendment were Alvah Bessie, Herbert Biberman, Lester Cole, Edward Dmytryk, Ring Lardner, Jr., John Howard Lawson, Albert Maltz, Samuel Ornitz, Adrian Scott, and Dalton Trumbo. They were cited for contempt of Congress for refusing to collaborate with the Committee, tried, convicted, and jailed.

13. Inscription included in correspondence, Arna Bontemps to author, October 29, 1970. Quoted by permission of Arna Bontemps.

14. Ralph Ellison, "Stormy Weather," *New Masses*, September 24, 1940, pp. 20–21.

15. Arna Bontemps interview with author, October 1970.

16. "Statement of American Intellectuals," *International Literature* 7 (1938), p. 104.

17. Lieber to LH, December 14, 1939 (Beinecke). Quoted by permission of Maxim Lieber.

Chapter 20: The Need for Heroes

1. LH to Thompson, January 19, 1940 (Private papers of Mrs. Louise Thompson Patterson). Quoted by permission.

2. LH to Sullivan, May 16, 1940 (NSP, Bancroft).

3. The text of the contract, together with correspondence expressing Hughes's dissatisfaction with the handling of *Cavalcade* by the American Negro Exposition, appears in *Arna Bontemps—Langston Hughes Letters (1925–1967)*, ed. Charles Nichols (New York, 1980).

4. Lieber to LH, July 14, 1940 (Beinecke). Quoted by permission of Maxim Lieber.

5. LH to Sullivan, July 19, 1940 (NSP, Bancroft).

6. Ibid.

7. M[ercer] C[ook], a review of *Langston Hughes: Un Chant Nouveau*, by René Piquion, *Phylon* 1, no. 4 (1940), p. 300.

8. Oswald G. Villard, a review of *The Big Sea*, by Langston Hughes, *The Saturday Review of Literature*, August 31, 1940, p. 12.

9. Milton Rugoff, a review of *The Big Sea*, by Langston Hughes, *The New York Herald Tribune Books*, August 25, 1940, p. 5.

10. Henry Lee Moon, a review of *The Big Sea*, by Langston Hughes, *Opportunity*, October 1940, p. 312.

11. Richard Wright, "Forerunner and Ambassador," *The New Republic*, October 28, 1940, pp. 600–601.

12. Jack Conroy, "Memories of Arna Bontemps, *Friend and Collaborator*," *American Libraries*, December 1974, p. 602.

13. The full text of Hughes's press statement appears under the title "Concerning 'Goodbye, Christ' " in *Good Morning, Revolution*, 133–35.

14. "Personal," *The Crisis*, October 1933, p. 238.

15. Lieber to LH, January 9, 1941 (Beinecke). Quoted by permission.

16. Bontemps to LH, January 4 [1941], in *Arna Bontemps—Langston Hughes Letters (1925–1967)*, ed. Charles Nichols (New York, 1980), p. 31. In a not uncommon lapse after the beginning of a new year, Bontemps inadvertently dated this letter 1940, instead of 1941. It is clear that the letter could not have been written in January 1940, inasmuch as Hughes did not distribute his statement on "Goodbye, Christ" to the press until January 1941. Nichols did not catch Bontemps's error.

17. LH to Louise Thompson Patterson, January 25, 1941 (Private papers of Mrs. Louise Thompson Patterson). Quoted by permission. (Louise Thompson became Mrs. William Patterson in September 1940.)

18. From FBI documents on Langston Hughes obtained through the Freedom of Information Act.

19. Hoover's lecture was presented at the Conference of Methodist Ministers, Evanston, Illinois, November 26, 1947. Eleven years later, in 1958, the Commission on Ministerial Training of the Methodist Church chose to delete Hoover's quotation of the poem from a volume, *The Christian Faith and Secularism*, following correspondence with Hughes about the poem. (From documents obtained through the Freedom of Information Act.)

20. The author is grateful to the poet Sterling Brown for bringing to her attention significant poetic similarities between Sandburg's "To a Contemporary Bunkshooter" and Hughes's "Goodbye, Christ."

21. LH to Louise Thompson Patterson, November 3, 1940 (Private papers of Mrs. Louise Thompson Patterson). Quoted by permission.

22. LH to Louise Thompson Patterson, March 10, 1941 (Private papers of Mrs. Louise Thompson Patterson). Quoted by permission.

23. After Hughes wrote "One Friday Morning" (first titled "Inside Us") in 1939, it was rejected by several editors and lost by *The New Anvil*, which had intended to publish it before the magazine became defunct in early 1941. Hughes gave it to *The Crisis* as part of his "twentieth anniversary" tribute to the NAACP periodical. It subsequently became one of his most widely reprinted short stories.

24. A summary of the dispute between W. E. B. Du Bois and Walter White appears in the introduction to *The Emerging Thought of W. E. B. Du Bois*, ed. Henry Lee Moon (New York, 1972). See also *The Autobiography of W. E. B. Du Bois* (New York, 1968).

25. Mrs. Amy Spingarn (Mrs. Joel Spingarn) in an interview with the author in 1971 acknowledged that it was her belief that "Christ in Alabama" was the major reason that Hughes was not seriously considered for the Spingarn Medal before 1960, when he became the forty-fifth medalist. He was the first recipient to be given the award directly by a member of the Spingarn family. Arthur Spingarn, brother of Joel, and then president of the NAACP, made the presentation at the fifty-first annual NAACP convention, Northrup Auditorium, University of Minnesota, in Minneapolis, June 26, 1960. The first Spingarn Medal was presented in 1915 and every year thereafter, except 1938.

26. Lieber to LH, April 23, 1941 (Beinecke). Quoted by permission of Maxim Lieber.

27. Hughes was represented in the *Mulatto* arbitration by a client of Lieber's, playwright Albert Maltz, who was succesful in eventually winning $300 for Hughes from Martin Jones.

28. For the purpose of the *Negro Revue*, Hughes produced a number of theatrical skits and lyrics which were considered "collaborative efforts," although they were his individual works. Among them were the librettos "Mad Scene from Woolworth's," "Run Ghost Run," "Hollywood Mammy," "Madame, How Can I Fall in Love," "Third Floor Airshaft Blues," and "Hey! Hey! Hey!" He had divided his material into three categories, since the Hollywood Theatre Alliance could never quite decide on the slant of the production while he was the script director.

29. Lieber to LH, March 11, 1941 (Beinecke). Quoted by permission of Maxim Lieber.

30. LH to Louise Thompson Patterson, March 10, 1941 (Private papers of Mrs. Louise Thompson Patterson). Quoted by permission.

31. The League of American Writers antiwar statement was circulated for signature among members (and some nonmembers) in the spring of 1941 while Hughes was traveling on a three-month lecture tour. He was a late signer and not included when the statement and a partial list of signers was first published. *New Masses* published the statement under the title "The Writers Don't Want War: Three Hundred Explain Why They Don't Want America Again to 'Engage in Foreign Adventure,' " June 25, 1940, p. 21.

32. The officers elected at the Fourth American Writers Congress were Dashiell Hammett, who succeeded two-term president Donald Ogden Stewart, who became a vice-president, and John Howard Lawson, Meridel Le Sueur, Albert Maltz, George Seldes, Erskine Caldwell, and Richard Wright.

33. LH to Bontemps, July 24, 1941, in *Arna Bontemps—Langston Hughes Letters (1925–1967)*, ed. Charles Nichols (New York, 1980), p. 86.

34. LH to Bontemps, August 27, 1941, in *ibid.*, p. 87.

35. Bontemps interview with author, October 1970.

36. LH to Bontemps, February 14, 1941, in *The Arna Bontemps—Langston Hughes Letters*, p. 75.

37. LH to Bontemps, September 28, 1941, in *ibid.*, p. 89.

38. "Banquet in Honor" was published in *The Negro Quarterly* 1, no. 2 (Summer 1942), pp. 176–78. The same title appears over a different story in *Simple Speaks His Mind*.

39. The title of "The Bottle of Wine" was changed to "On the Way Home" when it was published for the first time in *Story Magazine* (May/June 1946), and later anthologized in Hughes's collections *Laughing to Keep from Crying, The Langston Hughes Reader*, and *Something in Common*. "Mysterious Madame Shanghai" was first published in *Afro Magazine*, May 15, 1952, and reprinted in *Laughing to Keep from Crying* and *Something in Common*. "Two at the Bar" appeared in *Negro Story* (August/September 1945), and was not anthologized. "Sailor Ashore" was printed only in *Laughing to Keep from Crying* and *Something in Common*. "The Star Decides" was never published, despite numerous revisions.

40. *Arna Bontemps—Langston Hughes Letters*, p. 83.

41. LH to Bontemps, October 29, 1941, in *ibid.*, p. 91.

42. LH to Sullivan, December 15, 1941 (NSP, Bancroft).

43. LH, "Aesthete in Harlem," *Opportunity*, June 1930, p. 182.

Epilogue: Full Circle

1. *The Sun Do Move*, which was originally and alternately titled *Sold Away, Outshines the Sun*, and *Before I'd Be a Slave*, when Hughes drafted it in Carmel during 1940–41, had its premiere at the Skyloft Theatre of the Good Shepherd Community Center in Chicago, April 24, 1942. Hughes helped to produce the play and was later identified as having helped to organize the Skyloft Players, although the theatre itself existed before the play opened.

2. Langston Hughes, "Simple and Me," *The Chicago Defender*, October 13, 1945; reprinted in *Phylon* 6, no. 4 (1945), pp. 340–53.

3. "My America" was first published in the *Journal of Educational Sociology*, February 1943, pp. 334–36, and reprinted in *What the Negro Wants*, ed. Rayford Logan (Chapel Hill, N.C., 1944), pp. 299–307. Hughes condensed the essay for *The Langston Hughes Reader* (New York, 1958), pp. 500–501.

4. Langston Hughes, "A Poem for Jacques Roumain (Late Poet of Haiti)," n.d., signed copy to Arna Bontemps (Fisk). Quoted by permission of the Langston Hughes Estate.

5. Quoted in a letter dated December 28, 1944, from Newbold Morris (chairman of the board of directors, the City Center of Music and Drama) to Arthur Spingarn (ABSP). *Troubled Island* was conducted by Laszlo Halasz, the artistic and music director of the New York City Opera Company.

6. *Congressional Record*, April 1, 1948, vol. 94, pt. 3, pp. 4011–12. Albert Wahl Hawkes (R., New Jersey) was Senator from 1943 to 1949.

7. Lieber to LH, December 3, 1948 (Beinecke). Quoted by permission of Maxim Lieber.

8. Maxim Lieber, who was active in progressive causes and represented numerous well-known authors, chose not to subject himself to questioning about them before the HUAC. Once an avowed Marxist, he was accused by Whittaker Chambers, a former Communist, of once belonging to a Communist cell, in testimony before the HUAC and later in his autobiography, *Witness* (1952). Lieber lived in exile in Mexico for some four years and in Poland for thirteen. He returned to the United States in 1968, disillusioned with Communism.

9. Frank D. Reeves interview with author, March 1971.

10. See Faith Berry, ed., *Good Morning, Revolution* (New York, 1973), pp. 143–45.

11. Hughes was represented during the early 1940s by the New York lecture bureau of William Feakins. When Feakins died in 1946, Hughes and many of his clients transferred to Colston Leigh. Maxim Lieber, who had led Hughes to Feakins, tried afterward to have him go to the lecture bureau of Charles Pearson, a well-known agency which represented Carl Sandburg. Hughes later regretted not taking that advice.

12. After Du Bois's death in 1963, Hughes paid homage to him in "Du Bois: A Part of Me," which was published as "Tribute to W. E. B. Du Bois" in a commemorative issue of *Freedomways*, Winter 1965, p. 11.

13. Lieber to LH, July 8, 1954 (Beinecke). Quoted by permission of Maxim Lieber.

14. Professor Stanley Cyrus, editor of the *Afro-Hispanic Review* at Howard University, graciously made available to me the Spanish text of Pilar Barrios's poem "Voces," which he calls an "Ode to Langston Hughes." The poem is also cited in Richard Jackson, "The Shared Vision of Langston Hughes and Black Hispanic Writers," *Black American Literature Forum*, Fall 1981, pp. 89–92.

Unfortunately, little attention is given to Afro-Hispanic poets in Edward J. Mullen's *Langston Hughes in the Hispanic World and Haiti*, an edited collection (1977) which includes an evaluation of Hispanic criticism and translations about Hughes; it also reprints his English-language writings about the Hispanic world, but none of his Spanish translations or much evidence that he did any translations.

The most thorough assessment to date of Hughes's translations remains John F. Matheus, "Langston Hughes as Translator," *CLA Journal* (Special Langston Hughes Number), June 1968, pp. 319–30; reprinted in *Langston Hughes, Black Genius: A Critical Evaluation*, ed. Therman B. O'Daniel (1971).

15. Elizabeth Staples, *American Mercury*, January 1959, pp. 46–50.

16. Hughes's review essay, "Name, Race and Gift in Common," *Voices*, Winter 1950, praised Gwendolyn Brooks's second poetry volume, *Annie Allen* (for which she won a Pulitzer

Prize); his review of Julian Mayfield's first novel, *The Hit*, appeared October 20, 1957, in the *New York Herald Tribune Book Review*, where he also reviewed the author's second novel, *The Long Night*, on October 26, 1958.

17. LH to J. Griffith Davis, June 13, 1961 (Langston Hughes Papers, Schomburg).

18. Poston interview with author, and letter, May 14, 1971, to author.

19. LH to Bontemps. March 20, 1965, *Arna Bontemps—Langston Hughes Letters*, p. 473.

20. Hughes appeared with Paule Marshall, William Melvin Kelley, and Jean Wagner at the Centre Culturel Américain in Paris, May 19, 20, 21, 1965, for the Ninth Annual American Seminar on American Literature.

21. LH, "Flotsam," *The Crisis*, June/July 1968, p. 194.

22. In 1971 the author sought information about the Hughes medical records through a New York physician formerly on the staff of the Polyclinic Hospital. He was told the case was closed and that the records were not available to the public.

23. LH, "Tower," *Opportunity*, July 1930, p. 235. The poem was reprinted a year later in the collection *Dear Lovely Death*.

Permissions

Grateful acknowledgment is made to the following for permission to quote excerpts of previously unpublished correspondence and papers:

GEORGE HOUSTON BASS, Surviving Executor/Trustee of the Langston Hughes Estate, for letters and works in full or in part by Langston Hughes in the Moorland-Spingarn Research Center, Howard University Library; the Bancroft Library, University of California, Berkeley; Manuscript Division, Library of Congress; Special Collections, Fisk University; personal collections made available by the owners to the author; and the Wallace Thurman Papers, James Weldon Johnson Memorial Collection, Beinecke Rare Book and Manuscript Library, Yale University Library.

DR. EDMUND RANDOLPH BIDDLE for the correspondence of Mrs. Rufus Osgood Mason from the Estate of Katherine Garrison Chapin Biddle (Mrs. Francis Biddle) and the Alain Locke Papers.

HOWARD UNIVERSITY, Legatee of the Alain Locke Papers, Moorland-Spingarn Research Center, for the correspondence of Alain Locke and Zora Neale Hurston to Mrs. Rufus Osgood Mason and to Langston Hughes; also for the Arthur B. Spingarn Papers, Moorland-Spingarn Research Center.

MAXIM LIEBER for his literary correspondence with Langston Hughes and related sources, Yale University Library.

SI-LAN CHEN LEYDA for her personal correspondence with Langston Hughes, Yale University Library.

UNIVERSITY OF CALIFORNIA, Berkeley, The Bancroft Library, for use of the Archives of the League of American Writers, the Noel Sullivan Papers, The Marie Short Collection, and The Roy Blackburn Collection.

THE ESTATE OF CARL VAN VECHTEN for Carl Van Vechten's manuscript note, printed from the original in the Van Vechten Papers in the James Weldon Johnson Memorial Collection at Yale University by permission of the Beinecke Rare Book and Manuscript Library, of Donald Gallup, Literary Trustee for Carl Van Vechten, and of the Estate of Carl Van Vechten, Joseph Solomon, Executor.

Index